MINDS OF FEAR

A Dialogue with 30 Modern Masters of Horror

MINDS OF FEAR

A Dialogue with 30 Modern Masters of Horror

by Calum Waddell

Midnight Marquee Press, Inc.
Baltimore, Maryland

Interior and Cover Design: Susan Svehla
Copyright © 2005 Calum Waddell

Without limiting the rights reserved under the copyright above, no part of this publication may be reproduced, stored in or introduced into a retrieval system, or transmitted, in any form, or by any means (electronic, mechanical, photocopying, recording, or otherwise), without the prior written permission of the copyright owners or the publishers of this book.

ISBN 1-887664-57-2
Library of Congress Catalog Card Number 2005923722
Manufactured in the United States of America
First Printing by Midnight Marquee Press, Inc.,
                                                                                 June 2005

I wish to dedicate this book to Los Angeles. The city that was imperative to obtaining most of the interviews here—and which made for a truly enjoyable adventure.

TABLE OF CONTENTS

9   Foreword
13   Introduction

CHAPTER 1
MODERN CLASSICS
Five Landmarks of the Contemporary Fear Film

18   An American Werewolf in London
31   Black Christmas
39   Death Line
47   The Hills Have Eyes
56   Rabid

CHAPTER 2
CREATURE FEATURES
Five Examples of First-Rate Creature Carnage

64   Alligatror
72   The Blob
78   Cujo
85   Eaten Alive
92   The Hidden

CHAPTER 3
SLASHER FILMS
Perhaps the Most Popular Slice of Horror Cinema

100   Alone in the Dark
108   Intruder
115   Silent Night, Deadly Night
124   The Slayer
130   A Stranger Is Watching

CHAPTER 4
HORROR AND HUMOR
A Selection of Films That Exhibit an Especially Sinister Wit

- 140   Brain Damage
- 148   Motel Hell
- 156   The Texas Chainsaw Massacre 2
- 165   The Toxic Avenger
- 174   Two Thousand Maniacs!

CHAPTER 5
ECLECTIC GEMS
Weird and Wonderful

- 181   A Boy and His Dog
- 192   Cronos
- 199   Dead and Buried
- 208   Evilspeak
- 218   Strange Behavior

CHAPTER 6
FUTURE CLASSICS
Recent Cult Horror Films That We Might Just Be Discussing for Years to Come

- 226   Ginger Snaps
- 237   Jeepers Creepers
- 250   King of the Ants
- 258   R.S.V.P.
- 265   Wrong Turn

- 275   Footnotes

About the Author

Born and raised in Fife, Scotland, Calum Waddell graduated with an upper second class Honors Degree in English from Stirling University and gained a Masters in Broadcast and Film Studies from Bournemouth University.

Calum has contributed features and interviews to some of the world's biggest horror and fantasy film magazines including *The Dark Side*, *DVD World*, *Dreamwatch*, *Fangoria*, *Filmfax*, *Impact*, *Neo*, *Rue Morgue*, *Shivers*, *Shock Cinema* and *Videoscope*. The author also edited his own acclaimed small press magazine, *Firelight Shocks*, from 1999 until 2003. He acts as Head of Programs for the annual Fearless Tales Genre Festival in San Francisco—which in its two-year running time has honored Tobe Hooper, John Landis, Jeff Burr, Jack Hill and many others. More information on the festival can be had at www.fearlesstales.com.

The author is also involved in freelance acquisitions for a number of DVD labels, has contributed an audio commentary to the Lion's Gate DVD release of Tobe Hooper's *The Toolbox Murders,* and currently works as an independent producer on a number of film projects in various stages of development and funding.

Outside of writing about the films that disturb your sleep, the author's interests include classic Disney, the independent music scene, politics, roller coasters and wildlife. His next book, also for *Midnight Marquee*, will be the definitive guide to the work of his friend and all-round living legend, Jack Hill.

Without Whom

First, I would like to thank Joe Venegas of Creative Talent Communications in Los Angeles, who is one of my best friends. He secured many of the interviews for this book through his numerous contacts, and was nice enough to act as my tour guide when I lived in Los Angeles in 2003. I'd also like to thank Chris Otter for his sterling proofreading job, Mark Anthony Galluzzo for his excellent foreword and Elaine Tod. I wish also to thank Gary and Sue for their loyalty to this book, their hard work on it and their trust in me to produce this publication.

Thanks also to

William Alexander, Jace Anderson, Rachel Belofsky, Craig, Mark and Nick at the Anchor Bay UK forums, Del at Dark Delicacies (please check out www.darkdel.com), Josh Davidson at Elite Entertainment, Angelica and Michael Davidson, Geoff Garrett, Adam Gierasch, "Gwangi-Boy" (Mark), Kelly Hargraves, Jim Harper, Duffy Hecht, Joe Kane, Sean Keeley at Lion's Gate Entertainment, Andrew Kirkham at Screen Entertainment, Anthony Masi, Marc Morris, Iain Robert Smith for his help with HG Lewis, and every genre celebrity who agreed to participate in this book. And a special thanks to John Landis for still endeavoring to call me even after getting my answering machine five times.

Foreword

by Mark Anthony Galluzzo, Director of *R.S.V.P.* and *Trash*

Ah yes, the Horror Flick. What exactly is it about this well-worn genre that—despite some of the poorest displays of filmmaking ever committed to celluloid, *including porn*—still manages to pull audiences back for more? Go to any modern film market (AFM, Cannes, MIPCOM) and you can be assured that nearly every single booth on the floor will be flogging at least one, if not dozens, of horror films. Slashers, thrillers, creature features, supernatural epics, macabre comedies, you name it and you'll find it. As a wizened old sales agent once croaked at me, "You find yourself a serial killer that no one has made a film about yet, and I can guarantee you six figures in Japan alone."

Overhearing conversations such as that and getting an eye-full of the menacing blood-soaked posters lining the floor, one would not be wrong to ask oneself, "What does all this grisly content say about our modern society?" Indeed, what does it mean when a good leisurely night out for many apparently normal upstanding members of our community often involves: a) consuming a large bucket of buttered popcorn, and b) watching a half-dozen beautiful coeds get hacked to pieces for their viewing pleasure? Have we, as a modern people, become so jaded and hardened that we lust to witness the fictionalized suffering of others (*The Passion of The Christ* notwithstanding; those viewers are just plain cuckoo)? Or are horror films nothing more than a natural and much less barbaric progression from the blood sports of old? No longer throwing Christians to the lions in front of a bloodthirsty crowd at the Coliseum, do we now just settle for throwing big-breasted blondes to killer zombies via a glowing screen? Have we replaced two gladiators' fight to the death with "Freddy vs. Jason"?

Undoubtedly this is probably part of the mystery, but in my mind it does not sufficiently answer the core question. From an evolutionary perspective, I would argue that another reason for the longevity of the horror genre is that perhaps our lives have become so soft and predictable that we yearn for that primitive, protective, and yes, even addictive emotion of raw unadulterated fear (residents of war-torn Third World countries and totalitarian regimes excluded). An emotion that was once crucial to avoiding the jaws of a saber-toothed tiger is now used to simply entertain us. Yes, it's true ladies and gentlemen,

Scary Movie 2 spoofs modern day horror films, much to the delight of horror film fans, studios and theaters.

FEAR is now officially on sale at a theater near you. Our cowering caveman brethren might be gobsmacked at our audacity, but a look back at art in any medium over the centuries will clearly show that, from ancient Greek theater to the modern haunted house, Gothic novels to trashy paperbacks, mankind has always found quality entertainment in scaring the *beejezus* out of his fellow man.

Stephen King made a mint by proving over the course of three decades that the audience was insatiable when it comes to the macabre. Like the best horror masters, King effectively tapped into the primitive side in all of us that wants to go back to being that kid whose heart used to race at a strange noise in the night or an amorphous shadow in the closet. Back to a time when you might find yourself cowering on your bed, talking yourself into paralysis as you slowed your breathing, pulled the covers tight and hoped/prayed that when you put your foot on the floor to take a pressing wee, nothing would grab it. Thus, yet another *raison d'etre* for the horror film—it is a way to reach back and channel our innocence.

Yes, there are plenty of scary things in the real world (war, famine, pestilence, disease, Republicans), but for most of us, life is insulated and mundane, surrounded by safety glass, airbags, and innumerable warnings (e.g., Warning! Do Not Stick Babies in Bin-Liners! *Gee, thanks.*). Horror films provide that missing thrill and are a jolt to remind us that we are indeed still alive…which consequently means we will eventually die. Just preferably not on the business end of some lunatic's chainsaw. In other words, enjoy it while you still can.

I myself never actually intended to make a horror film (albeit some would argue, yours truly included, that *R.S.V.P.* is more of a stealth-parody than a horror). *R.S.V.P.* just sort of happened. I had just debuted my first feature film, *Trash*, a coming-of-age drama set in the trailer parks of the Deep South, and was dead broke. A money man came to me with the idea of doing a loose remake of *Rope*. Not really thrilled about the idea of taking on Hitchcock in a head-to-head battle, I agreed to make it as long as I could do something drastically different, i.e., turn the genre on its head and simultaneously poke the audience in the eye. Much to my surprise he actually gave me the green light to do just that, and *R.S.V.P.* was born. Thus I set out to not only explore the *Leopoldian* theme of Fame vs. Infamy in our modern fame-obsessed culture but also to dissect the genre itself as described above. Using the metaphor of a bullfighting aficionado as a character, I sought to draw a parallel with the horror audience itself. Asking the question, if we know how they're both going to end (the bull gets killed vs. Neve Campbell gets away), why do we still watch?

Mark Anthony Galluzzo

Like most of the young filmmakers who are currently taking their own a stab at the horror genre, I came of age at the dawn of the VCR and the birth of premium cable television such as HBO and Cinemax. Two new delivery mediums that, like many before and after them, turned to the old standbys of breasts and blood to attract their initial audiences. Wandering through my local rental shop in backwater Florida, the pickings were slim: James Bond, soft-core porn, and…horror. Having already seen most of the Bond collection while watching Sunday afternoon matinees with my dad, and being unable to convince the clerk to let me walk out with *Hollywood Hot-Tubs III*, I was naturally drawn to the horror aisle where the likes of Freddy, Jason and Michael Myers awaited. I was vaguely familiar with the R-rated horror films via their ad campaigns in the cinema, but being only about 10, I was never allowed into the theater to watch. My only contact with them was when the naughty 16-year-old girl from down the street came over to baby-sit and would make out with her brace-faced boyfriend to the romantic backdrop of the *Evil Dead* flickering on my Dad's wood-paneled Sylvania. But joy, oh joy, when I found out that while the video clerk in my tiny Bible-belt town was firmly against handing over any flick involving the baring of female flesh, he was more than happy to let me walk away with buckets of blood and human depravity.

Much to my mother's dismay (especially when I came home with a fresh copy of *I Spit On Your Grave*), I devoured the entire aisle in a matter of months. She would occasionally duck her head into the TV room with offers of snacks and a disapproving gasp as my friends and I watched some poor sap get shredded for the tenth time in slow-motion rewind. But for the most part, she let my horror phase run its course. She assumed that it was just a kid thing and that eventually I would grow more sophisticated tastes. And you know what, she was halfway right. I did develop more sophisticated tastes, moving on to study Welles, Lang, Hitchcock, Stone, Scorsese, Spielberg and such. And much to my surprise not only did I discover their Oscar-winning classics, but also some early works in the horror/thriller genre! Furthermore, as my education moved forward, as well as the better part of a decade, I started to recognize that not only was the horror genre a launching pad for directors but also a tremendous number of mainstream actors as well. From Johnny Depp in *A Nightmare on Elm Street* to Renee Zellweger and Matthew McConaughey in *Texas Chainsaw Massacre: The Next Generation*, the horror film is almost a cinematic rite of passage. Oliver Stone's *The Hand*, starring a young Michael Caine, comes to mind as a prime example on both sides of the camera.

The notorious *I Spit on your Grave*—one of the earliest "video nasties."

Further evidence of the demise of horror's reputation as catering only to the dregs of cinema is the fact that even the fictional characters from our modern horror franchises have seeped their way permanently into pop culture: Freddy, Jason, Carrie, Pinhead, Michael Myers, Leatherface, and my personal favorite, Maliki from *Children of the*

LOTR Viggo Mortensen in *Texas Chainsaw Massacre III*

Corn—don't ask why. Taking their place right alongside veterans such as Dracula, Frankenstein and The Mummy.

So ingrained is our desire to be scared that even after genre-busting films such as *Scream* and *Scary Movie* pulled back the curtain on horror flicks and let the audience in on the method behind the madness, we still flock to see them. So much is the horror movie part of our mainstream culture that it is nearly impossible to write characters in a horror film that *do not* reference classic slasher movies when trapped in their own "horror" situation. *"Wait, don't split up, you morons!" "Hey, don't smoke that joint." "Shit, I'm the only the black guy in the haunted house! I'm never gonna make it out alive!" "Hell no! Don't even think about picking up that drifter in the middle of the fucking desert! Didn't you see* The Hitcher*!?" "Go in the basement? Are you out of your freaking mind!"*

Yet still these characters make the same mistakes as their predecessors (smoke pot, have sex, split up) while we sit glued to our seats, merrily shouting at these bloody fools to run or cringing at the ludicrously predictable by-the-numbers plotline...

Either way it doesn't matter, for every now and again a genuine horror classic comes along that reaffirms our love for this redheaded stepchild of a genre. This fine book is an in-depth collection of those select horror gems—the good, the bad and the comically ugly.

Just remember, though, to paraphrase the words of Jonathan Banks in my own genre-busting horror/comedy *R.S.V.P.* "To truly enjoy, horror fans must learn to appreciate 'the details.' For it is the details that separate the aficionado from the masses."

Having already picked up this horror film history chock-full of such details, one can only assume that you are indeed well on your way to becoming an aficionado of cinematic macabre.

—M.A. Galluzzo

Introduction

So what makes *Minds of Fear* any more interesting than the many other horror film books vying for your attention? Well, aside from the fact that this little labor of love has involved conducting a number of exclusive interviews with top genre names, what you have in your hands is the perfect guide to 30 horror flicks that are each well worth your time. You may even discover a little gem that you otherwise might never have given the time of day—hence the focus, throughout this publication, on movies that haven't yet suffered from overexposure. As tempting as it may have been to dedicate sections to *Night of the Living Dead, Last House on the Left* (already the subject of a tremendous book release from the UK's FAB Press) or *Halloween*, the wealth of information available on these titles arguably reached saturation point a long time ago. However, from such classic benchmarks as *An American Werewolf in London* and *The Hills Have Eyes* to guilty pleasures like *Evilspeak* and *Silent Night, Deadly Night* and finally to the modern hits *Jeepers Creepers* and *Wrong Turn*, there should be something in here to satisfy every scary-movie addict. And even if you have seen every feature discussed in this tome, the variety of actors/directors/producers/writers and special effects maestros interviewed to accompany each entry should—at the very least—reveal a few interesting, even thought-provoking, secrets about the making of these cult favorites.

Of course one person's gold is another person's garbage and it is worth noting that horror film fans are possibly the most argumentative bunch you'll ever come across... just go to a convention or a genre movie festival and see for yourself. Better yet, take a trip onto an online horror message forum—sooner or later things will get messy and expletives thrown around as passionate fans argue over whether or not, say, Fulci's walking dead have held up better than Romero's. Well, that's been my experience anyway. Horror movie followers are dedicated and opinionated and so are the genre's critics—and who would have it any other way? The conflicting essays and reviews inherent in many a genre publication or online web site are what makes the horror scene so exciting, invigorating and thought-provoking. The loyalty of its fans (who often carry an encyclopedic knowledge of their subject) is usually nothing less than startling, and for those filmmakers, special effects artists and performers who work in the genre, one can only imagine that it is a rewarding experience to encounter such devotion. However, it is rare to find that "unified" horror gem that brings together fans and critics alike in deeming it as an undisputed classic. As such, the 30 films discussed in this book are likely to cause

The Exorcist—trash or treasure?

a number of disagreements among readers. In answer to any complaints about leaving out "such and such" a film in favor of a movie of lesser quality, all I can say is that each title contains a critique whereupon I have tried, as best I can, to put forward my own favorable defense. Even so, one would be stupid not to be prepared for any resulting controversy…

For example, for everyone, such as myself, who proclaims *Scream* (1996) to be a contemporary great, there will be many others to state the opposite, perhaps arguing that it is little more than a glossy retread of the films that it sets out to spoof. While it is probably safe to consider *Night of the Living Dead* (1968) an undisputed masterpiece and the benchmark of modern terror (it is certainly difficult to find any critical dismissal of it), everything else falls onto far trickier ground. *The Exorcist* (1973) might be a classic to Mark Kermode, who writes at length about the movie in his British Film Institute book on it, but to Phil Hardy in *The Aurum Film Encyclopedia* it is full of flaws. Likewise, *The Texas Chain Saw Massacre* (1974) might be considered an untouchable milestone to many—but Leslie Halliwell largely dismisses it in his popular *Film Guide*. Stanley Kubrick's *The Shining* (1980) seems to attract the same level of hatred as it does support, and while *Friday the 13th* (1980) was a huge (and influential) hit in its day, few would consider it worthy of being discussed in the same breath as *Night of the Living Dead*.

As such, each movie written about in the forthcoming pages is a personal choice—a film that has, in some way, etched its way into my collection (and my heart) since my love affair with the genre began at five years old and a showing of *An American Werewolf in London*. "Were your folks crazy?" asked John Landis when I revealed this to him. Well, you can blame it on my older sister and the family's investment in a video recorder rather than on my parents, but seeing horror films with childhood eyes is something that I personally miss. Plot holes, stupid characterization and incompetent filmmaking could be swept aside back when I was a wee 10-year-old feasting on a diet of *Amityville, Basket Case, The Evil Dead* and *Friday the 13th*. Looking at these films now, with adult eyes, I don't honestly know that I'd let a child see them—but when I was younger these were the greatest things ever and they never, for one second, did me any harm at all. Well, except for causing me to write about them…

A Few Words About the Modern Horror Film

The modern horror film is largely seen to have begun with *Night of the Living Dead* (interested readers should check out Kim Newman's essential *Nightmare Movies* for further discussion), although the first horror film to really take terror out of the realm of the Gothic and the supernatural and place it in our present, everyday lives was undoubtedly Alfred Hitchcock's *Psycho* (1960). Herschell Gordon Lewis went further by inventing the "splatter film" with 1963's *Blood Feast*—and Lewis gets acknowledged in this very publication through his 1964 classic *Two Thousand Maniacs!* In Italy, Mario Bava mixed *Psycho* with added blood and gore and the result, 1963's *Blood and Black Lace*, is probably the very first "body count," or slasher, movie. Where George Romero really changed things, with *Night of the Living Dead,* was with his finale. Up until 1968, horror films invariably featured a "wrap up," whereupon evil was defeated and the audience could comfortably leave the theater without feeling too distraught by the onscreen unpleasantness. Yet, when Duane Jones is shot dead in Romero's film—after having done everything correctly in order to fight the zombie plague—and his body mercilessly burned by a group of gun-toting rednecks, things changed. Suddenly horror did not have to follow any rules at all. Romero broke every rule. There was no happy ending in *Night of the Living Dead.* The terror is not destroyed at the end, and the audience has faced so many macabre, disturbing images (even today, the undead little girl stabbing her mother to death remains among the most horrifying sights in genre history) that the movie is genuinely difficult to shake off. Predictably, Romero's influence is present in almost every film in this book.

The realistic brutality of Wes Craven's *Last House on the Left* (1972) is certainly a further turning point for horror cinema's depiction of graphic violence, and the full-color disembowelments make even *Night of the Living Dead* look tame. How things had changed in only four years. Tobe Hooper's *The Texas Chain Saw Massacre* took Craven's stark realism one step further by combining it with genuinely credible filmmaking and, surprisingly, actually managing to attract an enormous audience in the process. If William Friedkin's *The Exorcist* did anything, it was to reaffirm Satan as

 a threat during the decade of *Last House*-inspired contemporary, real life, serial killer villains and produce a modern blockbuster. The movie also ushered in a new era of grisly special effects that would be followed up by the gory excess of *Dawn of the Dead* (1979)—perhaps still the definitive landmark of "splatter" cinema. *Halloween* (1978), and later *Friday the 13th* and *A Nightmare on Elm Street* (1984), would inspire the general direction of American horror cinema during the 1980s (witness even the slasher film coda in 1987's *Fatal Attraction*) for better and for worse. After these three hits, anyone with a money-spinning horror character would tire themselves out with two or three sequels—witness the direct-to-video schlock of the *Sleepaway Camp* (1983) and *Slumber Party Massacre* (1983) series. The slasher film movement is focused upon with five of the better examples in Chapter Three.

Italian horror cinema would find itself indebted to Dario Argento, Mario Bava and Lucio Fulci, although their impact on the English-speaking world was largely undervalued for a considerable length of time. That Argento's *Suspiria* (1977) is the forefather of *Halloween,* and his early giallo films the inspiration behind a number of mainstream thrillers, from *Dressed to Kill* (1980) to 2004's *Saw*, now goes without saying. That everyone from Tim Burton to Scorsese now credits Bava as a master filmmaker seems to have secured his reputation—as does the lingering influence of his *Twitch of the Death Nerve* (1971) upon the stalker movie genre. Fulci, meanwhile, remains the darling of low-budget independent filmmakers everywhere—his influence even managing to spread to the Far East, as fans of 1988's Japanese oddity *Evil Dead Trap* will attest. My recent visit to the Los Angeles-based special effects house "Spectral Motion," which has worked on *Hellboy* (2004) and *Blade 3* (2004), confirmed that Fulci's reputation has finally begun to penetrate the mainstream as the makeup artists sang the late director's praises.

The 1980s also saw the rise of David Cronenberg's weird form of "body horror," which reached its peak with 1982's outstanding *Videodrome*—a sure influence on the gory visuals of, among many others, Clive Barker's *Hellraiser* (1987) and Brian Yuzna's *Society* (1989). As a new decade was ushered in, the nineties were initially a quiet time for the genre. 1991's *The Silence of the Lambs* succeeded in advertising itself as something it was not (i.e., a top-rate thriller as opposed to a big-budget psychological thriller), although its presence on any number of direct-to-video serial killer movies is immeasurable. 1995's *Seven*, likewise, chose not to advertise itself as a horror movie despite its giallo roots and often disgusting visuals. The subsequent influence of David Fincher's movie on horror has not been especially vital, despite its commercial success, and it was instead Wes Craven's *Scream* (1996) that reinvigorated the genre. *Scream* spawned a number of copycat movies ranging from *I Know What You Did Last Sum-*

mer (1997) to *Halloween H20* (1998) as well as its own sequels. A few years later and 1999's *The Blair Witch Project* and *The Sixth Sense* allowed the genre to be more adult again—the scares in each film being far more imaginative, mature and primal than those seen in, for instance, 1998's awful *Urban Legend*.

Since *Blair Witch* and *The Sixth Sense*, it has been difficult to point a finger toward another original horror title that has, in effect, broken new ground or inspired a new confidence in the genre at the box office. However, this may be a rash conclusion. After all, it can take a few years before a film's influence can really be measured and the recent success of, for instance, *Open Water* (2004) might well create a renewed interest in shark movies and even the release of *Jaws 5*. Hey, it couldn't be any worse than *Jaws: The Revenge*, could it? What is for sure is that, post-September 11th, there has been an unmistakable rise in the popularity of horror flicks—and especially fantasy-based horror features whereupon the viewer is transported into a living, breathing comic book full of macabre violence. Just check out some of the films that reached number one at the American box office during 2003 alone: *Freddy Vs. Jason, Jeepers Creepers 2* and *The Texas Chain Saw Massacre* remake. Terror is big business yet again...as long as it remains far enough adjusted from reality. With the possible exception of *King of the Ants*, Chapter Six showcases a small selection of horror movies, made since the turn of the new millennium, that are decidedly removed from the brutal reality that previous trendsetters such as *Last House on the Left* reveled in.

Disagree with the choices in this book? Well you can either write your own follow-up or take solace in some of the films that were considered but ultimately left out of this first chapter. 1973's *The Wicker Man* was definitely one movie that, had Allan Brown not written his own excellent book on it, would have been included here. 1980's Italian classic *Inferno* is another horror title that I hold a lot more highly than most, although including a Euro-horror title is arguably taking this book down a whole other street. After all, European horror is almost a genre unto itself—with its own star directors and subgenres. 1974's *Deranged* was also played around with, since it remains a powerful slice of nastiness all these years later. For the "Future Classics" chapter I deeply regret not being able to write about Marc Evans' excellent *My Little Eye* (2002), which left me feeling, to put it bluntly, pretty damn fucked up when the end credits rolled in the cinema. Only my failure to nail down Evans for an interview on the film (having already discussed his new movie, *Trauma*, at length with him) stopped this excellent title from inclusion. 2003's *May*, another modern cult hit, was also thought about as a possibility for this chapter but, looking back, I don't regret the films chosen here. Each entry is a fine film, and a cult classic, in its own right and if this publication manages to alert at least a handful of readers to the merits of, say, *Death Line*, then it is a job well done.

—Calum Waddell

CHAPTER 1
MODERN CLASSICS

Five landmarks of the contemporary fear film

An American Werewolf in London

Director: John Landis
Produced by: George Folsey Jr.
Written by: John Landis
Cast: David Naughton; Jenny Agutter; Griffin Dunne; John Woodvine; Lila Kaye; Joe Belcher; David Schofield; Brian Glover; Anne-Marie Davies; Frank Oz; Don McKillop; Paul Kember
Special Effects: Rick Baker
Year: 1981

Plot Synopsis
David (Naughton) and Jack (Dunne) are two young Americans backpacking across Europe. In England, the two begin their trek across the vast Yorkshire moors. They arrive at a small local pub called The Slaughtered Lamb. When they enter they meet with a cold reception. Nevertheless, Gladys (Kaye), the barmaid, serves them a cup of tea and the two Americans take a seat.

Jack notices a pentangle on the wall and mentions to David that it is "the sign of the wolf." He asks his friend to raise the subject but David objects. "Remember the Alamo," comments Jack—which is overheard by Gladys and leads to a Mexican joke from one of the men in the pub (Glover). Jack finally asks what the pentangle on the wall is for and the pub goes quiet. The two boys are told to leave and warned, "beware the moon and stick to the road."

Outside, the two backpackers opt to get as far away from The Slaughtered Lamb as possible. As they do they wander onto the moors. Soon they find themselves lost and followed by a mysterious animal that growls and stalks them. Back at The Slaughtered Lamb, Gladys tells her customers that they should not have let the two Americans leave. She tells the men to go and help them.

Jack falls over on the moors. When David attempts to help him up to his feet, a huge wolf attacks and begins to devour his friend. David turns to run but, hearing Jack's screams, he doubles back where he, too, is attacked. The men from The Slaughtered Lamb arrive and shoot the wolf dead. David has been mauled. He sees his attacker appear in human form, just before he blacks out.

David (David Naughton) and Jack (Griffin Dunne) as two young Americans backpacking in England.

Three weeks later, David regains consciousness at a London hospital. Two nurses are present: Alex Price (Agutter) and Nurse Gallagher (Davies). David is under the care of a friendly male doctor called Hirsch (Woodvine). David blacks out again and dreams about running through some woodland. When David wakes up, an obnoxious man from the American Embassy (Oz) arrives to grill him. David explains that it was not a lunatic that attacked him but a wolf.

Two men from Scotland Yard (McKillop and Kember) arrive in Hirsch's office to investigate the case. They then interview David, who restates that he was attacked by a wolf. However, the case is deemed closed because the body of his attacker was found. David again dreams about running through the woods. This time he is naked and he beheads a deer with his bare hands.

Alex brings David some food to eat. They flirt. David has another nightmare—this time he dreams that he sees himself turn into a vampire while being attended to by Alex. When he wakes up he informs Doctor Hirsch that he'd rather not be left alone.

Alex spends the night looking after David. He tells her that she is very attractive and falls asleep again. David has a nightmare in which a gang of maniacs kills his entire family. When he awakens, one of the maniacs arrives in the hospital room and kills Alex. He wakes up again, having had a nightmare-within-a-nightmare.

The next morning David sees Jack—who appears to him as a decaying corpse. Jack warns David that he will turn into a werewolf at the next full moon. David screams for Alex, and when she arrives he kisses her. Alex asks David if he would like to stay with her when he is released from hospital the following day. The next evening David and Alex make love at her house. When David wakes up during the night, he is again greeted by Jack, who then repeats his warning about David's metamorphosis into a lycanthrope. Alex goes to work the next day and leaves David alone. Doctor Hirsch investigates The Slaughtered Lamb where one customer (Schofield) warns him that the "boy is in danger." At Alex's apartment, David changes into a werewolf and prowls the night. His first victims are a young couple (Geoffrey Burridge and Brenda Cavendish) and their friend (Christopher Scoular). Hirsch is concerned for David's safety and asks Alex to call home—when she does there is no answer.

Jack tries to convince David to commit suicide before he transforms again.

Three tramps are attacked and killed by David. His final victim is a businessman returning home via the London underground (Michael Carter). The next morning, David wakes up naked in London Zoo's wolf den. He escapes and, after stealing someone's jacket, makes it back to Alex's house. Alex hails a taxi to return him to the hospital, but when the taxi driver talks about the previous evening's murders, David insists on being let out of the cab.

Alex chases after David as he shouts that he was the one responsible. David tries, and fails, to get himself arrested. He tells Alex that he loves her and kisses her goodbye. David rings his house in America and talks to his young sister. He fails to slit his wrists in the phone booth, and notices Jack beckoning him into a pornographic movie house. In the cinema, Jack introduces David to his latest victims, who all tell him to commit suicide. However, it is too late and David begins to transform again.

The police barricade up the cinema after David mauls a customer. The werewolf escapes, killing one of the men from Scotland Yard and wrecking havoc around Trafalgar Square. The police corner the wolf, but Alex breaks through their firing squad. She tells David that she loves him, but when the wolf attempts to pounce at her, the police open fire and kill it. David's dead, bullet-ridden body lies on the ground as Alex weeps and Dr. Hirsch runs to her side.

Critique

An American Werewolf in London is a movie that hits so many high points that it is difficult to even know where to begin, but this is likely to be one of the most biased critiques that you will ever read of the feature. Simply put, *An American Werewolf in London* is rivaled only by *Fantasia* and the first two *Godfather* movies as this author's favorite film of all time. Yes, it really is *that good* and if you have—as unlikely as it

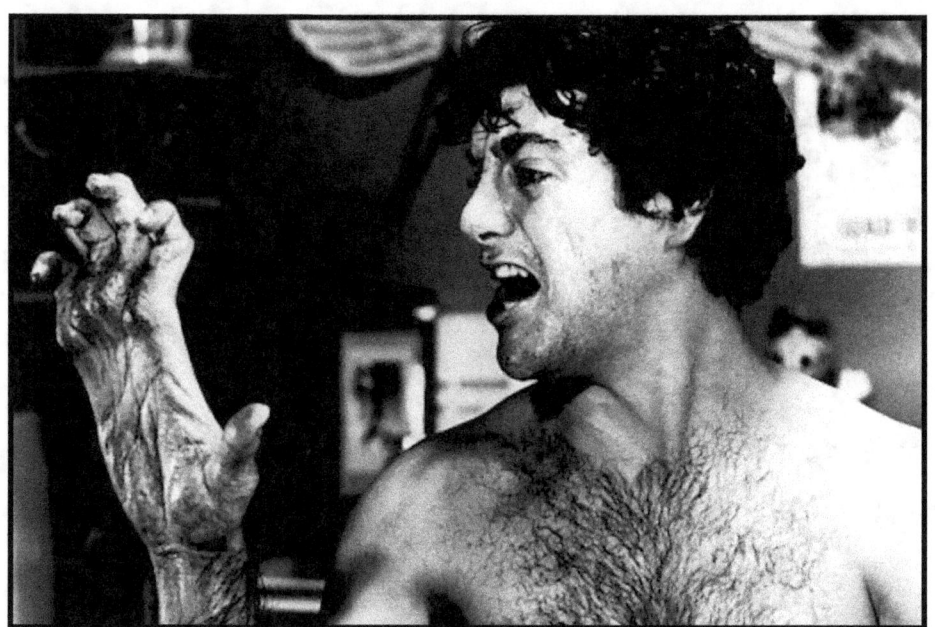

David Naughton's incredible metamorphosis into a werewolf is still amazing to watch.

is—picked up this book without having seen the movie, then one can only emphasize his envy at the thought of once again viewing this classic for the first time.

From the endlessly quotable script ("A naked American man just stole my balloons" or "Have you ever tried talking to a corpse? It's boring!"), to the groundbreaking man-to-beast transformation courtesy of Rick Baker, the movie is every bit as entertaining now as it was 25 years ago. While new breakthroughs in digital special effects have allowed for the sort of realism evident in productions such as *The Lord of the Rings* trilogy (and, indeed, permitted for such horrific cinematic experiences as the *Star Wars* prequels), there remains a huge satisfaction in knowing that what you are watching was actually constructed by someone from the ground up. Moreover, it is a testament to the skills of Baker that David Naughton's incredible metamorphosis into a four-legged lycanthrope is still amazing to watch, especially as it takes place with full lighting, and the sequence certainly puts to shame the computer-generated transformations that informed the 1997 in-name-only sequel *An American Werewolf in Paris*. Even when one looks at the werewolf design for 2003's awful Goth blockbuster *Underworld*—a film with budget to spare—the end result is not even fit to lick the boots of this movie[1]. While some have argued that Joe Dante's 1981 classic *The Howling* has the superior lycanthrope[2], this writer is inclined to disagree simply because of the sheer length of the special effect that Baker creates, not to mention the emotional involvement that we have in David Naughton's character. His portrayal is so accomplished, and his character so likeable, that his pain becomes our pain—undoubtedly the sign of a classic picture. Furthermore, breaking the rules of the genre, Landis makes it clear from the get-go that his werewolf does not need silver bullets to die. This is very much a movie that drags an old literary and cinematic genre into the contemporary age and, in doing so, recreates everything that went before it.

John Landis

The special effects aside, what really makes *An American Werewolf in London* such a delight is its obvious humanity. Credible, unforgettable characters drive a narrative that flips between humor and horror with an ease that most other genre movies can surely only envy. Certainly, neither emotion ever clashes with the other—such is the skill of Landis as a director and the beauty of his script. It is remarkable that the director creates some of the most nightmarish moments ever filmed, such as the dream-within-a-dream set piece and the shocking moment in which Naughton tears a deer's head asunder with his bare hands, yet he also crafts a number of laughs and a genuinely moving romantic subplot.

The number of laugh-out-loud moments is too vast to comprehensibly list; however, it should be noted that Landis' eye for documenting the personalities and culture of England is impeccable. The cheery Cockney couple, the straitlaced policeman at Trafalgar Square, the tackiness of British sex comedies from the 1970s, the all-male Northern pub, the overworked National Health Service staff and the grim hospital meals all lead one to conclude that this is somebody whose knack for satire is unparalleled. Perhaps the film's standout comedy moment involves the initially silent welcome that the two Americans are greeted with when they enter "The Slaughtered Lamb," an isolated Northern English pub. The entire scene will likely have most British viewers in hysterics and yet, this hilarity quickly turns to something altogether more sinister at the blink of an eye. What is at first lighthearted and amusing begins to seem conclusively more mysterious—and our laughs turn to nervous anticipation as Dunne and Naughton are forced to leave the pub and walk into certain danger.

Landis' casting choices are all excellent. Jenny Agutter makes for an inspired choice—her natural beauty shines throughout the movie, although she is not too glamorous (one might say that she really is a brilliant example of the girl next door) for us to find it impossible to believe her spontaneous romancing of a strange American man. Agutter embeds her character with a sad-eyed hint of misfortune that is perhaps inevitable from an overworked and underpaid NHS nurse. When she tells Naughton about her failed relationships, it adds a real emotional impact to the movie's sudden, tragic ending. There is evident chemistry between the two stars, and the end result

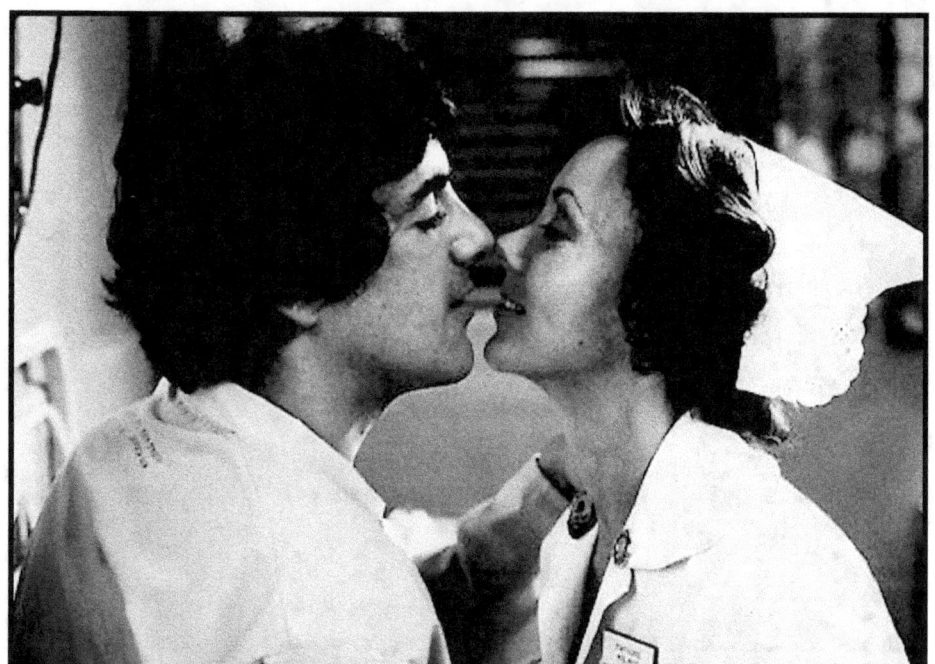

David and Alex (Jenny Agutter) share a rare happy moment in their doomed romance.

makes for one of the most believable onscreen romances this side of *Casablanca*. When Naughton is shot dead at the finale of the movie, it is following Agutter's pained "I love you," which in the hands of many lesser filmmakers could all too easily descend into farce (she is, after all, *speaking to a werewolf!*). Instead, the emotional performance by Agutter actually makes her lover's death as bittersweet and moving as anything ever put on screen and infinitely more effective than such redundant "romantic comedies" as *Pretty Woman* (1990) or *Sleepless in Seattle* (1993). It is indeed difficult, if not impossible, to think of any other horror movie that can boast an honest, powerful romance to accompany the inevitable carnage—making *An American Werewolf in London* a truly unique experience. Exactly how this hodgepodge of so many different emotions and ideas did not end up as a farce is beyond belief, and on account of this movie alone one feels that a case could, and should, be made for Landis to be listed as one of the finest directors to ever walk onto a film set.

If all of this praise seems somewhat overbearing, then keep in mind that this is the movie that also features a cameo from the Muppets, a naked David Naughton running around London Zoo, a killer soundtrack and, perhaps best of all, a jovial talking corpse—without a doubt one of cinema's most inspired sights. Dunne's performance is flawless as the dead Jack Goodman, appearing to forewarn Naughton's character about his imminent transformation, and one wishes that he had gone on to do more in front of the camera (although appearing in this film and then working with Scorsese on 1985's masterful *After Hours* is boasting right enough by anyone's standards). However, perhaps the greatest tragedy of *An American Werewolf in London* is that Naughton never went on to become a leading man even in spite of the talent that he showcases in this feature. Considering that his performance is the standard by which every subsequent,

It's unfortunate that David Naughton never received more film roles of this calibre.

and even previous, werewolf film should be measured upon (even Jack Nicholson's turn in 1994's *Wolf* does not hold a candle to Naughton's complex and tormented leading role), it is unfortunate that the actor never received further opportunities in films of this size. Moreover, for those of us who have little fondness toward the commotion, inwardness and quagmire of the U.K.'s capital city, it is a cathartic experience to see a werewolf trash the entire area.

An American Werewolf in London not only forced the Academy Awards to recognize makeup effects as a genuine art form, it also paved the way for a short spell of lycanthrope movies that included *The Beast Within* (1982) and the Stephen King adaptation *Silver Bullet* (1984). Although no future movie could ever come close to recreating the special magic that is evident in Landis' feature, it is pleasant to know that 2000's *Ginger Snaps* and 2002's *Dog Soldiers* have, at the very least, made an admirable attempt to do so.

And remember: "Beware the moon and stick to the road."

Standout Moment

Could it be Jenny Agutter's now-legendary shower scene? Not quite. Rick Baker's amazing transformation sequence is still an incredible accomplishment.

Memories of the Film

Following the classic comedies *Animal House* in 1978 and *The Blues Brothers* in 1980, John Landis would enter the horror field with a bang with *An American Werewolf in London*. "Well, I'd written it in 1969," reveals the director. "I was out in Yugoslavia working on *Kelly's Heroes* and when I made the movie in 1981 it was almost exactly the same." So what changed? "Well, there was this cartoon theater...the first time I was in

London was 1965, and then in 1975 I was hired as one of the writers for *The Spy Who Loved Me*, which at the time was to be directed by Guy Hamilton—who later pulled out. It was back then that I spent a lot of time in London, it was the time when [Bond franchise owners] Cubby Broccoli and Harry Salzman were at each other's throats all the time…and I went to these cartoon theaters. There was one in Piccadilly Circus, one in Victoria Station, one at Trafalgar Square and one at Leicester Square. They had these perfect prints of the Warner Bros. and Disney cartoons, and they showed all the classics—Ward Kimball, Tex Avery, Friz Freleng—and at that time in the U.S.A. you only saw them on television. So I was frequenting these cartoon cinemas and the only other people there were the homeless or children, whose mothers had left them there so they could get away to work. Anyway, when I wrote the movie I set the end sequence at Arrow's Theatre in Piccadilly and I originally had the carnage unfold to Road Runner cartoons. Then when I went back to shoot the film, the theater was showing porn—and so we changed that and that's the only difference between the script I wrote for it back in 1969 and the one that made it to the screen."

As for why it took so long for the film to make it to the big screen, Landis remains candid. "In the movie business—well, it's called the biz, or the industry—it's not about quality, it's about success and when you have a bit of success it gives you some power. So *Animal House* was successful, which allowed me to make *The Blues Brothers*, which was also successful and they didn't expect it to be because it was this twisted comedy, and that led to me being allowed to make *An American Werewolf in London*. Virtually every studio had turned down the script since 1969—it was considered to be too weird. Then I finally got to make it." *An American Werewolf* features Griffin Dunne and David Naughton, both unknown actors at the time, in fantastic performances. All the same, was there any reason for casting unknowns in the lead roles? "This was a different time," states Landis. "In the movie business now it's the cart before the horse—you develop a franchise or make movies out of comic books and everything is pre-sold. It was a better time then, you could still make films from your own platform, but now it's either you make it big in the first three days (of release) or you don't. I wanted people to accept these two boys as just being two boys. That's my reason. With Jenny (Agutter)…I had known her for years and I was a big fan of her early stuff, right from *The Railway Children*. It was an insane part for her to play because she invites this patient back home with her and I wanted to cast someone that the audience could take seriously in that role and not just think she was a slut," laughs the director.

From the spoof of the film in the Guinness television advertisements to the consistent television showings on U.K. television, *An American Werewolf* secured its place in the British consciousness a long time ago. However, it did not fare quite so well in the States. Why does the director think this might

Landis wanted Naughton and Dunne (pictured with Lila Kaye) to be accepted as just being two boys.

An American Werewolf...is considered a horror film rather than a comedy in the U.K. because of the gore.

be? "Well, first of all it did quite well here in America," maintains Landis. "It wasn't a big hit...people were taken aback by the graphic violence. In the U.S. it's considered to be a comedy, while in the U.K. it's considered to be a horror film, which is correct—I wanted to make a horror film and it's not really a very funny film. It has some humor in it—I mean, it's a British film, it was financed in Britain." Not that the film went without acclaim in America— and Landis admits that he was "thrilled to bits" when Rick Baker received an Oscar for his work on the movie.

To this day, *An American Werewolf* and John Carpenter's remake of *The Thing* are the movies that are usually held up as examples that you don't need CGI for good effects— surely this is something of an honor? "*The Thing* came out a year later," states the director. "I thought it was great. But it got terrible reviews and no one went to see it and I never understood why. It was a wonderful movie....But, you know—if I did *Werewolf* now I'd do a combination of both. I think when it's done well it works—like with some of the scenes in *Lord of the Rings*—that [series] has marvelous CGI." Speaking of computer effects—what did Landis think of the truly woeful digital werewolf that informed the in-name-only sequel, *An American Werewolf in Paris*? "I've never seen it," insists the director— although Landis did write his own sequel. "Yes, I wrote a sequel to *An American Werewolf*—but Michael Kuhn at Polygram hated the script. It was set 10 years later." With the original cast returning? "Of course they return. Even the dead guys in the theater" laughs Landis. Although the director admits that it's probably "a bit late now" to see a proper sequel to *An American Werewolf*, he is happy to share a little bit about what could have been. "The sequel that was made, that was not a true sequel, I believe that's the case anyway," states Landis. "With my sequel, it involved the girl from the original that they are speaking about at the beginning...Debbie Klein. We meet her in Beverly Hills and she is assigned to her company's London branch. She keeps asking herself, 'Whatever happened to David?' See, the official explanation is that a lion got loose from the zoo. What we don't see in the first film is that the day David spends pacing Alex's apartment, he writes Debbie a letter and it's very weird and mysterious. So Debbie pursues what happened but she keeps hitting a brick wall, and then she finally finds out the truth, and it goes from there…"

One of the things that shocked audiences and critics is the finale to *An American Werewolf*, and the way the jovial, upbeat version of *Blue Moon* kicks in after the somber ending. Of course, to many of us, it's a classic finish to an outstanding film, but did Landis ever think that the intrusive nature of the music might alienate some viewers? "What? Is that a serious question?" asks the director with notable shock. "It's called irony. If they don't get it then fuck 'em." Was it a surprise that the biggest star to come out of the film was the barely glimpsed Rik Mayall and not David Naughton? "No, I don't think it's bizarre," answers the director. "With David I'm actually surprised he never took off. He was in a Dr Pepper commercial in America, and I liked his personality. Rik Mayall is not really all that well known in America, but I think he's brilliant." *An American Werewolf* was unique in mixing comedy and horror—was Landis aware at the time that he was breaking new ground? "No, not really…. I knew what we were doing was unorthodox though." And is it true that Cat Stevens refused the rights for one of his songs to be used in *An American Werewolf*? "Yeah, that's true. I wanted to use his song *Moon Shadow* and he wouldn't let us use it. He had just converted to being a Muslim at that time, he was very religious and he disapproved of the film. It's funny though because now I find out that he's allowing car companies to use his music in their commercials."

An American Werewolf received some further reappraisal upon its eagerly anticipated DVD release in 2002. However, Landis was not part of the audio commentary for his finest film. Why was this? "I don't like them," he insists. "I've recorded two of them now but I don't like doing them. I always want to say 'Shut up, I'm trying to watch the movie.'" Has the director listened to the audio commentary that the stars, Griffin Dunne and David Naughton, did for the DVD? "Yes, and I thought it was very funny," he states. Even with the huge gaps of silence when neither actor says anything? "Yeah, well they're watching the movie. That's what you're supposed to do!" laughs Landis. So how does the director react when someone like me approaches him and mentions that *An American Werewolf* is his favorite horror film of all time? "Well, you know—you meet an interesting cross-section of fans that appreciate different films you've done. I never know which movie someone is going to talk to me about. I mean, obviously I had an idea of what it was in your case," answers the director. "But I was quite taken aback recently when I met a guy from the Czech Republic and he told me about the incredible impact one of my films has had on his life. So I'm thinking of my most well-known ones—*Blues Brothers, American Werewolf, Trading Places, Animal House*—and he tells me it's *Spies Like Us*. I didn't think that was such an important movie—I mean, it was Bob Hope's last film, but I had no idea why he picked *Spies Like Us*. Well, he told me about the time when soldiers occupied Czech and there was strict censorship and his father had recorded *Spies Like Us* from a satellite station they picked up from abroad. It turns out people would come over and watch it in secrecy and everyone loved it because it made fun of the Russians and the Americans and just everyone really. So you have no idea how your films are affecting other people."

David Naughton will forever be associated with starring in *An American Werewolf in London*, without doubt the most prestigious role of his long acting career. "I was in this Dr Pepper commercial that was very popular at the time," explains Naughton. "John Landis was an avid Dr Pepper drinker, although he was shipping in Tab as well. Well, I got discovered from these commercials and I remember going to John's office at Universal. It was a curious opportunity because back then this was *the* guy—he was the whole deal, he wrote the script, he was casting it—with the help of a casting director—this was not like my television experience where there were so many people involved. John had the final say. I met with him, it was a very social occasion and we got along well. He told me about Rick Baker, who had worked with him on *Schlock*, and he said, 'Whoever plays this part is going to be working with Rick (Baker) a lot.' I told him I'd lived in London and traveled all around Great Britain, and he said 'The character's backpacking, have you done that?' I said, 'Oh sure," that's what every actor says to get the part—'You're going to wake up naked in a zoo, you ever done that?'—and you say, 'Oh sure.' 'Ever jumped out of a plane?'—'Oh sure' (*laughs*). You just assume you'll pick everything up as the film goes along—it's usually a personality test to see if you fit the profile of the character. John was not particularly big on having stars in the film, although there were well-known people who wanted to be involved in 'The next John Landis film.' It was his pet project for years, and he said to me at the interview, 'Call me tomorrow.' I remember thinking, 'That's unorthodox,' because usually you have to go through agents, do a screen test, meet executives.... John and I were of the same generation and of the same age, primarily. So the next day I called him and he said, 'So, do you want to be a werewolf?' I said, 'Well, what does that entail?' and he told me I'd have to go meet Rick immediately. This was October and they started filming in January."

So how did Naughton react to the script, which called for the actor to be naked three times? "Well, it was really only three times, just like you mentioned," he answers. "You read it in the script and it's, like, only an eighth of a page. You read something like, 'He turns into a wolf,' you go, 'Well, okay,' and then 'They make love passionately'—there's not much more detail. 'He wakes up naked in the zoo.' It's only when you get on set that you realize—'As in naked? With real wolves?' You get told, 'Oh yeah, there will be real wolves and it will be zero degrees out there' (*laughs*). I remember going to meet Rick and he said to me—'So you're playing what part?' and I told him I was the lead. He says, 'Oh, I feel so sorry for you,' which wasn't really the reaction I was expecting (*laughs*). Well, little did I know I'd have to go through all this painstaking makeup, which was not like anything I'd ever done, and I had to be in shape so I was working out and always out jogging...Rick Baker—he's as much of a perfectionist as anyone I've ever met—it doesn't matter how long it takes, he wants things perfect. I'm not sure he even does makeup anymore. I remember saying to him, 'Are we ever going to be ready? It's been 10 hours,' and he'd say, 'No, not yet.' It would drive you crazy, but he won the Academy Award for it, and now he says, 'Of course I could have done better' (*laughs*). I think the biggest criticism he had was that he wasn't a fan of the wolf. When it was out on the street it had this fixed, locked jaw that he wasn't crazy about. He wanted a working jaw that he could control, but there was nothing like that at the time. The transformation part, this was back in 1981 and we had *Wolfen* and *The Howling* coming out soon, these rival films, and to this day I think our film holds up. With the love scene it's best to do something like that on the first day. That's the time when everyone is most nervous, and you're not familiar with each other, so there are not any personal problems yet. Not that there were any personal problems on this film, but that can happen. You end up saying, 'Oh God and I have to make love to this person?' But on the first day everyone is new and you can just get it done and put it behind you."

Was the love scene shot first? "No, in fact it's interesting because we actually started shooting at the beginning of the film," answers the actor. "All that stuff on the moors was the very first scene—coming down the road with the sheep. We wanted to establish these two guys and the friendship of these two guys, to prepare the audience for the horror scenes that were to come. We actually practiced speaking our lines a lot because at the beginning there were no sets built, Rick's makeup was not ready. Griffin [Dunne] wore more makeup than I did—and that wasn't ready yet, so we just went out and shot all the scenes on the moors."

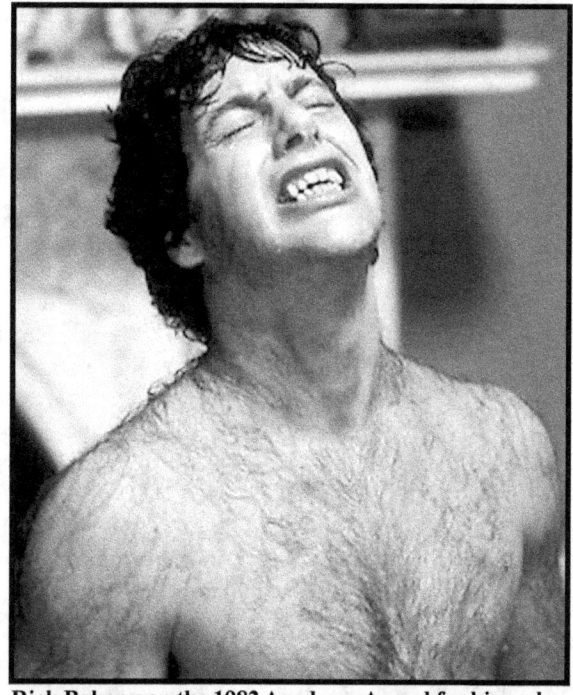

Rick Baker won the 1982 Academy Award for his make-up effects in *An American Werewolf in London*.

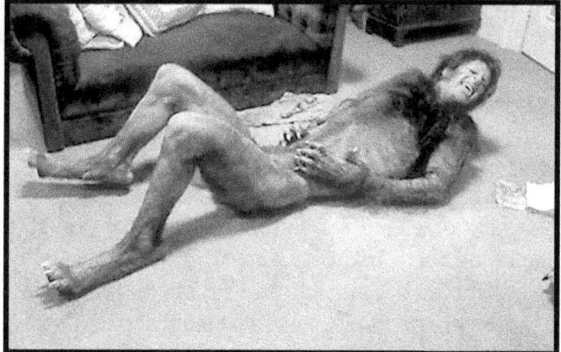

It is surprising to speak to Naughton and find out that, unlike many filmmakers or stars, the actor is extremely forthcoming and willing to chat about his career. However, in the DVD commentary track that he did for *An American Werewolf in London*, there's a lot of silence. "Is there really a lot of silence?" he asks. "I don't know...it had been a long time since I'd seen it and I'd never seen the film alongside Griffin before. Griffin was in L.A. for some specific length of time and they never said to us, 'Everything you say will go into the commentary track.' We thought we were just providing sound bites...and then of course they did use everything we said. I wasn't sure of the fan opinion of it, but I'm not even sure Universal knew at the time if they wanted a running commentary track or just some sound bites. I mean, why would you want to watch the film and listen to us? And how much do you say? I found it interesting to do it...before we started, Griffin and I said, 'Let's not talk too much about the people in the scenes—you know, let's not be too candid.'"

A Dialogue with 30 Modern Masters of Horror

How on earth did Naughton get away with shooting the scene in Trafalgar Square where his character calls Prince Charles a faggot and Queen Elizabeth a man? "That was all shot right there, on the spot in Trafalgar Square," laughs the actor. "I was quite embarrassed by it and, in fact, you can see that—it was done with a lot of energy, with me spinning away from the camera shouting, 'Queen Elizabeth is a man.' I thought they might want to dub all that, which is why I spun away from the camera. 'Surely they won't use that?' Yeah, it was uncomfortable...you know, it's bizarre because I remember the first thing that John shot was the porn film that plays in the cinema. I was reading the script and asked him, 'All this porn stuff, you don't actually see any of that?' and he said, 'Oh yeah, we shot that already—people even turned up to audition for it.' I just said, 'You can't be serious!'"

Did Naughton ever hear much about the sequel to *An American Werewolf in London* that John Landis always hoped to make? "Not really," he states, "There was talk—and there was a tentative deal. They signed us for a sequel, in the initial contract. There was no script, per se. I was talking to John and I said, 'If there is a sequel and Jenny is running down the alleyway, is there a chance I might live at the end and be in the next one?' And John just said, 'No you die, cut to the music.' And so...boom! Dead! Movie over! Get out! That's just the way it goes...But I did see *An American Werewolf in Paris*. I was really upset that they would call it a sequel. I always thought sequels had something to do with the original! It's not a sequel as such, and it didn't do well, it had a CGI creature. It was quite different and I was happy not to be involved."

Alternate Critiques

"On one hand the, the scenes in which Naughton seeks to persuade other people, including the nurse (Agutter) who has fallen in love with him, of the fate that has befallen him, are played for gentle humor. But the passages involving his change into a werewolf...and his attacks on sundry victims are handled unexpectedly straight. To some extent, this means that the film suffers from a split personality. But at times the two styles come fruitfully into conjunction..." (Phil Hardy, *Aurum Film Encyclopedia: Horror*, Aurum Press, 1993)

"John Landis' masterpiece to date. The transformation of David (Naughton) from nice New York Jewish boy to very scary werewolf is an outstanding achievement..." (Dan Millar, *Cinema Secrets: Special Effects*, Quintet Publishing, 1990)

"Certainly the horror and laughs don't always sit well side by side.... Perhaps the whole thing is a brilliant cinematic joke, Landis' way of pointing out the impossibility of making a horror movie in the modern age." (Pat Reid, *Empire: The Greatest Horror Movies Ever*, 2000).

Black Christmas

Director: Bob Clark
Produced by: Bob Clark
Written by: Roy Moore
Cast: Olivia Hussey; Keir Dullea; Margot Kidder; John Saxon; Marian Waldman; Andrea Martin; James Edmond; Doug McGrath; Art Hindle; Lynne Griffin; Michael Rapport; Leslie Carlson
Special Effects: Bill Morgan (Makeup Artist)
Year: 1974

Plot Synopsis

A stranger climbs through the top window of a sorority house. The sorority girls are packing up to go home for Christmas. A strange phone call is made to the house—with the male caller making bizarre sounds down the line to a perky girl called Barbie (Kidder) before stating obscenities. He finishes the call by telling Barbie that he is going to kill her. Mrs. MacHenry (Waldman), the alcoholic sorority mother, arrives at the house. Clare (Griffin) goes upstairs to her room where she is assailed and killed by the mysterious inhabitant.

Jessica (Hussey) receives a call from her boyfriend Peter (Dullea). She mentions that she has something important to tell him, but it will have to wait until they meet the next day. Clare's dead body now sits in a rocking chair, with plastic wrap pulled tight over her face.

The following day Clare's father, Mr. Harrison (Edmond), waits outside the university for his daughter. When she does not turn up he is directed to her sorority house, where he meets Mrs. MacHenry and is shocked to learn that his daughter has a boyfriend named Chris (Hindle). Mr. Harrison agrees to join some of the other girls, and Mrs. MacHenry, at a party for some local orphans.

Jessica meets Peter and tells him that she is pregnant. Peter is in a conservatory where he rigorously practices to become a professional concert pianist. He asks her to keep the baby, but Jessica has decided to have an abortion. Peter tells her to leave—stressing that he has an exam and that

Olivia Hussey is terrorized by a mysterious telephone caller in *Black Christmas*.

Jessica's revelation has come at the worst time. When Jessica comes back to the sorority house, she receives another strange phone call.

Mr. Harrison reports his daughter's disappearance at the local police station, but Sergeant Nash (McGrath) refuses to take the report seriously. Jessica meets with Chris to tell him of Clare's disappearance, and he insists that he has heard nothing from her. At his music exam, Peter belts out a ferocious composition on the piano, while his examiners look on unimpressed. Back at the police station, a woman (Martha Gibson) tells Lieutenant Fuller (Saxon) that her daughter is missing, but she is interrupted when Chris and Jessica charge into the office and ask why their report about Clare's disappearance has not been taken seriously.

At the sorority house, Mr. Harrison eats dinner with Mrs. MacHenry, Barbie and another young girl named Phyllis (Martin). A drunken Barbie asks if the other house residents blame her for Clare's disappearance, focusing upon how the two never got along. Once her rant is finished, she goes upstairs to her bed.

Jessica, Phyllis and Mr. Harrison leave the house to join in the police search for the missing girl. While they are away the assailant in the house kills Mrs. MacHenry.

The missing girl is found dead, her body discovered in the snow by Mr. Harrison. Jessica and Phyllis return to the sorority house and Peter tells Jessica that he is leaving the conservatory, although his girlfriend still will not agree to have her baby. After another obscene phone call, Lieutenant Fuller taps all the calls into the house. Barbie is murdered when the killer enters her room and stabs her to death.

After Peter makes a pained call to Jessica, Fuller becomes suspicious and a search is called to find the student. Phyllis enters Barbie's room to check on her and is murdered. The calls are traced, and Jessica is alerted—by phone—that the murderer is in the house. She does not run outside, but instead tries to warn her (now dead) friends.

The killer chases Jessica and she hides in the basement. Peter knocks on the basement window and enters. Having not seen the killer, Jessica presumes it is her boyfriend. When Lieutenant Fuller arrives, Jessica has killed Peter. A few hours pass; Jessica lies

Hussey takes a rare (if unwilling) moment of rest during a night of carnage.

sedated in her bed, as a police officer stands watch outside. However, the calls begin again—and the killer is still loose in the house.

Critique

Released in the same year as another pivotal horror classic (*The Texas Chain Saw Massacre*), *Black Christmas* is largely overlooked as the important genre landmark that it undoubtedly is. Not only does the film pre-date the short-lived fad of Christmas-related horror movies (c.f., *Christmas Evil,* the *Silent Night, Deadly Night* series and *To All a Goodnight,* to name just a few), it is the precursor to the slasher film boom that was kicked off by *Halloween* in 1978. Indeed, while using the camera to demonstrate the killer's point of view had been done previously in the Italian shockers *Blood and Black Lace* (1964) and *Cat O'Nine Tails* (1971), *Black Christmas* was almost certainly the first English-language horror movie to introduce this now overused device. That it does so in its opening sequence indicates that a young John Carpenter just might have been watching. Bob Clark himself states (see below) that Carpenter actually wanted to see a sequel to *Black Christmas,* and that Clark was the person who suggested the title *Halloween* to the now-legendary filmmaker. Certainly, *Black Christmas* features all the slasher film prototypes—from the mysterious killer to the young, attractive female victims and from a claustrophobic location to a series of shocking, unresolved murders. Unlike the vast majority of films that followed *Halloween,* however, Clark's movie has an interesting plot, drama between the characters that is central to the story and superior acting and direction. Although *Halloween* is the better film, the slasher genre may well have erupted earlier had *Black Christmas*—and not Carpenter's classic—swept up at the box office. In at least one previous interview the film's star, John Saxon, has maintained that the film's lack of success in the U.S. was down to a series of problems that held back the release for a year[3].

Black Christmas is, also like *Halloween*, a film that relies on suggestion and sound rather than on graphic violence. The murders either take place offscreen or are expertly

Margot Kidder (future Lois Lane in *Superman*) and Olivia Hussey could have used the help of a superhero in *Black Christmas*.

(even theatrically) staged without the graphic gore that would become the norm in the genre following 1980's hit *Friday the 13th*. The most disturbing thing about the film, then, is not a series of amputated limbs but rather the horrendously convincing sound of madness that bellows from the movie's maniac over the phone. Part-voiced by Clark, the killer shouts out random names—"Agnes," "Billy"—that bear no relation to the plot but succeed in giving the psychopath a suitably unhinged personality. Talk of "killing the baby," and sexual obscenities as well, give the screaming voice on the end of the phone a far more fleshed out, albeit mysterious, persona than any number of slasher screen villains hiding behind a mask.

Through the killer's random phrases and outbursts, viewers are able to pin their own preconceptions upon why he is carrying out the random killings—and this is arguably far more effective than any hamfisted back-story. Ultimately we know very little about the person slaughtering the sorority girls, but Clark presents—through the calls—just enough information for us to be fully aware that this is someone on a very loose end. The killer's reference to "killing the baby" is also, perhaps, the flip side of Hussey's cool, confident attitude. She is someone who has not given abortion a second thought—but the person on the other end of the phone appears to have been driven, at least partially, to madness through losing a child. In saying this, Clark's film, perhaps sensibly, dodges taking any real side over Hussey's decision to abort her child, and her character is presented as a sensible, modern woman. It is always made clear that she is looking toward the best option to take for her own future. In complete contrast, it is her boyfriend (Dullea) who is unable to handle his girlfriend's independence—with him believing that he knows what is best for her and that she would be best served by a child, a mortgage and a husband.

With the drama involved in *Black Christmas*, it is important to point out that the film manages to flesh out involving, believable characters. Each character is given a distinctive personality, and we believe in everyone on the screen. This is a far cry from what the slasher, or body count, genre would degenerate into. With *Black Christmas*,

Only one of the female sorority sisters from *Black Christmas* will make it through the night—in one piece...

Clark crafts a film that we actually want to follow (in the case of most stalker movies the viewer may choose to fast-forward to the next special effect, usually rendering the genre comparable to pornography). Consequently, although *Black Christmas* features many of the elements that would be groomed into movies like *The Burning* (1981) and *Splatter University* (1984), the film has a classy, Hitchcockian feel to it, and a genuine feeling of unease permeates the events. Furthermore, the use of the telephone as a weapon of terror would be redone in 1978's *Are You in the House Alone?*, 1979's mediocre *When a Stranger Calls*, and then in the later sleaze-fest *Don't Answer the Phone* (1980). The phone would also reappear in the genre when no less than Wes Craven paid homage to Clark with 1996's instant classic *Scream*. Not being a fan of the slasher genre, no doubt Clark would be delighted to learn of his influence upon successive movies. Even the sorority setting of *Black Christmas* is, when viewed today, overly familiar from a long list of horror titles that includes *Hell Night* (1981) and *Sorority House Massacre* (1986). Unlike these films, Clark does not include the sort of elements that might have sunk *Black Christmas* into being just another cheap exploitation movie. Instead, Clark's film is an exercise in prolonged suspense and tension, with an atmosphere that is so chilling that even when watched in the midst of summer can transport the viewer to a far colder climate.

Influence aside, however, *Black Christmas* is a truly unnerving experience, with a deeply unsettling ending. Despite Hussey's likeable portrayal of Jessica, she still ends up killing the wrong man and, judging from the bleak final moments, she herself appears likely to be murdered. As with *The Texas Chain Saw Massacre*, and later *Halloween*, Clark's film leaves the audience in no doubt that the bogeyman is still out there. It dares to let the audience hang on thin ice, with no explanation given as to what might be Hussey's fate. Neither a thrill ride of special effects nor a cavalcade of carefully set up scares, *Black Christmas* is instead the sort of movie that creeps under your skin and stays there. Although Clark would shy away from further horror movies, spearheading another exploitation juggernaut with 1981's raunchy teen comedy *Porky's*, there is

Claire (Lynne Griffin) never makes it home for the holidays, she becomes the first victim of the mysterious caller.

little doubt that he left a blood-stained paw print over the genre. One hopes that in the years to come, more critics will see *Black Christmas* as an important classic that has stood the test of time.

Standout Moment

The final, chilling coda when it becomes clear that the murderer is still on the loose, and the phone rings once again....Never has a telephone call carried so much terror.

Memories of the Film

"It's definitely not true—I had never seen any of them," maintains Bob Clark when questioned about whether or not the Italian giallo films were an influence upon *Black Christmas*. "I now know what they are," continues the director, "but I'm not lying—I didn't avoid the homage of *Night of the Living Dead* in (my earlier film) *Children Shouldn't Play with Dead Things*, so I wouldn't be afraid to say I was influenced by these movies. I now know of the Bava films, my son is a big fan of them, but they did not influence *Black Christmas*." Today, Clark remains proud of his film: "I couldn't make a better movie," he states. "Now they're planning a remake of *Black Christmas*—a company up in Canada is working on it. They have a very good screenwriter—I will certainly see it and read their script, but it's their film, and I really wouldn't know what to do to change it. Many people hated the ending and, okay, fair enough—but I don't."

Clark also notes that, despite its mediocre box office in America, *Black Christmas* was a huge hit in its native Canada. "The movie did extraordinarily well in Canada," he begins. "It was the first big Canadian hit and Warner Bros. picked it up (for America) and changed the title, which I thought was a mistake, and they changed the marketing approach to the movie. In any case, they did a good job of distributing it...it was many, many years before I realized that people were recognizing that it came quite a few years before the others. I think I've told the story many times and I'm told John Carpenter still gets offended, but he shouldn't....John loved *Black Christmas* and he asked me,

Actress Margot Kidder would become a star later in the decade.

'Are you ever going to do a sequel to it?' And I said, 'John, I won't be doing another horror film if I can help it, I'm not ashamed of them, but I have many more films in mind and I would never do a sequel to *Black Christmas*. However if I did, and I have thought about it, it would be a year later. They would have caught the killer but he would be in an asylum, he would escape and he would go back to the college campus and I would call it *Halloween*.' But look, John Carpenter wrote a script, he directed the movie, he edited it, he wrote a different score for the movie—he owed me nothing. I'm sure I wasn't the first person to think of calling a movie *Halloween*—although I wonder why no one ever did because it is a great title. *Halloween* gave a little nod of an idea to *Black Christmas*, and that's nothing." The director admits surprise when told that several slasher films set during the festive period followed *Black Christmas*. "There were others? I didn't know—I'm not being coy, but give me some names…" Told about such releases as *Don't Open 'Til Christmas* and *Silent Night, Deadly Night* (both 1984) the director affirms, "I didn't see *Silent Night, Deadly Night*. In fact, I didn't see any of these."

Conversation turns to the downbeat ending to *Black Christmas*, and whether Clark felt—at the time—that the gloomy climax might have damaged the film's box office potential. "Yeah I was worried about that," he admits. "It was the ending I had in mind, and it was the ending that was in the first draft of the script that I read. I'm not credited with much influence on the writing, but I did do a considerable amount—not that there wasn't a good script to begin with, because there was. I knew it was bold, I knew Warner Bros. really wanted to change it—they may have been right. It was just so horrifying and chilling. The one thing I felt, and I've said this many times over, is that she deserves better—Olivia Hussey played a wonderful and brave character. She didn't do any girlie running and screaming—she went back into the house, she did not leave her friends alone and she was a noble character. So to leave her in doubt was not quite fair—to the audience or to the character."

Coming straight from the horse's mouth then—does Clark believe that Hussey is murdered once the end credits finish? "No I don't," he states. "Because I think she's

been so resourceful. I had one idea that I would cut to John Saxon's car and have him stop and think for a minute, and then turn around and start back to the house—but that was open ended and the audience would kill me (*laughs*) and rightfully so! We know the phone is in the house, and there is a cop in there and a cop outside, so if ever there was a set-up for a sequel you would think that was what I was doing." With *Black Christmas* being light on gruesome set pieces, is this the sort of horror movie that Clark prefers? "*Black Christmas* has one scene where you see a small statue plunged into flesh, but other than that it's all done with cuts and I think it is more intelligent for being done that way," mentions the director. "*Children Shouldn't Play with Dead Things* is pretty grisly but it's also a comedy. My other horror film, *Deathdream*, again had some grim things, but they were also subliminal."

Alternate Critiques

"For viewers tired of the nineties take on the campus slasher, *Black Christmas* is a good lesson in how it should be done. A true classic." (Jim Harper, *Legacy of Blood*, Headpress, 2004)

"In retrospect, *Black Christmas* seems to be merely a compendium of slasher film cliches, but this is the film that introduced these cliches.…*Black Christmas* has had a huge influence on the genre and is the only movie that can actually lay claim to prefiguring *Halloween* on almost every level." (The Goremet, *Rue Morgue*, July/August 2002)

"This genuinely disturbing film prefigures and is superior to virtually all the slasher film canon. It was not a commercial success. *Halloween* (78), which borrows extensively from it, was." (David Henry Jacobs, *Toxic Horror*, Issue 4, June 1990)

Death Line

American Title: *Raw Meat*
Director: Gary Sherman
Produced by: Paul Maslansky
Written by: Ceri Jones/Gary Sherman
Cast: Donald Pleasence; Norman Rossington; David Ladd; Sharon Gurney; Hugh Armstrong; June Turner; Clive Swift; James Cossins; Heather Stoney; Hugh Dickson; Jack Woolgar; Ron Pember; Christopher Lee
Special Effects: John Horton
Year: 1972

Brief Plot Synopsis

James Manfred (Cossins) leaves a strip club in London and heads for Russell Square tube station. When he arrives, he propositions a prostitute (Suzanne Winkler), who kicks him between the legs and steals his money. Shortly afterwards the man is assaulted by someone offscreen.

Meanwhile, two young students—Patricia Wilson (Gurney) and her American boyfriend Alex Campbell (Ladd)—return from a date. In walking off the train, they discover the body of Manfred, sprawled across the staircase of the deserted train station. Campbell suggests that they mind their own business, but an appalled Wilson urges him otherwise. After checking the man's identity through looking in his wallet, Alex is convinced by his girlfriend to help the man. By the time they return with police help, Manfred has disappeared. Patricia has a sleepless night as she wonders what has happened to the man.

Inspector Calhoun arrives in his office the next morning, and is told by Detective Sergeant Rogers (Rossington) about the missing man at the tube station. Records show that this is not the first disappearance of someone at Russell Square. The man was a member of the Ministry of Defense, lauded with an Order of the British Empire, and Calhoun orders Rogers to bring Alex and Patricia in for questioning. Alex is brought into the station to be grilled by Calhoun—who sneers at the student and seems suspicious of him. Back at Alex's student flat, Patricia packs up to leave, upset at her boyfriend's lack of concern for Manfred.

At Calhoun's office, Inspector Richardson (Swift) speaks about a tunnel rumored to still be present under-

Death Line was not a big success when it first came out, but time has been kind.
Below: Norman Rossington and Donald Pleasance

neath the London underground station. The station began construction back in 1892, until the workers were buried alive after a deadly cave-in. With the company behind the construction forced into bankruptcy, the workers were left to die, and the underground railway was never finished. However, due to the presence of air pockets, some of the workers managed to stay alive by feeding off their dead colleagues.

A cannibal man (Armstrong) and his dying, pregnant partner (Turner) are the last ancestors of the dead laborers, living underneath the tube station in squalor and killing for food. We see the cannibal slit the throat of Manfred and drip the blood into his partner's mouth. The man's lair is covered in dead bodies.

Calhoun and Rogers arrive in Manfred's spacious house, still investigating the disappearance. Calhoun derides the man's wealth and materialism. A man from MI5 (Christopher Lee) arrives and informs Calhoun that the case is now closed.

Returning to the cannibal's lair, we see that his partner has died. The ghoul takes a shovel and sets out to murder three men at the tube station. One of the men beats the cannibal to the ground with a brush, but the three men are finally overpowered and slaughtered. Two of them are left on the station floor, and one is taken for food. Calhoun is awakened by a phone call relating to the discovery of the two bodies.

At a medical lab a scientist (Dickson) identifies a fourth man's DNA, presumed to be the DNA of the killer. Calhoun learns that the fourth man's DNA reveals that the killer is carrying the plague.

Alex is called in to identify some pictures of Manfred, which he does. Later, he takes Patricia out to dinner to help patch up their relationship. Following their meal, Alex and Patricia are separated at Russell Square Tube Station when Alex jumps back on the train to obtain a book that his girlfriend has left on the seat of the train. The door closes and he is taken to the next station. However, the cannibal kidnaps Patricia shortly after the vehicle leaves. Returning to their apartment and finding that his girlfriend has not returned home, Alex immediately goes to the police.

At the killer's lair, Patricia awakens in a small room and fights with her adversary before passing out. The next morning, a brash and obnoxious Calhoun, suffering from a hangover, is of little help to Alex. Alex decides to return to Russell Square Station and asks a guard for information regarding a possible underground lair. He is told the story of the cave-in back in 1892. Alex searches for the secret tunnel.

Although never especially gory, *Death Line* still has its fair share of rotten corpses!

When a rat bites her neck, Patricia awakens. The cannibal kills a number of rats, some with his bare hands, while Patricia tries to escape. The ghoul grabs her and attempts to slash her throat. However, seeing her as a possible replacement partner, he instead tries to communicate with her. All he can say is "mind the doors" in a variety of different tones. Patricia beats the ghoul on his head wound, sending him into agony, and makes a run for it.

Alex comes closer to the killer's lair. The ghoul finally catches up with Patricia and tries to rape her. Alex, who uses his searchlight to beat the cannibal across the head, saves her. The wounded killer stumbles back to his lair, to die next to his dead partner. Calhoun and Rogers arrive. Everyone leaves the underground station, as the cannibal lets out one last scream of "mind the doors."

Critique

Retitled *Raw Meat*, and edited by its North American distributors, AIP, for U.S. audiences, *Death Line* is a remarkable horror film that in recent years has finally begun to be seen as a vital addition to British horror cinema. Director Gary Sherman presents the screen with one of the finest sequences of terror as a lengthy, but slow, tracking shot treads through the villain's underground lair. Showcasing a host of decaying and mutilated bodies, the scene culminates in Armstrong's physically repulsive monster slicing the throat of his newest victim (played by Cossins) and allowing his dying spouse to drink the man's blood. With only the intrusive dripping of water to accompany the soundtrack, this is horror in its purest, rawest form—and the quagmire of Armstrong's lair only adds to the putrid, "you can almost smell it" feel of the film. The movie's creation of its monster's underground habitat is nothing short of startling in its theatricality, with its slightly too-marvelous architecture suggesting a set that could just as easily be presented onstage at the city's legendary Old Vic. Regardless of such theatricality, the movie captures a sinister, Gothic beauty in its set design, which is all the more remarkable when one considers that *Death Line* looks to have been done on a minimal budget.

By the end of *Death Line*, Armstrong's monster has become sympathetic and tragic, with even the terrorized Gurney screaming, "leave him alone" to her boyfriend as he violently bludgeons the villain to death. Having been beaten with a brush by one earlier victim, Armstrong nurses a bruised skull during the finale of the film, and screeches out in pain whenever his injured area is touched. Director Sherman seems intent on making the viewer connect with the monster's pain, as the beaten ghoul writhes on the ground howling in agony—his shrieks of pain sounding horrifically real. Raised in the underground tube, *Death Line*'s monster has only the words "mind the doors" in his vocabulary—a comical touch but also something that adds to the character's mystique and tragedy. His awkward attempt to express his attraction toward Gurney through only the use of this phrase (repeated in different, more frantic tones) is both horrible and sad.

However, this does not make Armstrong any less frightening. When first seen, the beast of a man is truly repulsive in his appearance, and his viciousness is in complete contrast with his attempts to connect with Gurney during the movie's climax. Sherman ultimately places the viewer in the situation of feeling compassion toward Armstrong's demise (which comes from a brutal beating at the hands of Ladd), but also relief at Gurney's escape. While this could have made the final scenes of tension difficult (whom does one root for?), Sherman expertly pulls it off—with the viewer only really coming to sympathize with Armstrong during the very final moments of his life. Having been witness to Armstrong's squalor, and the loss of his partner, the monster's death comes with an air of relief. At the end of the film, the villain's once-imposing demeanor has been reduced to a confused, lonely cry and a clumsy brawl with Ladd.

Donald Pleasance cuts a despicable presence throughout *Death Line*.

Donald Pleasence's role, as Inspector Calhoun, is miles away from his likeable portrayal of Doctor Loomis in the *Halloween* films—and the late, great British actor cuts a despicable presence throughout *Death Line*. His brief onscreen time with Christopher Lee, who has a cameo in an essentially irrelevant role as a member of MI5, is likely to bring a touch of warmth to any self-respecting horror film fan. Furthermore, Sherman does at least permit Pleasence to be seen in a briefly comical light during the movie—temporarily offsetting his obnoxious persona. For instance, following a night of heavy drinking, the Inspector (boasting a hangover) finds it hard to stomach Ladd's warranted concerns for his missing girlfriend, and the Inspector's put-downs are certainly amusing.

Playing up the rude, even xenophobic, London stereotype of his character, the actor also gives notice of his own working-class background (which is put down by Lee during their memorable onscreen encounter), and engages with bitterness toward the ruling classes that some viewers may sympathize with. His insistence that something will need to be done about a missing upper-class, OBE winner (when the Inspector's records show other, uninvestigated disappearances at the Russell Square tube station) is largely done to save his own neck. After all, a man of status comes with a level of importance not afforded to Joe Public. In this instance, at least, the beleaguered cynicism of Pleasence is understandable—especially when one learns that Armstrong comes from a lineage that involves those who were killed building the underground station. Left to die by a city that simply abandoned the construction of the new station and those trapped in the wreckage, Armstrong's run-down living conditions and lack of basic provisions are perhaps an exaggerated comment on a London that was still to surface.

An underground train station is effectively used to create a sense of claustrophobia and menace in *Death Line*.

Along with Robin Hardy's better-known *The Wicker Man* (1973), Sherman's movie demonstrates a move away from the Gothic period drama that informed the Hammer films of the 1950s and 1960s. Had bad distribution not plagued both movies, it is possible to imagine that British horror may not have crumbled in the wake of its more lavish, special effects-heavy Hollywood cousins such as *The Exorcist* and *The Omen*. Fittingly, *Death Line* is a superior movie to either of these contemporaries, and one of the most interesting horror films of its decade. Its visuals of decay and its (very British) story of a hidden society were likely of some influence on Clive Barker's *Hellraiser* (1987). Sherman's movie also approached the subject of human cannibalism before any of its more famous cousins did, whether American (*The Texas Chain Saw Massacre, The Hills Have Eyes*) or cult Italian (*Cannibal Holocaust* et al.).

Standout Moment

Armstrong chases the terrified Gurney through the catacombs of the old, deserted tube station, frantically hollering, "Mind the doors."

Memories of the Film

"I was really fascinated by how the London tube got built." begins director Gary Sherman, an American who was living in London as a director of television commercials at the time of making *Death Line*. "It was a really horrific time, there were these competing companies basically in a rush to build these big tunnels under London, and people were killed working on building the underground stations; it was really tragic. I thought about combining that with the legend of Sawney Bean. I heard about that story and I was interested in it, it was very gory as well. So I came up with the story for *Death Line*...I was about 22 or 23 years old when I made it."

As for whether or not Sherman expected that *Death Line* would find cult, if not commercial, success, the director admits that this was never expected. "I never actually thought it would be a cult film. For one thing I never thought it was understood. I didn't actually set out to make a horror film for a start—people just told me to write one because I could probably get it made. But *Death Line* was very political, I wrote a very political story and audiences and critics completely missed the political ramifications of the movie. I tell you who did get it—Robin Wood. As for the other critics, they just went on about how it was one of the goriest films ever made. *Death Line* did unbelievable business in London as part of a double bill with another movie called *Night Hair Child*, which was an awful movie. Eventually that got dropped, and *Death Line* played as a single feature. It did amazingly well throughout the U.K. and all around Europe. Then it went to the U.S. and we got it bought out from under us by American International Pictures...who created *Raw Meat*."

"Mind the Doors," screams *Death Line*'s classic monster.

With the title changed to *Raw Meat*, the film bombed in America, and the director remains notably upset when remembering the scenario that saw his impressive directorial debut given an exploitation movie title and being re-edited. "I was very upset. Robin Wood, who was a big promoter of the movie and who really loved the film, wrote an article for *The Village Voice* and *Rolling Stone* called 'Butchered.' They cut out the whole tracking shot in the tube station, cut out all of the British humor...they restructured the film, and it disappeared in the U.S. It was received terribly. Twenty-eight years later and MGM ended up with it, and they put it out on late-night television. It was still called *Raw Meat* at this point, but the film being shown was the original version at least. People were now beginning to see it in America and they were excited about it."

Death Line's cannibalistic killer is a creature who is also sympathetic, even in spite of his horrendous actions. Was this presentation of the movie's villain something that originated with Sherman, or with *Death Line*'s other screenwriter, Ceri Jones? "I don't actually know," replies Sherman. "The whole idea of the man being sympathetic was the basic idea for the whole film. I can't remember who came up with that line

('Mind the doors') though. I recall when I first came to London, being an American living in England you start to notice things that Brits probably don't even pay attention to. 'Mind the doors'—the way it's said on the tube—was just so British...and I thought it worked, it was very funny in the film. It was certainly risky to present the killer sympathetically. Whether it was going to work or not was always a big question. The idea was that the cannibal represented everyday society and that everyday man had been crushed by society in general. When the accident in the tube tunnel had happened, the developers had just shrugged and said 'it's working-class people down there—who cares?' and this was their punishment. You know, society can live on the opposite side of a wall from one another and not even know that the other side exists.... The rich just kind of thumb their nose at the poor and when the poor rebel, they call in the police, who are of course employed by the rich to keep order. Look at London—you can have the wealthy living just across the road from an impoverished housing estate and they'll never even go near that area. That society can live so close to each other and not even speak is so strange...whenever you deal with an urban setting you get this impression of these glass walls."

Genre icon Christopher Lee has a short cameo in Gary Sherman's classic.

Working with Donald Pleasence was also a thrill for the director. "Well, I was a huge fan of Donald's. Donald wasn't that well known back then, and he was seen as a serious actor and not a horror film star at that point in his career. I first came across Donald in the Polanski picture he did—*Cul de Sac*, which I caught back when I was a student. He was also onstage a lot, and I thought he was the greatest. I said to the backers, 'I want Donald Pleasence to play the roll of Inspector Calhoun,' and they said, 'He'll never do it.' So I went to New York where he was acting onstage in *The Man in the Glass Booth* and I talked to him and basically convinced him to do the movie. He said to me, 'I don't care about the rest of the film, I love this part and I want to do it,' and he was happy to be back in England with his family. Once Donald agreed, people started wanting to be involved with the film. We got Christopher Lee because he knew Paul Maslansky, the producer, and Paul called him and told him what we were planning on doing. Chris told him that as long as he didn't have to wear fangs he'd do the movie. At the time he was tired of playing Dracula and he wanted to act opposite Donald Pleasence. However, there were problems because Donald is about five-foot-four and Christopher is maybe six-foot-seven and I wanted them to have a scene face to face. Donald wouldn't stand on a box and Christopher wouldn't kneel down, so I shot them at opposite sides of a room...it came out well."

"Donald Pleasance's role in *Death Line* ranks up there with the late actor's finest screen appearances."

Despite seeing his film "butchered" by its American distributors and never coming to the commercial forefront as he had hoped, the director is rightly fond of his debut. "I look back at *Death Line* and think it was way ahead of its time, and people didn't connect with it back when it was released—they didn't comment on the social signals that were embellished in the movie. One of the things people say about my movies is that they were ahead of their time; for example, *Vice Squad* was so far ahead of its time people just weren't ready for it. In saying that, if I could go back and change the pace of *Death Line* I would—the pace is the only thing that dates it. It has that grinding pace of British films of the late 1960s and early 1970s. It's a very British movie.... When they changed the title of *Death Line* to *Raw Meat* in America, that upset me. I believed in *Death Line*, and it was important to me. Although the film got attention throughout Europe, *Raw Meat* was just such a piece of crap...."

Alternate Critiques

"A minor classic of straight-for-the-jugular British horror...fast-moving, irreverent chiller...a long way from Hammer horror." (Allan Bryce, *The Dark Side*, Issue 46, June 1995)

"...directed with a visual flair and precision that most British horror films can only envy...the film is peppered with little touches of directorial detail which make it an unusually rewarding experience." (Oliver Berry, *Kamera*, Issue No. 2, 2003)

"One of the most original and imaginative films made on the subject of circumstantial cannibalism in the last 30 years." (Mikita Brottman, *Meat Is Murder*, Headpress Publishing, 1997)

The Hills Have Eyes

Director: Wes Craven
Produced by: Peter Locke
Written by: Wes Craven
Cast: Susan Lanier; Robert Houston; Martin Speer; Dee Wallace-Stone; Russ Grieve; John Steadman; James Whitworth; Lance Gordon; Michael Berryman; Janus Blythe; Cordy Clark; Brenda Marinoff
Special Effects: Greg Auer/John Frazier
Year: 1977

Plot Synopsis

Fred (Steadman) runs a gas station in the California desert. He is ready to abandon his location when a young girl named Rudy (Blythe) appears and asks him for food. Noticing his luggage, she asks to go with him.

Shortly thereafter, the Carters, a middle-class suburban family led by retired policeman Bob (Grieve), arrive to obtain some gas. Mrs. Carter (Vincent) explains to Fred that the family's late aunt has left them a silver mine. Fred warns the family to turn around, explaining that the desert is now used as an Air Force gunnery range. Shortly after the Carter family leaves the garage, Fred's car is blown up and he locks himself away—evidently in a panic—after discovering a bloody paw print left for him on the wall of the service station.

The Carter family is run off the road when they swerve to avoid a rabbit. As they retreat from the vehicle, mysterious onlookers watch them through binoculars. After a word of prayer, Bob Carter agrees to walk back to the service station. His son-in-law Doug Wood (Speer) decides to walk in the opposite direction in the hope of reaching a military base for help. "Easy pickings now," cackles one of the unseen onlookers. The family's only son, Bobby Carter (Houston), is left in charge and given a gun. His sister Brenda (Lanier) protests.

The family's two Alsatian dogs, Beauty and Beast, get loose and Beauty runs into the hills. Bobby chases after her and hears a loud yelp. When he reaches the top of a steep terrain, he sees the animal's mutilated body and is pounced upon from behind a bush. Bobby falls down the hill. Back at the camper van, Mrs. Carter hears heavy breathing when she tries to radio in a message for help.

The crazy family from *The Hills Have Eyes* like to share their pets with visitors.

At the gas station, Bob finds Fred trying to hang himself. The man is drunk, and when he is pulled down he tells a story about the death of his wife and daughter at the hands of his young son, who was born as a physical freak. After the boy burned down his house one day, at 10 years of age, and killed Fred's daughter, Fred smashed his son's face in half with a branding iron and left him in the desert to die. However, the boy lived and has grown up in the desert wilds with a prostitute as a wife, preying on passing travelers for food. Fred's son, the now grown-up and monstrous Jupiter (Whitworth), crashes into the station and kills his father. Mr. Carter runs as fast as he can, but his heart problems cause him to fall, making him easy prey.

Doug returns to the van with some rope and practical supplies, having been unable to locate anyone. Bobby's attempts to tell his brother-in-law about Beauty's death are interrupted by Doug's wife Lynne (Wallace-Stone).

Shortly afterward, Jupiter's sons Pluto (Berryman) and Mars (Gordon) invade the van. Brenda is raped and Lynne is shot dead when she tries to stop Mars from stealing her baby. Mrs. Carter is also shot.

In the distance, Jupiter crucifies Bob and sets him on fire. Bobby and Doug cannot save their father. The remaining family dog, Beast, runs into the hills and pushes Mercury (Gordon), the most retarded of the cannibal clan, to his death. At the cave where the family lives, Mama (Clark) chastises Rudy for trying to flee from the family. The young girl is tied up.

With only two radio transmitters left, and with little ammo, the family accidentally gives away their lackluster resources—via radio—to Pluto when they believe him to be one of the military. When morning dawns, Doug goes into the hills with Beast. Bobby and Susan stay put in the camper van. Beast attacks and kills Pluto. Rudy takes the kidnapped baby and gives it to Doug. Jupiter reaches the camper van, but he steps into a trip wire that drags him toward the spinning wheels of the Carter family's car. Unfortunately, the gas runs out before they can pull him to his death. Switching to plan B, Bobby and Susan lure Jupiter into the camper van, which is prepared to explode as soon as the front entrance is opened. The explosion does not kill the cannibal, and he is finally shot dead by Bobby.

Mars chases after Doug and Rudy to retrieve the baby. He scuffles in the desert sand with Doug, but Rudy grabs a rattlesnake and forces it to bite her brother. Mars rolls over in pain as Doug stabs the man to death. The screen fades to red.

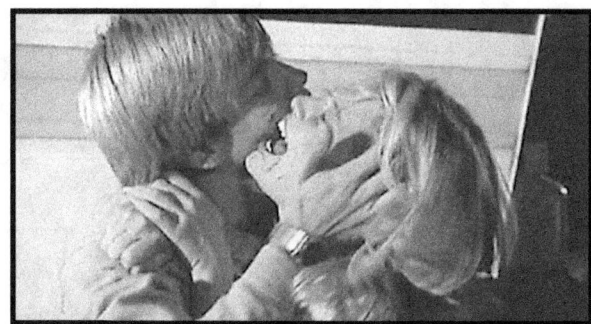

Wes Craven's classic, *The Hills Have Eyes,* is full of carnage as the family vacation becomes a hellish nightmare.

Critique

Following on from Craven's own *Last House on the Left*, the director's second full-length feature is not quite as brutal or graphically violent as its immediate predecessor, but remains a far grittier and more harrowing experience than any of the director's subsequent efforts. As such, *Last House* and *Hills* are usually spoken about in the same sentence—as the sole examples of when Craven's cinematic outlook was still unpolished and as nihilistic and unpleasant as horror films come. The director himself has noted a continuation in tone between the two movies, and admitted that he has no intention of returning to such raw, up-front depictions of cinematic brutality[4]. While both of Craven's most famous horror titles, *A Nightmare on Elm Street* and *Scream,* are undoubtedly accomplished pieces of work, it is difficult to associate either with the mind that gave us either *Last House* or *Hills*. Indeed, these two early works upset Stephen King enough for him to dismiss a pre-*Elm Street* Craven as nothing more than a director of "porno-violence."[5]

A young Wes Craven (far right) behind the scenes on *The Hills Have Eyes*.

Considering the filmmaker's current shining reputation as one of the founding fathers of the contemporary horror film, and certainly its most commercially bankable name, such criticism now appears ludicrous.

Hills, itself inspired by the classics *Deliverance*, *The Texas Chain Saw Massacre* and the story of Scottish cannibal Sawney Bean, would spearhead other films that pitched middle-class travelers against backwoods maniacs with violent results (further examples include 1981's *Mother's Day*, 1982's *Just Before Dawn* and, more recently, *Wrong Turn*). The feel of people "trespassing" in areas of North America that they do not belong is prevalent in each of these titles and echoes the tone of a fairy tale moral. As the monstrous Whitworth notes in *Hills*, "How dare you come out here and stick your life in my face?" (The actor screams this line while somewhat ghoulishly eating human flesh.) However, Craven's movie differs from its influences and prototypes in at least one important way: *The Hills Have Eyes* is set in the California desert, as opposed to a Southern area of the United States that is synonymous with an unfriendly redneck stereotype. Fittingly, therefore, the movie's surroundings add to a false sense of security for the Carter family, who separate almost immediately following their car crash and end up as "easy pickings" for the ravenous mountain men. Craven also shows his villains rape Lanier, reminding the viewer of a time when this taboo was still explored in horror films (albeit often in a graphically exploitative fashion, as with 1978's amateurish *I Spit on Your Grave*, which bears some indication of being influenced by *Hills* and *Last House*).

What makes *Hills*, like the less technically accomplished *Last House*, a major classic is its ability to not let up as soon as the film's terror begins to break out. Following the murder of Steadman, Craven's movie barely allows the viewer to register a breath—with characters frequently biting the dust and the air of horror increasing to almost unbearable proportions. Similar to the aforementioned *Texas Chain Saw Massacre*, *Hills* presents us with a mirror image of the America nuclear family—a wild, savage and untamed group of relatives that are unaffected by materialism or modern capitalism. Thus, when the rogue murderers pillage the Carters' caravan, it is not in their interest to seek out the family's wealth or possessions because they just want to feed and copulate. It is this savagery—and basic survival instinct—of a family living outside of modern civilization and surviving on the most base of animal instincts that helps to make *Hills* such a frightening piece of cinema. The fact that the middle-class, suburban white family eventually turns the tables on the cannibal clan, and does so with such ferocity, is clearly in line with *Last House*'s exploration of the untamed beast that exists in all of mankind, regardless of our social class.

At least one critic has made note of a "cosmic" link in *Hills*,[6] although aside from the villains' names (Jupiter, Mars, Pluto et al.), Craven does little to make this assumption relevant. Indeed, there is no supernatural feel to the film at all—and when the villains are killed they invariably stay dead (at least until the director's horrendous 1985 sequel, which resurrects Michael Berryman). Craven extracts wonderful performances from everyone in *Hills*, and unlike *Last House*'s botched scenes of humor, which mix heavy moments of rape and mutilation with slapstick parody, the director's second movie contrasts scenes of dark comedy with the overtly sadistic narrative far more successfully. For instance, Berryman's confused rants about the "devil dog," whom he presumes is the ghost of the wolfhound that he has already gutted, are comical in nature and subsequently invite the audience to laugh at the character's stupidity. However, this is not to say that Craven turns his villains into cartoon figures; instead, such fleeting moments of bleak comedy allow the audience a rare chance to relax amidst the sustained atmosphere of horror. Likewise, the cannibal clan's mother (Clark) sarcastically hollers, "Maybe you're too good for dog," at her turncoat daughter Rudy when she refuses to eat the remains of the animal that the family has cooked. It's a brief, but comical, reflection of any "civilized" mealtime around the world, with Rudy perhaps reflective of the child that drives her more traditional parents mad with a sudden switch to vegetarianism.

Undoubtedly, the cannibal clan is the most fascinating aspect about Craven's film. The Carter family is a little bit too perfect—beautiful, blonde Lanier and the equally attractive Stone sit alongside clean-cut, handsome Houston—and the end result is a bland selection of characters. Ironically, they only become of interest to the viewer when they are forced to protect themselves from their mountain-dwelling counterparts. At this point, the director expertly allows us to empathize with a family so utterly drab that, for the film's opening segments, we are left to wonder how on earth anything thought provoking can come from a movie featuring such a boring bunch of people. Of course, this is exactly the point Craven seeks to make—that deep down, no matter how predictable or rudimentary our lifestyles may be, human beings remain indebted to the primal urge to survive. The final scenes that show the maniacal face of Speer consistently bringing the knife down on his fallen counterpart, as turntable clan member Blythe looks on

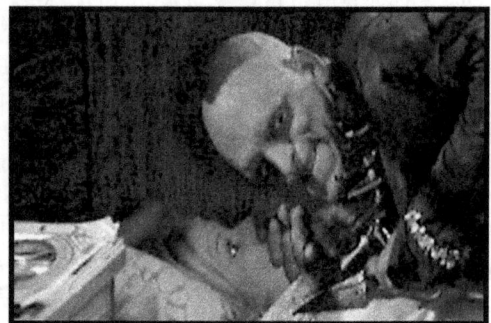

Michael Berryman is a sinister villain in *The Hills Have Eyes.*

in terror, is likely to echo in the viewer's mind for some time after the end credits have rolled. *The Hills Have Eyes* remains one of horror's greatest classics.

(As an interesting side note, original *Texas Chain Saw Massacre* star Gunnar Hansen was offered a part in the film which, to his later regret, he turned down.[7])

Standout Moment

"We have to be sure," screams Lanier, returning to the remains of the family's camper van after it has been blown asunder and, presumably, taken the imposing figure of Whitworth with it. Of course, no horror film is this simple, and Whitworth is still alive....

Memories of the Film

"I think it holds up, as they say, and it keeps you on the edge of your seat and the performances are great. I think everybody did a terrific job....I've directed a lot of films since, but I think these performances are right up there with the best of them," claims Wes Craven. "There's no secret to it," states the director in relation to making such a horrifying and unrelenting film. "Just break every set rule, we just went out there and did exactly that." Michael Berryman, who plays the savage villain Pluto, and whose face highlights the movie's original cinema poster, has similarly high opinions of the film. "All of the strong elements of the film still strike me right between the eyes," the actor insists. "I've got the film memorized and I can do everybody's part and it's always juicy. Entire subplots and the themes, the psychological elements...the things that just root you to your seat, they always strike home—and I can only credit that to my boss, Wes Craven."

The "civilized" family in Craven's influential hit quickly falls apart.

Naturally, talk turns to the genesis of the project, something that Wes Craven is happy to delve into. "The producer Peter Locke was working around Las Vegas and he was always telling me, 'You gotta make another film like *Last House on the Left*,' and I was always trying to do something different. Then at a certain point I was broke...and he approached me and said, 'Come on, let's do something scary—I live right up in the desert. Why don't you write something based there?' So, I went to the New York Public Library and I found this story of the Sawney Bean family. They were a 16th-century cannibalistic family that lived in some part of Scotland. There was a whole area that was considered haunted, very much like in this movie, and a husband and wife were coming through on horseback and they were attacked, and the husband got away, which was apparently pretty unusual. The husband got back home and described the events in such detail that the King sent an expedition. The bloodhounds eventually found these people who were living down at the base of a cliff, in a cave, and when they went in they found all these bodies that had been pickled in seawater—it was the most extraordinary thing! They took the family back to London...where they hung them and quartered them. And I remember thinking, 'You have this violent family and then you have these civilized people doing even worse things to them'—so you had this great switch-around and that's where the idea came from."

The shooting of *The Hills Have Eyes* took place on location in the California desert. At least one of the film's performers admits to having come prepared. "I had an advantage because I was living in the desert at the time," states Berryman. "Some of my memories of the film were that it was very cold at night and very hot in the daytime. It was very athletically demanding because running up and down the side of the hills—they were very steep and everyone else had army boots on. It was a very gritty, challenging film." Furthermore, the finale of *The Hills Have Eyes* features the manhandling of a rattlesnake—an experience that Berryman recalls with nervous laughter. "Oh that rattlesnake…

The shooting of the film took place on location in the California desert.

nobody knew it, but it was a Mojave Green! I said to the handler, 'That's not a regular rattlesnake, that's a Mojave Green—they've got cobra venom!' and he said, 'Yeah, I know—her name is Mary,'" he laughs. "And literally, one day, the snake was on ice to keep it slowly moving and I said to the guy, 'Did you put a suture through its mouth so it can't open up and strike us?' and he said, 'I'd never do that to my sweetheart!' (*laughs*). I couldn't believe it! Then the snake got loose during lunch one day and started wiggling along—which as you can imagine was kind of fun!"

Unlike Craven's subsequent films, *The Hills Have Eyes* has a far more sadistic and uncomfortable streak to it—making it more in the vein of his earlier shocker *The Last House on the Left*. Indeed, both films feature rape—something that, for viewers of more contemporary American horror films, seems incredibly out of place and almost foreign. While Craven admits that it is uncommon to see rape explored in the genre nowadays (although it's worth nothing that *Scream* has a murder-mystery that is based on this very arc and is all the more uncomfortable for it), he jokes about another taboo broken in *The Hills Have Eyes*. "You don't see much baby cannibalism either," laughs the director. "In fact I remember one guy was watching it and he said to me, 'If you kill the baby then I'm gonna kill you!'" Michael Berryman also mentions that the *Hills* cast was not quick to break character after a day's shooting, "At the hotel, the cannibal people hung together and the white-bread family hung together. It was nothing personal, just the dynamics kind of fell that way."

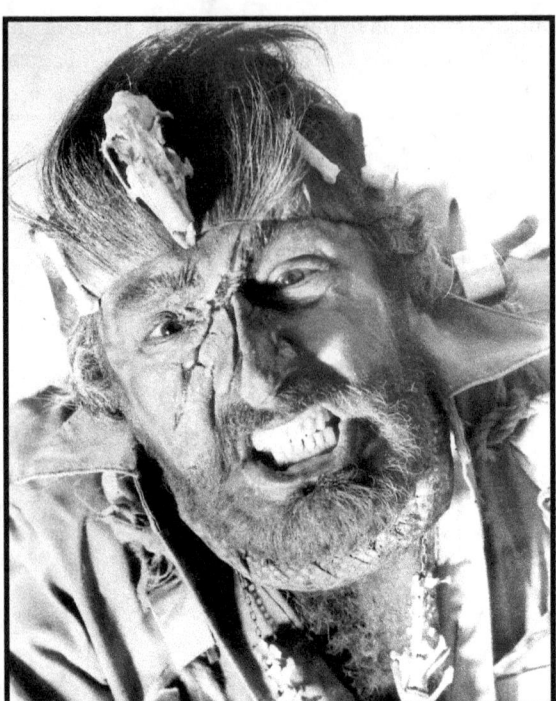

The Hills Have Eyes' villain Jupiter (James Whitworth) is one of the 1970s scariest villains.

What helps to make *The Hills Have Eyes*, and many of Craven's other famous titles, so successful is the cast. Think of David Hess as Krug in *Last House on the Left*, Heather Lagenkamp as Nancy in *A Nightmare on Elm Street* or Neve Campbell as Sidney in the original *Scream* and you get the picture of a director with a fine eye for great performers. "A film really lives or dies by its actors," admits Craven, going on to sing the praises of the hero in *The Hills Have Eyes,* who is played by Robert Houston. "Bobby was a champion skier and acrobat, so he could run down these canyons at full speed…which was amazing….Actually I don't know what they were looking for in our cast—I think we were probably looking for someone who looked a little different (to play a cannibal)." When it came to casting Berryman's role of Pluto, the director says, "I wanted someone who was smart and scary and very athletic." Berryman maintained that while *The Hills Have Eyes* was a great experience, it remained physically draining for him. "I had two open wounds under each arm because I was having major surgery on and off for about three years, he reveals. "We kept them stitched up, but I would have to change my dressings during the course of the work."

Acting in a horror classic of his own has become like a dream come true for Berryman, who claims to have always been a fan of scary movies. "I would grow up watching *Dracula* and all the classic horror films," the actor maintains, "and I would always love that I knew I was going to have nightmares—I actually liked that. During my dream I could keep a voice inside that said, 'This is a dream and you will wake up in the morning.'" Fans of *The Hills Have Eyes* may also be surprised to find out that it began life under another guise. "The original title was *Blood Relations*," explains Craven. "An old friend of Peter (Locke) and mine came up with *The Hills Have Eyes*—I think we had a list of about 45 titles and I didn't like any of them." Neither, as it happens, did Craven like the original ending to the film, and he admits that much of what you see in the finished climax was subject to re-shoots. "I know we went back and blew up the family's trailer bigger—the first time we blew it up big there wasn't much rubble around," comments the director.

Of course, similar to Craven's *Nightmare on Elm Street* and *Scream, The Hills Have Eyes* spawned a sequel of its own. Sadly, 1984's *The Hills Have Eyes Part 2,* which featured the return of Berryman, Blythe and a cameo from Robert Houston, was an enormous disappointment that even Craven himself admits he felt let down with. "You know I don't remember all the details," states the director in relation to the turbulent production of the second movie. "I know it was made on a real shoestring. It didn't quite come off as strongly as the first one. The reason maybe is that the story wasn't that good—it's not a family story; that made a difference too. But I know we were just out of money all the time." *The Hills Have Eyes Part 2* has, however, become famous in its own right for providing viewers with a flashback sequence by a dog! Craven laughs when reminded of this incredibly daft scene, and admits "Yes, the dog had a flashback—it had to be put in a movie at some time!

"The film, in a way, was about 'the other,' the third world, the people that we put down as savages, and then realize that they're trying to scrape by too," states Craven. "I think it's an interesting thing....I have a theory that the most powerful horror films have to do with families, you know *Last House* is that way, *Hills* is that way and *Scream* is that way." The director has long been a critic of censorship as well, and recalls that the MPAA, in America, removed two scenes from *The Hills Have Eyes* that are now probably "lost." Fans may be interested to know that these are the death of Papa Jupiter's father, in the gas station, and the crucifixion of Mr. Carter. "The whole thing with censorship is that it's unpredictable and there's no rules and you never know what you're going to get hit with," concludes the director.

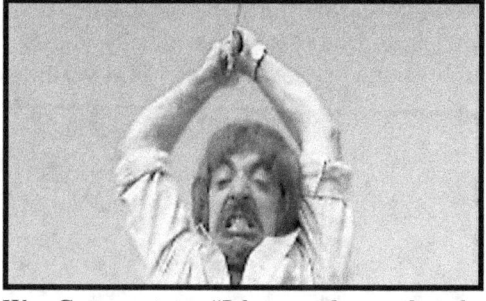

Wes Craven states "I have a theory that the most powerful horror films have to do with families."

Alternate Critiques

"Like most splatter movies it's less violent than you remember...but it always hits the unease button." (Kim Newman, *Empire: The Greatest Horror Movies Ever*, 2000).

"*The Hills Have Eyes* is, in a word, great...one of the most savage, suspenseful and gripping thrillers of the 70s." (*Fangoria's Best and Bloodiest Horror Video*, 1988).

"I rather liked *The Hills Have Eyes*. It was apparent to me that Wes has access, somewhere, to a very twisted fantasy world." (Robert Shaye, *The Nightmare Never Ends*, 1992).

Rabid

Director: David Cronenberg
Produced by: John Dunning
Written by: David Cronenberg
Cast: Marilyn Chambers; Frank Moore; Joe Silver; Howard Ryshpan; Patricia Gage; Susan Roman; Roger Periard; Lynne Deragon; Terry Schonblum; Victor Désy; Julia Anna; Gary McKeehan
Special Effects: Al Griswold
Year: 1977

Plot Synopsis

An attractive young girl, Rose (Chambers) and her boyfriend Hart (Moore) are driving along the Canadian countryside on a motorbike. They pass by the Keloid clinic where Dr. Dan Keloid (Ryshpan), his wife Roxanne (Gage) and his business partner Murray Cypher (Silver) discuss the possibility of expanding their privately operated plastic surgery clinic.

A family pulls over on the motorway to read a map. Rose and Hart swerve to avoid hitting the vehicle, but Rose ends up underneath the fallen motorbike, which then explodes. One of the patients of the Keloid clinic spots the accident from afar, and Dr. Keloid rushes to the scene of accident. The doctor concludes that Rose has just half an hour to live—"It's us or nobody," he says. Hart recovers in a hospital ward, while Rose is undergoing surgery. "What we are going to do is a little out of the ordinary,"

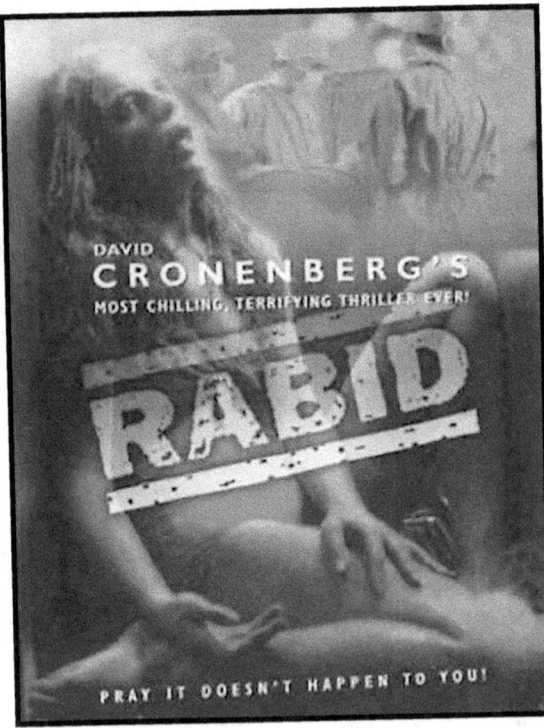

explains Keloid, as he practices a "radical technique" on the girl, whereby skin tissue from parts of her body will be reproduced onto injured areas and begin to grow seamlessly into the wounds.

One month later, Rose awakens and seems fine. Keloid explains to Hart that he cannot move her to a city hospital as she is still in a state of shock. Hart leaves the clinic and is driven back to Montreal by Cypher.

A patient at the clinic, Lloyd (Periard), hears Rose scream for help. He enters her room and the topless girl asks him to hold her. Unable to resist, he does so, and is attacked by her. Blood runs down Rose's arm as she cradles the man in a tight hug. Lloyd returns to his wife, pale and ill—explaining that he cannot remember what has

Even though she's not working with The Mitchell Brothers anymore, *Rabid* star Marilyn Chambers still drops her top in Cronenberg's cult classic.

just happened to him. Keloid examines Lloyd's wound, puzzled by the attack. A nurse believes that Lloyd must have tried to molest Rose in her sleep and that the girl may have struck back without realizing it.

Suddenly during the night, Rose gets dressed and escapes from the clinic. She hides out in a nearby barn, where she attacks a cow. The farm owner (Terence G. Ross) catches her in the act and tries to rape her, but he too ends up being attacked by the girl. We briefly glimpse something stab the man. Returning to the clinic, Rose enters a sauna and attacks a young woman named Judy (Schonblum). Meanwhile, Rose's first victim, Lloyd, leaves the hospital and violates a taxi driver, resulting in a car crash. Rose calls Hart and begs him to come and get her—her boyfriend then phones Murray in the middle of the night and voices his concern. Rose is taken back to her room, where Keloid examines her. For the first time we see an anus-shaped hole underneath her armpit. It spawns a sharp, mosquito-like point that Rose injects into Keloid. She then sucks the man's blood through it.

Hart and Murray begin their drive back to the clinic. Meanwhile, Rose's plague is spreading and a man enters a carryout restaurant, where he attacks another customer and bites the waitress on her arm. Keloid attempts to undertake an operation, but turning rabid, he suddenly attacks his coworkers. Rose leaves the clinic again, where she hitchhikes back to Montreal. A truck driver (Grant Lowe) picks her up. At the clinic, Hart and Murray pull up to the sight of police cars. Keloid is restrained in the back of a police van. The dead body of Judy is found in a refrigerator. Rose leaves the truck to vomit, and shortly thereafter a police car pulls up. The truck driver is found, sitting alone, with a wound on his neck. He cannot remember what has happened. Rose continues her trek back to Montreal, hitching another ride....

The clinic is now under quarantine. A manual laborer called Eddy (McKeehan) attacks some fellow workers. Rose's flat-mate and best friend Mindy (Roman) watches the news on television of a spreading rabies epidemic. The city is under martial law due to the number of people infected. Rose returns to her apartment and Mindy tells her about the plague.

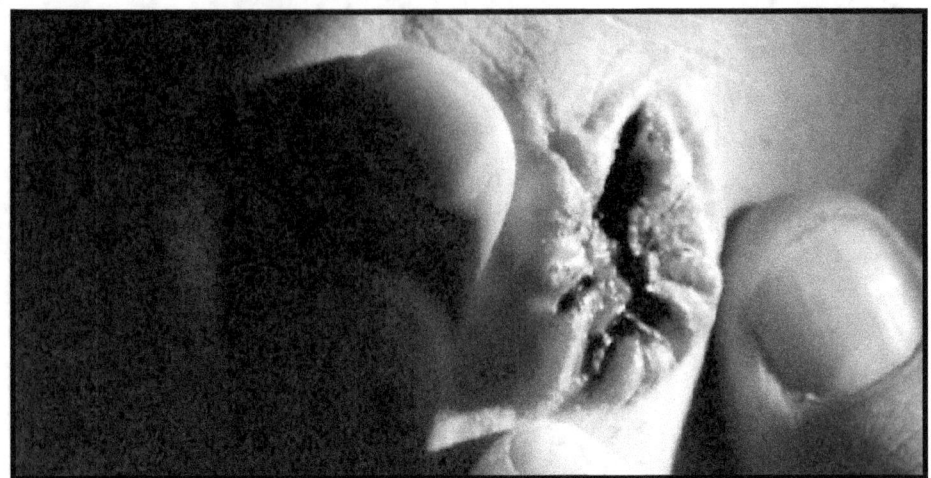

A different kind of 'penetration' for adult film star Chambers in *Rabid*.

Hart and Murray witness another rabid man shot dead at the clinic. Rose leaves her flat and goes to an adult movie theater. Once seated, she attracts the attention of one of the male audience (Miguel Fernandes). Encouraging the man's advances, Rose attacks him. She returns to her apartment, where she collapses onto the bathroom floor in pain.

Mindy witnesses a woman bite a man's throat on the train home. Some rabid workmen attack a car with authority figures in it. A report on television states that those already affected with the virus are considered to be "beyond medical help." Plastic identity cards are given to those who have had an injection against the disease.

Rose enters a shopping mall where she sees a stranger assaulted and bitten by an infected man. The man runs and is fired upon by a policeman, whose carelessness also results in a man dressed up as Santa Claus being shot and killed. When Mindy returns to the apartment, Rose is ill in bed. Hart and Murray struggle to get through the streets and back to their respective residences. When Murray returns home, his baby is missing and his infected wife attacks him.

Rose tries to leave her apartment again, but Mindy holds her back. When Hart arrives, he sees Rose sucking the blood from Mindy, whom she has just killed. The two struggle and have a fight. "It's all your fault," screams Rose to Hart, before pushing him down a staircase where he is knocked unconscious. Hart awakens and returns to Rose's apartment. The phone rings. Rose explains that she has attacked a stranger who currently lies near her. Hart tells her to leave the man's residence. The stranger awakens, infected by the virus. Rose screams into the phone that she is now afraid. The man attacks her. Hart screams, helplessly, as he hears his girlfriend meet her end.

The next morning, some men in a meat wagon pull over to see the dead body of Rose being sniffed at by a dog. Ushering the animal away, the two men take Rose's carcass and throw it into the back of the van.

Critique

Although not as accomplished as Cronenberg's later, more famous, films such as *Videodrome* (1983) and *The Fly* (1986), it is this writer's opinion that *Rabid* is the most entertaining of the director's first three horror films. Often pushed to the side in favor of the more critically acclaimed *The Brood* (1979), or the original body-horror of *Shivers* (1975), *Rabid* is arguably better paced than either film and commands a far more intriguing central figure in Marilyn Chambers, who gives an impressive portrayal of the doomed Rose. Chambers, the erstwhile porn queen of *Behind the Green Door* fame, manages a likeable and convincing performance which, sadly, she never followed up by branching into further legitimate film roles (she still appears in adult titles, and has undergone breast augmentation). This is something of a loss considering her genuine, natural sex appeal as a young woman and, judging from her role in *Rabid*, her obvious acting talent. In the film, Chambers realistically evokes a believable portrait of a woman who is unaware of her condition and who cannot recollect any of the horrific events that she has been a part of. As such, the viewer is led to both fear and pity Chambers—and the final, pathetic image of her dead body being nonchalantly thrown into the trash is a somber and nihilistic ending to a movie that does not exactly ooze with cheer.

As with most of Cronenberg's work, *Rabid* focuses on the metamorphosis of the body and the potential for the evolution of new limbs and diseases stemming from scientific irresponsibility.[8] The sequence where the mosquito-like point that protrudes from under Chambers' armpit is examined in close-up is truly uncomfortable—with the exit hole revealing itself to, unmistakably, resemble an anus and the limb itself mirroring a penis. In this sense, *Rabid* seems like a warm-up for the director's 1999 cult hit *eXistenZ*, which would also feature characters carrying anus-like holes on their bodies (in the case of *eXistenZ*, the holes are penetrated by virtual reality game leads). Whether the director has some sort of anal fixation is, therefore, open to considerable speculation, but impossible to ignore. In *Rabid*, for instance, the sight of Ryshpan circling his finger around the anus-like hole that inhabits Chambers' body, in full close-up, is undeniably sexual. Shown out of context, this moment would not be out of place in a porn movie—such is its graphic depiction. To further the inherent sexuality of this particular sequence, Chambers then penetrates the man in a bizarre scene of gender reversal.

It is also difficult not to acknowledge the heroin overtones of *Rabid*—where Rose needs her new "fix" of blood to stay alive. Cronenberg, a director who is seen by some critics as forever having one foot in the future,[9] shows the pale-faced Chambers spreading her disease whenever she needs a fresh hit of blood from another human. Perhaps an unintentional allegory for the future tragedies that would affect smack users, swapping needles with other addicts during the AIDS era, *Rabid* is a rare example of a film that becomes more potent with age. The sight of Chambers rolling around her bathroom floor, clutching her stomach in

David Cronenberg gets victimized in this gag shot for *Rabid.*

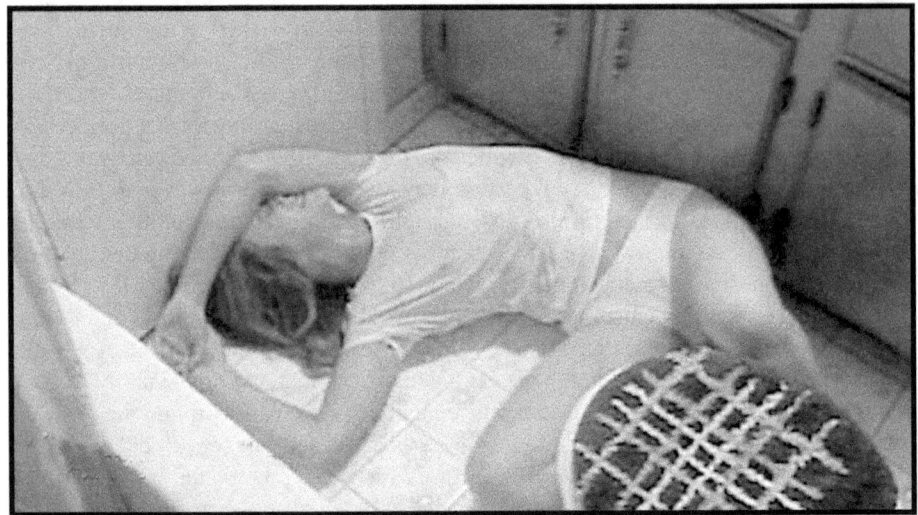

Marilyn Chambers writhes in pain—rather than pleasure—in *Rabid*. "Welcome to horror, sweetheart."

pain, and also vomiting after eating some proper food, only concludes the comparison between her disease and the horrors of smack addiction. Unlike, say, *Trainspotting* (1995), the end result is far from glamorized (even with a beautiful woman as the lead star) and there are no comical interludes in the movie that allow us to see the upside of Chambers' scenario.

At this early stage in his career, Cronenberg was not an especially stylistic director. However, his often-pedestrian set-ups give *Rabid* something of a documentary feel, not dissimilar to that of early George Romero. Indeed, if *Shivers* can be seen to most resemble Romero's masterpiece *Night of the Living Dead*, with its scene of pale-faced ghouls bursting through walls, *Rabid* has more in common with the zombie master's 1973 movie *The Crazies*. As with that film, *Rabid* shows the spread of a disease that turns people maniacal but, unlike in *Night of the Living Dead*, does not distinguish anyone physically from the person on the street. As a pre-AIDS-era movie, *Rabid* aptly predicts the paranoia that comes with uncertainty—with not knowing whether the person next to you is infected with a deadly disease. That the carrier of this lethal virus (Chambers) spreads it through penetration is a chilling premonition of a time yet to come where sexual acts with a stranger would actually carry an air of life-threatening risk. As a result, *Rabid* appears almost as an anti-sex film. Any attempt at intimacy by Chambers comes with deadly results. She is glared at and approached by many anonymous males during the movie, but none of them will get anything but her disease from the encounter. That Chambers, a performer in adult films lest we forget, portrays such a tragic figure is both chilling and ironic.

Consequently, the sight of Chambers in an adult movie theater, casually allowing herself to be fondled by a member of the raincoat crowd, is nicely staged, especially in the context of the actress' erstwhile day job. The audience is always in the position of knowing that men should stay well away from Chambers—leading to a knowing anticipation on the part of the viewer. While this is likely to be read as misogynistic by some critics, it actually lends the movie an air of fun that is otherwise absent. Even the moment where Santa Claus is shot, leading the bumbling police officer to utter, "Oh, Christ," carries a certain absurdity. However, what really makes *Rabid* one of Cronenberg's finest films is the unexpected, shattering ending. *Rabid* is one of these films where the viewer really cannot predict the finale—but with a climax as bleak as *Last House on the Left* or *Night of the Living Dead*, the movie etches itself into the status of classic. It's certainly not pretty, but who said horror films should ever be.

Standout Moment

The virus takes hold in a shopping mall, allowing for even Santa Claus to meet a grim demise. It's as bizarre as it sounds, but then this is a Cronenberg movie...

Memories of the Film

"The thing most people were interested in was Marilyn Chambers because she was quite an extraordinary porno star," says David Cronenberg, reflecting upon *Rabid*. "She was the Ivory Snow girl—and she was on all the boxes of Ivory Snow and the logo was '99 and 44/100ths percent pure,' and there was a picture of Marilyn holding this baby. For years, that was their emblem," adds the director, speaking about the famous Proctor and Gamble product. "And then it was revealed that this woman, who modeled for them, was a porno star! One of the most extreme ones—she did a movie called *Behind the Green Door*—it's considered a classic porno, and I swear I haven't seen it. I wanted to, but I never did see it. So that was an embarrassment to Ivory Snow, so she was famous not just for the porno films but for the Ivory Snow scandal."

"My producer Ivan Reitman was in Montreal at the time; he produced *Shivers* and *Rabid* for Cinepix, and we had gone to Cannes with *Shivers*. We had seen that the Cannes Film Festival is one thing, but the Cannes film marketplace was really where films got bought and sold. We saw this woman on a street corner and it looked as if she was doing a drug deal, but it wasn't drugs, it was movies, they were after film cans," remarks Cronenberg. "It was this amazing exchange going on, from countries all over

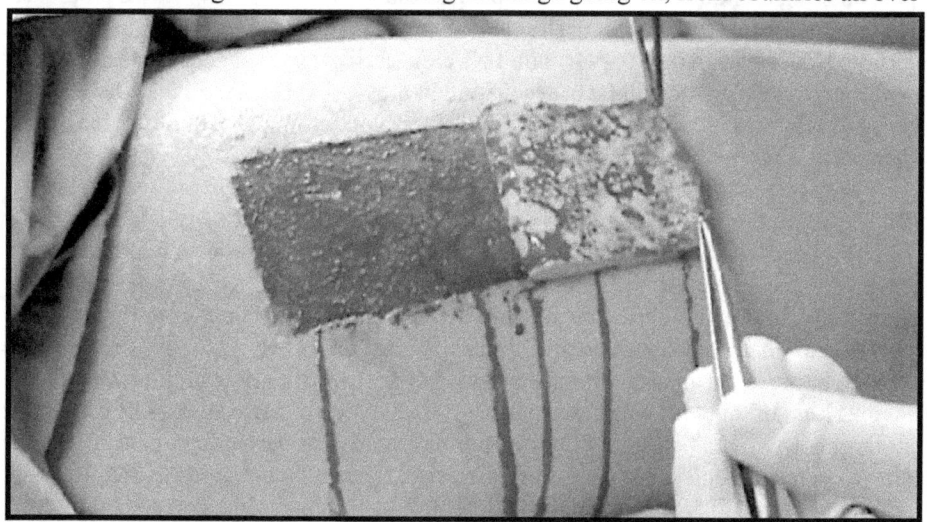

Cronenberg never skimped on the gore in his early shockers.

Rose selects her next victim at an adult movie house; hopefully they weren't showing one of her other films.

the world—there must have been over a thousand movies sold here at Cannes, and we said, 'Next time we come here with a movie, how are we going to get people to come and see our movie?' And the answer was, and it still seems to be the answer to major studios—'Yes, they have a star. They have a film star people want to see,' and that's how you distinguish a film in the opening weekend, and it seems to work now more than ever. So how do you get a star when you don't have any money, when you have a very low-budget horror film? For *Rabid*, I wanted Sissy Spacek, but she had just done *Badlands* and they said, 'No, she's got attention now.' So Ivan's idea was Marilyn Chambers because she was always the girl next door. She was this beautiful, pure-looking blonde who did these amazing sexually obscene things. It was fabulous," laughs the director. "So he said, 'The character in *Rabid* is supposed to be this beautiful girl-next-door type of thing—why don't we cast Marilyn Chambers because everybody will want to see her—it will be her first straight movie and I've heard that she wants to do a straight movie. So we'll audition her, and if you really don't think she can do it, then we'll do something else.'"

Thankfully, Chambers proved to be the right person for the part. "Well, she was really good at the audition," recalls Cronenberg. "So we thought, 'Let's do it,' and that was how Marilyn Chambers, porno star, did her only straight movie—and I don't know what happened, she was really quite good, and I had no idea why. Well, I had some idea, it had to do with her husband Chuck Traynor but that's another thing we won't talk about—that and the silver revolver...will I leave this? But, anyway, it was quite strange because her husband/manager was on the set all the time and he was, like, a famous kind of thug—it was very strange. But anyway, so that was just one of the few stories about *Rabid*." Despite moving on to far more commercially popular films, the director remains fond of his early horror movies, especially in regards to the bleakness presented by them. "*Rabid* has one of the bleakest endings I've ever seen and I don't how, for a low-budget horror movie, we got away with it. But it was quite exhilarating, I think, it's amazing."

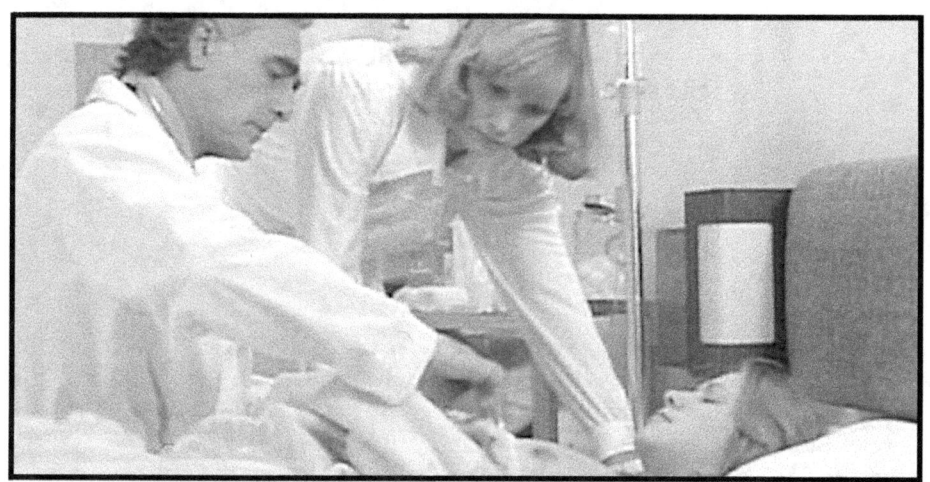
Scientific meddling causes the vampire-like plague which threatens the city.

Looking back on his early pictures, Cronenberg reveals only favorable feelings toward them. "Cinepix were originally my mentors, in a way and my teachers—because Ivan had directed a couple of movies and I never had. When I did *Shivers* anyway, I knew nothing. I had done my underground films where I did everything myself—shots and edited, there was no crew. The first time I sat down in a production meeting was for *Shivers*. I had no idea what a production meeting was, or what you did. I had no idea what a production manager was, I had no idea what an AD was, I didn't know what a production designer was, I had an idea what a costume designer might be (*laughs*). So I was really very fortunate that the pressure was intense because we were very ambitious in *Rabid* as well."

Cronenberg also states that there was a "Separatist group in Canada at the time, who wanted Quebec to become a separate state. So we had the spectacle of seeing troops and tanks on the streets of Montreal...and that was really quite shocking, because in those days you didn't see machine guns in the streets of a North American city. It was well understood, especially in Quebec of course, that *Rabid* was a subtle comment on the politics of the time. There were a lot of people on the streets, a lot of army guys in uniforms and stuff, and not much money to do it. So basically I had a lot of support from people who just wanted to see me do the best I could do. I thought that was the way it was going to be forever."

Alternate Critiques

"Although being his most disappointing film, it is still way above most similar fare. It is exciting, well-directed, gory and somehow manages to make its central character touching and sympathetic." (Michael Wesley, *Samhain*, Issue 1, Nov/Dec 1986)

"The film is essentially a bigger-budget retread of Cronenberg's own *Shivers*...and while Cronenberg's reputation for appalling violence isn't undeserved, *Rabid* frequently hints at the more esoteric direction his later films would take." (John W. Bowen, *Rue Morgue*, May/June 2004, Issue 39)

"Darkly funny and surreal...truly innovative horror classic." (Billy Chainsaw, *Neon*, July 1998, Issue 19)

CHAPTER 2
CREATURE FEATURES
Five examples of First-Rate Creature Carnage

Alligator

Director: Lewis Teague
Produced by: Brandon Chase
Written by: John Sayles
Cast: Robert Forster; Robin Riker; Michael V. Gazzo; Dean Jagger; Sydney Lassick; Jack Carter; Henry Silva; James Ingersoll; Bart Braverman; Leslie Brown; John Lisbon Wood; Robert Doyle; Patti Jerome
Special Effects: Robert Short
Year: 1980

Plot Synopsis

A little girl and her mother (Patti Jerome) attend a show where a man wrestles an alligator. The reptile gains the upper hand and savagely attacks the man. Following the show, the little girl convinces her mother to buy her a pet alligator, but the next morning the child's dad flushes the creature down the toilet.

Twelve years later, we meet David Madison (Forster), a police officer who complains to a pet shop owner, Luke Gutchel (Lassick), about the recent dog thefts that have been taking place. However, the officer's main priority is a dismembered arm, which is discovered by sewage workers. The workers also net the dead body of a rare species of dog. Chief Clark (Gazzo) explains to Madison that only three breeds of this dog were registered in the state of Missouri.

At Slade Pharmaceutical, a cold-hearted laboratory worker, Arthur Helms (Ingersoll), tells Gutchel that he needs more puppies to experiment on. Later, Gutchel takes some dead animal carcasses down to the sewers to dispose of them, but he is attacked and eaten by a huge alligator. His leg washes up at the sewage plant. Madison traces Gutchel to Jade Pharmaceutical, but Helms plays dumb and maintains that his dogs are all bred for laboratory use. "You just got caught with your pants down," says Slade (Jagger)—Helms' boss and future father-in-law—who urges the man to keep his cool.

At a press conference, it is revealed that Madison once lost a partner while on duty. When Madison asks for help to check out the sewer system, none of his coworkers respond, but a new officer, Jim Kelly (Perry Lang), agrees to help out. The two get off to a good start when they arrest a crazy man (John Lisbon Wood), who enters the police station claiming to have a ticking bomb attached to him.

Down in the sewer, the two cops walk deeper and deeper into the underground maze of tunnels, until they finally encounter the alligator. Madison fails to save his partner, and he later wakes up in the hospital. A journalist for the city's main paper, Thomas Kemp (Braverman), overhears Madison's story of the large reptile living underneath the city.

Madison and Chief Clark go to a nationally recognized herpetologist named Marisa Kendall (Riker) to ask about alligators. Marisa talks about the alligator she once had as a child. Kemp investigates Madison's story. Deep in the sewer he is also devoured, although he manages to snap pictures of the last seconds of his life. His camera washes up; photographs of the alligator now exist.

The mayor of the city (Carter) calls in a SWAT team to deal with the creature, but they fail to find it. Later the alligator finds its way into a suburb where it attacks a police officer. The beast then settles into an outside swimming pool. The SWAT team and a big-game hunter named Colonel Brock (Silva) comb a spacious lake for the reptile, but it is nowhere to be seen. When Madison arrives at the scene, the Chief informs him that he is no longer needed.

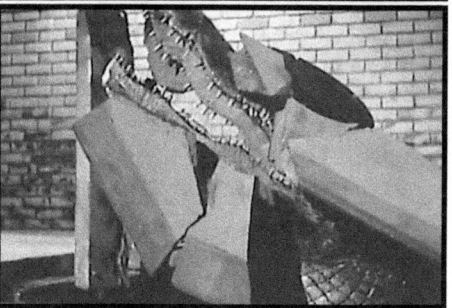

The film's title creature is surprisingly convincing—and ready to wreck havoc!

Madison drives to Kendall's place of work, and the two examine some cells from one of the dead dogs that had been swept up earlier. They discover that the animal had been injected with strange liquids. The two stop by Slade Pharmaceutical, where Helms talks about a testosterone he had been working on that had the adverse side effect of giving the specimens an insatiable appetite, although he denies any knowledge of the dead animals.

Slade is one of the prime fundraisers for the city's mayor. He asks the mayor to do something about Madison. Shortly afterward, Chief Clark tells Madison that he "pushed too far" and releases him from duty. Madison leaves the police building, but first grabs some dynamite from the evidence room.

Madison and Kendall explore the sewer, where they find another dead dog. The alligator still lies in a swimming pool. At a birthday party some young children force a blindfolded young boy into the water, where the reptile eats him. Colonel Brock hunts

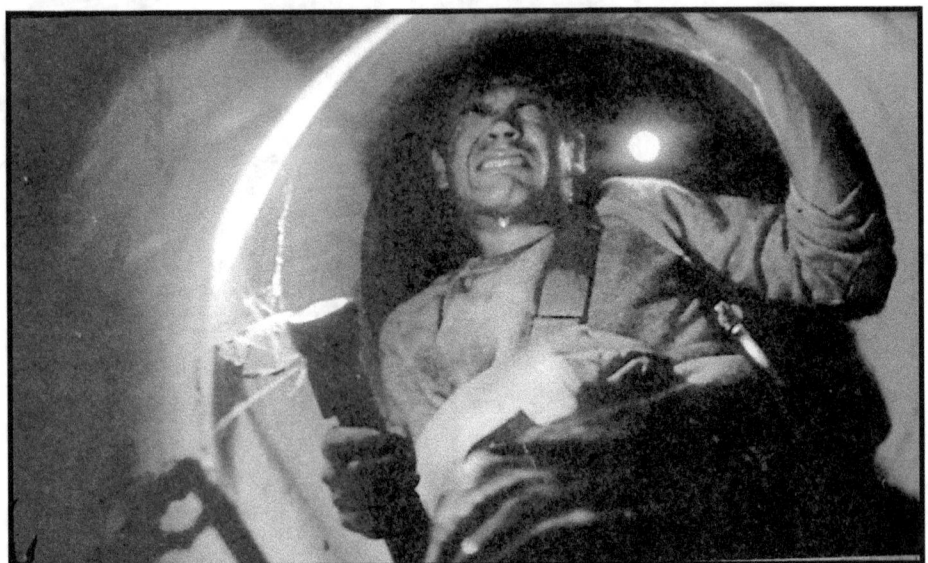

Madison (Robert Forster) takes to the sewers to save the city from the giant mutant killer alligator.

down the alligator to a rural suburb and, accompanied by three teenaged boys, he believes himself to have it cornered. However, the beast charges at him and eats him.

Having slept together, Madison and Kendall go out for supper. The two hear of Brock's disappearance, and Madison becomes cold—forcing Kendall to leave him for the night. The next morning Madison apologies to Kendall, and meets her eccentric mother (Jerome), the same woman from the film's prologue. The couple then set out to kill the beast.

Meanwhile, the alligator escapes from a lake and trashes the Helmses' wedding, killing Slade, the mayor and Helms himself. The reptile then returns to the sewer, where Madison uses himself as bait and attaches dynamite to the walls of the sewer. Madison escapes from the sewer just in time and the beast is blown apart—although another alligator lands in the sewers just as the film closes. It has also been flushed down the toilet.

Critique

It may seem unfair to some readers that director Lewis Teague finds two of his movies highlighted in this chapter. However, it is surely testament to the filmmaker's accomplishments in the genre that both *Alligator* and *Cujo* remain superlative monster movies, superior to most other comparable creature features. Riding on the coattails of both *Jaws* (1975) and *Piranha* (1978), and based on a famous urban legend, *Alligator* takes another "ferocious" creature and pits a small group of unprepared humans against it. As with Joe Dante's enjoyable *Piranha*, *Alligator* contains a literate, witty script by the veteran John Sayles, who also coscripted Dante's classic *The Howling* (1981). Never taking itself too seriously but nonetheless containing some first-class scares (the alligator's sudden attack on Lang is a jump and a half!), Teague's film is also brilliantly sequenced. For instance, there is never too long a stretch between the monster's carnage, and Teague also shows a lot more of the monster than many directors would ever dare attempt—especially considering the low budget of the movie.[1] Surprisingly, the alligator is a convincing critter; close-up shots of the beast's head are used for some more intimate moments of mayhem while the real thing is contrasted with miniature sets in other sequences—and viewers never have to suspend their disbelief for too long. Even after the arrival of CGI, and considerably larger production values, neither 1997's fantastically hokey *Anaconda* or 1999's risible *Lake Placid* could come close to rivaling *Alligator* in either excitement or in its depiction of a monstrous, carnivorous reptile.

Unlike so many other low-budget horror movies, *Alligator* benefits from a great ensemble cast. Future Academy Award nominee Robert Forster is always worth watching, but his performance in *Alligator* is at least as memorable as his better known turns in *Jackie Brown* (1997) and cult classic *Medium Cool* (1969). Make no mistake—this is Forster's movie, and the story is as much about him as a personality as it is about a ferocious animal. From the cool, confident cop who inhabits the first half of the movie to the far less suave, troubled being who finally comes to grips with his past demons in the last reel—Forster's character is nicely developed throughout. The movie's heroine, Robin Riker, remains one of the horror film's great one-shot deals—joining the same list occupied by Jessica Harper's Suzy Banyon in *Suspiria* (1976) and Zohra Lampert in *Let's Scare Jessica to Death* (1971). Teague also casts a fantastic supporting cast of familiar, and gifted, character actors that includes Michael V. Gazzo (instantly recognizable from his central role as Pentangeli in *The Godfather Part 2*), *One Flew Over the Cuckoo's Nest*'s Sydney Lassick and, of course, pivotal B-movie face Henry Silva. Teague's movie also marked one of the final screen appearances from former Oscar winner Dean Jagger. With such a stunning line-up of actors, it is hardly surprising that each performer takes his part seriously and approaches the film with the utmost professionalism. Silva is a special standout as the big-game hunter, who has just the right amount of stupidity and overbearing arrogance. His attempt to recite an "alligator mating call" to a bewildered television reporter is one of the funniest, and most memorable, moments in Sayles' excellent script.

Alligator also confronts vivisection, a subject that, despite growing protests and concern, was rarely acknowledged in 1980s cinema (and is similarly passed over in recent times, with exception given to *28 Days Later* and its preposterous prologue in which tabloid-friendly stereotypes of animal rights activists free some caged primates). Other films from the decade to at least touch upon this horrific taboo include *The Plague Dogs* (1982), *Day of the Dead* (1985) and, to a lesser extent, *Strange Behavior* (see Eclectic Gems). However,

The alligator crashes a wedding and causes the usual drunken wedding guest havoc.

The mutant alligator manages to snack on a reporter, policeman and a kid at a pool.

Alligator, along with the animated masterpiece *The Plague Dogs*, remains the only film of this period to address at face value contemporary scientific malpractice and its unmistakable link to animal cruelty.

Ingersoll's portrayal of Arthur Helms is as a coldhearted sleazebag whose only concerns are time and money. It is fitting, therefore, that because of his own carelessness the title reptile ends up expanding to such a huge size and causing so much damage. In dealing with a topic that has never aged (as evidenced by the recent debate over cloning), *Alligator* indicates that the end result of inexplicable "scientific" cruelty toward fellow creatures can only spell disaster, whether it is through the loss of humanity (Jagger, Ingersoll and Lassick have all lost any such feelings toward their animal subjects) or through the creation of something that is simply unnatural. When the ferocious and preposterously large alligator, ultimately a creation of man, ends up trashing Ingersoll's wedding and slaughtering its very creators, the viewer cannot help but feel these people have gotten their just desserts. Like the classic *Frankenstein* story, *Alligator* allows the viewers to—in at least this one sequence—enjoy the dreadful comeuppance of the film's other villains.

Whereas Teague's other great monster movie, *Cujo*, would have to battle hard to convince an audience that a formerly loveable Saint Bernard could be terrifying, here the director is given a far easier job. An alligator, obviously, conjures up some feeling of fear, and from the opening scene where a luckless performer tempts his own fate by wrestling one (and ends up being given a nasty bite), Teague does a good job of stressing the predatory nature of the animal. He is also careful not to demonize the reptile—as Spielberg did with Bruce the shark in *Jaws*. Instead, the movie's alligator is best viewed as the equivalent of Godzilla rampaging through Japan. The ludicrously sized behemoth has been created by man and is now taking its revenge. In one set piece, *Alligator* really does stress this connection to comical proportions. When the scaly carnivore invades a wedding party, it inexplicably trashes Jagger's limousine, crushing it flat with its huge tail, until finally Jagger is squashed and killed—suggesting that the critter is actually capable of planning a thoughtful revenge. In the crazed, delirious atmosphere of the entire wedding sequence, the movie actually manages to get away

A lesson for any independent filmmaker: During your film's slow points—throw in a car crash!

with such madness—and the viewer is pulled along into the climax without thinking too hard about the implausible scenario that has just passed by. Featuring all of the ingredients that make a monster movie great (and Spielberg's *Jurassic Park* certainly borrows the comical "alligator shit" scene), *Alligator* remains a virtual textbook "how to" on producing an exemplary creature feature.

(Note: As many articles on the film have mentioned, the graffiti at the movie's end is a nice touch—paying homage to *The Third Man.*)

Standout Moment

The alligator's attack on the wedding party. May hold some kind of record for the amount of people devoured onscreen in the shortest time.

Memories of the Film

"I found the idea amusing because it was based on a myth that we used to joke about back when I lived in New York City—that people had thrown baby alligators into the sewer and they had grown into gigantic, albino alligators," recalls Lewis Teague. "That was a famous New York story that goes back to the 1950s when people were actually selling baby alligators through the mail and advertising them as 'miniature alligators.' So if you sent them your $2.95 they'd mail you a little baby alligator in a plastic bag, and you'd give it to your child as a Christmas present. They'd usually die, but if they didn't die—if they were taken care of—they would continue to grow, meaning that people had to get rid of them. I guess a lot of them got flushed down the toilet and that's how the myth began." Teague also reflects upon how he got involved in directing *Alligator*. "I was sent a script by a man named Brendan Chase, and the script was one of the worst scripts I'd ever read in my life," laughs the director. "But it was an amusing idea—I found the idea appealing. So I agreed to do it, if I could rewrite the script and bring in John Sayles, who I'd had a good relationship with on (my previous film) *The Lady in*

Red. The producer agreed with that and so John read the script and we talked about the idea. I wanted to tell a story about a cop who has some ghosts from the past that are haunting him and, by being in charge of the investigation, to track down this giant alligator he is able to wrestle with these demons from his past and overcome them. So then John was on the way to Tokyo for some film festival and he wrote the script on the plane....Robert Forster, who starred in it, also wrote some funny bits."

Considering that Forster also appeared (uncredited) in *The Lady in Red,* was it Teague's own initiative that cast him in *Alligator*? "Yeah, he was another condition of doing the movie because I had worked with him on *Lady in Red*," replies the director. "I actually directed second unit on a film that he was in a couple of years earlier (*Avalanche*). I had to shoot a scene that he was in and I thought that he was such a terrific actor. I said, 'I'm going to be directing one day and I hope you will be in my movies,' and he said, 'When you direct, send me the script.' So when Roger Corman hired me to do his movie, *Lady in Red*, I sent Robert Forster the script and said, 'Pick any part you want,' and he picked the small part of the guy who looked like Dillinger. That was a lot of fun—he did it for no credit, and so when I was offered *Alligator* I thought, 'He's the ideal to play the lead.'"

Inevitably, speaking about any monster movie is going to lead to talk about the special effects. Considering the well-documented problems that Spielberg had with *Jaws* and Tobe Hooper had with his crocodile in *Eaten Alive* (covered later in this chapter), is it fair to assume that Teague also had a challenge on his hands? "Well, the experience was not totally unlike Spielberg's with *Jaws*," he laughs. "The producer had already constructed a giant alligator and inducted a designer who was, at the time, the Mayor of Beverly Hills. He had built this alligator and his concept was actually very clever—he built the framework out of rattan, which was light and covered with a very thin shell of rubber from a mold that he had made. However, it had been hanging in a warehouse for about six years, while they were out trying to raise the financing for the film, so they hooked it up to the ceiling and it disintegrated into dust. We hired a special effects man to work on the film and since we had the mold, we asked him to rebuild it and his concern was building something that would hold up to the rigors of working on the stage for six weeks. So he overbuilt it...the rubber shell was four times thicker than the original, it looked great and it was going to last, but it was too heavy for anybody. The original idea was to get a couple of NFL football players inside—two in the front legs and two in the back legs, like a Chinese dragon—and walk around with it. But these two guys—we hired the strongest two guys we could find and they got in it, and they could barely make it move. Not only that but a real alligator, even though it walks very close to the ground, when it walks its body barely scrapes the surface. Its legs extend very far to the front and rear as it's walking, but because of the proportion of the two men inside the giant alligator, it only took one or two mincing steps—so the first time we took a test everybody burst out laughing. We thought, 'We can't show this alligator—and whatever we do, it has to be a comedy—we can't take this too seriously.' I tried as much as possible to not show it. We had a full-size alligator which we used briefly in a couple of shots, we had a mechanical alligator head on wheels that we could move around for close shots of the alligator biting things, and we used baby alligators which were physically proportioned, and miniature sets too. There were some side tracking shots of a baby alligator in the sewer—just walking along."

Despite his pride in *Alligator*, Teague shows no signs of regret when questioned about why he did not choose to become involved in the largely forgotten about 1991 sequel, *Alligator 2: The Mutation*. "Why didn't I do it? Because I had moved beyond that kind of a film," states the director firmly. "I did agree to do a sequel if I could bring John Sayles back to write the script and Robert Forster to play the lead. And the producers weren't willing to spend the money to do that, so I wasn't interested. Besides, the sequel that they did make had nothing to do with the original."

Alternate Critiques

"The effects are barely passable but the film is done in such a good, high-spirited manner that you are quick to forgive and eager for more." (Chas Balun, *The Connoisseur's Guide to the Contemporary Horror Film,* Fantaco, 1992)

"Satirical, underscored with gallows humor, chock-full of sight gags and in-jokes, and surprisingly well directed....This is one that rises well above the sewer." (John McCarthy, *Official Splatter Movie Guide Vol. 2*, St. Martin's Press, 1992)

"Alongside the black humor, Teague creates some suspenseful moments, helped by a great exploitation cast..." (Stephen Jones, *The Illustrated Dinosaur Movie Guide*, Titan, 1993)

The Blob

Director: Chuck Russell
Produced by: Jack H. Harris/Elliot Kastner
Written by: Chuck Russell/Frank Darabont
Cast: Kevin Dillon; Shawnee Smith; Donovan Leitch; Jeffrey DeMunn; Candy Clark; Joe Seneca; Del Close; Paul McCrane; Sharon Spelman; Beau Billingslea; Art LaFleur; Ricky Paull Goldin
Special Effects: Tony Gardner
Year: 1988

Plot Synopsis

An American football game plays out at a California high school. Paul Taylor (Leitch), the lead player, notices that pretty cheerleader Meg Penny (Smith) is paying attention to him. After being roughly tackled to the ground, he asks her out. Brian Flagg (Dillon) has been released from Juvenile Hall and arrives back into town, to the disdain of Sheriff Herb Geller (DeMunn).

A homeless man (Billy Beck) sees what appears to be a shooting star. Upon closer investigation, however, the man discovers a pink-colored blob. The blob attacks the man and he later runs onto the highway—attracting the attention of Flagg and also Taylor and Penny, who are out on their first date together. The three take the man to the hospital, where the blob grows and consumes him. Taylor tries to call the police, but the blob crawls across the ceiling and swallows him. His screaming girlfriend cannot comprehend what has happened and the blob disappears. The police search for Flagg, believing that he may have had something to do with the night's events.

In the meantime, a young man (Goldin) sits in his car and tries to get past first base with his drunken date (Erika Eleniak). However, the blob arrives underneath the vehicle and attacks them both.

Penny manages to track Flagg down at a small cafeteria. The blob travels across the sewer systems and also arrives at the cafeteria, killing the cook. Flagg and Penny hide

Shawnee Smith is a pretty cheerleader who little realizes the nightmare awaiting her on her first date with football hunk Paul Taylor in The Blob.

in a freezer, where they notice that the blob is damaged by the cold. Moving outside, the blob attacks and consumes the cafeteria's waitress (Clark), who is trying to make a phone call. We see the Sheriff's face appear through the translucent skin of the blob, having also been devoured by it.

Flagg and Penny run into various men in laboratory costumes, led by Doctor Meddows (Seneca). The men assure them that they are safe and that the situation is under control. The scientists also insist that the two be transported back to town immediately. Flagg leaves Penny to go back into the woodland for his deserted motorbike and, once there, he overhears the scientists speak about the blob. They in fact created it, with the intention of ushering in a new era of biological defense against the Russians.

Back in town, Penny learns that her younger brother Kevin (Michael Kenworthy) and his friend are still in the cinema. She manages to escape the scientist's guard to get to the theater, where the blob is already beginning its attack.

Once Penny finds Kevin and his friend, the three of them flee down a manhole and into the sewer, where Kevin's friend is eaten. Both Penny and her young brother look likely to follow until Flagg comes to their rescue. However, knowing that Flagg is informed about his creation, Dr. Meddows does not want them to escape and tries to lock them down in the sewer.

When they finally manage to escape, the blob is also let loose. It digests Meddows and several other townspeople, before Flagg freezes the monster with a snowmaking truck, which the town had brought in to use for the upcoming ski season.

The film comes to a close with the local reverend serving his congregation with talk of approaching Armageddon. He keeps a still-living chunk of the blob floating in a glass of water.

Critique

As far as remakes go, Chuck Russell's *The Blob* is in the same vein as John Carpenter's *The Thing* (1982) and David Cronenberg's *The Fly* (1986), being an improved,

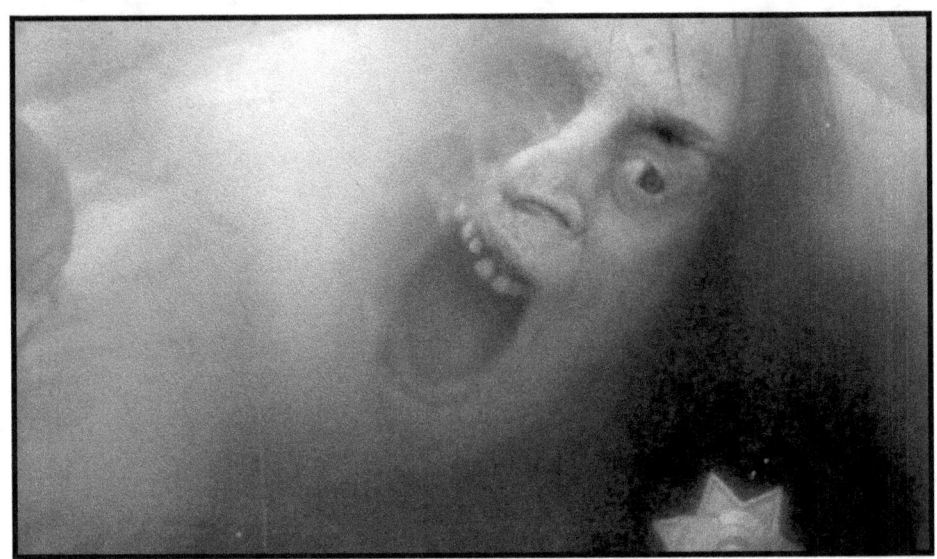

The special effects in The Blob are still amazingly gruesome and effective.

big-budget version of a decidedly average original. It has a tone that is, inevitably, very different from the 1958 version—Russell takes the premise of his movie very seriously, and the film never degenerates into comic relief or farce. Instead, with special effects that were radical for the time and remain superlative when viewed today, we see a wide variety of convincingly ghoulish special effects. Such delights include *Playboy* Playmate Erika Eleniak being consumed inside out, a luckless victim sucked down a plug hole head first and a child (who can't be much older than 12) die a surprisingly nasty death. How often does a horror film dare to slaughter a young adolescent? Not very often—but Russell pulls no punches with *The Blob*. This is Hitchcockian cinema at its best—with Leitch, who we are initially led to believe is the hero of the story, killed within the first reel and characters that we never think are going to die being brought to a sudden end. A further example of this is with Candy Clark's waitress, who is set up as a sympathetic and likeable character from the minute we meet her. Running to a phone box to call the town's sheriff, she finds herself trapped by the blob—its gooey mass surrounding the booth. Of course, we expect that her cries will be heard and that the creature will finally retreat but instead, after a slow and suspenseful few moments, the glass to the phone box caves in and Clark is heartlessly killed. This sense of unease carries the viewer throughout the movie, and we are never sure if any character is safe (the director even toys with this expectation in regards to the lead actress, Shawnee Smith, who looks increasingly likely to become blob food during the finale).

As with Carpenter's *The Thing*, *The Blob* was not a success when it first came out. Perhaps, like Carpenter's film, its outlook was too brutal and downbeat for many viewers. Even the film's original trailer seemed to forewarn of *The Blob*'s many moments of gruesome death. While the original movie was viewed in light of the Cold War—with the mass of goo that "invades" a peaceful, middle-class American suburb being equated, by some critics, to the nuclear paranoia of the time[2]—in Russell's film it is indigenous defense that is the real enemy. Created by man, to serve man, Russell's movie shows an entire town being served up as a guinea pig. "The civilians are expendable," notes Dr.

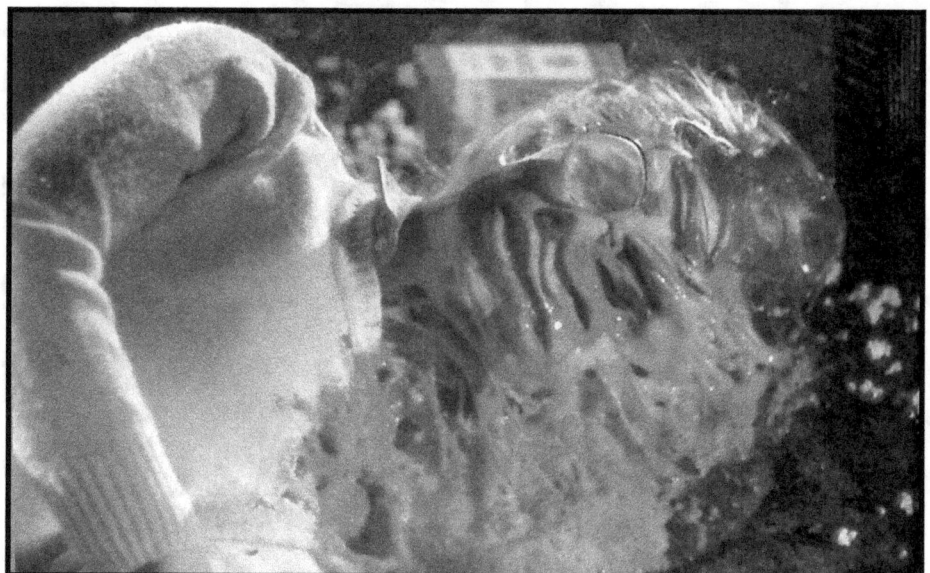

Although *The Blob* was a bit too gooey for audiences back when it first came out, it has long been a favorite of horror movie fans.

Meddows—mentioning that "this will put U.S. defense years ahead of the Russians." Although outdated now (and outdated even in 1988), *The Blob* is very much a film of its time. A period when Reagan was in the White House, and spending on increasingly bizarre forms of so-called "protection" from the Red Menace was plummeting America into debt, with the effects being felt on the poor and the working class. It is no mistake, certainly, that the blob's first victim is a homeless man (another product of the 1980s) and that, when taken to the hospital, he is questioned about having "Blue Cross or medical insurance." In other words, his life is secondary to whether or not he can actually pay for his treatment.

In *The Blob*, social class is also a driving factor for the film's hero, Kevin Dillon. Arriving in town clad in a leather jacket and riding a motorbike, the character is initially frowned upon by the law. Then he becomes the chief suspect for the film's first two murders. His outlaw appearance and anarchistic attitude make him the prime danger—although the real threat comes from the people who are in a position of power. Although science and the military are the chief evildoers in *The Blob*, the Church does not get off without criticism either. The film's reverend—played by Del Close—is a horrible man. He is someone who cheers the bloodlust of the college football game, is a practicing alcoholic and, in the final sequence, it is he who looks likely to resurrect the creature, keeping it bottled up in his church. Russell is suspicious of establishment in *The Blob*, and it is his creature that succeeds in bringing the town together—people disregarding class differences to bond with one another against a common enemy.

Russell would again go on to explore the mundane routine of suburban, middle-class America with 1994's *The Mask*—where Jim Carrey is permitted to "escape" from his ordinary life through becoming an exaggerated cartoon of himself. Although the director's career has since taken in shallow, big-budgeted action epics like *Eraser* (1996) and the more entertaining *Scorpion King* (2002), on the strength of *The Blob* and his *Nightmare on Elm Street Part 3* (1987), Russell could have been one of the great horror

Actress Shawnee Smith unloads with the heavy artillery in *The Blob*.

directors. Whether 2000's disastrously received *Bless the Child* marks an end to his time in terror is something we shall have to await. In the meantime, search out *The Blob* and check out one of cinema's most undervalued remakes. It's a delight.

Standout Moment

While many men would love the opportunity to fondle Erika Eleniak's chest, poor Ricky Paull Goldin comes up with a handful of blob and ends being swallowed by the monstrous title creature.

Memories of the Film

Beginning with *A Nightmare on Elm Street Part 3*, Russell showed himself to be a talented genre director. "*A Nightmare on Elm Street 3* was my first directing gig, and I really was a fan of the first one," mentions Russell—beginning to discuss the horror project that he embarked upon before making *The Blob*. "I pushed myself to find a way to make that movie….I didn't think that I could make it scarier then the first film—but I thought that I could find a way to make it thrilling and funny and to take what was surreal and funny about Freddy, and take that aspect a little bit further. I think the *Elm Street* series works because of the camaraderie of the teenagers. There's something magical there that we can all relate to—that time in life where no adults believe what you say. At that time I had also written *Dreamscape* and I had wrangled the rights to the remake of *The Blob*. I had actually written a script with Frank Darabont for *The Blob* when Bob Shaye (Co-chairman and Co-CEO of New Line) asked me to do *A Nightmare on Elm Street Part 3*, and I had 10 days to do a complete page one rewrite. That's the way it happens—when it happens, it happens fast!"

Following his work on the third *Elm Street*, which was a larger commercial success than its two predecessors, Russell began production on *The Blob*. "The thing about *The Blob* is that I had been optimistic about CGI. I thought that if I really focused these guys, this was very early on in the game, in a couple of key scenes with master shots I could be there right when the technology caught up," states the director. "But I was too early. They couldn't do it." (*laughs*) "It was one of these times when I had guys coming back to me and saying 'It can't be done—*at least it can't be done yet.*' So I was always a little disappointed that the effects didn't live up to what I had imagined.... But the film is a guilty pleasure, you know—again, I pushed myself on a project like that and I pushed myself to be wild with things like story and character...and then I wouldn't know how to support it." Despite the challenges involved with making a film dominated by difficult special effects sequences, Russell insists that *The Blob* did not discourage him from working with cutting edge visuals again. In fact, the director maintains that he does consider another film of his—1996's Arnold Schwarzenegger vehicle *Eraser*—to have been ahead of its time with its special effects. "You know one of the things that I didn't even think of myself until recently—as a friend of mine mentioned it to me—was that the real time effects that we developed in *Eraser* may have been a first....It's since been perfected in the *Matrix* movies. But I was just pushing myself, it all came out of my own concern that I'd seen everything that our star, Arnold, could do already in terms of gunfights. So I had to come up with something new."

The Blob **will knock your socks off!**

Following enormous mainstream success with 1994's *The Mask* ("New Line was actually looking for another kind of Freddy story. I convinced them it should be a comedy and that it should star this guy, Jim Carrey,") and *The Scorpion King* (2002), Russell looks back on his two early horror films fondly. "When I finished these early films on a short schedule there was always this little whirlwind of publicity that happened...and it's a shame because sometimes, even now, I'm not able to be in touch with how the audiences are really enjoying the film," reminisces the director. "So it was all a blur to me, but what's interesting is that ever since the film's release—it's such a prevalent credit that it always surprises me that if I don't mention it people will always ask me about *The Blob*. It blows my mind! It's such a little show, but I put my heart into it, and I believe the cast put so much into it as well, and I think that audiences appreciate that. I'm proud of the film, and I think it shows in the horror and science fiction stuff that I care. That to me it's not just a campy romp, and that I'm trying to go someplace that's really fun—but that I still give a shit about these people in the film."

Alternate Critiques

"Despite its admittedly jaw-dropping FX work and ferocious attack sequences, Chuck Russell's *The Blob* took a $250,000 idea from the '50s and let it simply rattle around in the overblown, rarefied environs of a $19 million budget." (Chas Balun, *Gorezone*, Issue 8, July 1989).

"Not as disgusting as John Carpenter's version of *The Thing* or as creepy as Cronenberg's remake of *The Fly*, but this delivers a fair amount of good gooey fun." (L.A. Morse, *Video Trash and Treasures*, HarperCollins, 1989).

"*The Blob* is a horror film with everything going for it, never boring and always scary, with a hugely satisfying climax and a fiendish closing twist." (Gary Bennett, *Samhain*, Issue 18, December 1989)

Cujo

Director: Lewis Teague
Produced by: Daniel H. Blatt/Robert Singer
Written by: Don Carlos Dunaway/Lauren Currier
Cast: Dee Wallace-Stone; Danny Pintauro; Daniel Hugh Kelly; Christopher Stone; Ed Lauter; Kaiulani Lee; Billy Jayne; Mills Watson; Sandy Ward; Jerry Hardin; Merritt Olsen; Arthur Rosenberg
Special Effects: Rick Josephsen
Year: 1983

Plot Synopsis

Cujo, a loveable Saint Bernard, chases after a rabbit at high speed. The rabbit takes shelter in what looks to be its warren, but when Cujo pokes his head through the hole in the ground he discovers a coven of bats. One bat bites Cujo on the nose.

Cut to the Trenton household, a middle-class family living in suburban America. Tad Trenton (Pintauro) cannot sleep, as he believes there is a monster in his closet. "There's no such thing as monsters," his father Vic (Hugh Kelly) assures him, finally chanting a short verse that he has devised to keep the "monsters" away from his son. Convinced, Tad goes back to sleep. The next morning at breakfast Steve (Stone)—a local handyman—stops by the house. Tad boasts to Steve that his father designs the televised advertisements for a famous breakfast cereal. Tad's mother Donna (Wallace-Stone) appears bothered by Steve's presence.

Vic stops at a mechanic's shop run by a stern man called Joe (Lauter), who also owns Cujo. He asks when the man might be able to fix his car and is told to come back the following day. Meanwhile, Donna and Steve make love at the Trenton household. That evening at the family meal, Vic tells Donna that he wants another child. The next morning the Trenton family stops by Joe's again to secure an appointment. Donna sees Cujo and becomes threatened by the dog's size. Joe's young son (Jayne) explains that the dog is harmless and playfully hugs the animal.

The company that Vic works for has a new cereal product on the market. A news report mentions that it is said to cause internal hemorrhaging. As a result, Vic is to be sent out of state to an emergency board meeting. Donna stops by Steve's house to tell him she wants to end the affair. Returning home from work, Vic passes the two fighting in the street. Back home he plays dumb.

At Joe's house, his wife Charity (Lee) nervously asks her husband if she can leave the house to visit her sister in Connecticut for a week. She has just won $5,000 in the lottery. Joe goes to his friend Gary's (Watson) house where he is in high spirits about his wife's departure and hints about having an affair.

How do you make a lovable Saint Bernard scary? *Cujo* gives you the answer.

Joe's son comes across Cujo prowling the fields around the house, and the dog is now fully rabid. The boy backs away. He tells his mother about the animal, but she tells him not to worry his father—there is every indication that Charity does not intend to return to her husband. Cujo arrives at Gary's house, where the dog chases and kills him.

Vic catches his wife at the conclusion of a heated argument with Steve. She admits to the affair, but Vic leaves her and Tad for his meeting the next morning. Joe stops at Gary's house where he sees his friend's dead body. Cujo attacks and kills him as well.

Shortly afterward, Donna and Tad take their broken down car around to Joe's to be fixed. As soon as Donna stops the car, Cujo attacks the vehicle and tries to claw his way inside. When the car will not start, Donna and Tad find themselves trapped inside it. Cujo sits in wait as day turns to night and back to day.

Vic tries to call home but there is no answer. He phones Joe's house, but the ringing frustrates Cujo and the dog smashes a window in Donna's car as he aggressively tries to break inside. Tad begins to asphyxiate. Donna leaves the car but Cujo attacks her and leaps into the vehicle, savaging her leg. She finally beats the dog outside, slams the car door shut and passes out.

Unable to get his wife on the phone, Vic leaves the board meeting and returns home. When Donna awakens, Tad can barely catch his breath. Steve breaks into the Trenton house. When Vic arrives home, his bedroom has been slashed to pieces and the family photographs cut up. The police have caught Steve, but he denies having seen Donna in days. A policeman stops by Joe's garage, where Cujo attacks and kills him.

When Tad will not wake up, Donna leaves the car. She grabs a child's baseball bat from Joe's lawn and beats Cujo. The dog leaps on top of her, pinning her to the ground. When the baseball bat snaps, Donna impales the animal on it and Cujo appears to die in her arms. She takes the policeman's gun and carries Tad inside of Joe's house. Tad awakes when Donna splashes some water on him.

Cujo is not yet dead and he bursts through a window. Donna shoots the animal dead, just as her husband turns up.

Critique

Stephen King notes that he barely remembers writing the original novel of *Cujo* but—being the masterful storyteller that he is—the end result is still rewarding and results in a great horror movie.[3] One long-debated factor about the film adaptation of *Cujo* is whether or not the finale should have stayed loyal to the book and allowed for the little boy, Tad, to die. While King's original novel showcased the death of the child in order to symbolize the boy's parents' realization of their own neglect—of each other and of their offspring—the film suggests that Tad's survival opens up a new door of hope for his parents. While *Cujo* is unlikely to be the last book that finds itself undergoing changes en route to the silver screen, it does have to be said that it seems almost unthinkable that the movie could work as well as it does with such a downbeat coda intact. Instead, Teague's film encourages the audience to applaud the death of its monster and leave the end credits on a high. Had we seen the child's demise, the movie would likely have left viewers feeling somewhat depressed and cheated—such a climax would have completely overshadowed the rush of adrenaline that comes from cheering Wallace-Stone's heroics in the face of adversity. Had *Cujo* retained the ending of the novel, it is perhaps comparable to finding that just as Chief Brody swims to safety in *Jaws,* the Great White lunges up from the depths for one last meal. Surely more than one movie house may have encountered a riot after this kind of conclusion.

However, as with the book, the dog in *Cujo* is shown to be the catalyst that brings the Trenton family together again, although King's original, literal symbolism of the animal with Stone's sexual prowess was always going to be a bit trickier to adapt to the screen. Only a brief, aggressive sequence between Wallace-Stone and her lover hint at the animalistic passion that may have driven them into an affair. The mirror image of the Trenton family is that of the working-class household of Joe the mechanic and his wife and young boy. Teague brilliantly understates the scene at Lauter's dinner table

where the man's wife trembles and spits out her desire to leave her husband for a week. The class difference is obvious through the contrast between the two surroundings—the mechanic is dirty, his lawn unkempt, his wife unwashed while the Trentons own a lavish suburban residence and Hugh Kelly's character is every bit the successful businessman. However, despite the diversity in income and social class, both families are shown to have the same problem—corrupt marriages and a broken down family unit. It seems that money cannot buy happiness, and Wallace-Stone's onscreen lover is every bit the rugged slice of rough that her more carefully ironed, wealthy husband is not. Interestingly, had Teague not made *Cujo* so indiscriminate in regards to the people he kills (which include his owner), the animal could very well have been symbolic of a working-class attack on the privileged.

As for the actual tone of *Cujo*, Teague's movie makes for an extremely tense viewing experience, and the essential feeling of claustrophobia that Wallace-Stone and Pintauro experience while locked in their broken-down Pinto is captured well by the director and really resonates upon the audience. When the dog attacks, it does so with ferocity, and the feel of an impending attack is never far away. As with Spielberg's *Jaws*, the director sets up some first-class jumps (the dog leaps, suddenly and without warning, at the car just as Bruce leapt at the passengers on the Orca),

Dee Wallace Stone must fight the beast to save her child's life in *Cujo*.

and there is a prevalent feeling of mounting desperation on the part of his heroine. The location of the mechanic's, which looks to be in the middle of nowhere, is perfectly apt—and allows for the viewer to draw upon the helplessness of the film's two main characters.

Inevitably, any film that has a child's life in danger as its central motivation in the scenes of horror is likely to elicit a strong emotional response from the audience, but strangely Teague does not exploit this factor too much. Instead, he focuses more on Wallace-Stone and her desperate, and eventually hopeless, attempts to start her car and remain calm for the sake of her young son. Despite her affair, she is shown as a caring and guilt-ridden woman, left empty by a marriage that is clearly no longer working. For all intents and purposes, this is her movie—and the actress puts in perhaps her finest screen performance to date. The finale between Cujo (let us not forget—a rabid Saint Bernard!) and the actress could have turned into something comical in the hands of a less-talented filmmaker, but here it is a perfectly fearful conclusion. The movie is also boosted, to no end, by imaginative cinematography from future blockbuster director Jan De Bont (*Speed, Twister*) including a stylish 360-degree camera turn in the back of the car (done just as Wallace-Stone faints). The dog's-eye-view shots are always convincing and smooth and used especially well in the lead-up to some violent attack sequences.

The most difficult aspect of the film, for Teague and the makeup effects crew, was presumably making the cuddly figure of a Saint Bernard dog scary. The answer seems to have been to show the animal's attacks in fleeting detail—with close-ups only being revealed when Cujo does battle with Wallace-Stone near the end. It works well because we are made aware that the predator is lurking near the film's leading characters, and so we do not have to be reminded of its presence every few seconds. Sometimes the horrors of the mind, just like the unseen "monsters" that lurk in Tad's closet, are the most terrifying element of a scary movie. An underappreciated terror masterpiece, by a director who can boast at least another two works of genre brilliance in his resume (1980's *Alligator* and 1984's *Cat's Eye*), *Cujo* is one of the best King-to-screen adaptations.

Standout Moment

Yeah, it is very much "of its time," but the *Friday the 13th*–type, "he's not quite dead yet" ending still works well and even the most cynical genre viewer is likely to get a fresh burst of adrenaline from Teague's expert set-up.

Memories of the Film

"On the contrary—it was Stephen King's idea for Tad to survive in the film, and I agreed," states Lewis Teague when asked about whether or not he wanted to keep the book's original ending intact. "It made sense, and it was definitely less of a downer. If you've read King's book *About Writing*, you know he wants his stories to unfold honestly—and given the circumstances, the story could have gone either way. I, on the other hand, wanted to make a point, and that point was that we can survive our fears: real and imaginary." Teague explains that the basis for this rationale is self-evident in the film. "As you remember, everyone in the story was motivated by fear—fear of financial ruin, fear of growing old, fear of monsters in the closet, and eventually a real monster in the form of a rabid Saint Bernard," the director explains. "Now it is my experience that fear can become a self-fulfilling prophecy if we believe it and surrender to it. And it is my opinion that within every person exists the power to overcome fear, if we only have the courage to look for it. So I wanted Tad to survive in order to illustrate that positive outlook."

"I was pretty much trying to follow the tone of the book. And, yes, the subject matter was serious," confirms Teague when asked about the challenges of making the movie. "It was a challenge to make the film scary for one, and also it was a challenge to tell two parallel stories at once—because the dog is the metaphor for the poisonous fear that the family was suffering from," adds the director. "Stephen King's brilliant at writing about people with everyday problems. The husband was afraid of financial insecurity, he's scared of losing a major account (and) his wife is scared of growing old and being bored, and so she's having an affair. And the tension in the family was filtering down to the son—whose tension manifested itself in his idea that there were monsters hiding in his closet. All of those fears are very ordinary, everyday fears that a lot of people could share and identify with. And the dog becoming sicker and sicker with rabies and eventually turning on them was, to me, symbolic of how poisonous fear of relationships can be and how it can eat someone up from inside."

The director also admits that he had to be careful dealing with the subject matter of a rabid animal that must, ultimately, meet its demise at the hands of a human. "I did show Cujo's attacks onscreen," recalls Teague. "But I did not show the attacks on Cujo. There's a double standard on the part of audience when it comes to animals versus humans. You can show humans being flayed, but audiences are revolted when they see animals being harmed. I guess there are two reasons for that. One is, animals are usually more innocent than humans. The other is that people have more difficulty suspending disbelief when they see animals getting hurt onscreen. Probably because few animals have really been hurt onscreen in the past. So, anything you do with animals is a big challenge." The director then explains some of the intricacies of completing the final showdown between Wallace-Stone and the vicious Saint Bernard. "We shot that scene in post-production, with a small crew, so we could take the necessary time," begins Teague. "The animal trainer, Karl Miller, did an extraordinary job.... You never see Dee Wallace, when she was hitting the dog. We never showed the club making contact with the dog and by the time (Cujo) crashes through the window and she has to shoot it, hopefully the dog has become evil enough where the audience is happy that she is able to destroy it."

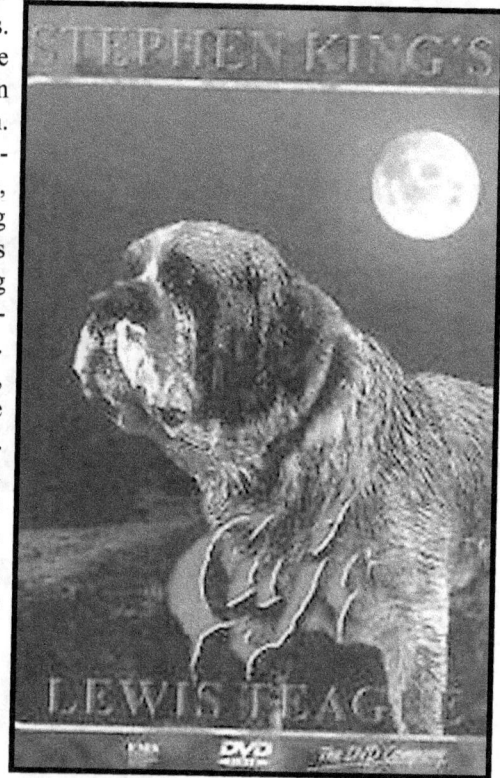

Teague would know about audience reaction to animal cruelty. In the case of Monte Hellman's 1974 shocker *Cockfighter*, which the director edited for Roger Corman, Teague found himself working on a movie that showcased real roosters engaged in gruesome battle (the movie is still banned in the U.K.). "Well, that's what I'm talking about when I mention killing the dog in *Cujo*," says the director. "People couldn't stand *Cockfighter,* that picture made no money. It's a funny story—Joe Dante, another famous director, was working for Roger editing trailers at the same time as I was editing *Cockfighter*. Roger had this idea that *Cockfighter* was going to make a lot of money in the South. As he said, 'Cockfighting is very big in seven states and I think this film has a built-in audience down there.' Then the Monday after the weekend the grosses came in and I was in the editing room putting away things and cleaning up and shutting things down. Roger called out, 'Well, Lewis, I was wrong. Nobody went to see the film.' He said, 'I guess they don't want to see chickens tearing each other apart. So we're going to change the trailer, we're changing the title and I want you to take every shot of sex and violence that you have and put it in the movie. Find every scene of sex and violence and give it to Joe Dante because he's cutting a new trailer.' I said, 'Roger, Monte didn't shoot any sex and violence,' and he said, 'I don't care where you get it, I want you to get sex and violence and give it to Joe.' Now Roger had made a lot of student nurse films, genre films, car chases, nurses ripping off their bras—and I started collecting all of these scenes and giving them to Joe and he cut a trailer and it bothered my conscience. I called Roger back and said, 'Roger, I don't think the director would want a trailer with all these scenes that aren't in the movie.' He

"I wish I was back working for Spielberg", thinks *E.T.* star Dee Wallace Stone, during the intense horror of *Cujo*.

said, 'You know, Lewis—you're right. Put it in the movie.' So there used to be a scene where the actor falls asleep, face down, and he wakes up in the morning with the birds chirping. Now he dreams about cars racing and student nurses....I put it in as a dream sequence. It makes absolutely no sense. But it justified putting it in the trailer and still no one went to see it."

Alternate Critiques

"The film builds up gradually to an extraordinarily horrific climax. It is probably not to everyone's taste, but the horror fans rank it highly." (*Hoffman's Guide to SF, Horror and Fantasy*, 1991, Corgi)

"Genuinely frightening adaptation of a Stephen King thriller about a woman and her son terrorized by a rabid St. Bernard dog." (Leonard Maltin, *Movie and Video Guide*, Penguin)

"Director Lewis Teague added more hydrophobia to

Dee Wallace finds W.C. Fields was right—don't work with kids or animals!

his massive mutt, so the film lacks the demented dog's-eye-view of the book. But the tale of the 170 pounds of canine pain and fury trapping an adulterous mother and her young son in their Ford Pinto for two days... is confrontation at its most primal." (Peter Guttmacher, *Legendary Horror Films*, 1995, Metro Books)

Eaten Alive

British Title: *Death Trap*
Director: Tobe Hooper
Produced by: Mardi Rustam
Written by: Alvin L. Fast/Kim Henkel/Mardi Rustam
Cast: Neville Brand; Mel Ferrer; Carolyn Jones; Marilyn Burns; William Finley; Stuart Whitman; Roberta Collins; Kyle Richards; Robert Englund; Crystin Sinclaire; Janus Blythe; Betty Cole
Special Effects: Bob Mattey
Year: 1976

Plot Synopsis

Clara, a prostitute (Collins), refuses to engage in sodomy with a client called Buck (Englund). The brothel owner, Miss Hattie (Jones), hears their argument and throws Clara out.

The girl takes shelter in the nearby Starlight Motel, a run-down building owned by Judd (Brand). Judd is initially kind to the girl, but when he recognizes her as "one of Hattie's girls," he begins to brawl with her. Chasing her outside, Judd slashes her up with a rake and throws her body to his pet crocodile—which lives in a small swamp outside the building. Following the murder, Judd retreats inside his motel, singing to himself.

Shortly afterward, Roy (Finley) and Faye (Burns), a married couple who do not get along, turn up at the Starlight with their young daughter Angie (Richards) and her pet dog Snoopy. The little girl notices a dead monkey in a cage. Because she takes her eyes off Snoopy, the dog is eaten by the huge crocodile. Angie goes into shock, and her parents take her upstairs, whereupon they continue to fight.

Roy leaves the motel, takes a shotgun from his car and attempts to shoot the reptile, but Judd stops him by slaughtering the man with a scythe and then throwing him to his pet. In the process, Judd is shot in his wooden leg. Faye goes for a shower, but Judd breaks into

A Dialogue with 30 Modern Masters of Horror

Texas Chain Saw star Marilyn Burns finds herself back in a similar situation during *Eaten Alive*.

the bathroom and beats her, gags her and ties her to a bed. Angie escapes and hides under the rafters of the motel.

At the Sheriff's office, Harvey Wood (Ferrer) arrives with his daughter Libby (Sinclaire), inquiring as to the whereabouts of his other daughter, Clara. They go to the brothel, where Miss Hattie states that she does not recognize the photograph of Clara presented to her. At the Starlight, Judd crawls under the motel to try to attack the little girl, but he is interrupted by the Sheriff's car, which pulls up to drop off Harvey. On the way to his bedroom, Harvey stops to investigate the screams of Angie and is scythed through the neck by Judd. The man finally dies when he is thrown into the crocodile's pit.

The Sheriff takes Libby out for some food at a local bar, but has to eject Buck from the surroundings when he is causing trouble with his new girlfriend Lynette (Blythe). Buck and Lynette go to the Starlight to make love, but they are distracted by the sound of Faye's struggles upstairs. Buck goes to find out where the noises are coming from. Outside the residence, he hears Angie's cries for help. Judd creeps up behind him and throws Buck to the crocodile. Lynette runs out of the Starlight and is chased by Judd through the woods. She finally escapes to freedom in a passing car.

Libby returns to the Starlight. As she is getting undressed in her bedroom, she hears Faye struggling in a nearby room. Judd cuts the fencing out from the crocodile's lair, allowing the reptile to crawl further under the motel and closer to Angie. Libby finds Faye and unties her from the bed. Judd enters the motel and chases the two girls, cutting Faye's leg with his scythe.

Outside, Angie tries to climb to safety over a mesh fence. Libby helps the little girl escape. Faye nudges Judd into the crocodile's pit where he is eaten. The Sheriff pulls up just in time to see Judd's wooden leg float to the surface.

Critique

Any film that begins with the line, "My name is Buck and I'm ready to fuck," must have something to offer fans of bizarre movies—and in the case of *Eaten Alive* you would be correct. Despite going either unseen, or having been largely

Don't go near the house if you want to avoid being *Eaten Alive*.

dismissed by horror fans, Tobe Hooper's follow-up to *The Texas Chain Saw Massacre* is a startling piece of renegade filmmaking, evidently made on a higher budget than its predecessor and featuring a haunting Gothic atmosphere that remains virtually unrivaled in modern American horror cinema. While Brand's cackling hotel owner is the central villain of *Eaten Alive*, the ad campaigns for the initial release highlighted the movie's crocodile, crafted by Bruce the Shark's creator Bob Mattey. The film's creature is certainly a valid threat throughout the picture (especially to poor Richards, who spends the bulk of the movie trying to avoid ending up as its lunch) and actually remains quite a convincing beast by B-movie standards. Without the use of any stock footage, or live animals, Hooper ambitiously attempts to use only his fake critter for the many moments of crocodile carnage, and the end result pays off, although one imagines that perfecting such sequences must have been a nightmare.

Cowritten by *Chain Saw* scriptwriter Kim Henkel, the movie has much in common with its predecessor, not the least of which is the presence of actress Marilyn Burns and momentary lapses into near-identical set pieces, including a chase through some punishing woodland and a gibbering lead villain. The feel of poverty, impending death and rot is also carried over from *Chain Saw*—with Judd's residence being effectively run-down and a depressed-looking monkey dying in its tiny cage early on in the film. Even the apocalyptic rumbles of *Eaten Alive*'s soundtrack appear to be a close relative to the aurally similar groans that blast from *Chain Saw*. To make the link between the two films even more conclusive, *Eaten Alive* is also loosely based on a horrific true story—that of Joe Ball, who owned an inn during the late 1920s where he would murder women and animals, often throwing them to his pet alligators. However, this is not to say that these similarities are a negative thing, especially when *Eaten Alive* manages to be, again not unlike *Chain Saw*, both effectively scary and darkly comic. This is something of an accomplishment when one takes into consideration the shooting of the film which was, according to whom you listen to, such a disaster that the movie was taken out of Hooper's hands and finished by either Carolyn Jones and editor Michael Brown or Marilyn Burns.[4] When asked about this (see below), Hooper denies such rumors and instead maintains that *Eaten Alive* was actually wrapped by himself. He also remains proud of the movie, preferring it to the bulk of his later work.[5]

What really helps make *Eaten Alive* stand out as a classic genre film is its surreal studio set backdrop. Imbedded in deep, garish red hues, the scenes outside the Starlight feature a clearly simulated landscape and resemble—with such bright primary color illustration—something out of a comic book. Indeed, it is hardly surprising that some critics have likened the movie, in plot and visuals, to the EC horror comics of the 1950s.[6] Coupled with these frankly gorgeous mist-shrouded atmospherics is the presence of a future star name. *Eaten Alive* sees Hooper working with "proper" actors for the first time in his career—including a young Robert Englund. Given a small but memorable role as a reactionary redneck hick, Englund—a vastly underrated character actor—shines and offers a glimpse of the villainous charm that would surface to more prominent effect later in his career.

One of Hooper's trademarks is coaxing deranged, standout performances from his villains. Even in the director's more lackluster works such as *Invaders from Mars* and *The Mangler*, he manages to bring out crazed turns from his evil leads (Louise Fletcher and Robert Englund, respectively) that go some way to making each movie redeemable and even enjoyable. Of course *Chain Saw*'s Jim Siedow and Ed Neal, not to mention *Chainsaw 2*'s Bill Moseley, are rightly revered as trademark screen psychopaths—but Neville Brand's Judd remains woefully overlooked. More realistic than the ghoulish *Chain Saw* villains, Brand looks to be enjoying himself in amongst the swampland, mist and screaming female victims and really lets rip with a maniacal screen turn. With his character's prevailing sense of madness, from blasting old Country/Western tunes out of his radio at high volume to mask the screams of Marilyn Burns, or his cackling, nonsensical mutterings, Brand is never short of compulsive viewing. Whatever was happening behind the scenes of *Eaten Alive*, the onscreen craziness certainly hints at a movie that is out of control and completely unsure of where the hell it is heading. Even the split personality of the movie, one part monster movie and one part backwoods slasher flick, works well—resulting in a film where not one onscreen moment feels safe or relaxed.

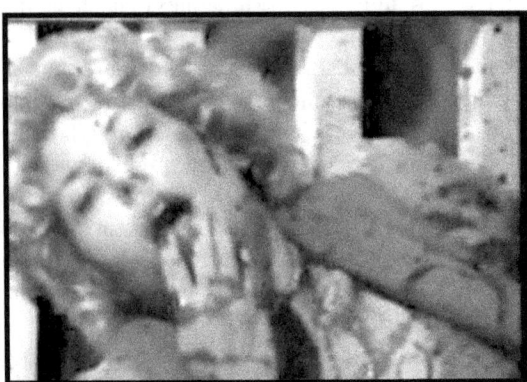

Hooper stretches believability to the maximum with his "all in one day" scenario.

Despite the above accolades, however, *Eaten Alive* does contain one major flaw in its recreation of the *Tales from the Crypt* comic strips that so thrilled the youngsters of the director's generation. As with the EC comics, Hooper stretches believability to the maximum with his "all in one day" scenario. Indeed, it is difficult to comprehend how Brand could ever have run any sort of business, small or otherwise, when visitors are summarily sliced up and served up as crocodile treats. However, with its nasty death sequences, menacing oversized reptile, and theatrical surroundings, *Eaten Alive* is hard to resist and—even three decades later—looks and plays out marvelously. As an interesting bridge between *Chain Saw* and the beginning of Hooper's short-lived career as a bankable genre director (*Salem's Lot*, *The Funhouse*, *Poltergeist*), the movie prevails with its horrific landscape of highly animated characters, cruelty and impressive visuals. So much so that the director would attempt to recapture *Eaten Alive*'s reptile carnage with 2000's *Crocodile*—a movie that went straight to video and, despite the odd moment of B-movie charm, is largely without worth.

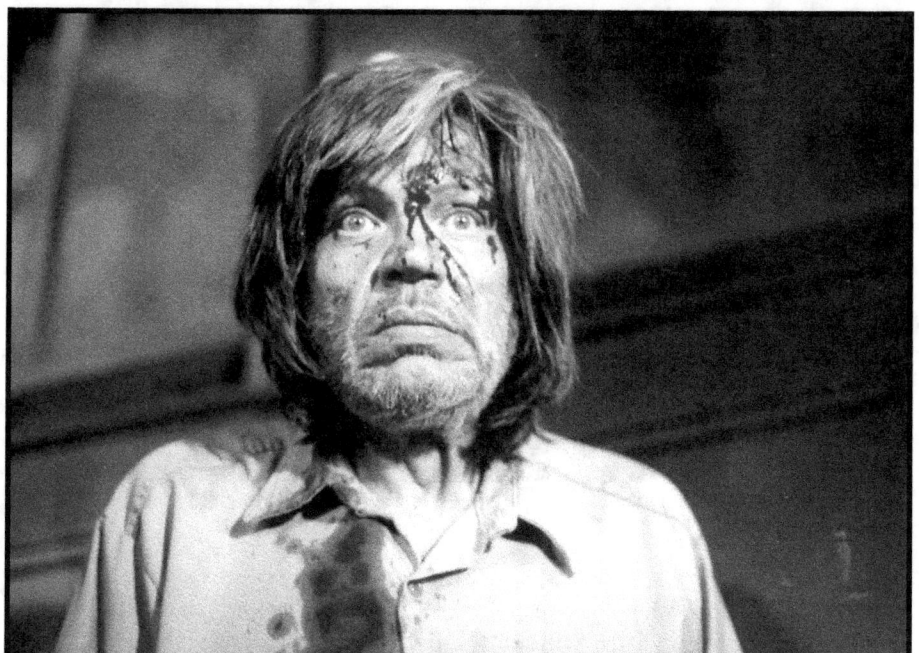

One of Hooper's trademarks is coaxing deranged, standout performances from his villains such as movie vet Neville Brand.

Standout Moment

Judd's crocodile rolls out of nowhere to attack a little girl's pet dog. Taboo breaking and still shocking.

Memories of the Film

"Tobe got canned on that, and that's the problem with that movie," explains actor Robert Englund when questioned about *Eaten Alive*. "I walked on the set and I had never done a horror movie before—I was quite a serious Hollywood renaissance actor like Jack Nicholson in *Five Easy Pieces*, I was a real 1970s character actor. And the set was unbelievable! It was all dead monkeys and dead birds in cages and iguanas...and there's this old Texas motel and a 1952 Cadillac convertible with bullet holes in the side of it and old rotting leather—and cactus in the background. It's a two- or three-story set! Neville Brand is sitting shirtless with a full body tattoo painted on and he's got his cigarette in the eye of one of the monkeys and he's screeching 'this is going to be amazing,' and we started making it and they fired Tobe Hooper! After making *The Texas Chain Saw Massacre*, they fired him for not being sexy or scary enough! I have friends in Japan that have seen it there with added scenes including a monster shot of me in a hardcore porno scene and it's not me! The guy's not even as well-endowed," laughs the actor. "I auditioned for a part in *Kill Bill*," continues Englund. "I fucked it up and didn't get the part, I had forgotten my glasses, but *Eaten Alive* is one of Quentin Tarantino's favorite films. That was the movie he sat and spoke to me about at the audition."

"Oh—well, yeah, you got me there," states Tobe Hooper when Robert Englund's statement about the director's dismissal from *Eaten Alive* is mentioned to him. "The producers came in with new ideas—they kept trying to change things. Kim Henkel and

Despite the wishes of male viewers worldwide, Marilyn Burns stays clothed in *Eaten Alive*'s shower sequence.

myself wrote the original script. It was like a domino effect—there would be something really cool, I'd be shooting it and then they'd call me and ask to change stuff. We were doing the ending and we had Neville outside fighting this big sponge rubber beast when the producer came in one day and told me his daughter had just seen *Jaws*. Then he says to me, 'Go get a grenade and throw it down the alligator's throat,' and I was wondering, 'Well, where would anyone find a grenade in this film?' This happened three or four times a day. I was a naïve artist at the time—*Chain Saw* had done well and I had raised money on the success of this, so I was in a compromising position. Every day I felt like it was ruining me, but I did finish the movie and I finished cutting it—only one scene ended up being directed by the second unit and it was just a little scene." As for the hardcore inserts that Englund mentioned, Hooper remains in good spirits when speaking about the foreign tampering that his film has encountered. "Yes, it was Robert on top of Janus (Blythe) and it cuts right out of a pornographic movie. Vibration and penetration—locomotive style," laughs the director.

"Well, what can I say?" adds Hooper, before revealing some information about the creation of *Eaten's Alive* crocodile. "It's really funny, we shot it at Rawley, just across from Paramount. Bob Mattey, who made Bruce the Shark, made this big alligator, and it looked as if it had been sitting in storage for about 12 years. Some special effects crew left it in a tank all night and it soaked up all the water! Actually, we shot it at a historic location—the place where William Holden was floating in the water with the photographers taking pictures above (from Billy Wilder's classic *Sunset Blvd.*). It was a totally surreal experience. I did like working with Neville Brand, he had that kind of weird…crazed state about him, not just an eccentric—but rather what you're seeing is what you think he's actually like. You begin to think that there might be people just like that…."

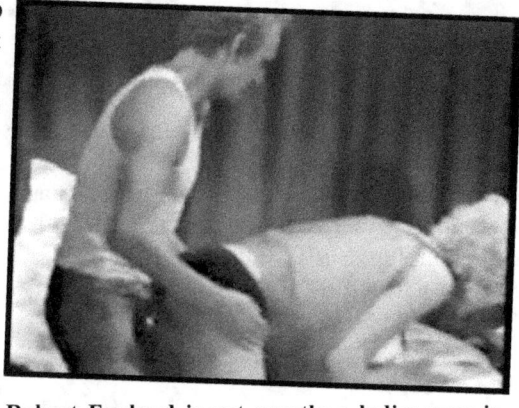

Robert Englund is not exactly a ladies man in Hooper's second horror feature.

So why make another psycho-reptile film almost 25 years later with *Crocodile*? "I should have known from the first one that these damn crocodiles hate me," laughs Hooper. "So I don't know why I did *Crocodile*. It was like being struck by lightning twice."

With *Texas Chain Saw* and *Eaten Alive* there is this very "by the teeth," frantic-looking direction at work. Both films look quite spontaneously directed—so did Hooper ever use storyboards? "No, in fact I don't work with storyboards," answers the director. "I do use them with special effects. You have to do that with storyboards to have, for example, ILM make a bid…you have to tell them how much each shot will cost. Since I was a kid with my 8mm camera, I've had an understanding of the language of film—so that's second nature to me, I might for instance doodle in a script to remind me of how to set something up. I grew up with a camera so exiting and movement—I've done all that for a long time. I was a Director of Photography in films as well. I don't use storyboards because I know what I want—I know what lens I want to use. If I was making something like *The Matrix*, I'd be stupid not to use them, on a special effects film like that you have to. But if it is a scene that is sensitive, with a lot of subtext, I like the actor to discover their way through this subtext—I like to give the actor more space. I think dialogue makes a movie, and I think you get a better performance from the actor this way. Trying to match storyboards with an actor—actors hate this, they find themselves placed in unnatural positions trying to push the story along…."

Alternate Critiques

"Hooper's flawed follow-up to *The Texas Chain Saw Massacre*. Hooper tries in vain to recreate the atmosphere of his vastly superior debut." (Kerekes and Slater, *See No Evil*, Headpress, 2000)

"Hooper was obviously trying to recreate the grimness-level of his first film, but instead of severe dementia, he only achieves an EC-Comics-style Flee-For-Your-Life feature. No big scares on board…it's all derivative as hell. At least Tobe keeps the story moving, and it's never too boring." (Steve Puchalski, *Slimetime*, Headpress, 1996)

"While almost every aspect of the picture is fatally compromised, of all Hooper's films it best captures the sleazy, twisted atmosphere of the EC comics he loved." (Stefan Jaworzyn, *The Texas Chain Saw Massacre Companion*, Titan, 2003)

The Hidden

Director: Jack Sholder
Produced by: Michael T. Meltzer/Gerard T. Olsen/Robert Shaye
Written by: Jim Kouf
Cast: Kyle MacLachlan; Michael Nouri; Claudia Christian; Clarence Felder; Clu Gulager; Ed O'Ross; William Boyett; Richard Brooks; Larry Cedar; Katherine Cannon; John McCann; Chris Mulkey
Special Effects: Kevin Yagher
Year: 1987

Plot Synopsis:

In Los Angeles, Jack DeVries (Mulkey) shoots down a couple of bystanders in a bank, before fleeing in his car. A lengthy chase follows, until finally—cornered by the police—DeVries is riddled with bullets. At the hospital, where DeVries is on life support, we meet Detective Beck (Nouri). DeVries has been on a two-week murder spree without any apparent motive, and Beck is not sad to learn that he "probably won't make it through the night." At the police station, Beck meets Lloyd Gallagher (MacLachlan) from the FBI—the agent claims to be trailing a murder suspect.

At the hospital, DeVries suddenly awakes and spits out a huge slug-like creature into the mouth of Jonathan Miller (Boyett), an overweight man who is also on life support. The terminally ill man rises up. Miller subsequently stumbles into town and enters a record store, where he beats the owner to death. He then retreats to a cafeteria with a stolen portable stereo and, with interest, watches some news about the senator from the city on the television.

Miller notices a red Ferrari zoom past the window and he walks to a nearby garage, where a sleazy car salesman (James Luisi) is finalizing a deal with a customer (Frank Renzulli). Insistent that he obtain a red Ferrari, Miller opens the car's door and sits in the driver's seat. The owner of the business sends his muscular bodyguard Eddie (Duane Davis) to sort out Miller, but the man is shot dead. Miller then shoots and kills the salesman and his customer, before stealing the Ferrari.

Unable to understand the new trail of bodies, Beck looks to Gallagher for some help, but the FBI agent is not forthcoming with the facts. Back at Beck's house, Gallagher meets his wife (Cannon) and young daughter (Kristen Clayton). Gallagher tells Beck that the same person who is responsible for the current murders also killed his wife and child.

Kyle MacLachlan is the mysterious FBI agent who helps detective Michael Nouri battle a strange alien.

Miller sits in a strip club watching an act by a dancer named Brenda (Christian). After her performance is finished, he corners her in a dressing room and the alien parasite swaps bodies once again. After leaving her employment, Brenda makes love to a stranger in the front seat of a parked car. The man dies during sex. Gallagher oversees the event and orders Beck to follow him.

Beck and Gallagher chase Brenda to the roof of a warehouse, where a shoot-out ensues. The stripper appears to fall to her death. However, the parasite enters the body of a dog belonging to Lieutenant Ed Flynn (Gulagher). Back at the police station, Beck arrests Gallagher, having found out that he has taken on the identity of a dead FBI agent. At his house, Flynn's dog attacks him. The alien swaps bodies again.

Gallagher tries to explain that he is from another planet and hunting an alien that can only be killed with a special laser gun that he has in his possession, but Beck believes him to be crazy and locks Gallagher up. The following day, Flynn enters the station, with the alien inside his body, and tries to kill both Beck and Gallagher. Realizing that there might be some truth to Gallagher's story, Beck frees the man and returns his weapon. They both escape from a brutal shoot-out with Flynn.

The alien's true motivation is to enter into the body of presidential candidate Senator Holt (McCann). With a political rally being held in the city, Flynn manages to swap the alien with Holt. A shoot-out at a press conference ensues, and Gallagher finally kills the alien with his laser gun when it crawls out from the mouth of Holt.

Beck ends up on life support, but Gallagher comes to his rescue and swaps his life force with that of his friend, killing himself in the process.

Critique

A creature feature crossed with a cop movie—*The Hidden* is an oddity that deserves more than the minor cult success that it has obtained. Kyle MacLachlan may have gained lifelong infamy for splashing about in a Jacuzzi with Elizabeth Berkley mounted on top of him—both of them participating in probably the worst sex scene in film history—during *Showgirls*, but for 1980s horror buffs, he will always be FBI Agent Lloyd Gallagher. The actor puts in an excellent performance as the tragic space visitor,

MacLachlan will go on to play another FBI agent in cult fave *Twin Peaks*.

tracking down the alien life form that has claimed his wife and child. The "good cop, bad cop" routine is completed by Nouri, who brings his confused and cold character a final vulnerability that gives *The Hidden* an emotional depth unusual for its genre, and indeed unusual for director Jack Sholder. An eloquent, downbeat climax to *The Hidden* provides the feature with a peculiar power and an unexpected resonance. It is also refreshing to see a horror movie end on a deeply sad note—MacLachlan's act of self-sacrifice bringing the film to a perfect finish. However, with this acknowledged, it is hard to deny that most viewers will carry away images of the feature's considerable carnage with them. Indeed, *The Hidden*, with its slam-bang combination of car chases and shoot-outs, is almost nonstop in showcasing its action set pieces, barely leaving the audience with time to catch their breath.

Made after Sholder's largely disastrous *A Nightmare on Elm Street Part 2: Freddy's Revenge*, which was a critical—if not commercial—disappointment, *The Hidden* fulfils the potential that the director showcased with his debut movie *Alone in the Dark*. There are moments in *The Hidden* that, even by B-movie lore, are deliciously bizarre and original. Take the gorgeous Claudia Christian literally fucking someone to death—or the alien parasite being vomited from one character's mouth into another. The creature is unseen for most the film—hence the title—but once it is glimpsed (thanks to a remarkable scene devised by makeup legend Kevin Yagher), it remains on the viewer's mind for the rest of the movie. Cleverly, Sholder stages this special effects highlight early on and, in doing so, he does not need to remind us of the creature's gruesome physicality until the end of the picture. When watched again today, the sight of what can only be described as a giant slug escaping from the mouth of McCann is an absurd, but fascinating, spectacle and a reminder of a time when horror movies did not lapse into CG effects. Certainly, *The Hidden* is a standout genre release from its decade (especially when one remembers that the late 1980s was a time of creative bankruptcy for the horror film, with seemingly endless sequels) and very well directed. That the film's potential as a lucrative, and interesting, franchise was largely fudged by the appearance of 1993's dire sequel remains disappointing.

Of course, it is difficult to deny that *The Hidden* takes at least some of its influence from 1956's *Invasion of the Body Snatchers*—although without the symbolism that the original, Cold War-era *Body Snatchers* carried with it. Instead, the creature in Sholder's film invades the bodies of humans, forcing them into psychopathic murder sprees—although we are never given a reasonable explanation as to why the alien life force should encourage this. While the invaders in Don Siegel's *Body Snatchers* come to earth to breed and to exploit the planet's resources, *The Hidden* is a real "sit back and enjoy the ride" experience—a popcorn film that does not pretend to be anything other than B-movie fun.[6] Ultimately, Sholder could have used the invasion theme to comment on the innermost monster that is inherent in his characters, but this potential is not exploited. In some ways this is frustrating, being that *The Hidden* is set in 1980s Los Angeles, a time and place ripe for symbolism (imagine a typical suited-up Hollywood producer being turned into a drooling blood and sex craving maniac!). Even when the alien parasite chooses to inhabit a presidential candidate, Sholder does not attempt to explicitly equate the process with a politician's outer, public personality—and that same person's hidden self. Then again, such symbolism may have derailed the roller coaster-ride fun of *The Hidden* and, ultimately, the movie is a fine example of how to make an unpretentious and just plain enjoyable action-packed horror flick.

The Hidden also contains what has to be classed as one of the all-time great movie openings. Allowing the audience the point of view of looking through a bank's security camera, the film then erupts into sudden violence as a possessed man opens fire on a couple of bystanders, finally escaping into his car and driving away at high speed. What follows is a *French Connection*-influenced car chase around the city that, for a relatively low-budget movie, is nothing short of outstanding. This slam-bang action gives the viewer little time to comprehend what the hell is going on—and Sholder wisely slows the pace down (if only for a short while) following this invigorating opening sequence. As a film that shifts along at lightning pace and never offers a dull spot, *The Hidden* is an essential entry in this publication. Even more so, for *Babylon 5* star and *Playboy* pin-up Claudia Christian's seductively nasty femme fatale—one of the sexiest sights the genre has ever offered.

(It is worth noting that 1993's *Friday the 13th* sequel, *Jason Goes to Hell*, plays out as a glorified remake of *The Hidden*.)

Standout Moment

The opening double-whammy of a bank robbery followed by one of the best low-budget car chases ever committed to celluloid, just narrowly edges out special effects whiz Kevin Yagher's amazing "alien parasite down the throat" set piece.

Memories of the Film

"When it came time for *The Hidden*, one of the executives at New Line said, 'There's this terrific script and you should see about directing it.' So she gave me the script and I thought, 'Wow, I would give anything to direct this movie,'" laughs Jack Sholder, reflecting back on directing *The Hidden*. "I loved the script and I loved the fact it was kind of a cop movie, I was a great admirer of the films Lumet did like

MacLachlan is excellent in *The Hidden*—his character's act of self-sacrifice brings the film to a perfect finish.

Actor Chris Mulkey gets ready for war in *The Hidden*.

Serpico and *Dog Day Afternoon*, I loved that genre. So here was a chance to do it—it was a very smart script, but they had another director in mind. Fortunately he decided for one reason or another not to do it, so that left the field open for me. I thought, 'This is really a movie about what it is to be human.' The bad alien comes to earth, and the good alien learns what it is to be a good human. If you look at the film that was always in my mind—the bad alien is always looking at his body—like 'Wow, I got breasts,' when he swaps bodies with the stripper," he laughs. "There's one scene that I really love, where Kyle MacLachlan goes into his partner's house and has this very soulful look when he sees the picture of him with his wife and daughter. There were a lot of those moments. Like when the old guy goes to the strip bar and he looks at his hands—kind of an odd moment—because he's inhabited this strange vehicle, this human body. I had seven different versions of this alien—the guy in the Ferrari, the old guy and the girl and the detective and so on. I thought, 'This is one character—so it has to be directed as the one character but in a different guise.' So what I did was to gather all the actors, and the dog, and have some rehearsals for them to work on character."

The Hidden has one of horror's greatest openings, although Sholder is remarkably humble when offered this opinion. "Well, it's not for me to say it has one of the all-time great openings, but I'll take your word for it," he laughs. "It certainly has a good opening though—in the original script it was a bank robbery and it was written as a bank robbery. Then New Line, for budget reasons, said 'Let's cut out the bank robbery. We've all seen a bank robbery before and who needs to see another bank robbery? It's going to take another day or two to shoot it and it's not going to add to the film.' So we never shot a bank robbery and the idea was that the film would start with the guy exiting the bank, being shot at, and jumping in the Ferrari and taking off, allowing you to figure, 'Okay, he's robbed the bank.' When the film was cut together we realized that you didn't know what was going on—and so I shot it all through a security camera. I told New Line, 'That will be cheap and we can do it all in one day, we'll just stage it and it can be done in one shot.' So that is exactly what we did, it's one of those things that came out of adversity, but I have to say that it was a good idea. Much cooler...one of the things about *The Hidden* is that it doesn't do things the obvious way; if we had done the opening the way it had been scripted, it would have been a far less interesting opening."

Did the car chase sequence prove a challenge to stage for the director? "As far as doing a car chase, I had never done one before," he admits. "Bob Shaye said, 'Ah, forget about the car chase—you've never done one, they are all kind of generic anyway.' A friend of mine is a very good writer and any time he had to write a car chase he'd just put down 'add car chase sequence.' But I felt challenged and I thought, 'I'm going to do the best damn car chase scene that's ever been done.' I had my assistant go out and find all the movies with great car chase sequences and assemble all of them on a tape so I could study them." The car chase in *The Hidden* looks to have been taken from *The French Connection*. "You're very insightful," replies Sholder. "I thought that the greatest car chase of them all was *The French Connection,* and the reason that it is great is because the camera is always with the car. The one that Walter Hill did uses a lot of telephoto lenses, a lot of geography and with (William) Friedkin the lenses are very wide, so the car comes right at you—as if it's going to hit you. Consequently, you are moving with the car, and I mean nowadays the state-of-the-art has gotten pretty good, and when you compare *The Hidden* to what you see now it's not as big, but it has a great kinetic energy. So yes, absolutely I stole shamelessly from Friedkin."

Aside from the exciting car chase opening, *The Hidden* also features the jaw-dropping special effects sequence in which the alien parasite slowly crawls from one character's mouth into another's. "We only did that effect once and I used Kevin Yagher for it," remembers Sholder. "I had used Kevin to do *A Nightmare on Elm Street Part 2*, I hired him. He was a young guy who was just starting out. I used two people—Mark Shorstrom, who was more the *Fangoria,* 'more blood, more gore' kind of guy. But Kevin was an artist—he had studied sculpture. He didn't have books of brains cut in half and arms lopped off and people burned up. I mean, he had some of those—but he had pictures of this guy, an actor in his 20s, and he made him up as a 60-year-old guy and took him out to the park to play with kids. Nobody knew it was just a 20-year-old guy in

Prison life gets too much for one convict in *The Hidden*.

makeup. So I was really impressed and he became the Freddy guy—redesigned Freddy's makeup from the original film. I hired Kevin for *The Hidden*, and he came up with an idea of what the creature should look like. He came up with a parasite and right at that point some new materials had arrived, so he did a mold of the old guy's face where the creature was going to come down his mouth and it was the most realistic thing I'd ever seen. Literally every pore—it was so perfect that when the actor saw it he fled the room! That was actually the last thing we ever did, we spent a whole night trying to get the creature out of this one guy's mouth and into the other guy's mouth. The interesting thing is that we only did that once—and then right at the very end when it pops out. That's because a) it's not really about that and b) once you've seen it once you don't need to see it again."

Surprisingly, Sholder is not aware of 1993's *Jason Goes to Hell: The Final Friday*, a film that takes a lot from *The Hidden*. "No, I never saw it—you know, I saw the first two or three *Friday* movies and then I stopped because I didn't think that they had much left to offer. But a lot of people have stolen from *The Hidden*, including that film that Denzel Washington was in—*Fallen*. In fact, New Line even sued somebody, there have been several things. There was a time when I was trying to set up *The Hidden* as a TV series, and someone told me, 'Oh, Sci-Fi Network is going ahead with something really similar,' it was the same thing. I'm not a hysterical guy when it comes to plagiarism, as you've already figured out, but there were seven or eight things that were direct steals from *The Hidden*. With this television proposal it

The Hidden is as much a buddy movie as it is a genre classic.

Down but not out... one of *The Hidden*'s many city natives who are taken over by the vengeful alien.

was like they went and rewrote it, so I went to New Line and they said they'd look into it and I think they sent a cease and desist letter. It's a very powerful idea and I think it has entered the culture. So people like yourself might say, 'This all started with *The Hidden*,' because so much has come since then that it is almost like a genre now—an alien that goes into other people's bodies."

Sholder also admits that he has no regrets about turning down the chance to direct the sequel to his original movie. "They basically just wanted to do a cheap ripoff of *The Hidden* for one quarter of the budget and then just get it out," he shrugs. "They had to offer me the opportunity but I turned it down. It wasn't a serious attempt to do it and also I felt that I had already done it and I wanted to move on to something else. It really is eminently sequel-able."

Alternate Critiques

"A really good movie which blends action, horror and sci-fi to near-perfection." (Allan Bryce, *Dark Side*, Issue 61)

"Smart, fast-paced thriller effectively blends horror, sci-fi, and action with humor; good acting and savvy direction." (Leonard Maltin, *Movie and Video Guide*, Penguin)

"This is a very well-made and quite entertaining movie....My only real quibble is that we only get a few seconds of the creature, which is so thoroughly creepy it would've been nice to spend a little more time with it." (L.A. Morse, *Video Trash and Treasures*, HarperCollins, 1989)

CHAPTER 3
SLASHER FILMS
Perhaps the Most Popular Slice of Horror Cinema

Alone in the Dark

Director: Jack Sholder
Produced by: Robert Shaye
Written by: Jack Sholder
Cast: Jack Palance; Donald Pleasence; Martin Landau; Dwight Schultz; Erland Van Lidth; Deborah Hedwall; Lee Taylor-Allan; Phillip Clark; Elizabeth Ward; Brent Jennings; Carol Levy; Keith Reddin
Special Effects: Tom Savini, Tom Brumberger, Don Lumpkin
Year: 1982

Plot Synopsis

Byron (Landau) enters into "Mom's Cafeteria." Inside he meets the chef (Pleasence). Suddenly chains grab Byron by the feet and haul him upside down. With his legs split wide open, the chef swings a machete down toward his crotch...but before the weapon can make impact Byron awakes. It has all been a dream.

Dr. Dan Potter (Schultz) is at home with his wife Nell (Hedwall) and daughter Lyla (Ward). They appear to be a happy, middle-class family. Later at the asylum where he is starting work, Potter meets the facility's owner, Dr. Leo Bain (Pleasence) and Ray (Jennings), the building's security guard. Bain talks about a "special security system" that the asylum utilizes—whereby everything is controlled by electricity.

Potter is introduced to some of the inmates that will be in his care. Along with Byron, a former preacher, is Jack Hawkes (Palance) a paranoid former P.O.W., and Ronald Elster (Van Lidth), an obese child molester. Another inmate is Skaggs (Clark), who hides his face from strangers. He is also known as "bleeder," because of his violent rage whenever he obtains a nosebleed. After Potter leaves, Hawkes becomes convinced that the new doctor is out to kill them, and may even have murdered Harry Merton, who was their previous psychiatrist.

Nell collects Potter's sister Toni (Taylor-Allan) from the airport and brings her back to their home. Toni is a hippie, with a history of mental illness. She urges Nell to attend a punk rock concert later that night.

Meanwhile, at the asylum, Elster steals a letter that has Potter's address on it. Later that night, Potter agrees to attend the punk rock concert with his wife and sister. During the gig, the lights go out; there is a blackout around the town. With the electricity down, the inmates are able to leave the hospital. After murdering Ray, Potter's five patients go on a looting spree, taking whatever weapons they can from the burgled stores that litter the neighborhood. Wearing a hockey mask, Skaggs has a nosebleed and slices a pedestrian's throat. He then runs away from the rest of the group.

Famed for his portrayal of "Howling Mad" Murdoch in *The A-Team*, actor Dwight Schultz takes on a more serious role in *Alone in the Dark*.

The next day, Toni and Nell attend a protest rally against nuclear war and are arrested. Back home, Lyla arrives from school to the imposing figure of Elster, who claims to be her new babysitter. He urges the little girl to go upstairs with him. From jail, Nell calls Bunky (Levy), the family babysitter. When she arrives, Bunky finds Lyla in bed asleep and calls her boyfriend (Reddin) to the house. The two make out until they are attacked and killed by Elster and Byron.

When the family returns, with a new friend of Toni's called Tom (Clark), there is no sign of the babysitter. Potter calls in the town's Police Inspector (Frederick Coffin) when he learns of the presence of one of the asylum escapees in his house. Soon they all settle down for dinner but are distracted by noises outside. As darkness looms, the Inspector leaves the house to investigate, whereupon he is shot with an arrow. Bain turns up at the Potter residence soon after and asks his patients to return to the asylum, but he too is murdered.

Before long, the maniacs begin to stalk the family and Potter is forced to kill to defend his loved ones. Tom is revealed to be the "bleeder," and he strangles Toni before Nell comes to her rescue and stabs him to death. With only Hawkes left, and the family cornered, the electricity comes back on and the lunatic notices a news flash about the asylum escape on the television. His former doctor, Harry Merton, appears onscreen to give an anchorwoman a rundown on his former patients.

His assumptions about Merton's murder proven wrong, Hawkes leaves the Potter household and attends a punk rock concert at the same venue from earlier in the film. He punches out the show's ticket vendor and then meets a girl who appears to be even more insane than him. As he draws a gun on her, the girl presumes this is part of his act and sucks the barrel of the weapon. Hawkes looks on, smiling and perplexed.

Critique

A welcome variation from the more familiar plot of a masked psychopath in a lone vacation spot (or old dark house) hacking away at a small cast of attractive teenagers

without any apparent motivation or reason, *Alone in the Dark* is a suspenseful and well-made stalker film. It is perhaps its lack of adherence to traditional generic values that ultimately makes *Alone in the Dark* such a standout movie all these years later. The film certainly manages to evolve into a taut and well-directed slice of mayhem, with a prevailing feel of claustrophobia as Schultz and his family find themselves trapped in room after room of their own house by a group of escaped lunatics.

Most interesting is Sholder's projection of a society gone mad, perhaps most implicitly demonstrated in the scene where a punk rock group called The Sick Fucks perform a song with the chorus "Chop Up Your Mother," to an evidently delighted crowd of teenaged misfits. Moreover, it is during the outbreak of looting that Skaggs (clad in a hockey mask in, ironically, the same year Jason would don his for the first time[1]) kills someone, only for passing members of the public—more concerned with the capture of their new goods—to pay no notice. This atmosphere of hysteria is further played out during the film's ending, where Palance's violently schizophrenic character finds his way into the same punk rock venue that the Potter family had visited earlier. After viciously beating up an obnoxious ticket vendor, to the applause of bystanders who take advantage of the scenario and enter the concert for free, Palance meets a young lady who takes a fancy to him. Unable to comprehend her fascination with him, and evidently feeling quite threatened by the girl's aggressive sexuality, Palance takes out a handgun...only to have his female acquaintance place the weapon in her mouth in an attempt to simulate fellatio! Sholder wisely ends the film at this moment, driving home the idea that the world really has gone crazy.[2]

Donald Pleasance offers up some slice & dice mayhem.

In these surroundings of madness, *Alone in the Dark* offers up only one truly sensible adult character—Schultz's Dr. Dan Potter (oddly enough, Schultz went on to gain international fame by playing "Howling Mad" Murdoch in *The A-Team*). Always the voice of reason, Schultz is a lone, rational mind in the landscape of Sholder's film. Even his wife, looking to find an escape from her predictable household activities, is easily led by the arrival of her hippie, college student sister-in-law. One suspects that the director may be poking fun at the doctor's proclaimed pacifism during the final home invasion, where Schultz is forced to defend his family against the aggressors but, if so, it is a somewhat futile point. On the other hand, Schultz does do virtually everything correct throughout the movie—and none of the film's villains would have made their escape if Pleasence had only listened to the doctor's sensible doubts about his asylum's electronic locking system. Indeed, when we first meet Pleasence's Dr. Leo Bain, the old man is so patently nuts that it is uncertain if he actually is one of the inmates. The doctor's rosy idealism is in stark contrast to Schultz's wise acceptance of the patients as dangerous men, and it is curious indeed that such a character should run an asylum.

Pleasence aside, Sholder expresses an unmistakably cynical outlook toward authority in *Alone in the Dark*. For example, one scene highlights Hedwall and Taylor-Allen in prison, having been arrested during a street protest against nuclear weapons. Again, this seems in step with the movie's portrait of a world with haywire values—where peace protestors are actually seen as a threat but, when the chance arises, looting and theft are deemed to be acceptable by the general public. Whether or not it is intentional, given this cynical outlook toward authority, it is at least fitting that the maniacs' early victims include not only Pleasence but also an asylum security guard and a police Inspector. Likewise, Martin Landau's insane, "hellfire and brimstone" preacher does not exactly paint a positive picture of one of the oldest institutions of them all—the Church.

The violence in *Alone in the Dark* is, contrary to the bulk of genre films of the period, restrained. Only a briefly seen throat slashing warrants any kind of grimace, and Sholder—contrary to the more special effects-laden slasher action in his *Nightmare on Elm Street* sequel—uses the plot to build tension. Certainly, the invasion of Schultz's home is malevolent and scary, while the scene where the monstrous Erland Van Lidth urges the doctor's young daughter to come upstairs with him is just plain ugly. Rarely has a director ever placed a child in such an awful situation, with the viewer's knowledge of Van Lidth's past crimes (child molestation) causing the sequence to be truly uncomfortable viewing. Even at the nastier end of the slasher cycle (for example *Maniac* or *Nightmare*—both 1981), the psychotic was never portrayed with these sort of sinister, repulsive urges—giving *Alone in the Dark* a somewhat dubious honor, but certainly adding to the villain's air of terror. Landau and Pleasence are also in top form throughout; suc-

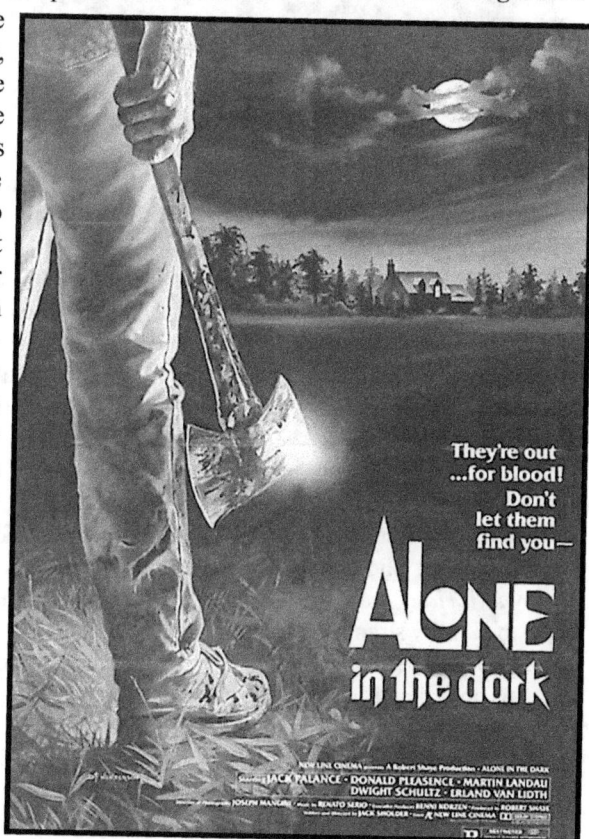

"I loved you in the A-Team" —Dr. Leo Bain (Donald Pleasance) gets cozy with his new co-star.

cessfully evoking the feeling that these are desperately violent men, and—unlike so many masked stalkers in copycat films such as *Graduation Day* (1981) and *Slaughter High* (1985)—these characters are genuinely fearsome. It is to Sholder's credit that he should write and direct a horror film that presents villains without masks and with (God forbid) personality during a time when every screen killer seemed to be decked out in some kind of ridiculous gimmick. Alas, the initial advertising campaign for the picture did not stress the film's originality and, instead, played it safe with its portrait of a mysterious killer descending upon a house, axe in hand (the U.K. visual was even more shoddy with a black glove pictured gripping a knife).

Of course, *Alone in the Dark* has the privilege to feature two future Oscar-winning actors in Landau and Palance, alongside genre veteran Pleasence in a role that suits him well. Eagle-eyed viewers might also spot future star Lin Shaye, from *There's Something About Mary* and *Boat Trip*, in a small role as the asylum's receptionist. Schultz, meanwhile, is excellent throughout—and such a perfectly thought-out cast gives the impression that Sholder really was aiming to make a classic horror film and not just a copycat *Friday the 13th* spin off. The feature also pulls off a nice, unexpected twist when the kindly stranger Clark turns out to be "bleeder"—one of the escaped inmates.[3] Sure, this does rely on a preposterous coincidence (the man meets Taylor-Allen when they are both being held by the police following the nuclear weapons protest) and an unlikely personality switch, but when the payoff is as sudden, and frightening as this, it is hard to feel cheated. *Alone in the Dark* was Sholder's first effort as a director (he had previously edited the violent, *Friday the 13th* remake/ripoff *The Burning* in 1981) and it still holds up as an accomplished debut.

Standout Moment

The revelation that "bleeder" is in the Potters' very household is unexpected and results in a bloody good scare!

Memories of the Film

"I had a long association with New Line Cinema," states Jack Sholder, commenting on how the studio came to finance his first horror picture. "They were a small company that was basically just distributing films to colleges—that was their main thing. Then they started to move into theatrical distribution and production; they figured that was where they needed to go because it was increasingly hard to get movies. So they said, 'Gee, if we could do a low-budget horror film for about $1 million then we could definitely make money on it.' So I said, 'What about this for a story—a bunch of mental patients escape from a mental hospital during a blackout and they terrorize Little Italy. Then they are rounded up by the Mafia.' They said, 'That sounds like a good idea, why don't you give us a treatment?' A week later they asked for the treatment again, and I said, 'Oh—so you were serious?' (*laughs*). Then they said, 'We can't do it in New York because it is going to be too expensive.' So I came up with the idea of what we have in the final film—and so they said, 'Okay, we'll pay you a small amount of money to write the script and if we make it we'll pay you to direct it.' They liked it, but it kind of sat on the shelf. In the meantime, because I was working as an editor, I got hired to edit the first film that the Weinstein brothers did, called *The Burning*. Which is a fairly dreadful film—they just ripped of every film that made money, the campers and the weird guy and their little creative twist was that the killer had garden shears."

Stating that he never knew *The Burning* was one of the U.K.'s famous "video nasties," Sholder does admit that his time editing the film proved valuable. "By editing that film I ended up learning quite a bit about how the genre works," he says. "Prior to that I had done work for New Line, mainly on action trailers—kung fu and stuff. After I finished editing *The Burning*, New Line said, 'We'd like to see if we can make your film this summer.' So I said, 'Let me go back and do a rewrite,' so I did and I think that improved it because I now knew how the rules of the genre functioned. They tried to get the budget down to a very low figure, which was kind of unrealistic, and basically the whole production was kind of a mess—no one knew what they were doing. Everyone was working one category above what they were supposed to do. It was the first film New Line distributed on their own, so it came out in small markets. It initially opened in Detroit and Cleveland and (producer) Bob Shaye comes from Detroit. It opened there, and it didn't really set the world on fire—it got mediocre reviews. Some people liked it but it didn't knock anyone out. I have a great fondness for it. It's nice to hear that it has fans because I always thought it was a pretty interesting film. The one thing that was

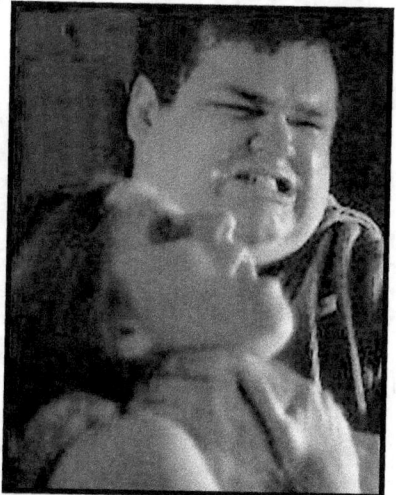

Erland van Lidth portrays one of the escaped killers.

Martin Landau isn't afraid of the dark – but frogs are another matter.

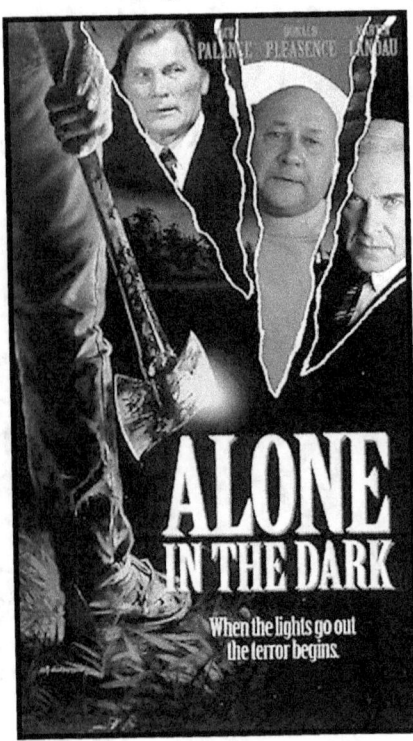

kind of successful, obviously, was the casting."

Indeed, *Alone in the Dark* is probably the only slasher film to have two Oscar-winning actors in the cast. "Yeah, but we caught them at absolute low points in their career," laughs Sholder in response. "Martin Landau actually campaigned for the role. Donald Pleasence, I was thrilled at because I had been a gigantic fan of his. I think he had just done *Halloween* so he had the credentials for the genre, and I was very excited. We ended up with a very good cast. Part of what happened with Jack Palance was that he had been told there would be no night shooting. It's called *Alone in the Dark* but there's no night shooting—'Yeah, don't worry about it Jack,' (*laughs*). And he arrived in a very bad mood because in the meantime he had gotten an offer to do something that he could have done in Florence instead of Jersey. He wanted out of our movie but we wouldn't let him, so he was in a bad mood, and he also thought that he was doing the Donald Pleasence part. He really didn't want to play a psychotic killer." For children of the 1980s, it is also strange to see Dwight Schultz in a serious role, far removed from his more famous turn in *The A-Team*. "Dwight is a really good actor," replies Sholder. "At that point he had done a lot of serious stuff, a lot of really good stage work on Broadway. He was a really fine actor. He had kind of an odd sense of humor, which became exploited later in his career, and he has kind of disappeared over the last 10 years, which is a shame. The woman who played his wife was also an excellent actress."

Alone in the Dark hit theaters in the same year as *Friday the 13th Part 3*. Was it more than just a coincidence that both featured a hockey mask killer (Jason first donned his iconic get-up in the third *Friday the 13th*) or was someone ripping off someone else? "I don't think so," says Sholder. "You know we were all stealing from everybody else anyway. I knew all those guys—I didn't know John Carpenter—but I knew Sean Cunningham and Wes Craven and all those people.

I'm sure I stole just as much from *Friday the 13th*—just in terms of approach as opposed to specifics. It was very successful, I mean now it is kind of spoofed—'Oh, there's a maniac out in the woods and they just shot Suzy with an arrow, let's go out and see if we can find him,' but at the time it was still new. Then what happened was that any body part that could be lopped off, burned or pierced was done onscreen so, I mean, it just became a bore eventually."

One of the film's most memorable set pieces is the old 'knife through the bed during sex' trick...

Sholder also explains why he might be considered an unlikely director of horror films. "It seems like there are three kinds of people who do horror movies," he says. "There are the people who grow up reading *Fangoria* and are just into it and a lot of those guys end up being special effects experts. Then you have people like Wes Craven, who really has a vision that's very dark. And then there are people who get their start doing it just because it was a way to get in, and that was me. Because left to my own devices and given a budget, I would not have done a horror movie. The idea with the movie was to touch on some cultural issues—there had been some blackouts and people running amuck, R.D. Laing—he had a mental institution in Scotland actually, he thought that mental patients, schizophrenics, were healthier than normal people. So instead of treating them as sick he treated them as if they had some greater insight and gave them a lot more freedom. He had a certain level of success, but his opinion was, 'The world is crazy and they are reacting to the craziness of the world.' It was certainly meant to be more than a slasher movie, it was meant to be a commentary on a whole lot of things. For instance, the diner in the beginning is called Mom's Diner and the guy gets castrated and it goes on and on—the very final scene with Palance and the girl. The purest statement—'What is crazy?'"

Alternate Critique

"...an above-average entry in the already crowded maniacs-on-the-loose subgenre, thanks to its tight, crisp look, imaginative use of sound, excellent playing by its veteran cast, and a nice line in humor." (Phil Hardy, *The Aurum Film Encyclopedia: Horror,* Aurum Press, 1993)

"... one can't help but think that this film should have been lots funnier or lots scarier. Still, though, a nice piece of work with plenty of good moments and enough visceral shocks for even the most demanding, jaded audiences." (Chas Balun, *The Connoisseur's Guide to the Contemporary Horror Film,* Fantaco, 1992)

"Three psychos are better than one. Well, that's what director Jack Sholder must have thought when he put together this lucid shocker....Good performances help. The final scene is a real weirdie." (Allan Bryce, *Dark Side,* September 1993)

Intruder

Director: Scott Spiegel
Produced by: Lawrence Bender/Douglas Hessler
Written by: Lawrence Bender/Scott Spiegel
Cast: Elizabeth Cox; Renee Estevez; Dan Hicks; David Byrnes; Sam Raimi; Eugene Robert Glazer; Billy Marti; Burr Steers; Craig Stark; Ted Raimi; Alvy Moore; Tom Lester
Special Effects: Howard Berger, Robert Kurtzman, Gregory Nicotero (KNB Effects), Sean Rodgers
Year: 1988

Brief Plot Synopsis

It is business as usual at the Walnut Supermarket. Linda (Estevez) and Jennifer (Cox) speak about boys and serve some late-night shoppers as their shifts come to a close for the evening.

Jennifer's violent ex-boyfriend Craig (Byrnes) turns up and aggressively confronts her. Linda calls for help; some workers and the shop's co-manager Bill (Hicks), arrive to assist her. After a lengthy fight with Bill, Craig escapes. His presence is reported to the police and the shop crew searches for him. Craig manages to avoid being caught and confronts Jennifer again, but this time he is forcefully ejected from the building by some of the workers.

Following this scuffle, Bill's partner in the shop—Danny (Glazer)—breaks it to the staff that the Walnut Supermarket is being sold and that they will soon be laid off. "I own 49 percent of the shop and he owns 51 percent," complains Bill to his disappointed staff.

Shortly afterward, Jennifer receives a call from Craig, but she hangs up. She tells Linda that her ex-boyfriend has been in prison for a murder, which she labels "accidental." Two policemen show up (Moore and Lester) and reassure the workers that if there is any more trouble with Craig, they can be reached for help.

Linda packs up for the night and is stabbed by an unseen stalker. Later, Bill brawls with Craig outside the supermarket

Jennifer (Elizabeth Cox) faces the horrors of the supermarket in *Intruder*.

and is knocked out with a hammer. Danny, who is reviewing documents in his office, is impaled through the eye. Jennifer's new love interest Dave (Marti) kisses her as their colleague Tim (Stark) spies on them. It becomes apparent, however, that someone is in fact watching Tim. The shop's butcher, Randy (Sam Raimi), fails to notice an eyeball in a pickle jar. The supermarket's meat cutter, Produce Joe (Ted Raimi), is stabbed through the head. More workers die—one after the other: Tim is stabbed in the gut, Bub (Steers) has his head squashed, Randy is hung on a meat hook and Dave has his head sawn in half by a band saw.

Jennifer becomes aware of the murders, and is the only person left alive. She sees Craig and beats him to the ground, thinking he is the killer. The real murderer is Bill—angry that he has been forced to sell his shop. He stalks Jennifer through the store, and uses a decapitated head as a talking puppet. A deliveryman (Spiegel) comes to the front door of the store, but Bill stabs him. Craig comes to help his ex-girlfriend and Jennifer escapes through an open window as the two men fight.

Outside the shop, Jennifer takes the knife from the dead body of Linda and uses it to stab Bill. She phones for the police. Bill is still not dead, but Craig comes to the rescue and hacks him with a knife. Two police officers (Bruce Campbell and Lawrence Bender) arrive. Craig and Jennifer are both arrested, while the dying Bill insists to the officers that the two survivors of the massacre are, in fact, the guilty party...

Critique

Opening with an ominous shot of a full moon, *Intruder* is one of the goriest slasher films ever made.[4] Produced on a very evident shoestring budget, the film is nonetheless

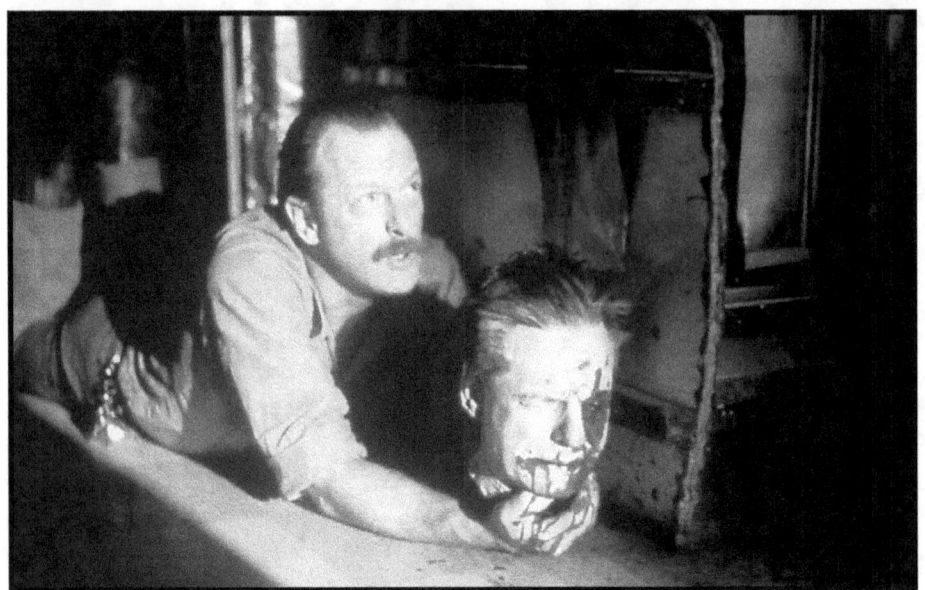

Produce Joe (Ted Raimi) loses his head in *Intruder*.

notable for the amount of future talent involved. *Spider-Man* director Sam Raimi has a sizeable role in the movie and *Evil Dead* icon Bruce Campbell makes a brief cameo toward the end of the film. KNB Effects, now one of Hollywood's major FX studios, also work their considerable talents on this early production with a variety of juicy demises for the young cast. Perhaps most startlingly, *Intruder*'s producer and cowriter is none other than Lawrence Bender—the man who would produce such landmark blockbusters as *Pulp Fiction* and *Kill Bill*. Director Scott Spiegel also went on to gain a considerable level of success in his own right—directing the straight-to-video sequel *From Dusk 'Til Dawn 2*, befriending Quentin Tarantino by helping to see the classic *Reservoir Dogs* produced, and also acting as a producer on *2001 Maniacs*. With such talent present, it is hard not to view *Intruder* as a training ground for those who went on to bigger and better things. Even the cast is not without interest—Martin Sheen's attractive daughter Renee Estevez followed her brief stint in slasher cinema (she also played the lead in 1988's *Sleepaway Camp 2*) with mainstream work in the likes of *Heathers* and her father's television series *The West Wing*. Meanwhile, Sam Raimi's brother Ted, who meets a brutal death in the film, will be recognizable to horror fans from his many minor roles in his sibling's subsequent directorial efforts and most recently 2004's *The Grudge*.

Naturally, it is the many gruesome deaths that make *Intruder* stand out as a stalker movie. At a time when fans were used to seeing R-rated slasher flicks such as Paramount's neverending *Friday the 13th* series cop out at showing anything even remotely explicit, *Intruder* does not let up—with one visceral jolt after another. The deaths in the film include such "highlights" as a spike in the eye, a head being slowly squished, a meat hook through the jaw and—in the movie's most unforgettable set piece—a face torn apart by a band saw. All of these murders are shown in incredible detail and likely to entice a genuine "Holy shit—did you see that?" response from the viewer. Very few of the film's murders take place offscreen (the early death of Estevez is a rare exception) and Spiegel really rubs the audience's face in the gore. However, this is not to say that *Intruder* should be classed with the sleazier, misogynistic side of the slasher genre. Aside from the fact that, atypical for an 1980s teen-kill movie, it is almost all men that are killed—the death scenes are so excessively over the top that the film soon ceases to carry even a remote sense of seriousness. Take the scene where Ted Raimi is killed, for instance—sliced through the head with a knife—his static demeanor and wide-eyed expression hints at a comical stupidity that is far removed from the explicit nastiness on show. It is easy, at this point, to remember that the same people responsible for *Evil Dead 2* are also behind this flick.

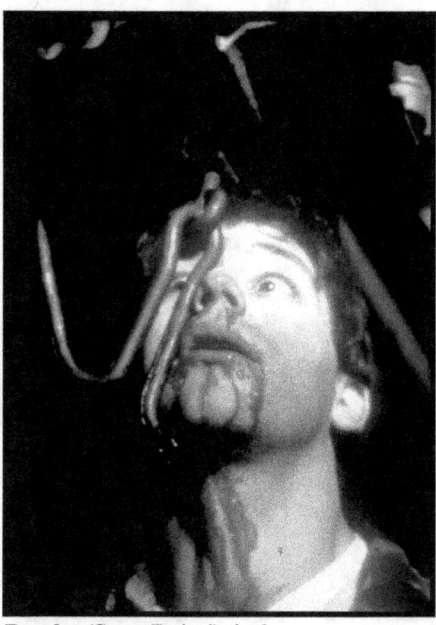

Randy (Sam Raimi) is hung on a meat hook in *Intruder*.

Also worth noting is how Spiegel chooses to give inanimate objects a point of view shot throughout the movie. Adding a humorous visual sheen to the proceedings, point of view shots from such diverse articles as a door handle, a telephone, a shop shelf and a shopping trolley are nothing short of amusing. One may argue that such technical trickery pulls the viewer out of the movie momentarily—but such camera angles also allow otherwise-pedestrian dialogue, or "filler" scenes, to transform into something unfamiliar and fascinating. No doubt even Dario Argento would admire the over-the-top camera calisthenics, and such instances as when a bucket of water takes on the eye view of the audience are silly enough to remind the viewer that nothing here is supposed to be taken with any mean-spirited intent. However, this is not to say that *Intruder* fails to pull off an air of suspense. The final chase sequence between heroine Cox and villain Hicks is when the director really begins to shine—taking the darkened aisles of the supermarket and lending them a sudden uninviting, dangerous feel—Spiegel succeeds in bringing a nicely realized air of panic to the proceedings.

As well as tight direction and fantastic special effects, *Intruder* also gives the viewer possibly the most preposterous explanation for a killing spree ever put onscreen. When the surviving Cox asks Hicks why he would kill so many people, his reasoning is nothing short of bizarre. "I couldn't let that son of a bitch take the store away," he tells her, alluding to his business partner. "This store's my life. I had to kill him." A bewildered Cox replies, "The night crew didn't have anything to do with this"—to which Hicks shrugs and answers, "I guess I just got a little carried away."

The ending, in which it looks as if the film's two survivors are going to face the heat for the killing spree, is both unexpected and witty. In other circumstances it might have seemed quite cruel to finish the film like this, but somehow *Intruder* never gives this impression. Perhaps it is because, in amongst the slaughter (which is almost non-

Employees, and not prices, are slashed in *Intruder*.

stop after a deceptively quiet first half hour), we never really get to acquaint ourselves with the personalities of the characters to such a degree that our sympathies are played upon to a high extent. More likely it is because the film carries such a slapdash sense of excessive mania that it appears entirely appropriate that the final joke should be on us, the audience. Thus, Spiegel closes his feature with his dying murderer cackling—fully aware that only we, the hapless viewers, are aware of whom the real perpetrator of the film's carnage is. With neither logic nor reason to the slaughter, Spiegel's first full-length feature is nonetheless a thoroughly enjoyable, low-budget thrill. Released at least five years too late to cash in on the boom of *Friday the 13th* clones, *Intruder* nevertheless takes the fundamental appeal of the genre (sudden, violent death) about as far as it goes.

Standout Moment

Although it is tempting to say the band saw death, Spiegel shows himself to be much more than just a director of spurting crimson, when he masks the identity of his killer by imaginatively shooting one murder through the gaze of an empty beer bottle.

Memories of the Film

"I remember showing the film to some friends at the time and someone said, 'If this came out in 1980 you'd have a huge hit,'" recalls Scott Spiegel. "The script people actually ended up crying when we did the buzz saw scene," adds the director. "Even when we were shooting it I was thinking, 'How do I make the world a better place by doing this?' Cast member Billy Marti even said, 'If my mom saw this she'd freak out!' It is what it is I guess. KNB effects really did a spectacular job on it—that was one pretty disgusting gelatin head. Just gross! That just goes to show you how good KNB is—we had the script people crying because they were really upset by it."

Spiegel also talks enthusiastically about working with Renee Estevez. "She was just the sweetest," he states. "I remember calling her and Martin Sheen picked up! Martin is just one of the nicest human beings on the planet, and he goes, 'Oh, is that Scott? Renee isn't here just now.' I kind of forgot when I was calling her that she was actually Martin Sheen's daughter. I was like, 'Oh, is this Martin Sheen? How cool!' That was just absolutely the coolest thing—and she was such a good sport. All the cast members

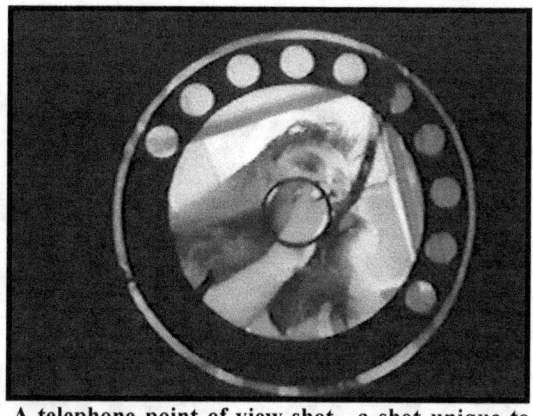

A telephone point of view shot—a shot unique to Intruder.

were great. Even Sam Raimi surprised me because I never knew he was so serious as an actor—he would always be saying, 'Scott, was that okay?' I think he was intimidated by the really meaty actors that we had, because this was before he did *Darkman*—and I think he was intimidated by us having 'real actors'—we had Tom Lester, who had been on *Green Acres*, for example.

"We weren't throwing the humor in the audience's faces," maintains the director when asked about his decision to include so much dark comedy in the film. "I don't think the humor is overt—it's not slapstick. If you watch *The Evil Dead* there's these little things like where Bruce steps in the puddle of blood and we see a Band-Aid on the shelf above him. It's kind of ironic, but with a lot of the things people laughed at in *Evil Dead*—Sam didn't mean for them to be funny, but people needed something to laugh at during this intense horror movie. Like the line, 'We can't bury Shelley, she's our friend'—people just thought, 'What the hell?' But you hope people will find humor in the film. *Intruder* is what it is...the bit with the scene of the chopped-up body on the butcher's block and you cut to a sign that reads 'meat.' That's kind of Hitchcockian—there's nothing scary about a grocery store, but when you see a sign that reads 'meat' and there's a human body chopped up, lying there... well, okay, then it becomes disgusting and scary."

Spiegel looks back on his gimmick for giving various objects point of view shots with fondness. "Yeah, we tried to give every inanimate object a point of view shot," he laughs. "We originally wanted a point of view from a dead guy, we tried putting a mask over the lens so it felt like you were looking through someone's eyes, but it never quite worked with our camera...so instead we just had the actor swing at the camera. Visually horror films are fun—you can do all sorts of wacky things with the camera...." *Intruder* also went through a variety of name changes, as the director explains. "It was originally called *Night Crew: The Final Checkout*. What happened was that I liked *Night Crew* and Charlie Band, who was going to release the film, liked *The Final Checkout*, so we came to the agreement of calling it *Night Crew: The Final Checkout*. Then Charlie sold his company and with it three movies, including mine. Of the other two, one was called *I Was a Teenage Sex Maniac* and the other was called *Cannibal Women in the Advocado Jungle of Death*. So they made a deal with Paramount and it got renamed *Intruder*. I think that's a pretty generic title. I think they considered calling

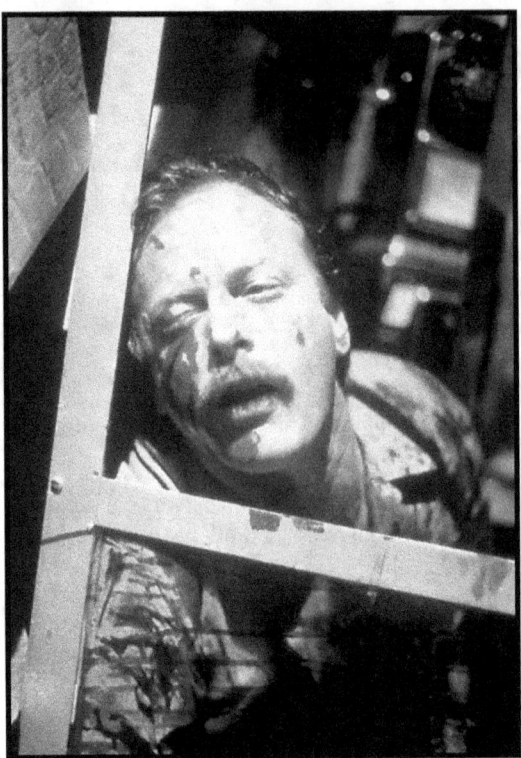

Intruder's odd camera angles and POV shots earned praise from critics.

it *Nerve Endings*—which was a very appropriate title. *Nerve Endings* is pretty good...."

Inevitably *Intruder* was always likely to garner is largest appeal from horror viewers through the vast amount of blood spilled onscreen. "KNB Effects had worked on *Evil Dead 2* and without us having any big stars for *Intruder*, I knew we needed to have good special effects," states Spiegel. "We were very fortunate to have KNB—we couldn't afford them...I mean, I called up KNB's Greg Nicotero and said, 'Greg, would you know any low-budget special effects artists who might want to work on *Intruder?*' and he said, 'Yeah, we'll do it.' I said, 'What?' It was great to have them, and the effects still hold up. We never had any CGI either. It's just amazing what they did—often you see an older horror film and there's no impact left....I think that's so fucking cool that we have the goriest slasher movie of the 1980s. We shot it in two weeks, well I think we got 15 days if we were lucky, but as fast as we shot it we were still going for quality. We weren't just trying to do *Sleepaway Camp Part 5* or whatever. I've always had a huge love of horror films, including the classics like William Castle and *I Saw What You Did, Psycho, Play Misty for Me*. Even stuff like *The Prowler* and some *Friday the 13th* movies....It's really cool to me, that I made this little cult film."

Alternate Critiques

"...in its uncut form, *Intruder* is one of the most stylish and creative slasher films in years." (Tim Lucas, *Gorezone*, Issue 11, January 1990)

"The first thing that strikes you about *Intruder* is the odd camera angles; cameras peer out from inside telephones, beneath the floor and inside buckets, making for an odd atmosphere....It's worth looking out for the longer version, since it transforms the film from an average slasher to a pretty good (and underrated) gore flick." (Jim Harper, *Legacy of Blood*, Headpress, 2004)

"To make up for his surprise-free, slasher script, Spiegel resorts to trick shots, filming through a bottle, from underneath a telephone dial or wastepaper basket...." (Phil Hardy, *The Aurum Film Encyclopedia: Horror,* Aurum Press, 1993)

Silent Night, Deadly Night

Director: Charles E. Sellier Jr.
Produced by: Ira Richard Barmack
Written by: Michael Hickey
Cast: Lilyan Chauvin; Gilmer McCormick; Toni Nero; Robert Brian Wilson; Britt Leach; Nancy Borgenicht; H.E.D. Redford; Linnea Quigley; Leo Geter; Randy Stumpf; Andy Will Hare; Tara Buckman
Special Effects: Richard N. McGuire
Year: 1984

Plot Synopsis

It's Christmas Eve. A married couple (Buckman and Geoff Hansen), accompanied by their young son Billy (Jonathan Best) and newborn baby Ricky, drive to the Utah Mental Facility. Billy's grandfather is being kept at the institution in a state of catatonia.

Upon arrival, the parents leave young Billy with the old man (Hare)—who suddenly awakes and scares the young boy by telling him that Santa punishes children who have not behaved. He asks Billy if he has behaved himself all year long. When the child admits that he has not, his grandfather warns him that Santa will punish him. When Billy's parents re-enter the room, the man sinks back into a state of false catatonia.

Nearby, a man in a Santa outfit (Charles Dierkop) holds up a gas station and shoots the cashier dead; however, shortly afterward we see the maniac stranded at the side of the road with a broken down car. Stopping to help, Billy's father is shot dead and his mother is raped and killed. Billy looks on from a distance, with his baby brother Ricky in his arms. The killer gives up searching for the boy and leaves the scene of the crime.

Four years later, it is December 1974. Billy is now eight years old (played by Danny Wagner) and at a strict, unforgiving Catholic school for orphaned children. He draws a picture of Santa murdering people and is scolded by the harsh Mother Superior (Chauvin).

For Billy (Danny Wagner) punishment is the key word in *Silent Night, Deadly Night*.

Later Billy looks through a keyhole and sees a young couple making love. He is caught spying by the Mother Superior and the two youngsters are beaten. Billy is later caned and told that what they were doing was "very naughty." That night, following a nightmare, Billy is tied to his bed—despite the concern of the kindly Sister Margaret (McCormick).

On Christmas Day Billy punches a man dressed as Santa Claus in the face and runs into a corner to hide. He says the word "naughty" over and over again.

Ten years pass and Billy is now fully grown (played by Wilson). Thanks to Sister Margaret, he obtains a job in a toy store and he seems to have settled down well. However, come Christmas time at the store, the boy is beginning to have flashbacks to his horrific childhood memories. Things become worse for Billy when he is asked to dress up as Santa on Christmas Eve by his boss (Leach). He does so, and frightens at least one child by threatening "punishment" if she does not quiet down.

When the shop closes late on Christmas Eve, Billy becomes unhinged. He sees a smarmy coworker (Stumpf) trying to rape a girl called Pamela (Nero), whom Billy is attracted to. With a flashback to the sexual act he witnessed as a child, and the Mother Superior's insistence that this is "naughty," Billy slaughters them both. He then kills his boss and another coworker.

Wandering the streets, Billy breaks into a house where two teenagers (Quigley and Getter) are making out. He kills them both, hanging the girl on the antlers of a reindeer's head that hangs from the wall. Next in line is someone who steals a sled—the thief is decapitated as he flees down a hill.

The next morning the local police force is warned to keep an eye out for Billy, who Sister Margaret believes will head back to his orphanage in order to kill the Mother Superior. One police officer opens fire on a man dressed as Santa Claus, who was attending the orphanage for Christmas Day. It is a fatal mistake, and witnessed by a horrified Mother Superior.

Billy (Jonathan Best) becomes traumatized by his grandfather (Andy Will Hare) when he visits the nursing home.

The officer investigates a cellar, but there is still no sign of the killer. Billy surprises the policeman as he walks out from the cellar, and kills him with an axe.

Entering the orphanage, Billy attempts to decapitate the Mother Superior, but the police arrive just in time to foil his plan and shoot him down. As he dies, Billy sees his young brother, Ricky (Alex Bunton). Ricky utters the word "naughty," evidently sympathizing with his older brother.

Critique

Guilty pleasure time with this nasty little slice of Christmas mayhem! Although largely dismissed, *Silent Night, Deadly Night* is a far more interesting film than its detractors would have you believe. Although it is, admittedly, not the best-directed of horror movies (although the various Christmas-related set pieces are well staged and carry a strong sense of menace) the film does contain an indisputable anger at religious authority that makes it worth more attention than many of its other psycho-flick colleagues. The real monster in *Silent Night, Deadly Night* is the Mother Superior, who is portrayed as an evil, heartless woman—administering a brutal caning to young Billy because he catches two teenagers making love. The woman never appears to find time to show warmth to the boy and governs her Catholic orphanage on fear. It is little surprise that when the grown-up Billy (Wilson makes for an imposing figure in the role) attempts to conclude his murder spree, it is by beheading his former nemesis. One wonders if many audience members sighed in perverse disappointment when the miserly old lady remained intact at the end credits (she finally receives her comeuppance in the movie's sequel). *Silent Night, Deadly Night* does—at its heart—reveal criticism at how cruelty can be justified as a means to an end, under the guise of organized religion. As a result, the film plays out a mean-spirited first reel that is both involving and slightly betrays the movie's later trash sensibilities.

"Punishment" is the key word in *Silent Night, Deadly Night*. Not only does Wilson chant the word whenever he is in the midst of slaughtering a fresh victim, it is also a word

The now-adult Billy (Robert Brian Wilson) has issues with Christmas in *Silent Night, Deadly Night*.

repeated by the Mother Superior. Chauvin, who plays the Mother Superior, is probably the best performer in the film, convincing in her role and giving her character a necessary sense of righteous dictatorship. She believes that for Billy, punishment is the only solution, and instead of trying to understand the child's condition, the Mother Superior can only relate to his problems through violence. The film portrays a woman who cannot reason with the human condition, and who cannot confront anything or anyone whom she considers to hold a world view different from her own without flying into a brutal rage. This is shown in the aforementioned sequence where she physically abuses the young couple caught lovemaking. Her disgust toward sex reveals a lady who is deeply unhinged, albeit loyal to the strictest reading of Catholic rhetoric, and her desire to beat Billy until he reasons only through fear of yet another pummeling is nothing less than child abuse. While *Silent Night, Deadly Night* may attempt to show Gilmer McCormick's Sister Margaret in a sympathetic light (her body language and facial expressions reveal that she is uncomfortable with her superior's practices), she merely comes across as a coward. It is biblical sin that is the enemy of the Catholic Orphanage, and despite such "sins" as sexual activity outside of wedlock being long outdated, the Mother Superior permits herself to use this as the basis for harsh, violent abuse.

This dark portrait of religious institution aside, *Silent Night, Deadly Night* works well as a slasher film. When the film begins to document Wilson's murder spree, Sellier stages some ridiculous, albeit vicious, scenes of mayhem. The Christmas theme permeates the murders, with the highlight being an amusing sequence where a teenager steals a sled and rides down a snow-covered hill, only for Wilson to jump out from the bushes—axe in hand ("Punish!"). When the sled reaches the bottom, the boy's body sits upright, only without a head. In another memorable scene, Scream Queen Linnea Quigley's house is invaded (shortly after she finishes necking with her boyfriend) and the pretty blonde is chased around her living room, finally impaled on the antlers of a stag's head that hangs on her wall. The hunter becomes the hunted, so to speak. This

Of course there's breasts... it's got Linnea Quigley in the cast!

sequence is probably the most notorious moment in *Silent Night, Deadly Night*—with the actress running around topless and with the deer's antlers finally penetrating through from below her bare chest.

Misogyny is a common criticism of the slasher genre and often rightly so—with films such as *Don't Go in the House* (1980), *Maniac (*1981), *The New York Ripper* (1982) and *The Toolbox Murders* (1978) introducing attractive, young female characters simply so they can then be graphically killed.[5] Characterization and/or reason for their murder usually goes no further than that they are in the wrong place at the wrong time or, arguably most reprehensible, that they are dressed revealingly/showcasing sex appeal. The physical attractiveness of the actresses in these small roles seems taken for granted by the director (God forbid, after all, that a prowling psychopath would ever slay a fat/old/unattractive female). Admittedly, *Silent Night, Deadly Night* also falls into this trap and the murder of Quigley is undeniably trashy and exploitative. However, unlike the aforementioned movies, it may be worth arguing that the tone of Wilson's Christmas-related rampage has become so absurd by this point in the feature (and Quigley's acting is as excessive as usual) that it is hard to take the scene seriously. Moreover, from the beginning of the film, Sellier does emphasize that Wilson has been taught to fear sex and to treat the act with "punishment." As a result, the murder of a promiscuous couple does seem inevitable from the start.

The best slasher films manage at least a grain of suspense and *Silent Night, Deadly Night* pulls out some nicely staged jumps. However, it is the film's opening savagery that really puts the viewer on edge. As the young Billy looks on, his mother is raped and father killed by a maniac in a Santa suit. This brutal sequence, which is decidedly at odds with the later, more comical murders such as the decapitated sleigh rider, sets the tone for the child's awkward time in Catholic school. It also allows us to approach the fully grown Wilson with some sense of sympathy, and there is delicious dramatic irony when the storekeeper asks the 18-year-old hulk to don a Santa costume. It's the perfect moment, the scene where Sellier indicates to us, "Now you just know that this is going to send the poor lad over the top." Although more seasoned horror critics noted that previous films had dealt with a nasty Santa Claus (as seen in 1972's *Tales from the Crypt* and 1980's *Christmas Evil*, to name but two), no Christmas-set film had ever been quite so violent. Nor did we ever see someone in a Santa suit commit rape and murder! In this light, it is hardly surprising that *Silent Night, Deadly Night* caused a heap load of controversy in North America. Never released in the U.K., and certainly not a masterpiece of horror cinema, the film is still a firm favorite of this writer—although it is a guilty favorite all the same! Fans of trash cinema are also advised to check out the sequel, which replays a horde of footage from the first film but features enough hilarious moments to make it almost worthwhile.

Standout Moment

The decapitation of the sled rider...sure it's not high art, but even the most stone-faced critic is bound to have a giggle.

Memories of the Film

"Directing is very hard," reflects Chuck Sellier. "If you are filming a scene in the rain and mud then you, the director, are standing in the rain and mud. I achieved a lot of success early in my career so I decided I like writing and producing much more. I was able to choose what I did, unlike the many that must take what they get. I am, in fact, just a writer. In 1974 when they wanted to make my *Grizzly Adams* book into a movie, I told them they could not unless I produced. I did not have a clue what I was doing! Then the show opened to big grosses and I became a 'film genius.' It took me many years to get really good at producing. Today, I am one of the very best, but it took a whole career to achieve this."

Asked if he is surprised by the controversy that *Silent Night, Deadly Night* caused, Sellier answers in the positive. "I was indeed," exclaims the director. "There had been a lot of shows already out in this genre and this was just another slasher film. Yet it

Silent Night, Deadly Night **caused a heap of controversy in North America and was never released in the U.K.**

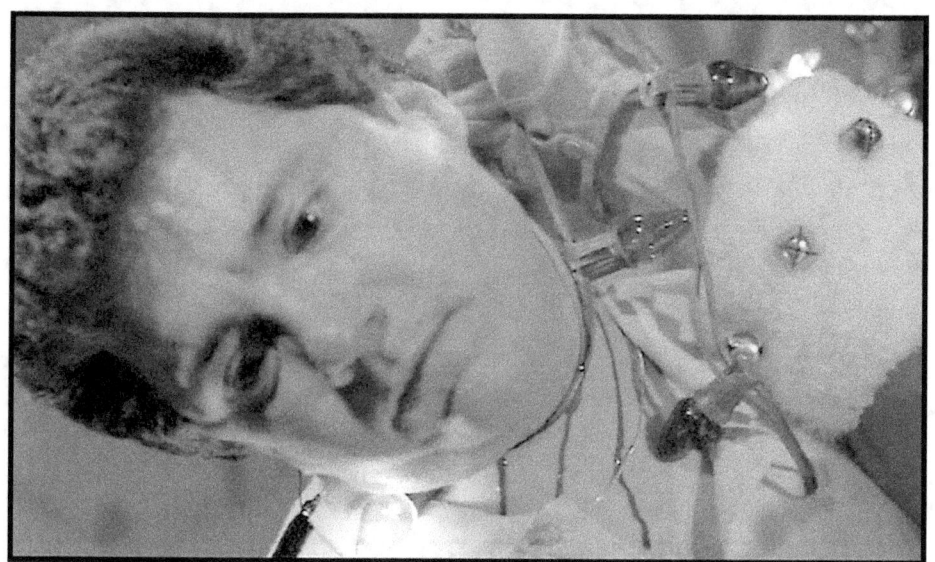

Not exactly what most people imagine when they think "deck the halls."

got the attention of protest groups that put the show on the map. The show is about a nice young boy who is raised in such a way that seeing Santa Claus makes him go nuts and this is the backstory," says Sellier, retelling the plot. "When he becomes 18 his employer asks him to put on a Santa Claus suit and because of what he had witnessed as a kid, it makes him go nuts and he starts killing people. Groups in America started picketing the film, saying that the film depicted Santa Claus as a slasher and this is not, in fact, true. It was about a young man dressed up like Santa Claus—the film makes this very clear. But parent groups saw it different. The minute the film was released, they started protesting, probably never having seen the film. This made the film an instant and major success."

The director is also unsure of how much money the film ended up piling in. "Many millions of dollars. The studio was Tri-Star. Because of the controversy, they never released gross figures. But I was told privately by studio execs that it did very well. Remember, it was made for only $750,000. I believe it has made millions over the years." As for why Sellier got involved with the film—"Tri-Star Pictures green-lighted the picture to a young producer named Ira Barmak. The studio president, Jeff Sagansky, was worried that Ira could not pull off a low-budget picture because this was his first. Jeff, who is a lifelong friend of mine, called me and asked if I would do him a favor and direct the film. They knew I was very experienced by then, having done many shows. My crew had just finished with the show we were working on and was available, so I said yes. The film is actually based on a book (*Slayride*). It is my understanding that the events in the book are based on real happenings."

The sequence where Linnea Quigley, topless, is impaled on stag antlers remains *Silent Night, Deadly Night*'s most notorious moment. When filming, was this a difficult scene to shoot? "Not at all," responds Sellier. "Making a horror film is not in any way a scary event. The scenes are broken up into many pieces and much of it makes no sense until it is cut together and the music is added. I had a great special effects crew. They were young and willing to experiment. Originally, she was to be just stabbed, but

Who would think the All-American boy Billy could turn into a deranged Santa?

when I arrived on set that night here was this giant elk hanging in the middle of the set. The lights had not been set up yet, and we were working with just one light that cast very long shadows on the wall. It gave me an idea. I went over to the elk and looked at my shadow on the wall. It looked truly scary. Henning Schellerup was my director of photography. I showed the shadows to Henning and told him I wanted to hang the actress on the elk—but that most of it would be covered by the shadows. The special effects crew came up with a latex torso of the actress that the horns could pop through, making it look like the actress had been stabbed with them. We shot the scene with a stuntman raising Linnea up in front of the elk—then we cut to the latex close-up of the torso and saw the antlers penetrate the body. It all looked very believable on film but in person it was all very hokey.

"By the way, I have a funny story about Linnea Quigley," continues Sellier. "When the stuntman raised her up to the antlers, the whole crew discovered that Linnea was not wearing any underwear! This was not acceptable for the rating the studio wanted on the film, and this really shocked me. The camera saw far more than was intended. I yelled 'cut' and called for wardrobe to complain. They informed me that 'Miss Quigley never wears underwear.' I went over and had a talk with Linnea, informing her that this would not work at all. We ended up calling my wife to rush over three pairs of her panties for Linnea to try on. When this problem was solved, the scene had to be filmed again. I wonder what happen to the other version?" Interestingly, Sellier denies that there is any anti-Catholic message in the film. "I have never heard that," he mentions. "The film does cover the boy's early life when he was in a convent and, while there, he was mistreated by a particular sister. This added to the boy's mental lack of stability. I do not feel the film was meant to state that all Catholic sisters were like that, just this particular one."

Silent Night, Deadly Night would spawn four sequels. Sellier was not involved in any of them and is happy to explain why. "I had a very creative crew working with me on that show," he affirms. "We were able to do some very good effects for not much money.

Michael Spence, my second unit director, was able to get some very creative footage for the show. After that, we all became very busy and most of us continue to be busy to this day. The offer to do the sequel was not a good one. We could all do much better at that point. So we turned down doing any more of them." Not that the abundance of sequels surprised the director. "No, I'm not at all surprised. Most of the shows in that genre have gone to multiple sequels. They seem to all develop a cult following."

Interviewed in *Fangoria* magazine,[6] Sellier mentioned that he would like to apologize to anyone who was offended by *Silent Night, Deadly Night*. Does this still stand? "Absolutely! I never intended for the show to do more than scare and entertain. If it offended parents and caused people to have problems

"Naughty or nice?" – Santa Claus punishes the bad-people in *Silent Night, Deadly Night*.

with it, then I feel very bad and want to apologize for that. We were all young filmmakers trying to do a good job without much money. We succeeded very well, apparently too well. Remember that the show had an R rating, which means it should not have been seen by anyone under 17. So the protests stating that it would scare kids and make them afraid of Christmas were probably not valid, but I felt very bad about the write-ups." Having never followed up *Silent Night, Deadly Night* with another horror hit, Sellier is forthcoming as to why this was. "I began to get older and my likes and values changed. Making horror films is for the young. It takes highly creative and fresh thoughts. Most of them have to be made on very small budgets. That means young filmmakers, just starting their careers, should make horror films."

Alternate Critiques

"*Silent Night, Deadly Night* is just another lesser entry in the slasher sweepstakes and nothing else...the Noel mayhem lacks suspense, imagination and peace on Earth..." (*Fangoria's Best and Bloodiest Horror Video*, 1988).

"Whatever the critics may have said, it's not a bad film....Shut off all brain functions and enjoy—after all, it's got a homicidal Santa, a fair helping of blood and gore, and a naked Linnea Quigley (again!). What more could you ask for?" (Jim Harper, *Legacy of Blood*, Headpress, 2004)

"Weak acting and outrageous psychology...this may be the worst horror film ever to inspire a series of follow-ups." (James O'Neill, *Terror on Tape*, Billboard Books, 1994)

The Slayer

Director: J.S. Cardone
Produced by: William R. Ewing/J.S. Cardone
Written by: William Ewing
Cast: Sarah Kendall; Frederick J. Flynn; Carol Kottenbrook; Alan McRae; Michael Holmes; Sandy Simpson; Paul Gandolfo; Newell Alexander; Ivy Jones; Jennifer Gaffin; Richard Van Brakel; Carl Kraines
Special Effects: Robert Short
Year: 1982

Plot Synopsis

The hands of a grand clock swing back and forth as Kay (Kendall) walks through an old house. She glimpses herself being throttled to death by the hands of a monster. It is all a dream and Kay—a professional artist—awakes, with her husband David (McRae) telling her that it is time to leave for their vacation.

Kay's brother Eric (Flynn) wakes up at his house, while his wife Brooke (Kottenbrook) takes a shower. Brooke mentions that she is far from thrilled about going on holiday with Eric's weird sister. Nevertheless, the two couples fly out to a tropical island by plane. When they land, their pilot—Mr. Marsh (Holmes)—is eager to leave.

The two couples pass by a run-down old theater on the way to their island retreat. Kay mentions that she has imagined and drawn the same dilapidated theater before. They finally arrive at the beach house and take a tour of the location, but are interrupted by Mr. Marsh. He tells them that a heavy storm is expected and that they should consider leaving right away, as he is unsure if and when he will be able to land again.

The foursome decides to stay. In the interim a local fisherman (Gandolfo) is stalked by a mysterious assailant and smashed on the back of the head by a boat oar.

As night falls, the two couples sit outside the beach house talking and getting

drunk. Eric tells Kay that he does not like her latest art work, labeling it "surrealist crap." Her husband does not defend her, telling Kay—"You draw what you dream." Eric leaves for bed and Kay tells David that she does not like it on the island and wants to leave. David reassures his wife that she has nothing to worry about. They retreat to bed, where they make love.

During the night David is awakened by a noise from downstairs. His investigation takes him to a leaking ceiling door, which he climbs up to shut. However, with his head poking up into the attic, the door is slammed shut and David is strangled to death. His body is then pulled into the attic.

Kay dreams that she is lying next to the decapitated head of her husband. She awakens in a panic and tells Brooke that she dreamed about David's death. Eric is dismissive and they all go to the beach. Kay draws an empty old room, but sensing this may have something to do with her dreams, she tears it up.

As night falls, there is still no sign of David. The next morning all three search for Kay's husband. Kay finds his headless body strung, upside down, in the theater. The room is the same one she previously drew. Kay becomes convinced that if she sleeps again her friends will die. Eric tells Brooke that his sister is mad and that when she was a child her parents gave Kay a kitten, which

The cast of *The Slayer* prepare for a rough evening ahead...

was later found dead in a meat freezer. Kay blamed her dream monster for the animal's death. Eric suspects that Marsh might have killed David. Eric goes out to the boathouse to get a flare gun. Someone impales him with a fish hook and hauls his body into the sea. Brooke searches for her husband and is impaled through the back by a rake. The next morning Kay finds their bodies and locks herself in the beach house. She attempts to stay awake, but the house comes under siege from her assailant. Kay sees someone coming up the stairs and fires a flare gun at him. It turns out to be Mr. Marsh.

With the house now ablaze, Kay tries to find a way out—finally running into the monster she has been dreaming of. A clock in the background indicates that this is the same house that she dreamed of at the start.

Kay suddenly awakens as a small girl (Gaffin) on Christmas morning. Her mother and father (Jones and Alexander) offer her a kitten as a gift. The events of the film have still to transpire...

Critique

As with a selection of other slasher films,[7] *The Slayer* is best known in the U.K. for being one of the notorious "video nasties." In actuality, the film is a surprisingly tame entry into the genre, with most of the movie's horror taken from the surreal threat of Kendall's dreams as opposed to lopped-off body parts. As detailed by the inclusion of the hands belonging to an anonymous monster in the prologue, it is clear that something is not quite right in the movie—that heroine Kendall is being stalked by a creature that is far from human. In this sense it is somewhat frustrating that Cardone and scriptwriter Ewing do not delve into their villain's background, or why the beast has chosen to stalk Kendall. Had they done so, then *The Slayer* could possibly have been catapulted into another type of film, but given the movie's budget it is understandable that the title monster is left unseen until it shows its face in the last five minutes. Perhaps learning a lesson from Jacques Tourneur's 1958 classic *Night of the Demon*, which throws its climax into a wayward spin with the appearance of a ridiculously unconvincing monster,[8] Cardone keeps his assailant offscreen and shows it only briefly during the climax.

Consequently, *The Slayer* plays out as a straightforward slasher picture for most of its running time, with the cast meeting their ends through the devices of an unseen prowler.

Unwilling to even showcase the monster's hands after the opening sequence, Cardone instead allows "The Slayer" of the film's title to slash its victims with a variety of weapons, nudging the movie further into *Friday the 13th* territory. The film also throws in a bonus body, presumably so that the pace doesn't slow down too much, in the guise of an unnamed fisherman who just happens to be in the wrong place at the wrong time. His link to the story, and to Kendall, is never explained or presumed—but the scene does throw something of a red herring at the viewer, preparing one for another run-of-the-mill stalker film when the ending suggests something that is considerably more imaginative and sinister.

Who would live in a house like this? How about a maniacal, bloodthirsty demon?

The Slayer can also be viewed as a skid row precursor to the *Nightmare on Elm Street* series—mainly because the film deals with the notion that dreams can be deadly. Although not anywhere near as expansive or as smart as Wes Craven's original *Nightmare on Elm Street* (1984), Cardone's film does manage to touch upon some of the same ideas. As a result, Kendall speaks of people being murdered because she dreamed of their deaths. Unlike with Craven's film, this is not visualized more than once (when the actress dreams of her husband's decapitation). The film's twist ending makes this reluctance understandable—the point remains that the victims in *The Slayer* die because of Kendall's ability to unleash some sort of creature through her nightmares. During the movie's finale, for instance, Kendall tells herself, "Just stay awake—that's all you have to do." Furthermore, the burning of her arm with a cigarette and her reliance on coffee are the same sleep deprivation techniques that are also used by the characters in the *Elm Street* series. Likewise, because *The Slayer* takes place within a dream reality, it is easier to forgive the film for some especially sloppy moments in the script. Therefore, it is possible to overlook such unlikely traits as Kendall's surprisingly calm reaction to her husband's death—while both Flynn and Kottenbrook respond to the murder with a demeanor that suggests the passing of a pet hamster rather than the slaughter of a family member. However, presuming that the monster only attacks those that Kendall is linked with, the aforementioned death of the fisherman does still seem illogical. Whether this was meant to be the case, or whether this might be down to lousy scripting is uncertain—but Cardone certainly covers his steps by concluding *The Slayer* with it the young Kendall waking up in bed, having dreamed the entire movie.

Stories that end with the hero waking from a dream are nothing new, of course, and are often inexcusable devices on which to base a narrative. The 1980s saw *Slaughter*

High (1985) and the higher-profile Demi Moore/Emilio Estevez film *Wisdom* (1986) both conclude in this manner. Even the original *Nightmare on Elm Street* seemed unsure of how to wrap things up, finally ending in a confusing "Is it all a dream or not?" finale. *The Slayer*, on the other hand, takes a far more sinister approach to its dream logic. By showing the young heroine waking up as a child—and being presented with the pet cat that we already know will die at the hands of the film's beast—the film manages a surprisingly effective shock.

The director's wife, Carol Kottenbrook, takes the obligatory slasher film shower scene.

Exactly where the young girl goes from here is uncertain. The conclusion of *The Slayer* marks the beginning of Kendall's slide into madness (her brother details that her dreams threw his sister into psychiatric care as an adolescent) and ends the film on a rather potent nightmare in its own right. As Kendall states midway through the film—"Sometimes as I drift off to sleep, I think that when I wake up my real life will be gone and my dreams will have taken its place." This is not to say that the ending is the only effective part of *The Slayer*, of course, because Cardone also stages some very elaborate set pieces. The director himself is especially proud of the death of Kottenbrook, his erstwhile wife no less, who receives a pitchfork through her back—with the prongs then emerging from under her breasts. This sequence (which was cut from the film's initial rerelease in the U.K., long after the video-nasty brouhaha had calmed down) is brutal and convincing, definitely one of the genre's standout demises. Although Flynn and McRae both meet rather vicious deaths, neither of them holds a candle to Kottenbrook's painful onscreen farewell.

Working with an unknown cast, *The Slayer* features perfectly apt performances, and the movie never has too much of a B-movie feel as far as dialogue goes. Clearly, Cardone was a director who was unlikely to fade into obscurity, and since *The Slayer* the director has made at least two more worthwhile genre films—1989's *Shadowzone* and 2001's excellent vampire fable *The Forsaken*. His latest genre picture is the acclaimed *Mummy an' the Armadillo* (2004). Although careful not be pigeonholed as a director of B movies (Cardone has also made such effective dramas as 1998's *Outside Ozona*), the director nonetheless admits a love for the genre (see below). This affection shines here, in his first film, and it is difficult to deny his desire to scare an audience in *The Slayer*, or his wish to take the proceedings seriously (under a less capable hand, the temptation to show more of the monster would surely prevail). Although *The Slayer* has largely sunk into obscurity outside of the U.K., where it has not had the benefit of being "forbidden candy," the movie deserves to secure a reputation as one of the most interesting slasher films to emerge from the early 1980s. It captures a *Twilight Zone* sense of the macabre and the unpredictable that is unusual for a film attempting to capitalize on the dwindling returns of the *Friday the 13th* audience.

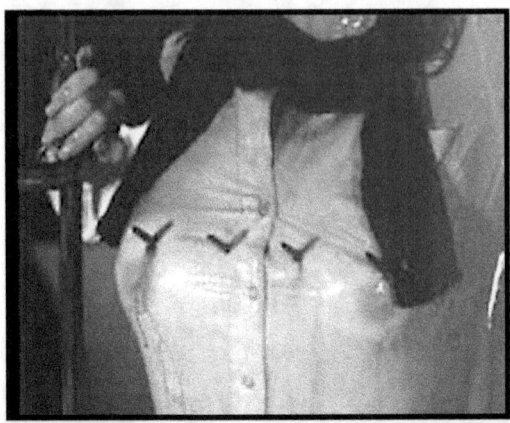

The director's wife also meets a gruesome death in the film—but over 20 years later the couple are still happily married!

Memories of the Film

"I love B films and always have. I love making them. When they get bigger budgeted like *The Forsaken,* they are what they are," states J.S. Cardone. The director's memories of making *The Slayer* begin with how fast the picture came to fruition. "Well, in that particular one, there was a lot to do" he admits. "I had been working in the studio system for a while and I had a pretty decent reputation for doing rewrites and stuff. It came along at a period of time where Irwin Yablans had produced *Halloween* and he had just hired me to do a picture called *Beautiful* for him, which was loosely based on *The Picture of Dorian Gray*, the Oscar Wilde story. And during that time I had written *The Slayer* because there was that glut of horror films and, with the popularity of *Halloween*, everyone was rushing to make a horror film. So I wrote *The Slayer* really quickly and we found the financing really fast through a small releasing group called The International Picture Show Company. And it all came together relatively quickly—in fact it came together so quickly that it took us all by surprise (*laughs*). We were very young and we set off to this tiny island off Georgia to make this picture. Obviously we were all inexperienced, but we just struggled through it from this position of inexperience and how naïve we were. But I think that from the standpoint of all of us that were involved, at the time—we still stand by the picture. We had fun making it, obviously it is your first picture, but you remain proud."

Cardone speaks with fondness about the special effects in *The Slayer* which, done on a low budget, are highlighted with admirable aplomb. The director is most proud of when Kottenbrook receives a pitchfork through her back—with the prong emerging from below her chest! "If you look at that scene very closely, there is no cutaway," he mentions. "Robert Short—the special effects guy on it, he went on to do the mermaid costume in *Splash*—it was his first picture. We tried to figure out how to do this, how to shoot this woman from the front—who happens to be my wife (*laughs*) and has been for 13 years and is a producing partner in our company. We thought about how to do it with her actually crawling through the boathouse window, with her blouse wet, so you can see the details of her breasts underneath. We thought, 'How can you actually see her from the waist up, without a cutaway, and the prongs coming through her and then retracting back out of her without doing an insert cut?'

"So Bob Short and I played around with some ideas and finally it was my brother, who was shooting some second unit, who said to us: 'You know the camera sees myopically—if you were to close one eye then you would get the field.' So, he said, 'If you shoot this dead on, you won't see the depth of field.' Then Bob built an apparatus that actually had false breasts and everything on top of it. That apparatus actually stuck out from her real breasts, I would say, probably eight to 12 inches, which allowed the prongs to be inside that. It was all designed and constructed to go in and come out with blood packs and everything, and then we just put an oversized blouse on top of her, wet it down and shot it straight on and it actually worked very well. I mean obviously she did a good job of selling it from the point of view of reacting to it and everything, but many years went by before anybody came up with any sort of retractable or expanding concept. In fact, we just used something that was much less complex...we just did the sequel to Carpenter's *Vampires* and we used a system that didn't work nearly as well as what Robert came up with."

Cardone himself remains a fan of B movies, although he mentions some so-called B filmmakers that might come as a surprise. "Oh, you can go back to the great noir filmmakers like Sam Fuller and those guys, Ida Lupino—she was a great filmmaker and an inspiration. But to me, the greatest B filmmaker to have ever existed, beyond Spielberg—if you look at his films they are B films, they are genre films—the greatest B filmmaker of all time, and who had no fear of it, was Kubrick. I mean look at his movies. He made horror films, war films, action films, sexual thriller, noir films—he made sci-fi films, he was a great B filmmaker, maybe the greatest of all. When you really look at it, he used genre to exploit his narrative and his story and it always worked extremely well. What I find most fascinating about B films is when you look back at the great genre films, especially during the 1950s when they were doing *Invasion of the Body Snatchers* or *The Day of the Triffids*, the British film. Then you look at *28 Days Later* and there is an incredible lift from *Day of the Triffids*. All of those films, the great things about them as opposed to studio films, is that they allow you to create characters that are real, that are everyday. They are the walk-of-life type of character and they can say things that studio characters cannot. If you have Julia Roberts you have to write for a movie star, and you are limited in the vernacular of their dialogue and stuff—as well as what happens to them."

Alternate Critiques

"Director Cardone strives for subtle psychological chills but sabotages his efforts with cheesily incongruous cheapo gore FX...and the joke-shop mannequin-like appearance of the titular beastie when he does finally show up." (John Martin, *The Dark Side*, Issue 58, 1996)

"Bloody, claustrophobic chiller.... Well produced on a low budget, and one of the few splatter films in which dream sequences are actually effective. The hideous monster makeup is also impressive." (John McCarthy, *Official Splatter Movie Guide Vol. 2*, St. Martin's Press, 1992)

"*The Slayer* is formulaic, but happens to be well made." (Kim Newman, *Screen Violence*, Bloomsbury, 1996)

A Stranger Is Watching

Director: Sean Cunningham
Produced by: Sidney Beckerman
Written by: Earl Mac Rauch/Victor Miller
Cast: Kate Mulgrew; Rip Torn; James Naughton; Shawn Von Schreiber; Barbara Baxley; Stephen Joyce; James Russo; Frank Hamilton; Maggie Task; Roy Poole; Maurice Copeland; Eleanor Phelps
Special Effects: Connie Brink
Year: 1982

Brief Plot Synopsis

Julie Peterson (Baxley), a little girl, sees her mother killed by a stranger who has broken into their house. The man snaps a photograph of the dead body and approaches the girl. Julie wakes up in bed two years later, having suffered a nightmare of the event. Her dad Steve (Von Schreiber) runs into his daughter's bedroom to calm her down.

At a television station, Sharon Martin (Mulgrew), who also happens to be Steve's new girlfriend, cuts together a news report on Ronald Thompson (Hamilton), who is due to be executed for the murder of Julie's mother. He denies having done it. At the Peterson household, Steve readies his daughter for school and catches Sharon's news report on television. He feels that it is exploitative and goes to Sharon's office to speak to her. The two settle the matter, although Sharon indicates that she does not approve of the death penalty.

Julie's driver Bill (Hamilton) drops her off at school, but a figure in a van watches from a distance. The van drives away and in a basement we see the stranger, Artie (Torn), take out handcuffs, a child's teddy bear and a picture of Julie. Later that night, the Petersons' neighbors Mr. and Mrs. Perry (Copeland and Phelps) recognize the figure of Bill outside the house, but assuming that as a friend of the family he is not up to anything, they forget about it.

Steve phones his daughter and tells her he will be home late, but Sharon is expected soon. As he is chatting with her, Artie—who has broken into the house—grabs the girl. Hearing his daughter scream, Steve naturally assumes something is terribly wrong. Sharon turns up at the house late and is faced with the sight of Julie being held by Artie. Told to do exactly what he says or else the girl dies, Sharon is

Television reporter Sharon Martin (Kate Mulgrew) is kidnapped by murderer Artie (Rip Torn).

forced to comply. When Steve gets back home he finds a message left for him—"I got the kid and the girl. You want to see them alive, don't get cute."

Artie transports the gagged body of Julie across the city and under a subway station. He carries her in a bag and attracts the attention of a homeless lady (Baxley). Artie then forces Sharon to walk to the station with him—telling her that if she does not act normally, the girl dies.

Inside the small room that he has prepared for them, Artie begins to caress Sharon. She asks him to unzip Julie from her bag. He does so and leaves them both imprisoned. A homeless man follows Artie and is beaten to death. Artie leaves a tape for Steven, who by now has called in the police, led by Detective Taylor (Russo), and demands £182,000—the exact sum that Sharon has recently been left in an estate. Mr. Turner (Poole), a defense lawyer for Ronald Thompson, turns up at the Peterson house to interview Julie but is turned away.

Sharon tries to open the door in the room that she and Julie have been left locked in. She breaks off a shaft of metal from under a table and uses it as a crowbar. However, when the door opens, she and Julie are faced with Artie. The man slaps Sharon to the ground. He pieces together an explosive and leaves it attached to the door so that the two cannot attempt to escape again. Julie suddenly recognizes his face and places him as the killer of her mother.

Sharon uncovers another exit when Artie leaves, but it leads to a dead end. Julie has a nightmare about her mother's death, this time identifying Artie, not Thompson, as the murderer. She awakes and tells Sharon that she was wrong to identify Thompson. Sharon now realizes that an innocent man is going to die.

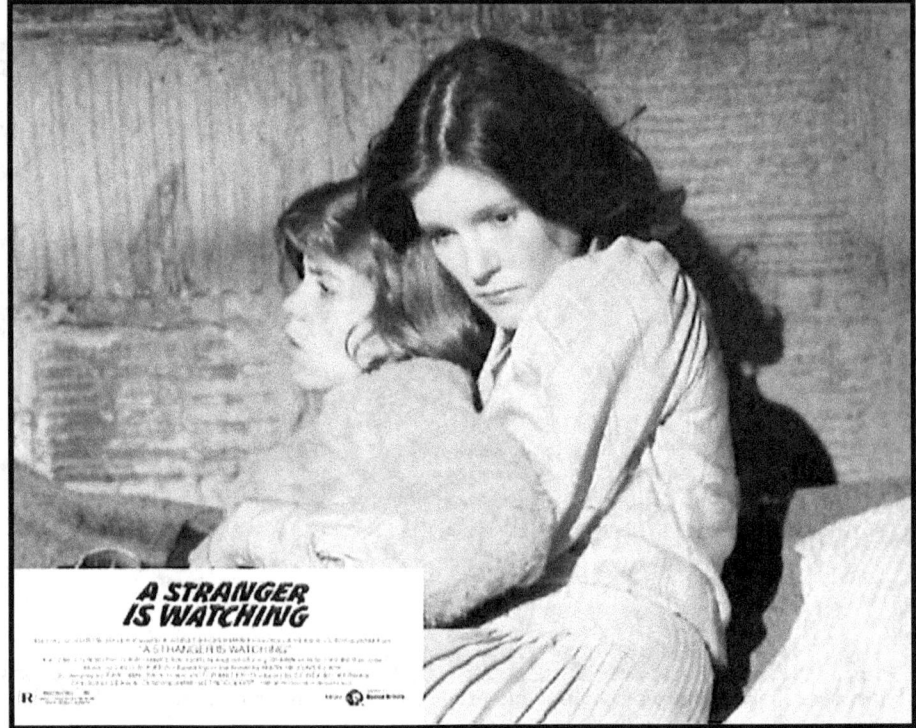

Sharon tries to comfort Julie (Barbara Baxley) in the tension-filled *A Stranger Is Watching*.

Artie makes a telephone call to Steve, telling him where to leave the requested cash sum. He is faced by a homeless man wanting change—after telling him to get away, Artie slips into a public toilet, where the man's friends approach him and beat him up. A policeman comes to Artie's defense and the thugs run away.

Artie returns to his secret room under the subway station, beaten up, and Sharon flirts with him—pretending to take an interest in his wounds. Having left the door slightly ajar, Julie makes a run for it and Sharon follows after kicking Artie between the legs. A homeless man (David Brooks) aids the two women, but Artie finally catches up with them. He kills the tramp and returns Julie and Sharon to the hideout.

Mr. Turner returns to Steve's house with a court order asking for Julie's assistance in the case of Thompson. He is informed of what has transpired.

Bill goes to Artie's house, where he is revealed to have been in on the kidnapping. However, he is horrified to learn that Artie intends to kill the girl and the woman. Refusing to have anything more to do with it, Artie stabs him. Sharon is now chained to a pipe, and Julie is tied to a bed. Artie returns to the hideout and forces Julie to crawl back into her bag. He stabs Sharon and leaves her to bleed to death. Artie calls Steve with a request of where to leave the cash. In the car, Julie manages to grab a metal pipe and smash Artie across the head. She escapes to freedom at a train station, but Artie gets away on the back of a train. Julie is reunited with her father.

Sharon is not dead and the homeless lady, from earlier, helps her to her feet. Artie arrives and beats the woman, knocking her out. Sharon grabs an iron bar and beats the man—finally impaling him through the neck. Julie and her father run through the

A Stranger Is Watching **explores the story from the victim's point of view.**

train station to get to Sharon. A coda reveals that Ronald Thompson was released from prison.

Critique

Having come off the success of *Friday the 13th*, one might have expected Sean Cunningham to follow up his smash with a similar type of effort but, instead, the director crafts this—one of the slasher genre's most endearing oddities featuring neither a mysterious killer nor a high body count. Indeed, only with the movie's finale, in which Torn is stabbed through the neck with an iron bar (and turns to the camera to showcase the effect so that the audience gets a gruesome full view of it), does the feature echo Cunningham's previous horror hit. While other stalker movies of the period did feature an unmasked, nonsupernatural killer (including 1980's sleazy *Don't Answer the Phone* and 1981's *Night Warning*), *A Stranger Is Watching* is different from these titles in exploring its story from the victim's point of view. Furthermore, there is very little violence in the movie—and the only gore effect is the aforementioned death of Torn—with the concentration on building a palpable sense of danger and suspense. Although the end result did not do well commercially, *A Stranger Is Watching* is a mature and well-directed film that features an impressive cast (including a pre-*Star Trek* Mulgrew and a fearsome Torn—far removed from his more well-known comical turn in the *Men in Black* movies). One imagines that the film may have been Cunningham's attempt to wash away the blood and thunder of Camp Crystal Lake and announce himself as a more serious filmmaker—although it is interesting to note that coscriptwriter Miller

A Stranger Is Watching **is one of the few slasher movies to put a child in the midst of the horror.**

is held over from *Friday the 13th*. Even so, the overriding atmosphere of *A Stranger Is Watching* is so dark and downbeat that it is understandable why the film failed to capture a wide audience; that it remains somewhat forgotten about among loyalists of the genre is, however, a crime in itself...

So where does Cunningham's film sit in the pantheon of the slasher genre? Interestingly, this is what makes the movie such a standout. While some of the action in *A Stranger Is Watching* seems fitting to the genre, including the victims who are suddenly and violently murdered by Torn and the extended chase sequences, the movie centers upon a kidnapping. None of the films that rode the wave of the post-*Friday the 13th* slasher boom would focus on this remarkably obvious situation of terror—instead opting for the more typical popcorn ingredients of teenaged victims, special effects and bare breasts. Situations of kidnap have been used to powerful effect in horror movies—from the trash sensibilities of 1973's *The Candy Snatchers* to the shattering brilliance of 1988's original *The Vanishing*—and Cunningham aims to get as much mileage from the situation as possible. There's an incredibly good jump-out-of-the-seat moment when Torn appears at the entrance to the room in which he has locked both Baxley and Mulgrew, just as they are about to escape. There are also two lengthy, and tense, escape attempts from the victims during the movie. Baxley, in her only screen appearance, pulls off a difficult role as the terrorized girl and it is hard for the viewer not to sympathize with her. Unlike many films of the genre, where the audience takes a perverse thrill in cheering the inventive deaths of cardboard victims, Cunningham places us in a situation where the victims are so helpless that we simply have to rally behind them. In this sense, the director may well have been attempting to put the very genre that he helped to create

Torn is certainly a strong enough actor to carry the film's much-needed sense of terror.

to its bed—asking us instead to view a more psychological tale of terror and confront the very real horror of a dangerous mind.

The film also acknowledges the homeless problem that was beginning to materialize in the United States in the 1980s. The movie's homeless are painted as genuine, but down on their luck, characters—far removed from the more tabloid-friendly stereotype of drug addiction or hapless drunkards. The fact that Mulgrew is finally saved from certain death by a homeless woman appears to highlight the futility of social class. Money counts for very little when one is stripped of material goods and placed in a situation of life or death—in which genuine human conscience and remorse comes to the forefront. The dirty, unwashed characters who call the subway system of *A Stranger Is Watching* their home are in stark contrast to Baxley's privileged lifestyle in which the girl is waited on by a maid, has a personal chauffeur and appears to want for little. Torn's decision to hold the girl, and Mulgrew, as ransom for money perhaps pinpoints the very greed that results in the social divide we see in Cunningham's film, whereupon "haves" and "have-nots" exist in the same city and yet remain as far away from each other as possible.

Although *A Stranger Is Watching* is not a fun film to view, it remains easy to become involved in. Torn is certainly a strong enough actor to carry the film's much-needed sense of terror—a decidedly cruel and frightening character, his rampage may be relatively low (and bloodless) when measured against the extremes of the genre, but his presence never ceases to frighten. It also makes for strong drama when Cunningham reminds us, in the midst of his kidnap story, of the impending death penalty imposed on the innocent man played by Hamilton. With only young Baxley aware of the upcoming miscarriage of justice, the little girl ends up racing against time to not only save herself and her father's girlfriend, but also to save someone who is about to be executed for a crime he did not commit. As a result, Cunningham does not need to focus on the morality of the death penalty in any great detail because, in this very scenario, he manages to implicate the flaws, and resulting danger, of such a system—where "guilt" can so easily be based on misinformation. While *A Stranger Is Watching* will not be to everyone's taste, it is a well-developed and scary film that should appease those wishing for a stalker film where the carnage is not the focal point.

Standout Moment

Even in spite of the almost unbearable build-up of suspense, Cunningham can't help but reward the viewer with at least one gruesome special effect—and Torn's demise is as brutal as they come!

Memories of the Film

"Well, it's nice of you to say that," replies Sean Cunningham when told that *A Stranger is Watching* is an underrated follow-up to *Friday the 13th*. "It had its own problems but (*pauses*) if you're going do business, you have to do business at the box office," he adds. "You have to find a way—you know watching a movie is fun—not just suspenseful or engaging and individual people may like it, but the metaphor that I always use is this.... When you create something that's incredibly riveting, then you can't take your eyes off it, and when other people are watching it you can hear a pin drop. That's when you've done it, when you've got them—they're in your story, they're yours and when they leave they are happy....So the answer is that—well, think of it this way: you're driving down a highway, you notice there's a terrible accident and you get to see it. You're looking at it, and going by you can't take your eyes off it, you're stretching your neck to see it and thinking, 'Oh my God,' and when you finally get past not many people say, 'That was so cool man, turn around and let's see it again!' You don't do that do you? That's what I'd call *A Stranger Is Watching*. The difference between that and the kind of genre picture that is successful is that instead of creating a car wreck, what you really need to do is to create is a roller coaster. What I mean by that is, you go you with a group of people up a roller coaster and there comes that moment when it goes over the top and even the bravest, you know, you are scared for that moment—but in a very safe place. And just for that moment you're given a release...but it's always done in the safety of the harness and in a way that you always know it's going to be alright even though your breath has been taken away. Successful scary movies do that—and that's the difference between a really successful film and a car crash movie..."

Of course, with *Friday the 13th* everybody was doing car crash movies... "Well, yes they did," answers Cunningham, "and that's one of the reasons I didn't want to." However, contrary to the director's description of *A Stranger Is Watching* as "a car crash movie," the film did not have any scenes of spurting gore. "No, I didn't have that because it's not needed," he states. Instead, the viewer is presented with a kidnap movie. "Yeah, and you get a lot of mileage with that," confirms the director. "I think part of the fun with *Friday the 13th* was that this was before we had CGI. So you were kind of seeing a magic show. You had Betsy Palmer standing there and someone swinging a machete at her and all of a sudden you saw Betsy Palmer's head come off, and blood coming out! Now this was 1980 and I promise you, you had never seen that before and it's sort of like a magician sawing his assistant in half. You know he didn't saw her in

Panic and suspense are commonplace for the characters in Cunningham's film.

half, but it sure looked like he did, so how did he do that? There's a kind of fun in that magic trick, right? And that's where we were in the history of special effects—in that it was still popular to do magic tricks. Kevin Bacon is lying on the bed and all of a sudden this arrow comes out of his neck—'Holy shit,' you know! Now, you know the arrow didn't actually come out through his neck, but 'How did they do that?'

"And that is kind of fun, but you can't do that anymore. You can't do magic tricks in movies anymore because when I did *Friday the 13th*...people would just act incredibly to it. From the audience's point of view the camera is a coconspirator....People go out and they do the most amazing special effects work—they do the most seamless stuff and they do stuff that is so hard to accomplish and they do it so well and the audience goes (*yawns*)—and now that's it, they don't care. They don't have any idea how hard it is to do this stuff, but they're not being surprised anymore because they are prepared for it to happen. And if you're prepared for it, then it's less fun. So anyway, I've grown to understand that by and large—gore, and the less gore you have, up to a certain point, the better off you are. And the less sex you have, the better off you are. When you think of Tom Cruise's first movie—*Risky Business*. *Risky Business* is a nifty, nifty movie the way it turned out..."

Indeed, *Risky Business* (1983) remains a cult classic to this day. "But it had a really interesting preview history," begins Cunningham—emphasizing his 'less is more' argument. "Because they had an incredible, hot sex scene with Rebecca De Mornay, who played the hooker, and there were other sex scenes but there was this one particular sex scene on a subway that was very, very risqué. The idea was just mind blowing, you'd never seen anything like it and it was so hot. And then when they screened the

Rip Torn makes for a believable psychopath in Cunningham's stellar shocker.

movie...there was trouble with the sex scenes, and in particular the one in the subway. After the preview they cut it in half and the audience thought it was much better. Then they previewed again, and then again after that—and the more they took out of it, the more the audience liked the movie. Even though you think you would love to see it, when you were presented with it—it was not what you wanted to see. So how it ended up was that all of De Mornay's scenes had a hint of sex, but they're not very specific at all, and it works better for the movie—and I think gore is similar."

Despite being best known for *Last House on the Left* and *Friday the 13th*, Cunningham has also made such family films as 1978's *Here Comes the Tigers* and *Manny's Orphans* (also '78). "I had never really wanted to do dark and ugly films any more than I wanted to do sex films," he explains. "What people don't understand is that you often look at people who go off and make movies as people who are driven to exorcise a particular artistic vision. And there may be people that are that way, but I didn't have that luxury. But by the time I made (1971's soft-core feature) *Together*, I was married and I had a kid, and during *Together* my wife was pregnant with our second child, so from that point all of my decisions were absolutely simple. I thought, 'I don't mind doing this, but how do I make some cash doing it?' because I had people who were depending on me to bring home money. It wasn't like I had to go service some great emotion in myself, because it had nothing to do with that. I wanted to make something for five dollars and hopefully be able to sell it for six or seven or 10. 'I'm going to make this for five bucks, where's the five bucks gonna come from? And can I sell it for 10, whatever it turns out to be like?' And that informed a lot of my decisions.

"For instance, would I have ever been involved in (1974's sex farce) *The Case of the Full Moon Murders*? No, except that I was owed this money and I had to figure out a way to get the movie out. If I didn't, then my family would suffer and so—now this is not meant to be an excuse or self-justifying—it's just an explanation of the world and of moviemaking. Also, what is particularly true...I was gypsy. I didn't have a job. You know—there were people who worked in the movie industry, but they might be working in a camera rental house, or they might be a grip or they might be a follow spot operator on a stage. With them, you got a job, you got  a paycheck and you got to go home. But if you're like me and you don't have a job, then you're always looking around going, 'Hey, you want to buy this?' Then someone says, 'Well maybe, you want to sell it?'—and that's kind of what you do. So I thought it would be fun to make children's movies and I wanted to make children's movies. There's a feeling that you get, especially when you're making 'snuff' movies (*laughs*)...'Do I have to do this? Can't I do anything else?' and so there are a lot of children—well why can't I make children's movies? And so I was looking at that, and I did a lot of work trying to put together some fairy tales early in my career. A new *Hansel and Gretel* in particular, and when we weren't able to make half of them I wound up putting together a tax shelter and moving to Spain, and then I came back and somehow or other I was given the opportunity (to make) *Here Comes the Tigers*.

"My conversation with the producers probably went something like 'Did you ever see *Bad News Bears*?' 'Yeah,' and then, 'Do you think you can make a movie like that?' 'Well, sure'—'But can you make it now?' 'Yeah, I can make it—but really, to give you a decent answer I'll need to read the script.'—'Then we'll get started on that right away.' And that was just before Labor Day, which is September in New England, and we were shooting three weeks later."

After a career spent in horror, Cunningham admits that he was looking for new challenges even after *Friday the 13th* and *A Stranger Is Watching* cemented his name in the genre back in the early 1980s. "Yeah, I thought, 'I don't want to spend all my time doing this.' I did that, and that's fine, but I didn't want to keep doing it, and I wasn't driven to do it...so, yeah, I always wanted to go in other directions. 'Can I have a challenging script please—can I have a challenging script?'—'No you can't,'" laughs the director.

Alternate Critiques

"Disappointingly lacking in gore, this plays like your average TV movie with only an effectively menacing performance from Torn to recommend it." (Allan Bryce, *The Dark Side*, Issue 107, January/February 2004)

"... this has first-rate acting from Torn and Mulgrew but often is needlessly sadistic." (James O'Neill, *Terror on Tape*, Billboard Books, 1994)

"I'm not sure why this doesn't work. The cast is good, it's well produced, and it has some interesting locations...While not really bad, this is just a little too flat and straightforward to have much impact at all." (L.A. Morse, *Video Trash and Treasures*, HarperCollins, 1989)

**CHAPTER 4
HORROR AND HUMOR
A Selection of Films That Exhibit an Especially Sinister Wit**

Brain Damage

Director: Frank Henenlotter
Produced by: Edgar Levins
Written by: Frank Henenlotter
Cast: Rick Hearst; Gordon MacDonald; Jennifer Lowry; Theo Barnes; Lucille Saint-Peter; Vicki Darnell; Joseph Gonzalez; Bradlee Rhodes; Michael Bishop; Ari M. Roussimoff; Kevin Van Hentenryck; John Zacherle (Voice)
Special Effects: Gabe Bartalos
Year: 1987

Plot Synopsis

"Elmer, din din," shouts Martha Ackerman (Saint-Peter) as she prepares a plateful of cow's brains for the mysterious recipient. Her husband, Morris Ackerman (Barnes) screams that "Elmer" has gone missing, and they both begin to search their immediate surroundings in a panic. When the couple cannot locate the missing creature, they fall to the ground and begin to froth at the mouth.

In a nearby apartment, Brian (Hearst) is feeling unwell and is unable to go out to a concert with his girlfriend Barbara (Lowry). He asks his brother Mike (MacDonald) to accompany her instead, and the two leave Brian to recover.

Brian begins to hallucinate that his bedroom is becoming swamped in crystal clear water, which finally washes over his face. He later wakes up from his strange visions and locates a tiny, bloodstained hole on the back of his neck. Suddenly a small, gruesome, turd-like purple creature (voiced by Zacherle) emerges from

Elmer—*Brain Damage*'s turd-like parasite.

under Brian's shirt and eloquently introduces himself. The creature calls himself Elmer and tells Brian that all his problems are now over. Having enjoyed his first "trip," Brian agrees to let Elmer inject him with his juice again.

High on Elmer's fluids and hallucinating, Brian leaves his apartment and enters a scrap yard. He screams out in pleasure and dances around the yard. His whoops of delight attract the attention of a security guard (Rhodes). Elmer attacks the guard, eating out his brains. Brian sees none of it, and encourages Elmer to give him another shot of fluid.

As Brian stays more to himself, locked in his room, his girlfriend and his brother become increasingly concerned about him. Barbara takes Brian out for a dinner date, but her boyfriend is still hallucinating from a recent dose of Elmer's fluids. He sees pulsating brains on his dinner plate and walks out of the restaurant.

Brian arrives at a punk rock club. Once there he picks up a busty blonde (Darnell), who takes him outside to perform oral sex, but when she opens his fly, Elmer leaps out at her and sucks the girl's brains out through her mouth.

Once sober, Brian discovers blood on his underwear. He learns about the previous two murders and consequently swears to give up Elmer's juice once and for all. Locking himself away in a cheap, grubby motel room in New York, Brian promises Elmer that he will never again succumb to the temptation of his fluids.

After two nights of hell and horrific visions, Brian begs for Elmer's help. The creature agrees to inject his fluids into Brian again, but only if Brian can supply him with fresh human brains to feast on. Brian goes to the motel's showers, where Elmer creeps into a toilet cubicle and slaughters another victim (Bishop).

Brian returns home and lies in bed. He hears his brother making love to Barbara. After a dream in which he eats Barbara's brains, Brian enters his brother's bedroom and tells the two that they should leave the apartment because they are in danger.

Walking the streets of New York, Brian hops onto a subway train. Barbara follows him and also boards the train. She tells Brian that she still loves him. Elmer leaps out of Brian's mouth and attacks her. Barbara's dead body is left on the train.

Trust us—this picture is not what it looks like at first...

When he returns to his apartment block, Morris and Martha Ackerman threaten Brian with a handgun and take Elmer from him. The creature responds by burrowing itself through the couple's heads. Following this grisly scenario, Elmer injects Brian through the back of his neck, but the dying Morris Ackerman muscles up enough life to squeeze the creature to death—forcing Elmer to penetrate Brian's brain with large amounts of fluid. His skull pulsating and ready to burst, Brian returns to his room and shoots himself in the head. Light and electricity beam out from his wound as the dying man falls into a final, lethal trance.

Critique

Brain Damage is the sort of horror movie that comes along all too rarely—disgusting and yet intelligent, horrible and yet hilarious—the film manages to balance opposing emotions perfectly, and considering the outlandish subject matter of the production, this is no small feat. Sadly, the film's director (Frank Henenlotter) has embarked upon very few movies during his career,[1] although he has spent a considerable amount of time working to restore and release extremely obscure horror movies for the American company Something Weird Video. *Brain Damage* is undoubtedly the highlight of his small oeuvre, towering over what remains probably his best-known movie—1982's *Basket Case*—by being both technically proficient and far more interesting. Where *Basket Case* was crude and badly acted (albeit still a great deal of fun), *Brain Damage* is competent, even stylish, and extremely well performed by an unknown cast. Moreover, the film details what appears to be a forceful anti-drug message—with lead character Hearst losing his girlfriend and any semblance of self-respect during the movie's running time, all because of an addiction to a mysterious fluid. Although Henenlotter denies that his film carries any such message on purpose,[2] the resulting picture still gives the impression of carrying a warning against drug addiction—with the film aptly depicting a habit that leads to paranoia, illness and finally death.

Despite being called "heavy-handed" and "hopefully unintentional"[3] by one critic, *Brain Damage*'s approach toward drug use clearly singles out heroin as its prime target—a soul-destroying addiction that deserves every piece of castigation aimed at it. Elmer's injection of Hearst through a lengthy needle that protrudes from his mouth apparently completes this equation. Furthermore, to anyone who has ever been in contact with an addict, it is refreshing to see Henenlotter emphasize that as soon as his lead character accepts the drug, his life spirals out of control, with no "upside" to Elmer's strange fluid except for the initial rush.

Whether the director may actually be spoofing the junkie lifestyle to power a gross horror tale is obviously open to consideration, but there are scenes in *Brain Damage* of real brilliance—with images that are more potent than anything in *Trainspotting* (1996). Whereas Danny Boyle's admittedly compulsive story of Edinburgh smack-heads details near-loveable, sexy, casual goofballs in the likes of Robert Carlyle and Ewan McGregor, *Brain Damage* is a far more forceful analogy of the "coming down" effect of drug abuse. There's no room in Henenlotter's movie for a hip soundtrack or moments of casual, comical aggression and, instead, *Brain Damage* details one of the most gut-wrenching cold turkey sequences in film history. As Hearst decides that he is going to attempt to withstand Elmer's fluids, the character begins to vomit and curl up in the corner of a filthy motel room. As night dawns he shivers profusely and, wrapped up in blankets, he begins to pick gray matter from his right ear. Finally Hearst reaches further inside his ear and pulls out a long string of brain, which concludes with his ear falling to the ground and buckets of blood pouring from the wound. The result is devastating. On the opposite side of the coin, Hearst's first "hit," in which gorgeous blue water rises up over him, is tranquil and poetic—and a rare moment of bliss in an otherwise nonstop parade of increasingly bizarre set pieces.

If all of this sounds horribly depressing and thus unsuitable for a chapter on "dark humor," then take solace in the fact that *Brain Damage* is actually full of hilarious set pieces. The film is (rightly) most famous for its deadly blow-job sequence, in which Darnell goes down on Hearst—only to be greeted by Elmer, who leaps down the young girl's throat. Largely shot from the back, Hearst grabs Darnell's head and tightens his grip on the young woman, mocking the standard filming of a pornographic oral sex sequence. Then, in fierce close-up, we see Elmer's body—purple and enshrouded in veins and muscle—rammed down the luckless female's throat—the blood trickling from Darnell's mouth taking the place of the

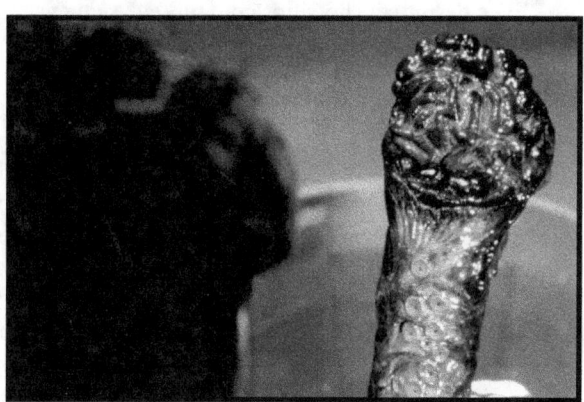

Elmer is a strangely endearing creature—just don't get on his bad side.

A Dialogue with 30 Modern Masters of Horror

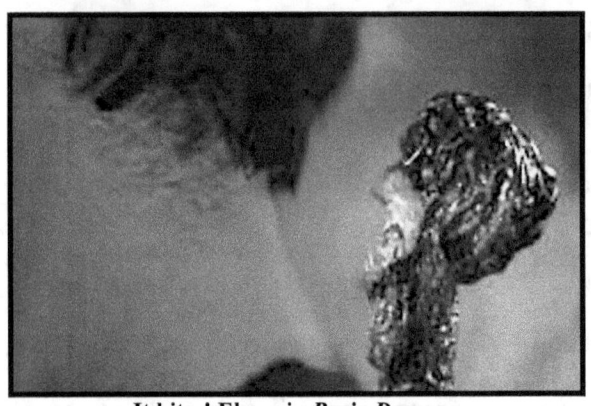

It bites! Elmer in *Brain Damage*.

semen that would normally accompany such a moment in an adult movie. Truncated from many prints, this scene ends with Elmer finally tugging Darnell's brains out through her mouth and into the trousers of Hearst. Sex and death are commonly linked in the horror film (from Bela Lugosi's seductive but deadly Dracula to the promiscuous teenagers who meet their deaths in the *Friday the 13th* movies), but perhaps never so blatantly, or explicitly, as in *Brain Damage*. Acting largely as a spoof of porn movies—right down to the build-up toward the final, climactic "money shot" whereupon Elmer graphically tears Darnell's brains asunder—this controversial moment is indeed extremely funny, but done with such bad taste that its notorious reputation seems inevitable.

Even despite the horrific "cold turkey" sequence, *Brain Damage* is a cavalcade of gross hilarity, and a moment of jet black humor is never too far away. Choice selections include the bizarre sight of Hearst taking a bath with Elmer, the creature singing "Elmer's

tune" to Hearst, and the fantastic shots of Elmer leaping out from Hearst's mouth in an attempt to attack his girlfriend, who remains blissfully unaware of her impending doom. *Basket Case* fans will also enjoy spotting that film's star Kevin Van Hentenryck in his cameo appearance where—complete with basket—he sits in front of Hearst but finally swaps seats when even he cannot fathom the strange-looking man in front of him. Even with an ending that should be as nihilistic as it comes, *Brain Damage* still pulls out some twisted comedy from its final moments. A spaced-out Hearst, with a huge chunk missing from his forehead, peers up at the bright light escaping from his brow and continues his trip, blissfully unaware of his certain death. The addiction may have finally destroyed him, but his spaced-out demeanor suggests someone totally unaware of the fact that half his skull is missing. Only in the strange world of Frank Henenlotter could something as absurd as *Brain Damage* play out as a totally logical morality tale. It's the perfect party movie, still waiting to be discovered.

Memories of the Film

"Frank had a lot of input into the creation of Elmer. He had in fact sculpted a really dynamic version of Elmer that was used on his promotional teasers when he and the film's producer, Edgar Levins, were raising money," begins special effects artist Gabe Bartalos. "He brought this to me and said, 'Make something not like this...but try and convey this energy.' So obviously Frank's input was huge. He would be right over my shoulder as I was sculpting and he'd say, 'Can I try something?' and he'd actually push the clay around a little to make a suction cup or something." Bartalos, a well-respected makeup artist, would follow *Brain Damage* by working on such films as 1989's *Fright Night 2*, the *Leprechaun* series (where he created the title character) and 1991's *Sometimes They Come Back*. He directed his first film, *Skinned Deep*, in 2002.

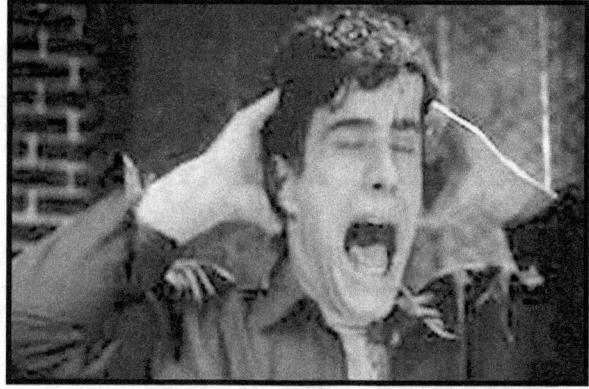

It can't be denied that Frank Henenlotter certainly has a unique vision.

"The nice thing about Frank is that he communicates very clearly. In designing a character, especially one as whacked out as Elmer, the less guesswork the better," continues Bartalos, who also regards *Brain Damage* as a largely underrated classic. "And Frank is very specific. As my sculpture advanced, he'd always be poking in, and I should really stress that this was not in a 'checking up way,' but in a way to keep the process collaborative and really fun! Once the sculpture of Elmer was done, we were both really psyched with him and I think most of the effects still hold up alright. There will always be some things you wish you did a little different, or wish you knew more about at the time. I think it's kind of cool though, that a film is a time capsule of where you and your talents are at that specific time." As for the anti-drugs message, Bartalos maintains that the film was always designed to carry this. "Of course that was the case," he states.

Perhaps inevitably, any conversation about *Brain Damage* results in talk about the deadly oral sex sequence. "It was a little surprising that the most controversial gore moment came from Elmer's zipper jump into the unsuspecting female's mouth. I mean, it's a little distorted for me because I always thought that effect was so outlandish that it hit comedy, but even on set there were people that thought that Frank and I had gone

Audiences spent half the film gasping and the other half laughing.

too far with the set-up. Compared to some of the other gore moments that were more violent in tone, I just didn't think that scene would freak people out that much. Maybe now, looking back, I do have a better understanding of ratings and how they pretend to come to their conclusions. This scene was clearly a fusion of two of the biggest 'no-no's'—graphic violence and sexuality, together in one great scene! But still, with that said, I feel that the careful way Frank shot it—it is more funny and bizarre than mean-spirited. One more great example of why people hate the ratings board and love Frank Henenlotter."

Bartalos also remembers back to *Brain Damage*'s North American cinema release. "Watching *Brain Damage* early in its release with an audience was an interesting viewing. I remember during the attack scenes that audience members' audio outbursts would start out the same way, with a big burst of shock, but then as the air continued to expel from their lungs, it clearly became two different reactions. Half fused it into disgust while the other half of the audience turned it into a laugh. This reaction could probably be applied to most of Frank's films, and maybe that's why we still remember and celebrate them." The special effects artist also explains why he believes the film never crossed over to a large audience. "Maybe the reason *Brain Damage* wasn't spotlighted early on is that Frank doesn't sell out his ideas in exchange for a quick buck. All of his films stand the test of time and he makes them to have pride in his library of work. That may mean taking a little less money or not having such a wide release because he feels that an up-and-coming actor is worth more than spending a shitload on an actor who will be forgotten in two years' time. This is nice, because all aspects of the film are done for the right reasons. A film with a giant release that is splashed all over the press may get that 'opening weekend' buzz, but doesn't guarantee a quality film, and these days that seems to be the warning sign

Director Frank Henenlotter

of a compromised product. A movie that is just screaming to make back its money before the reviews hit. Frank made a genuine film that was also technically very well done and people that scratch the surface of cinema and find it are even more appreciative of it. I think Frank likes and connects with this type of viewer anyway."

Bartalos went on to again work with Henenlotter on his next three films—*Basket Case 2*, *Frankenhooker* (both 1990) and *Basket Case 3*. However, the special effects artist admits to admiring the director even before *Brain Damage*.

Henenlotter keeps his films bizarre without becoming incomprehensible.

"I was a big fan of *Basket Case* before I ever met Frank," states Bartalos. "So to be able to contribute to his excellently deranged form of filmmaking was a real treat. I clearly remember falling off my couch in hysterics when the animation sequence happened in *Basket Case*. Here was the most unapologetic insanity I had ever seen boldly displayed across the screen and I could not help but be impressed. To then later meet him and see he is such a gentleman with an incredibly quick wit and bottomless imagination was very exciting. Frank holds what I call the 'Holy Grail' in horror filmmaking: he keeps it bizarre without being incomprehensible, he keeps it horrifying without being repugnant, and he keeps it fun without ever using comedy as a safety net. What more can you ask for?"

Asked about his favorite creation during his long and impressive career in horror films (which also includes makeup work on 1986's *The Texas Chainsaw Massacre Part 2* and 1996's *Little Witches*), Bartalos responds with affection toward his most recent project. "My personal favorite creations always tend to be the last one I focused on, so in this case it would be the Surgeon General from my own horror film that I wrote and directed, *Skinned Deep*. He has eerie welder goggles bolted to his head, a bear-trap as a mouth, and shriveled skin stretched over his disfigured skull, so yeah, right about now, Surgeon General is my favorite."

Alternate Critique

"Arguably the director's best work (and certainly his best written)." (Michael Gingold, *Fangoria*, Issue 188, November 1999)

"Extremely strange, oddly effective horror film....Clever parable about drug addiction." (Leonard Maltin, *Movie and Video Guide*, Penguin)

"Maybe a bit too esoteric to be a big hit, but it should cultivate a nice cult status in years to come. It's miles better than the usual trash on the market..." (Steve Puchalski, *Slimetime*, Headpress, 1996)

Motel Hell

Director: Kevin Connor
Produced by: Robert Jaffe/Steven-Charles Jaffe
Written by: Robert Jaffe/Steven-Charles Jaffe
Cast: Rory Calhoun; Paul Linke; Nancy Parsons; Nina Axelrod; Wolfman Jack; Elaine Joyce; Monique St. Pierre; Rosanne Katon; E. Hampton Beagle; Everett Creach; Michael Melvin; John Ratzenberger
Special Effects: Adams R. Calvert
Year: 1980

Plot Synopsis

Outside the "Motel Hello," the letter "O" flashes on and off.

A motorbike rider and his girlfriend skid off the motorway when a trap is set for them. The man (Creach) dies, but his girlfriend Terry (Axelrod) is saved and taken in by a local meat farmer called Farmer Vincent (Calhoun), and his sister Ida (Parsons)—even though the brother and sister had originally intended to kill them both.

The local sheriff, Bruce Smith (Linke)—who is also Vincent's younger brother—comes by to investigate the incident. He takes a liking to Terry and agrees that she can recover and work on his brother's farm. Terry asks what has happened to her boyfriend. Vincent surprises both her and his brother by explaining that he buried the man's dead body.

A health and safety inspector (Beagle) drops by the farm. The man soon leaves, but remains suspicious that all is not as it seems. The inspector creeps back at night and discovers a secret garden where live human beings, with their vocal cords slit, are buried up to their heads in the earth, played mellow music and fattened up for the kill. The inspector does not see Vincent creep up on him, and he is knocked unconscious.

Vincent sets up a trap on the road to catch more passersby. He bags himself a heavy-metal rock band and we later see the farmer's buried victims being force fed through a funnel.

Later two young girls (Pierre and Katon) who are out driving late at night come to a fake "road closed" sign. Vincent then chases them in his truck. They are forced off the road, but the farmer has to leave the bodies when his brother—on patrol—is alerted to the chase. When Vincent returns to his motel, a couple have arrived—under the impression that the "Motel Hello" is a swingers' club because of a fake invitation

One of the many sight gags in *Motel Hell*—a horror film with a nasty sense of humor!

that Vincent and Ida have drawn up to attract fresh victims. The couple let Vincent and Ida tie them up and they are then knocked out.

The next day, Ida and Terry go out in the lake and float on rubber rings. Jealous of her brother's attention toward Terry, Ida tries to drown the girl—making it look like an accident. Vincent saves her, however, and when Terry wakes up in bed she proclaims her love toward the elderly farmer. They agree to be married. The sheriff is jealous and cannot understand his bother's relationship with Terry.

Some of the buried humans are hypnotized and slaughtered by Ida and Vincent. Later in the evening, however, one of the victims gets free from the garden. Meanwhile, the sheriff finds out about the ambushed cars and investigates Ida and Vincent. The escaped victim attacks Ida, and soon more of Vincent's human cattle are free. Terry finds out about what her fiancé has been doing and is tied up to a meat cutter by the old man.

As she approaches the blades of the cutter, the sheriff and Vincent—who wears a pig's head—have a chainsaw duel. Vincent loses and is sawed deep into his stomach. Ida is buried face first into the ground by the escapees. The "O" in the "Motel Hello" sign finally explodes, as Sheriff Smith and Terry walk to safety.

Critique

Released just as the slasher film boom really began to take off, and marketed as being not entirely dissimilar to *Friday the 13th* and its ilk, *Motel Hell* was not a huge success. The film has, however, remained a cult favorite of horror fans for many years—not least because it manages to mix comedy with an effectively vile set-up. Surprisingly it works well, and the film carries some extremely amusing, not to mention engaging, lines of dialogue. Calhoun's dying words are especially memorable, as he informs both his girlfriend and his brother: "My whole life has been a lie. I'm the biggest hypocrite of them all. For my meats...*I used preservatives*." Delivered with beautiful timing and a sly wink at the audience, the actor looks perfectly comfortable with, and understanding of, the tone of the movie that he is performing in. Certainly,

Rory Calhoun as Farmer Vincent in *Motel Hell*

with this inspired climactic piece of scripting, the movie contains one of the greatest kiss-off lines from any screen villain in history. For that, it should be cherished as an undervalued classic for many years to come.

With its tongue placed firmly in its cheek, *Motel Hell* turns its satire toward the "God-fearing Christian," with Calhoun as the deluded moral philosopher. It is indeed strange to view the old man contemplating, with his sister by his side, whether or not it is morally "right" for him to be taking all those lives...just moments before he snaps a few necks. Admittedly it is not high art but, done with just the right amount of bad taste, it makes for an amusing spectacle. The presence of Wolfman Jack, in a small cameo as a popular evangelical preacher (albeit one not above reading *Hustler* magazine), leads to the assumption that *Motel Hell* might be set within an especially Christian area of America. There is certainly an atmosphere of sexual repression in the movie as indicated by Calhoun—who won't have sex before marriage out of respect to his religious values, but who thinks nothing of slaughtering a few innocent humans. His strict attitude toward sexual relations is also played out when Axelrod awakens and wonders why anyone would attempt to drive her and her boyfriend from the road. Calhoun casually asks the girl if she was married to her partner—presumably in an attempt to justify his actions to himself when she answer in the negative.[4]

Such sexual repression is not limited to Calhoun, however. For example, the local Sheriff cannot bring himself to admit that he purchased pornography to the town's preacher, who catches him with some adult literature. Instead, he chooses to tell a lie and mention that he confiscated the magazine from some children. The movie also shows a married couple secretly hiking around the middle of nowhere looking for a sex party. This takes them to "Motel Hello" and they are subsequently tied up in what they perceive as an act of kinky sexual relations. Of course, this is not true. However, since they are now helpless, they become easy pickings for Calhoun and his sister, who have the couple trapped in a John Wayne Gacy-style scenario.

Of course, sexual desires and taboos are hidden within every society (save perhaps for San Francisco!), but considering the actions of *Motel Hell*'s lead characters, it seems

Terry (Nina Axelrod) little realizes the dangerous consequences that wet T-shirt will set in motion as she enjoys the sun and water.

especially relevant here. Set within a township where murder can go unnoticed and is ultimately carried out by so-called Christian people, yet sex and pornography are deemed to be unacceptable—*Motel Hell* portrays a deluded sense of morality. As far as Calhoun and Parsons are concerned (especially when confronted by the two swingers), sex is a confusing, even irrelevant, issue that they appear unable to approach. Confronted with a beautiful, topless girl, Calhoun has to turn away, insisting that he can do nothing until he is married. To Calhoun and Parsons, all human beings are just meat, and violence is a basic necessity of their trade. The victims in *Motel Hell* die not for any so-called "moral" reason on the part of the psychopath, but rather because they will make for good food. Sex is an alien concept to the film's villains.

The grotesque and the comical blend together nicely in *Motel Hell*—as seen in the sequence where Calhoun and Parsons inject their helpless victims in the throat and then slit their vocal cords so that their "cattle" will not make any distracting noises. Such moments, because they are accompanied by sharp and funny dialogue, allow *Motel Hell* to offset the inevitable gore with bursts of inspired humor. Top of the list is undoubtedly Calhoun's many, somewhat dazed, outbursts in relation to his homicidal day job. "I wonder about the karmic implications of these acts," deadpans the actor before he goes in for the kill. A B-grade philosopher, Calhoun plays Farmer Vincent as a deluded, crazy old backwoods hick—always thinking of ways to justify his murder spree. For example, when his girlfriend finds out what he has been up to, Calhoun defends himself by saying: "I'm not trying to play God. I wouldn't even know how to begin…there's too many people in the world and not enough food, but this takes care of both problems." In such instances it is difficult not to laugh along with the bumbling madman and his crazy beliefs. Nothing less than excellent in the lead role, Calhoun shines in *Motel Hell*, creating a character that—as sickening as his actions are—is difficult to really hate. On the other hand, his obese sister Ida actually brings a more threatening persona to the screen. With a hint of incest between the two, as suggested by Ida's jealousy of her brother's new girlfriend, the late Nancy Parsons portrays a larger than life, impos-

Nancy Parsons, of *Porky's* fame, has a delicious grasp of the character she plays.

ing specimen who always appears eager to jump headfirst into a new act of violence. Parsons—most famous for her villainous role in the *Porky's* films—approaches her role with a delicious grasp of the character's immaturity.

Motel Hell also boasts tight direction from Kevin Connor, who stages a standout, thrilling finale in which Calhoun and Linke battle with chainsaws. This scene, taking place while Axelrod speeds toward the spinning blades of a meat cutter, is very much an homage to the familiar "damsel in distress" theme—where the heroine is typically tied to a train track as the hero rushes to save her life. The sight of Calhoun clad in a pig's head and letting loose with a deep laugh is certainly bizarre, but also weird enough to confirm a sequence that was always destined to attract cult favor. It also predates a similarly staged battle in Tobe Hooper's *The Texas Chainsaw Massacre Part 2* by six years.[5] One may also look at Connor's movie in light of vegetarianism for, despite searching for more "humane" methods to kill his victims, Calhoun's human cattle still live and die horrifically, force-fed the right ingredients and fattened up for extermination. There may even be some commentary on the "supply and demand" of the modern marketplace—where the demand for Farmer Vincent meats is so high that more and more bodies have to be collected from the roadside. Perhaps this showcases the inevitability of factory farming. Regardless of how one chooses to look at *Motel Hell*, the movie certainly benefits from its more "lived-in" villains and a well-developed, literate script. It remains a horror film that carries with it a whole host of delicious one-liners.

Standout Moment

How can anyone who watches *Motel Hell* possibly forget the already-discussed sequence where Calhoun, cackling wildly with a pig's head over his mug, takes the fight to his brother in the climactic chainsaw duel?

Memories of the Film

Having made such British films as *The Land That Time Forgot* (1975) and its sequel *The People That Time Forgot* (1977), *Motel Hell* was director Kevin Connor's first American film. "I moved to the States because I was feeling stuck in Edgar Rice—those

Sex before marriage is a big no-no for Rory Calhoun's Bible-bashing psychopath.

kinds of movies—and my producer and partner at the time didn't want to expand," states the director. "And what we should have done, of course, is have bigger budgets and go the way of Spielberg—we should have had bigger stars, kept getting bigger, but we didn't. So we parted company and I came to the States and couldn't find a job for a while and I only had one contact, so I went to see him. Now this is a Hollywood tale! I went to see my one contact because I had left my reel with him a few weeks before. So I went to collect my reel and when I went into his office, his door opened—now he was a very famous agent—and he came through and asked me, 'Kevin, have you got a job yet?' I said, 'No.' Then he said, 'Well, come in here, I'm going to get you a job.' He took me in his office, he picked up the phone. 'I promise you, Kevin,' called another agent and said, 'I've got a young horror film director sitting in front me, have you got anything for him?' Then his friend said, 'Funny you should say that because this morning we had a call from United Artists and they were looking for a horror film director...'"

Such a comment brought excitement to Connor—as one might imagine. "So, off I went, carrying my cans of *From Beyond the Grave* up to MGM/UA," laughs the director. "They saw *From Beyond the Grave*, they loved it, they gave me this script called *Motel Hell*. I took it home to read and the opening instructions were, 'Long shot, flashing lights of Motel Hello, cut inside is a fat woman with a dildo and she's cuddling a pig.' Originally, in the opening scene, Nancy Parsons' character was in bed with a pig and a dildo! I thought, 'And I've come to Hollywood to do this.' So I read it, because I needed the money and I needed the work, and I hoped to get my foot in the door. Eventually I said, 'I'll do this if we treat it as a black comedy.' So you never really see any cutting of throats or anything—everything is what you don't see—which is always more effective, more creepy and more disturbing. I said, 'As long as you take out all the stupid stuff like dildos'—and that's how I came to get it and I got on very well with the two boys who wrote it. I don't think I would change anything in particular if I could do the movie all over again—it was my first American picture and one of these lucky

An iconic image in the making – even fans that have never seen the film might find this bizarre image familiar… (it's been re-printed in genre magazines for years).

breaks. I loved the cast too—we cast Nancy and Rory together. Nancy was lovely and (Rory's) the old cowboy.

"I think that the movie has stood the test of time okay," continues the director. "But, of course, if I was to make it today then the audience would expect to see much more gruesome images. I deliberately stayed away from showing graphic stuff. I find that it is what you don't see that is more effective. Once you set your mind on how you're going to treat it…I mean, if you treat it straight—the actors can't take the piss out of it, they can't take the mickey out of the subject matter. So it's what they're saying, and the things they're doing, that becomes the dark comedy element. You know they bury people upside down in the ground and do this sort of thing, but it's just a way of life for them." Having gone on to direct several episodes of a variety of successful television series (including *Moonlighting* and *Remington Steele*), as well as the horror title *The House Where Evil Dwells*, Connor still has fond memories of making *Motel Hell*. "The movie was a lot of fun to make. Everybody enjoyed themselves so much, including the crew." Not that the director was inspired by the genre films of the time—"I cannot say that I was a fan of American horror movies in particular, I enjoyed Claude Chabrol's kind of horror more, so I wasn't really inspired by more recent films." Connors states that, contrary to rumors stating otherwise, there were not any censorship problems with *Motel Hell*. "I don't think we had any bother, but I really can't remember. They were probably posed photographs, I don't think we cut anything…we did cut down the disc jockey guy that we had at the beginning of the film—Wolfman Jack, we had to cut him down a bit. But he was a delight to work with."

Connor admits that he would like to do more horror in the future. "Oh yes, absolutely—yeah," he responds. "Horror-wise I've actually got a couple in my hand—some of Graham Masterton's work. I like his work. There's one called *Prey*, which I've just been working on the screenplay for, and the producer hopes to go with it next year in the Isle of Man and Pinewood, and another one of his books I'm adapting called *Outrageous*, and yeah, he's written a ton of stuff." Connor is also surprised to learn that his chainsaw duel turned up in the second *Texas Chainsaw Massacre* film. "Did it?" he laughs. "I don't know—I think I probably stole it in the first place. Yeah, we had the two chainsaws going—I tell you, the stink in that place was horrible because they were real pigs' heads.... We didn't shoot it in a real abattoir, instead we were out at some ranch, someplace—I can't remember where. We had a little hut on the location and we made that into the abattoir where they boil the bodies and things. So we did it all in there, but we had real pigs' sides and stuff hanging out and after about three or four days they got a bit wiffy."

Despite becoming a cult favorite in later years, *Motel Hell* was not a hit when it was originally released. "Sadly, it didn't do that well," says the director. "It didn't

The long arm of the law counts for little in *Motel Hell*.

put me on the map or anything, but it has become a sort of cult film. I think there were a lot of similar movies out at the same time, so it was like at the tail end of a cycle that you have in the cinema from time to time. Everything comes down to (the fact that) you've got to be at the right place at the right time, and that time was just the luck of the draw."

Alternate Critiques

"One of the most interesting aspects of *Motel Hell* is the film's presentation of a form of cannibalism that is anything but regressive." (Mikita Brottman, *Meat Is Murder*, Headpress Publishing, 1997)

"Seen today...the film's mix of broad comedy and authentically gruesome imagery only sharpens its brutal satire of all things American." (Jonathan Rigby, *Shivers*, Issue 54, June 1998)

"Obviously located midway between the Bates Motel and the Texas Chainsaw Barbecue, this one can't decide if it wants to go for shocks and chills or grotesque black humor, and doesn't quite achieve either." (L.A. Morse, *Video Trash and Treasures*, HarperCollins, 1989)

The Texas Chainsaw Massacre 2

Director: Tobe Hooper
Produced by: Yoram Globus/Menahem Golan
Written by: L.M. Kit Carson
Cast: Dennis Hopper; Caroline Williams; Jim Siedow; Bill Moseley; Bill Johnson; Ken Evert; Harlan Jordan; Kirk Sisco; James N. Harrell; Lou Perry; Barry Kinyon; Chris Douridas
Special Effects: Tom Savini
Year: 1986

Plot Synopsis

An opening narration explains that Sally Hardesty, the sole survivor of the original *Texas Chain Saw Massacre*, "sank into catatonia" following the film's events. Since 1973, "recurring reports" of chainsaw deaths have been filed around Texas, but no one has ever been found responsible.

Two college boys (Kinyon and Douridas) are on their way to the "Texas OU Weekend" ("the biggest party in the world"). They drive fast down the Texas roads, shooting at road signs. The boys phone a radio program hosted by Stretch (Williams), an energetic female DJ, and scream a tirade of nonsense down the line. Despite her pleas, they refuse to hang up and the radio station's technician, L.G. (Perry) cannot find a way to cut them from the air.

The two play chicken with a passing farm truck, finally hanging up their mobile phones. Later in the evening, the two boys phone Stretch again—but this time the college kids are distracted by the reappearance of the farm truck from earlier. The truck chases the boys' car and Leatherface (Johnson) appears from the roof with his chainsaw. The driver of the car has his head sawn in half, causing the vehicle to crash. Stretch records the entire ordeal.

Lieutenant Lefty Enright (Hopper) is the brother of Sally and Franklin Hardesty, from the first film. He appears at the site of the crash, and urges a local patrolman (Jordan) to put the story in the news. The patrolman believes that Enright is insane—spending his years hunting "chainsaw killers"—but agrees to do so.

Having read about the story in the newspaper, Stretch visits the alcoholic Enright at his apartment and tells him that she has the entire massacre recorded on tape. He sends her away—too drunk to comprehend what she is offering him.

The dead body of The Hitchhiker (who's killed at the end of Part 1) makes cameo appearances throughout Chainsaw 2.

Stretch and L.G. report from the "Texas/Oklahoma Chili Cook-Off Competition," which is won by Drayton Sawyer (Siedow), the psychopath cook from the first film.

Enright visits a chainsaw store and purchases some weapons. Following this, he visits Stretch and, sobered up, asks her to play her recording live on air. She does so, attracting the attention of Sawyer. Stretch's radio show closes down for the night.

The station is paid a visit by a member of the Sawyer family called Chop Top (Moseley). He is a Vietnam veteran who has a metal plate installed in his skull. He unleashes Leatherface, who corners Stretch in a room. Meanwhile, Chop Top beats L.G. repeatedly across the head with a hammer. Stretch notices Leatherface's attraction to her and asks him how good he is. The masked maniac responds by rubbing his chainsaw up against her crotch, finally seeming to achieve some form of orgasm by power-starting the weapon and carving up the studio. Leatherface indicates to Chop Top that he has killed Stretch, and the two leave with the body of L.G.

Stretch follows them to a closed-down amusement park. She arrives and is greeted by Enright, who states that he used the disc jockey as bait. Stretch falls through a trap door and ends up in the Sawyer family's lair. Enright responds by sawing his way into the derelict building and carving up the family's residence.

Stretch hides out in a small back room where Leatherface—busy cutting up the body of L.G.—notices her. He hides the girl, but ties her up in case she attempts to escape. He also places a mask of flesh (taken from the face of L.G.) on her features. He leaves the room after being shouted at by Drayton to work harder.

L.G. awakens and cuts Stretch loose, but he dies shortly after. The Sawyer home is crumbling, causing Drayton to complain about losing more and more money. Chop Top runs around with the dead body of his other brother (the hitchhiker from part one). He screams that they should reopen the amusement park as "'Nam Land." Enright finds the dead body of his brother and continues to carve his way through the family's hiding place.

"You mean it's a comedy?" remarks one angry viewer of *Chainsaw 2*.

Stretch runs past the family, causing them to send Leatherface after her. Following a lengthy chase Leatherface corners her, but he cannot bring himself to kill her. Instead Chop Top knocks her out, and she awakens at the family dinner table. Grandpa (Evert) is wheeled out—"137 years old"—to kill the girl, but the barely functioning old man cannot strike her. Drayton gets impatient and delivers a knockout blow to Stretch's head, just before Enright arrives to confront the family.

Enright saws Drayton in his backside and begins a chainsaw duel with Leatherface, which ends with the masked behemoth being sawed through the stomach. Drayton takes a grenade from the corpse of the hitchhiker and blows up the amusement park. Only Chop Top and Stretch escape.

Chop Top chases Stretch up a rickety old bridge and to the top of a small mountain. A room inside the mountain features the corpse of the family's grandmother, whose decaying hands hold a chainsaw. Chop Top slices at Stretch with a razor blade, but the girl finally starts the saw and kills the man. He falls to his death as Stretch stands bloodstained and victorious—the entire Sawyer family is now dead.

Critique

In a genre where sequels are synonymous with repetition and largely frowned upon as a result, it is shocking that *The Texas Chainsaw Massacre 2* should have met with such critical hostility upon its initial release. Somewhat miffed that so many viewers failed to notice the inherent humor in the first film, Hooper—and scriptwriter Carson—set out to make a spoof of the original hit, as well as the movies that it inspired. As a result, the first *Chainsaw* sequel is far removed from follow-ups to other modern horror flicks such as *Friday the 13th* and *Halloween* (both of which just regurgitated the same thing film after film). It is also a more effective lampoon of the genre than the more popular *Evil Dead 2* (1987), to which the tone of *Chainsaw 2* bears some resemblance. In this sense, it is understandable why audiences felt that they had been thrown a curveball by Hooper's sequel. Whereas legendary stories of viewers vomiting, or leaving the theater in a state of shock, abound over the initial release of *The Texas Chain Saw Massacre*, the follow-up is a very different experience. Played largely for laughs, the film is a brilliant and inventive satire on consumerism, multinational corporations and other facets of Reagan/Thatcher-era capitalism.

The Sawyer family undoubtedly represent the working class—they toil away day after day in a sweatshop-like environment with no windows, looking after their small but successful business. The only spoil of Chop Top and Leatherface is the radio, which acts as a form of escapism for the two men (boys?), who otherwise spend their every moment hard at work. "Thousands of dollars down the drain," hollers Siedow's cook as his house crumbles, "You got that kind of money?" In another scene the old man kicks Leatherface and screams, "Get back to work," adding, "More money lost, I never get a break." Siedow is very much the no-nonsense boss—the owner of an expanding business and the sole face of it. It is he, and he only, that collects the statewide prize for making the best meat. Symbolic of so many contemporary corporations (Disney is synonymous with Michael Eisner, as opposed to the hard-grafting souls who stitch together the company's clothing and soft toys for a living), the president soaks up the accolades while the workers toil and struggle with maintaining the company's actual output.

Leatherface especially, with his poor wide-eyed foolish expressions, is cast as something of a victim in the movie. No more the menacing, gruesome monster that Gunnar Hansen once played, the character is turned into an exploited factory worker—perhaps a symbol of the 1980s and the abuse of the blue-collar worker. Lest we mistakenly imagine *Chainsaw 2* as a Marxist tract, let us not forget that Chop Top himself has an eye on making money and escaping the daily grind. "'Nam Land," which he wants to convert the family's amusement-park hideout into, would surely be an even more perverse idea than the macabre, broken-down Disneyland that the Sawyers already inhabit in the movie. "It's what the public wants," bellows Chop Top (Moseley has unsurprisingly commanded a cult following through playing this role, which he takes to like a duck to water)—and how right he is. One of the biggest hits of 1986 was Oliver Stone's Oscar-winning *Platoon*.

If the comical death of the two yuppies driving a Mercedes at the beginning of the film signals the direction that *Chainsaw 2* will take, then it is nonetheless a surprise to see Hooper answer his own critics. Although the first *Chainsaw* features no nudity or sex, the film nonetheless hints at sexual assault on the part of the villains (most implicit in the notorious dinner scene where a bruised and bound Marilyn Burns cries, "I'll do whatever you want" to her aggressors). Refused a certificate by the British Censorship (later Classification) Board for nearly 30 years, and with one board member calling it "the pornography of terror,"[6] the film was almost certainly responsible for the "final girl" scenario that would inform a lot of subsequent horror, and especially slasher, films. With the male killer's implement of slaughter, be it a drill or a knife, being equated to a substitute penis by some critics[7]—and with the murders in this genre subsequently linked to sexual frustration—Hooper and Carson take this viewpoint and make it literal.

In doing so, the movie makes such criticism appear ludicrous. Balancing his chainsaw upon his groin, and thrusting it into Williams' crotch—

Tobe Hooper with the late, great Jim Siedow on the set of *Chainsaw 2*.

Leatherface grunts and groans before finally achieving what appears to be an orgasm through kick-starting his weapon. The sight of the masked psychopath in some form of sexual ecstasy, as he "ejaculates" via the roar of his chainsaw, is nothing less than hilarious. Inevitably, this sort of madcap reading of the whole slasher genre and its critics left many viewers befuddled. Leatherface is rendered as a goofball, and he is certainly no longer scary or threatening. Instead, the terror in *Chainsaw 2* is left to Moseley's Chop Top and, despite widely held proclamations to the contrary, the film finally manages to achieve some of the fright factor of the original movie in its closing moments.

During the movie's finale, Hooper belatedly introduces suspense and a truly creepy sense of out-of-control madness to the film. Leaving aside the comical chainsaw duel, culled from *Motel Hell*, Moseley's vicious, unrelenting chase of Williams informs the sequel with something close to the frantic pace and terror of its predecessor. Moseley finally lets rip with a believable sense of insanity in the movie's climactic sequence—taking in self-abuse and the prolonged torture of Williams with a razor blade. The actress' final stance, having killed her adversary, screaming and shaken, still manages to disturb, and the movie's closing images have a power to rival even the climax of the original.

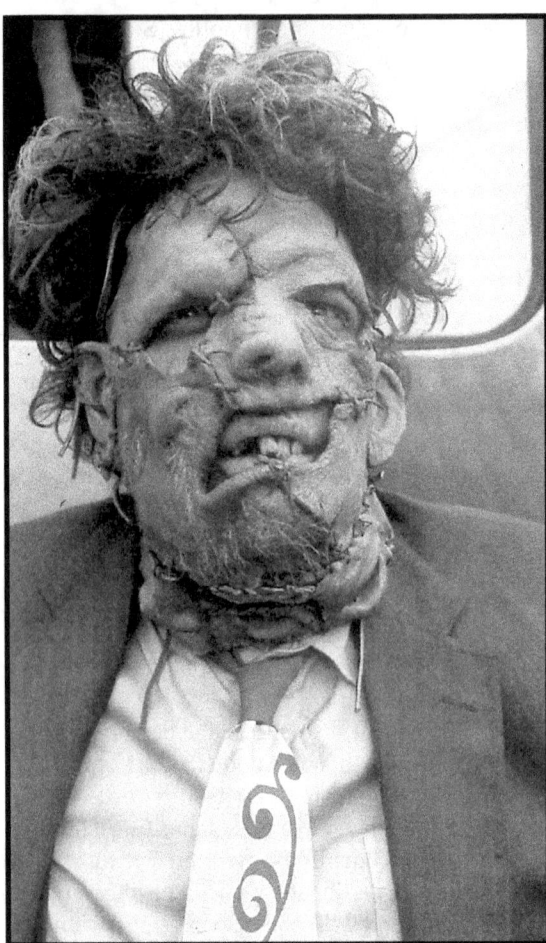

Tom Savini's Leatherface makeup added a whole new twist to the character's appearance.

Coming as a sequel to a movie that did not feature any graphic bloodshed, *Chainsaw 2*—under the expertise of special effects legend Tom Savini—presents us with a bucket-load of lopped up bodies, all showcased in grisly detail. Unsurprisingly, so as to not make the film overridingly sadistic and thus clash with the comical tone, Hooper stages the various spurting arteries with jovial abandon. One of the yuppie characters (Kinyon) feels around for the top of his head after it has been sawn asunder, and Perry simply refuses to die as Moseley continues to pummel him in the head with a hammer. At first bloodthirsty and nasty, the prolonged stupidity of the sequence—where blow after blow fails to kill Perry—turns it into something straight out of Monty Python.

This is typical for most of the violence in *Chainsaw 2*, and in retrospect it is difficult to understand why so many censorship boards—including the American, Australian, German and, inevitably, British—were repulsed by the film. This point is furthered by the genuinely funny dialogue that usually precedes the movie's violence, such as when Moseley chastises Leatherface for accidentally destroying his "Sonny Bono wig" with a chainsaw.

Actress Caroline Williams screams her mouth dry in *Chainsaw 2*.

Made at the tail end of a lucrative three-picture deal that Hooper signed with Cannon Pictures, *Chainsaw 2* was besieged by daily rewrites to the script, a slashed budget and a rushed shoot.[8] Hooper badly needed a commercial and critical hit after the hugely disappointing flops *Lifeforce* (1985) and his mediocre remake of *Invaders From Mars* (1986), but—coupled with the MPAA's refusal to give the film a rating and the death of the drive-in cinema—*Chainsaw 2* was another clunker at the box office. It is testament to the talents of Hooper and his cast and crew that the final film looks so good, and the cast is excellent (whether or not he was still wrestling with his own personal demons, Hopper brings a distant sadness to his role that works well). Viewed today, *Chainsaw 2* is nothing less than wonderful. Featuring some hilarious one-liners ("Lick my plate, you dog dick," "It's a dog eat dog world, and from where I stand there just ain't enough damn dogs," "Wiped out my younger years like a can of cheese whip") and brilliant comical sequences, the film is unforgettable. It's also of interest to see how the chainsaw family still remains together, through thick and thin. Even the barely mobile old Grandpa—"137 years old and still as fast as Jesse James"—is still at the side of his family. If the original film showcased a disturbed portrait of the American nuclear family—*Chainsaw 2* presents that same family nearing the point of mental saturation due to the demands of modern-day living. Largely misunderstood, but nonetheless a far superior film to the next two *Chainsaw* movies that followed, *Chainsaw 2* is one of the contemporary horror genre's finest sequels. It is also one of the most ambitious follow-ups to any successful film.

Standout Moment

With a wealth of razor-sharp dialogue and moments of seriously gruesome excess, it is hard to pick just one—but Perry being slammed across the head with the repeated blows of a hammer, courtesy of Moseley's horrific Chop Top, is perhaps the pinnacle of the film's bad taste humor.

Memories of the Film

"It is a hard X, and not an R-rated movie," states Tobe Hooper on *The Texas Chainsaw Massacre 2*. "I wanted a different film because of two things," he continues.

Played for laughs – few people were in the mood to watch a sequel to the terrifying original that aimed for the funny bone rather than the gut.

"Number one was that in the first *Chainsaw* we had very little special effects of the Tom Savini kind. There had been 10 years between making the original and *Chainsaw 2*, and in that length of time had come *Halloween*, Jason and the *Friday the 13th* films—and they were more visceral with what was on display. So I thought, 'Oh, maybe I should sprinkle a little of that in there.' I hired Tom Savini, and he's really the best at anatomically taking bodies apart onscreen (*laughs*). The second was that the first *Chain Saw* has this ironic, dark comedy in it, that comes totally out of the situations—I guess the most famous example is the bit where (Jim Siedow) goes, 'Look what your brother's done to the door.' It was played very natural, and only eight years after the film was released did people start tittering and laughing at these scenes as the film's stature grew. So I think *Part 2* was a kind or reaction to that—if the first was funny, I wanted the sequel to be funnier, but to remain dark. I wanted to go in the other direction and it came about one stage at a time."

Of course, *Chainsaw 2* did not attract the box office receipts of the first film. Why does Hooper think this was? "I think the original marketing on *Chainsaw 2* really missed the mark," he answers. "The film's poster had this *Breakfast Club* comedic aspect that really wasn't there. And at the end of the day the film was limited because it didn't get an R rating. It didn't get any rating. When I sent the film to the MPAA, as you can imagine, they just said, 'There's no way—there's nothing that you can cut out. Just put the titles in and that's it!' But that film was about the 1980s and that was its own weird time frame, you know? And they weren't able to advertise the film—so it later found its audience on tape and DVD." *Chainsaw 2*, like the first film and also Hooper's earlier *Eaten Alive*, was banned in Great Britain for some time. How does the director feel about this? "Not bad," laughs Hooper. "The interesting thing is that the first videotape I ever bought of the first *Texas Chain Saw* was at Harrods in London. Then it became one of the 'video nasties.'"

The only returning actor in the second film is Jim Siedow. Did Hooper never want to bring back original stars Gunnar Hansen, Ed Neal or Marilyn Burns? "Yes, I did," he maintains. "There were a few characters I wanted to bring back. With the first *Chainsaw* there was a lot of discourse, and misunderstanding, between the property owners and the participants. Well anyway, I got Dennis Hopper for less money—don't get me wrong, he still got paid handsomely...I hate talking about people's pay scale, but it comes down to 'How many movies have you been in and what does that make you worth?' And on our budget we couldn't afford to bring back all the stars that had been in the first *Chainsaw* and were now associated with that." The second film marked the last time Hooper would become involved in his hit property—with Jeff Burr taking over to direct the ill-fated *Leatherface: The Texas Chainsaw Massacre 3*. Is the director bothered that the franchise was taken out of his hands? "Well, of course in some ways you think it's great to see your creation live on and on, so there was always that aspect of it," admits the director. "But it never happened with me. I never made another one."

Following *Chainsaw 2*, Hooper's work would largely go straight to video. After directing such huge hits as the original *Texas Chain Saw Massacre* and 1982's *Poltergeist*,

Don't lose your head—it's going to be a cult classic in the years to come.

did this bother the filmmaker? "Well, you know these things happen," admits Hooper. "Sometimes it goes wrong. I think it would really have been cool to have a career where you don't have to validate yourself by making two movies every year. I ended up in television by accident—I directed an episode of *Freddy's Nightmares*, which acted as a prequel to the film series...I also did an episode of *The Equalizer*, which was an important episode because it was the first time television had addressed that America was beginning to be struck with a homeless problem. As far as TV movies go—I was in Brussels showing *The Mangler* and I got a script for a pilot called *Nowhere Man*. I read it and I thought, 'Oh cool,' it was very esoteric, reminded me a bit of *Prisoner*—how do you sustain it on TV for a while? So I did the pilot, and it featured a lot of suspense and drama and then it got picked up. Then I did *Dark Skies*—another pilot—then I finally did a comedy called *The Apartment Complex*. At the beginning, when I was a kid, I always thought more about doing comedies. I love that genre. *Chainsaw* was a reaction to going to a horror film and never quite getting what you wanted..."

Working with Tom Savini and complex special effects was nothing new to Hooper at this time. Previous to *Chainsaw 2,* the director had been responsible for such special effects-driven movies as *Poltergeist* and *Lifeforce*. From his more low-budget origins with the first *Chain Saw* and *Eaten Alive*, does the continuing reliance on special effects in films—and the advent of CGI (which Hooper would use for 2000's *Crocodile* and 2004's *Toolbox Murders*), bother the director? "God, I have mixed feelings about CGI, simply because they are no longer unique," he remarks. "*Jurassic Park* blew me away when I saw it back in '93. I just thought, 'Wow—technology certainly has developed,' I was viewing this world that could not happen without CGI. Since then it's become overused in creating things like dinosaurs. When you see other creations that are CGI you can usually tell. Even if it's a good CGI you can tell it's still a CGI—it's usually the only way to do these things. *Hulk*, on the other hand, was a different story—*Hulk* had some substance with its plot and I began to forget...I was so involved with the film that I forgot, I didn't think about the CGI. The trick is—total involvement, to try

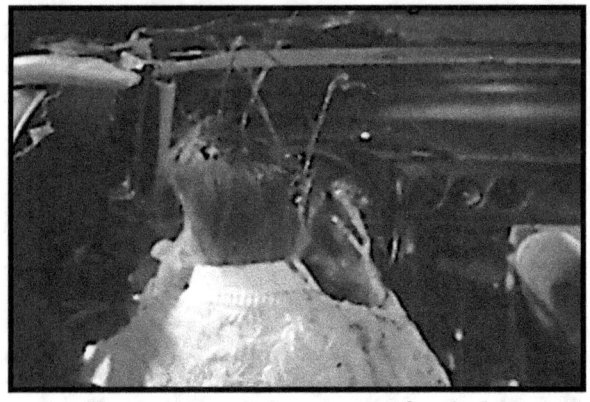
Hooper's sequel plays the gore for giggles

and pull the audience into the story and not insult anyone's intelligence. It should be the promise of seeing what is behind the door—you need a matrix, a structure, to pull the audience in—otherwise they'll just think, 'Why am I suddenly seeing all this stuff'?" I think using CGI elements can be very cool—they can be used to remove things such as wires or whatever..." So how would Hooper explain the recent returning interest in horror cinema, that includes a return-to-form from himself with 2004's *Toolbox Murders*? "It seems to me that in times that are politically charged, these things bubble up," he replies. "It's all a part of the alchemy of and the spirit of the time that we live in."

Actor Bill Johnson had the task of stepping into Gunnar Hansen's shoes for *The Texas Chainsaw Massacre Part 2* and he looks back on the role with pride. "We had a really good writer on *Chainsaw 2*, Kit Carson, and Tobe Hooper worked on the script as well," he explains. "Kit was relentlessly doing rewrites, I mean our script—as you know new pages have different colors—so we had a full rainbow going on! And Kit would be at the entrance to the set typing up his rewrites and ripping it out to give to us—'Here, learn this before you enter!' Fortunately I didn't have lines so I didn't have to deal with any of that, but Jim Siedow, he had these big speeches that Kit would give him, and he really came up with the goods. So that was pretty far-out." The actor is also shocked to find that the film was banned in the U.K. until 2001. "I just recently found that out," exclaims Johnson—"I didn't know that—I think that's pretty amazing." As for shooting a chainsaw duel with Dennis Hopper, the erstwhile Bubba Sawyer informs, "I wish I could tell you all about that—but it was the stunt double for me and the stunt double for Dennis that did the duel. Dennis did the close-ups, but it was just too dangerous for the actors to do that scene."

Alternate Critiques

"Viewed again in retrospect, and judged on its own merits, the movie is not quite a disaster, but it's a no more than competent and largely gratuitous rehash of the first film. There's only one truly effective sequence—the radio station invasion—and like so much else in the movie, it's dragged out too long, with humor that's overly self-conscious." (Michael Gingold, *Fangoria*, Issue 159, January 1997)

"*The Texas Chainsaw Massacre 2* does have its flaws. On its own, it seems a little lost and something akin to a punchline without a joke. Couple it with the first movie however, and the joke suddenly makes a whole lot more sense." (David Kerekes, *Fantasy Film Memories 3*, 1991)

"...if anything, even more of a study in derangement than the original—and a lot bloodier as well, for which it was routinely criticized." (John McCarty, *Movie Psychos and Madmen*, Citadel, 1993)

The Toxic Avenger

Director: Michael Herz/"Samuel Weil" (Lloyd Kaufman)
Produced by: Michael Herz/Lloyd Kaufman
Written by: Joe Ritter
Cast: Andree Maranda; Mitchell Cohen; Jennifer Prichard; Cindy Manion; Robert Prichard; Gary Schneider; Pat Ryan Jr.; Mark Torgl; Dick Martinsen; Chris Liano; David N. Weiss; Dan Snow
Special Effects: Jennifer Aspinall/Tom Lautten
Year: 1985

Plot Synopsis

New Jersey: a voiceover informs us about "pollution—the unavoidable by-product of today's society." Tromaville is introduced as the "toxic waste capital of the world."

A weedy young man called Melvin (Torgl) works at the Tromaville Health Club. At his workplace Melvin is always being harassed by Bozo (Schneider) and his girlfriend Julie (Manion), as well as the couple's two friends Wanda (Jennifer Prichard) and Slug (Robert Prichard).

Bozo, Julie, Wanda and Slug go out driving on a highway, where they play a game that includes running over children and people of minority race. A child rides his bicycle down the road, and Bozo speeds up his car—cheered on by Julie and his two friends. The child is knocked over and crawls across the road, covered in blood. Bozo reverses his vehicle and squashes the child's head. Julie and Wanda leave the car to take pictures of the boy's dead body. Bozo wants to continue the game, but Slug tells him he has to go home early to attend church the next day.

The next morning at the health club, Bozo and his friends hatch a plan to play a prank on Melvin. Julie seduces the wide-eyed cleaner and tells him to meet her later dressed in a pink tutu, as that really turns her on. A truck pulls up outside the Tromaville Health Club carrying barrels of toxic waste.

"Melvin the mop boy" (Mark Torgl) from *The Toxic Avenger*

Melvin arrives later to meet Julie, dressed in a pink tutu. He enters a dark room. Unable to see, Melvin ends up kissing a sheep and—horrified—he runs straight out of a window, whereupon he lands in one of the barrels of toxic waste. A nearby policeman tries to help him, but ends up on fire, as Melvin's skin turns green and begins to pulsate. Back home, the boy locks himself in the bathroom and finally transforms into a muscular, distorted monster (Cohen).

Officer O'Clancy (Martinsen) walks the streets where three criminals approach him—explaining that they want to pay him off. When the officer refuses, they threaten to shoot him between his legs, but Melvin comes to the man's rescue and brutally attacks the thugs.

At a press conference the next day, hosted by the town's Nazi chief of police (Weiss), O'Clancy talks about the monster that saved him. Tromaville's Mayor Belgoody (Ryan Jr.) is less pleased, however. The town's obese mayor is in on the extortion and theft that takes place throughout the town.

Melvin goes home to his mother (Sarabel Levinson), but she does not recognize her son and screams in horror. The Mayor tells some friends that he is going to set up a new toxic waste dump—this one only 20 feet away from the area's reservoir.

At a Mexican café, three robbers invade the food place, opening fire on a helpless victim. A beautiful blind girl called Sara (Maranda) has her guide dog shot and the leader of the gang (Larry Sulton) attempts to rape her, but Melvin enters the café and kills the three men. He takes Sara home, where the girl takes a shine to him. At the carryout place, the workers speak of being rescued by a "monster hero."

Another press conference is held, led by a crazy German academic called Dr. Snodburger (Reuben Guss). Back at the Tromaville Health Club, we see one of the Mayor's friends, Dennis (Dennis Souder) dealing heroin. Melvin enters the building and squashes Dennis's head in a weight-lifting machine.

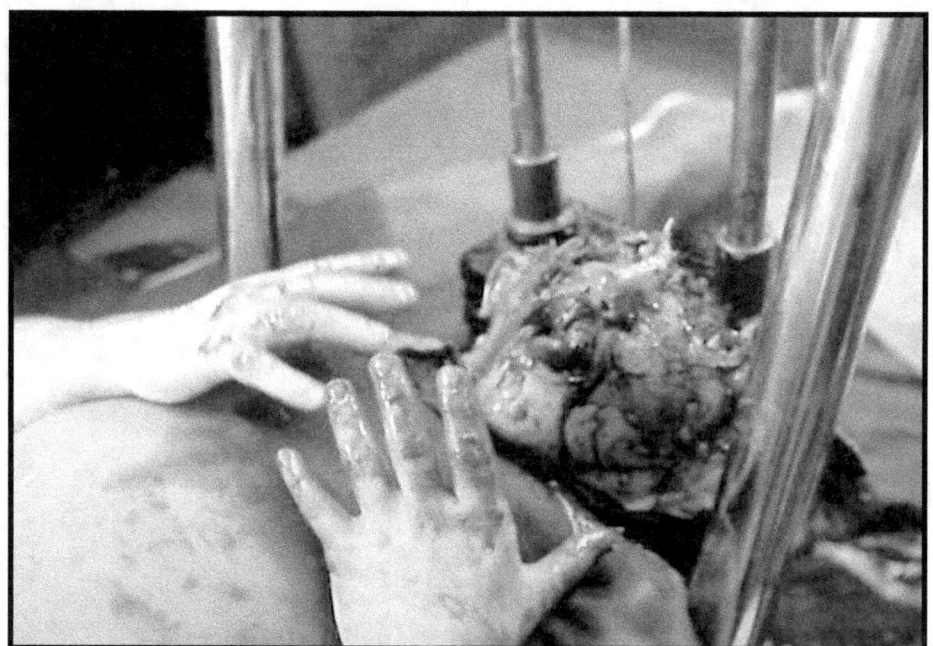

The Toxic Avenger takes bad taste cinema to an all new level.

Wanda lies in a sauna, where she masturbates over the pictures she took of the dead boy from earlier. Melvin arrives and kills her by burning her upon some hot coals. Later, Melvin saves a kidnapped girl by attacking the men that took her. Now gathering pace in his fight against evil, we see Melvin rescue children from being run over, help an old lady across the road and open a woman's jam jar. He is also beginning to fall in love with Sara, and a number of scenes show the two making love, moving in together and having fun. Melvin's work is not yet finished, however, and he returns to Tromaville Health Club to attack Julie with a pair of scissors. He also leaps into Bozo and Slug's car, throwing Slug to his death and forcing Bozo to drive off a cliff and to his doom. Later that day, Melvin tosses an old lady (Norma Pratt) into a washing machine. It later transpires that the old lady ran a white slavery ring.

Melvin goes home and explains to Sara that he is the "monster hero" and he cannot stop killing. As a result, the two agree to go for a holiday in an unspoiled local pasture.

The mayor puts out an army SWAT team to look for the monster. They find him in the pasture, living in a tent with Sara. A number of townspeople led by O'Clancy and Melvin's mother protest the killing of the monster and make a human shield around the tent. The army team drops their firearms, but the mayor opens fire on Melvin. His bullets are to no avail. Finally, the monster tears out the mayor's guts and the man dies. Melvin and Sara leave the site to the cheers of the gathered onlookers.

Critique

Troma has gained such a—justifiably—bad reputation for making awful films that is understandable why many fans now choose to avoid watching anything that carries the studio's name. However, unlike the truly banal *Class of Nuke 'Em High* (1986) or

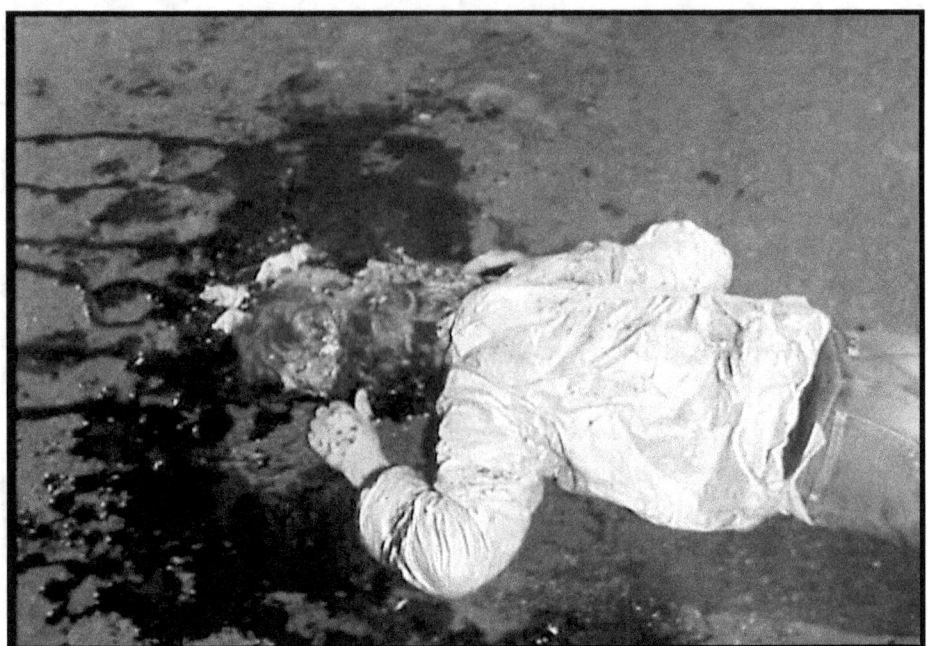

Troma never made another film even half as entertaining as *The Toxic Avenger*. Maybe the company shot all of its energy on the one movie?

Tromeo and Juliet (1996), *The Toxic Avenger* is a first-class bad taste romp that (with a mere 80-minute running time) never wears out its welcome. It is hard not to admire a film that is so exhaustive in its attempt to shock. With bad taste humor prevailing throughout *The Toxic Avenger*, rest assured that there is something in this movie to offend just about everyone. Even by today's standards, scenes such as a naked young girl arousing herself over pictures of a dead child—or a blind lady having her guide dog shot dead in front of her, remain truly shocking. That these moments are played for laughs should make the movie even more offensive, but within the cartoon-gore atmosphere of *The Toxic Avenger* it soon becomes clear that Kaufman and Herz are playing their own little game with the viewer. One can almost imagine the two men on set—daring one another to take things just one step further...to see how far the movie can push bad taste. However, because of the overriding slapstick nature of the many violent moments, a scene of pure political incorrectness is usually coupled with a ridiculous, gruesome gag—or some terrible overacting. As a result, even though it is hard not to leave *The Toxic Avenger* feeling slightly guilty for having laughed along with the movie, it is also difficult to remain disgusted for long. Nevertheless, this is surely a film that will split people's opinions in two. It is definitely not one to show to a new date, but as a movie to play at the end of a drunken party *The Toxic Avenger* has few rivals, and that should be recommendation enough.

Kaufman began production on *The Toxic Avenger* after reading an article in *Variety* claiming that the horror film was dead.[9] The resulting film not only helped to build a globally recognized studio, but also spent six months playing in New York alone.[10] Even so, *The Toxic Avenger* does seem like a weird movie to make in response to a statement declaring the burial of the horror genre. For a start, it is not scary—nor is it

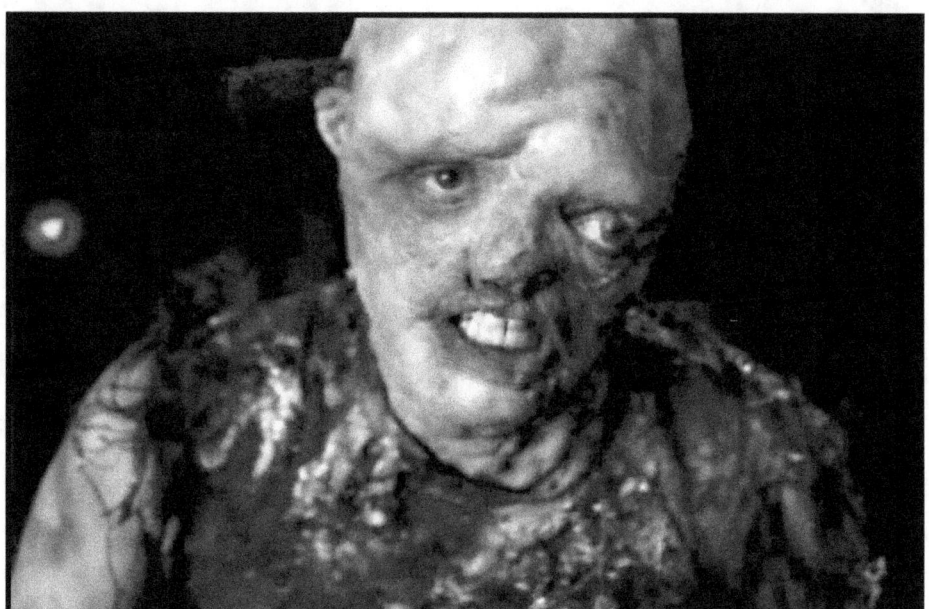
Hard to believe this ugly mug would later star in a children's cartoon series.

set up to be. Instead, the film has a wealth of Herschell Gordon Lewis-style gore effects that, however unrealistic, retain a certain power to them. Eyeballs are poked out, arms pulled off, guts ripped asunder, a young boy is run over twice—the second blow from the car crushing his head like a grapefruit—and a man has his face turned into an ice cream sundae. Such mayhem is graphic, but when combined with the slapstick tone of the film it does not seem as if anyone ever really suffers in *The Toxic Avenger*, even in spite of the often stomach-churning brutality.

The death of the child on the bicycle is probably the sole exception to this, however, and the episode remains the movie's only truly disturbing sequence. Herz and Kaufman are wise to conclude this unpleasant scene with the "I have to go to church" punchline, reminding the viewer that this is supposed to be funny after all, despite what we have just witnessed. Other examples of graphic nastiness are played for more obvious visual comedy. A man might lose his arms, but he is still up and fighting, and when Tromaville's mayor has his insides pulled out, he responds with a befuddled look and tries desperately to shovel them back into his wounded stomach. Even when someone is given a violent blow to the testicles, it does nothing but allow the man to speak in a high-pitched tone. This is the stuff of Tom and Jerry.

As with all of Troma's films, the acting in *The Toxic Avenger* is, for the most part, unimpressive. However, this said, there are at least a handful of performers who embrace their roles and overact in the manner required of the material, rather than in spite of it. Ryan Jr. as Officer Belgoody is a special standout, lending his huge frame to the role and coming across as believably sleazy. He seems to be the only proper, professional actor in the cast—and delivers a decent character portrayal. In her only screen role, the drop dead gorgeous Andree Maranda as Sara is never anything but physically pleasing to watch. While her attempts at acting blind become a little grating, and basically involve her mechanically rolling her eyes in the opposite direction from her costars, she is a

That population is set to drop once *The Toxic Avenger* is finished eliminating the bad guys!

far better actress than Pheobe Legere, who took over the part of Sara for *The Toxic Avenger Part 2* and *3*. The many jokes at the expense of the blind girl may appear a little obnoxious, but it is hard not to laugh when Maranda innocently pipes, "Watch the step," on the way into her house, before falling head over heels anyway. Kenneth Kessler lends his gentlemanly, English voice to the Toxic Avenger (yes, apparently being covered in toxic waste changes the way you speak as well!), and while the joke is somewhat obvious, it is also amusing. Although the rest of the cast is flat, or far too over-the-top, the script does give most of the characters distinctive personality traits to work with—something that would be sorely lacking in future Troma productions. Likewise, despite an obvious low budget, the film's direction is assured and confident—certainly not flashy, but neither does *The Toxic Avenger* ever give the impression of laziness, and the picture has obviously been crafted with at least some degree of thought.

The Nazi personae given to both Weiss as the Tromaville chief of police and to Reuben Guss as Dr. Snodburger can be seen to reflect Troma's, and Kaufman's in particular, cynicism toward authority.[11] The dominant villain in *The Toxic Avenger* is the town's mayor, and in line with Troma's general disdain of the control that big film studios have over Hollywood, it is hardly surprising that he should end up dead—having been seen to exploit the "little guys" throughout the film. Ultimately, one begins to suspect that the Toxic Avenger character is something of a fantasy figure for Troma itself. The studio commonly casts itself as the victim of corporate Hollywood, fighting the good fight for quality independent cinema. Hence, in the tale of *The Toxic Avenger* at least, Kaufman has his "monster hero" —who takes out the bullies and saves the good guys, such as the fast food employees or the hard-grafting police officers. Done in the twilight of a major city (New Jersey), perhaps "Toxie" is bringing his own little piece of socialism to America.[12] It is a fantasy of the studio's own making, and in light of the fact that Troma—despite their boast of saving independent cinema—invariably produce awful films, *The Toxic Avenger* is an enjoyable and imaginative farce.

Standout Moment

"Why don't you show a little guts?" screams Toxie as he hauls out the mayor's intestines. Sick and messy...

Memories of the Film

Speaking to Lloyd Kaufman and attempting to get him to stay on the subject of one of his movies is difficult, if not impossible. The result is the following conversation, recorded at Cannes 2004, where Kaufman was intent on promoting his company's salvation of what he likes to call "the independent spirit," as seen on such "making of" documentaries as the one found on the *Terror Firmer* (1999) DVD. "Umm...I think the truth is important," begins Lloyd Kaufman when asked about his very public profile as Troma's president and the fact that such exposés on his company often present him in an honest, but sometimes unflattering, light.

Everything from blondes in bikinis to Nazi police officers are served up in the name of laughs.

"You know, I think young people should learn how Troma makes movies and learn that you can be idiots and survive for 30 years making movies where people get their heads squashed. Making movies about incest—making movies that nobody wants to see. The point is that if Troma can do it and survive for 30 years, then

anyone can do it. You don't have to work for Harvey Weinstein at Miramax and make *Shakespeare in Love*. You know? You don't have to make baby food. *My Big Fat Greek Wedding* is an entertaining film, but it's a piece of shit—it's baby food. Independent film is dying...so I think it's important—even though the documentary is about how I make movies—maybe I look like an asshole, well so what? At least I'm a sincere asshole, and I take the movies very seriously. Yeah, I take the movies very seriously and I take myself very seriously...and I masturbate a lot (*pauses*) but that is the meaning of Christmas." That's Kaufman all over for you, he'll begin letting you into his character and then—almost protectively—take a U-turn and start talking nonsense again. It is, of course, very funny, but it also makes for a frustrating and unpredictable conversation.

Regardless of the criticisms toward Troma's releases, there is no denying that Kaufman has worked hard to strengthen his studio's visibility in what is an unforgiving and merciless industry. In a rare moment of reflection, Kaufman looks back at how he started out and the events that led up to the creation of Troma. "My first feature-length film was around 1967—we made *Rappaccini*, based on the Hawthorne short story called *Rappaccini's Daughter*. It was feature length and then I did *The Girl Who Returned*—which I directed when I was at Yale, and we shot that with a Bolex, wind-up

She's blonde and beautiful – and she's dating *The Toxic Avenger*? Oh, I see, she's blind as well...

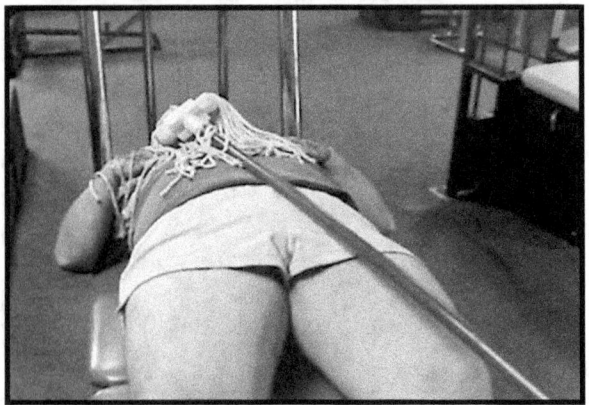

Another dead drug dealer at the hands of *The Toxic Avenger*.

camera. It was black and white, 16mm. Then *Sugar Cookies* in 1971, which was the first 35mm movie I made. I took it to Cannes and I slept on the beach that year, and I had the two 35mm cans. I couldn't even ship it—I carried it on the plane, I couldn't ship, couldn't afford hotel rooms. But we made deals, we rented theaters and buyers went in and we sold to Australia, the U.K. and I think Belgium.

"So that was sort of the early filmmaking days, instead of going to film school I attached myself to talented directors—or directors whom I felt were talented and who would go on to bigger and better things like John Avildsen, whom I met on *Joe*. Then we did *Cry Uncle*, I raised some money for that...and obviously I worked on *Rocky* and all that stuff, but that was basically learning. And it also paid the rent at Troma. I did production managing jobs too and for *Saturday Night Fever* I was the location executive—and it paid the rent and also taught me about movies." So is Kaufman still proud of these early movies? "Yeah, the only one I don't like is *Big Gus, What's the Fuss?* We gave that away—we didn't control it. We let other people control it—even though Michael Herz and I raised all the money. I met Michael when we did *Big Gus, What's the Fuss?* We shot it in Israel, and we made every mistake possible."

Focusing on *The Toxic Avenger*, how did Kaufman feel when his violent splatter movie was turned into a popular children's cartoon show called *Toxic Crusaders*? "Yes, well, that wasn't our fault," he states, apologetically. "The cartoon just arrived because the toy company had made some toys, but we made a movie where a little boy's head gets squashed by the wheels of an automobile and a girl masturbates over the pictures. People get their arms ripped off and naturally it is made into a children's environmentally correct cartoon show." Would Kaufman agree that *The Toxic Avenger* is his company's best work? "Well, I think *Terror Firmer* is my most personal film," he argues. "It's based on my book, *All I Know about Filmmaking I Learned from The Toxic Avenger*, and so I prefer that."

Kaufman remains proud of how Troma has influenced future generations of bad taste filmmakers. "You know, James Gunn—with whom I wrote *Tromeo and Juliet*, he went on to write the new *Dawn of the Dead*," he beams proudly. "Now when they do a Troma retrospective in the States, they put *Dawn of the Dead* in there because Troma is such an influence on that movie. I think what is interesting is that Quentin Tarantino is head of the jury here at Cannes and he's talking about Troma in the papers—we've got *Dawn of the Dead* playing here and that is a Troma influence. Eli Roth, who made *Cabin Fever*, did the commentary track for our DVD release of *Bloodsucking Freaks*. I think that makes me feel better than anything—knowing

that we have good people who are now working in the establishment. And talented people and they will hopefully restart the independent spirit, which we are losing."

Alternate Critiques

"Pushing (better make that *shredding*) the envelope of good taste, *Avenger* cracks jokes about the blind, elder abuse and aiming shotguns at children." (*Entertainment Weekly*, Issue 23, May 2003— voted the 24th "Top Cult Movie")

"As with all Troma product, the emphasis here is on creating a film of legendary cheesiness....Alas, this frequently translates to onscreen stupidity.

The gore is served up by the shovel load in *The Toxic Avenger*.

Joe Ritter's screenplay probably reads much funnier than the film that came out..." (*Fangoria's Best and Bloodiest Horror Video*, 1988).

"The mentality of this savage, enjoyable romp is captured in the exclamation of a would-be-rapist: 'I never cornholed a blind bitch before!'" (John McCarthy, *Official Splatter Movie Guide Vol. 2*, St. Martin's Press, 1992)

Two Thousand Maniacs!

Director: Herschell Gordon Lewis
Produced by: David F. Friedman
Written by: Herschell Gordon Lewis
Cast: Thomas Wood; Connie Mason; Jeffrey Allen; Ben Moore; Gary Bakeman; Jerome Eden; Shelby Livingston; Michael Korb; Yvonne Gilbert; Mark Douglas; Linda Cochran; Vincent Santo
Special Effects: None credited
Year: 1964

Plot Synopsis

Rufe (Bakeman), a young Southerner, sits hidden atop a tree, and looks at an approaching car through a pair of binoculars. He signals to his friend Lester (Moore), who watches from the ground. Lester brings out a detour sign and the approaching car disappears down another road. The road leads to Pleasant Valley, where it is the town's centennial (1865—1965). A group of three men sing a song about the South rising up, while a child (Santo) strangles a cat.

Two married couples arrive in the town—David and Beverly Wells (Korb and Gilbert) and Johnny and Bea Miller (Eden and Livingston). They are followed shortly afterward by another pair of guests: Tom (Wood), a schoolteacher whose car has broken down, and Terry Adams (Mason), a beautiful young blonde. Mayor Buckman (Allen) welcomes the new arrivals to Pleasant Valley and informs them that they are the guests of honor.

Shown to their hotel rooms, Johnny and Bea begin arguing. Bea is convinced that Johnny had his eye on one of the pretty locals called Betsy (Cochran), while Johnny believes that Bea was flirting with the rugged Harper (Douglas). The phone in their room rings and Johnny answers to find Betsy on the other end. She convinces him to come outside for a walk. He does so and shortly after, Bea receives a phone call. She is asked out by Harper and instantly obliges.

Harper and Bea walk to a nearby field, where Harper brings out a knife. Bea asks what he needs a knife for, and Harper cuts off her thumb. Bea arrives at the mayor's office with Harper, in a state of shock. Lester and Rufe arrive and pin her down to a table, where Bea has her arm cut off.

Back at Tom's hotel room, he voices concern to Terry—convinced that something is not right. Tom leaves to make a phone call and does not return—meaning that Terry attends that night's barbecue by herself. When she arrives, Betsy sits with John, who is

As an example of an early splatter film, *2000 Maniacs* has a charm all to itself.

drunk. Strange limbs are being fried on a spit. Suddenly Tom appears from the shadows and asks Terry to come and see something with him. The locals give chase but fail to catch them.

Tom finds a grave in memorial of the people of Pleasant Valley, who were slaughtered by Yankee soldiers during the Civil War. The grave claims to be "a testament to the vengeance pledged in their memory." Tom concludes that the "guests of honor" are to be sacrificed as an act of "blood vengeance." The two escape back to their hotel.

At the barbecue, John is tied to four horses and quartered. We see one horse run away with his arm. The locals seem unsure of what they have done, but Rufe rouses them into singing "Dixie."

The next day David is separated from his wife and taken to a barrel rolling event by Betsy. Once there he is placed in a barrel that has nails hammered into it by the mayor. He is thrown down a hill and dies.

Tom and Terry escape from their hotel and are chased by Harper—who falls into a pond of quicksand and drowns. Back at the events, Beverly is tied up under a huge rock. Whichever Pleasant Valley citizen hits a well-placed bulls-eye with a stone or a ball will see the screaming girl squashed. Rufus hits the winning ball, and Beverly dies instantly.

Tom and Terry con young Billy (Santo) into providing them with their stolen car, claiming they will give him candy if he can help. When the two retrieve their car they drive away, chased by the locals. Later at the police station, the couple take a breath analysis test and then they are told a local legend about the ghosts of slaughtered townspeople rising up to take revenge.

With Pleasant Valley now having disappeared into a wave of mist and the ghoulish locals back in their graves, Tom and Terry drive to the state line—beginning a new relationship together.

Critique

Two Thousand Maniacs! was the second film by director Herschell Gordon Lewis, following 1963's *Blood Feast*. With *Blood Feast* introducing graphic bloodletting to

Mayor Buckman (Jeffrey Allen) and Rufus Tate (Gary Bakeman) and Betsy Gunther (Linda Cochran) are the local yokels who terrorize two couples from out of town.

a cinema audience, and even today remaining a rather messy viewing experience, it was always going to be difficult for the filmmaker to top his previous film in terms of graphic violence. Moreover, when you've shown an audience something once, it is then difficult to grab the same amazed and/or horrified reaction a second time. Subsequently, when Lewis finally did attempt to top the carnage of his debut horror picture, the results (as with 1970's *The Wizard of Gore* and 1972's *The Gore-Gore Girls*) were so distasteful as to eliminate the charm that permeated his early movies. Therefore, with *Two Thousand Maniacs!* Lewis appears to take the opportunity to craft a more competent film—and the result remains the director's best and most accessible work. Neither as slow-moving as *Blood Feast* or *Color Me Blood Red* (1965), nor as misogynistic and distasteful as his aforementioned two films from the 1970s, *Two Thousand Maniacs!* has proven so endearing to its faithful cult following, that 2005 sees the release of a bigger-budgeted remake entitled *2001 Maniacs*. Although Lewis made films on a minuscule budget with varying degrees of competency, it is somehow endearing to note that a purveyor of low-budget, sleazy films has unwittingly created a legacy all his own and, in doing so, contributed to motion picture history. Thus, whenever someone comes to a gruesome demise onscreen (even with such a mainstream example as Dennis Hopper's decapitation in 1994's hit *Speed*), rest assured that one can trace the origin of such bloody stunts back to Lewis.

Two Thousand Maniacs! is, unlike *Blood Feast* and many of Lewis' subsequent splatter films, a well-paced movie with competent, tongue-in-cheek acting from the Pleasant Valley citizens (Jeffrey Allen as the mayor is a special standout). *Playboy* cutie Mason and her costar Wood, both carried over from *Blood Feast*, remain wooden, but strong support from Bakeman and Moore (who look to be having a swell time going overboard with their roles) more than make up for the dearth of thespian talent from the main players. Regardless of her lack of acting ability, the camera still loves Mason's

Local Harper (Mark Douglas) falls into quicksand while trying to lead a victim to the slaughter.

naturally striking looks, and there is a charmingly nostalgic moment when she pulls up her dress to bathe her bare legs in a lake. This brief moment of cheesecake acts as a subtle reminder that Friedman and Lewis opted to make graphic splatter films, as opposed to graphic sex features, because nudity was already deemed to be obscene back in the 1960s while the depiction of gruesome death had just never been attempted. Of course, the special effects in *Two Thousand Maniacs!* remain primitive and—as with *Blood Feast*—cutaway shots to onlookers are used to fill in the gaps between a limb being axed away or someone falling foul of a barrel full of spikes. By today's standards, these laughable depictions of gory mayhem are more likely to arouse a smile than revulsion.

Despite Lewis playing his murders for comic effect, when one imagines an audience of 1964 viewing the movie, it is easy to believe that many viewers were left reeling from the carnage on offer and letting the jokes pass them by. Southern, redneck stereotypes are in abundance in the movie, leading to some tough lines ("Having more fun than a beagle on a coon hunt")—and some brilliant moments of black comedy. Best of all is when, having murdered Eden, the downtrodden townspeople are aroused into a sing-along of "Dixie." Also of considerable hilarity are the ridiculous deaths, played out as carnival games. Hence, the "barrel rolling event" turns deadly when Korb is spun to his death in a barrel decorated with nails. His wife, Gilbert, meets the film's most prolonged end when she is placed in a bizarre variation of "hit the bulls-eye and win a prize," involving an enormous rock hinged over her body. Ironically, *Two Thousand Maniacs!* was filmed on the same plot of land that Walt Disney would purchase, shortly before his death in December 1966, for Walt Disney World.

If one thing is likely to remain in the viewer's head, long after *Two Thousand Maniacs!* has finished, it is the movie's insanely catchy theme tune—"The South is

Gonna Rise Again." Played by a group of men identified solely as "The Pleasant Valley Boys," and written by Lewis, the song introduces the movie in a unique fashion. Perhaps more appropriate to a small-town drama than a horror movie, the song has nonetheless become something of a cult favorite over the years. Although Lewis is an acquired taste, even among the most dedicated of trash film hounds, *Two Thousand Maniacs!* stands out from the rest of his repertoire in being both intentionally funny and detailing a plot that actually has a reason to showcase the buckets of blood synonymous with the filmmaker. Lewis never was one to spend time throwing messages or symbolism into his movies, always sticking steadfastly to his belief that cinema is a business, but even so—in the mid-1960s a mob of prejudiced, blood-crazed Southern Americans living in the past was ever so slightly topical. It might pain the director to hear this, but he does appear to have touched on at least one theme that was contemporary back in 1964. A redneck variation on *Brigadoon*, *Two Thousand Maniacs!* is likely to endure for another 40 years, especially in light of the bigger-budgeted remake *2001 Maniacs*, as future generations fall in love with its over-the-top mayhem.

"The barrel rolling event in *Two Thousand Maniacs* can only end in tears..."

Standout Moment

The death by a barrel with nails hammered into it. Now that has got to hurt...

Memories of the Film

"I see too many *auteurs* in the film business who care about themselves but not about those people out there, who may be sitting in the theater or watching a DVD. My attitude in both marketing and in filmmaking is that these are works aimed at others and their reaction is what matters, not mine," states Herschell Gordon Lewis. "The advice I might give to a young, aspiring filmmaker is not a piece of advice that that person wants to hear. It would be, 'Instead of looking in your mirror and admiring your own ego, look out the window and consider the people you are trying to entertain.' That's a clue that seems to leave some people clueless. The purpose of making a movie is not self-gratification. If that is what you want to do, then don't release it commercially. Show it to your friends, put it on some video so you can watch it late at night and say, 'What a great artist I am.' Starve in an attic somewhere, but don't call yourself a filmmaker. A filmmaker is someone who makes films for others, not for himself or herself."

Of course, some would argue that Lewis's many on-set duties during the making of his splatter films might make him something of an *auteur*. "I did a lot of the jobs because I didn't want to pay anybody," laughs the director. "Some people say, 'Well, you wrote the music for *Two Thousand Maniacs!* and it was your voice on the soundtrack.' But there is a rationale behind that which is strictly one of money. When I started to score the original *Blood Feast*, I did that because I was getting prices from musicians who were not Shostakovitch, they were just hack musicians. And their price to score the film was more than the movie cost. This was insane! Now, I had had some background in music and I said, 'I know exactly what I want.' So I sat down and tortuously scored that movie to the point where I was about to give up...not because I was an *auteur*, but because I didn't want to pay anybody! In fact, when it came time to record the musical background, I had a trombone, a cello, an organist, a fellow who played several woodwinds, and I had kettledrums. I had rented the kettledrums but I'd forgotten to get a kettle drummer, so I played the kettledrums myself! I didn't think anything of it. I thought any moron could do that. Now, I'm not trying to insult symphony kettle drummers, but I knew what I wanted. Knowing what you want and being able to project that out is worth a lot of money. If somebody else had scored that picture then I'd probably have hated what that person did. That person would have superimposed onto the score what he wanted. I used what I wanted."

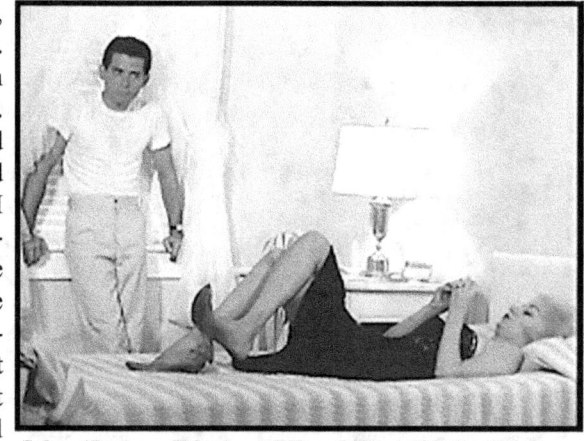

John (Jerome Eden) and Bea Miller (Shelby Livingston) have no idea what awaits them in Pleasant Valley.

Certainly, the film's theme music has stood the test of time as a well-remembered cult oddity. "When it came to *Two Thousand Maniacs!* I wrote the theme music for that because I knew what I wanted but I didn't want to use my voice for that. So I hired a musical group—they showed up and the film began with a singsong. It's almost like Rex Harrison in *My Fair Lady*, It's not really singing (*singing in deep voice*) 'There's a story you should know from a hundred years ago.' In came their singer and he started (*singing in squeaky high voice*) 'There's a story you should know...' I said "Wait a minute, it's not supposed to be done in falsetto.' He was a tenor and it didn't come off as a tenor. It had to be a bass baritone. I had the deepest voice in the room and I knew the tempo I wanted, so I did it. It wasn't an *auteur* intention at all...I didn't like having to hang the lights for these movies, that's one thing I was so delighted about in the new movie. I could sit in the director's chair and direct and say, 'Wow, I'm now an executive at last after all these years.'"

After the spurting crimson on show in *Blood Feast*, Lewis does admit that theaters were prepared for his next film. "Yes they were," he states. "Theaters went wild over *Blood Feast*, but many feared community reprisals. We heard repeatedly, 'I'd play that picture if it weren't so bloody.' So *Two Thousand Maniacs!* was a compromise. I think the psychology in the film works. Impending evil grows. Unlike with *Blood Feast*, the acting is passable. And I have an avuncular posture here, even using my own voice on the theme music—which I still can sing song today...Also, the comedy—that was why this film was received on a higher level than the watershed *Blood Feast*. Even some critics who had given a brutal reception to *Blood Feast* relented after seeing this one. At no time did I ever predict the longevity this movie would enjoy. I really do feel like a proud parent whose child has won major recognition."

The director also confirms that he did not know that Walt Disney World was forthcoming on the site where the shoot took place. "I had no idea. I even remarked, 'I'd like to own some property down here.' How I wish I had carried through on that idea!" Lewis is also happy to discuss his favorite moment in the movie. "My personal favorite is the barrel-roll. For some reason, audiences start to cringe as the first nail goes through the barrel. I was part of that effect too, crouching inside a rolling barrel with a hand-held camera. From an audience point of view, the first effect of 'the thumb and then the arm' have the greatest impact, probably because people aren't expecting it.

"Even today, when they have seen so much, when films have gone so far beyond what I did in terms of gushing blood, *Two Thousand Maniacs!* still has an effect on people," comments the director. "Of all the films I've made, *Two Thousand Maniacs!* is the one I didn't want remade. I'd certainly like to remake *The Wizard of Gore*, but ownership has been out of my hands for years, and now a production company is making *2001 Maniacs*..."

Alternate Critiques

"With a wry (and this time intentional) sense of humor, *Two Thousand Maniacs!* once again offers a catalogue of carnage, but this time backed with a vaguely interesting plot and a bevy of eccentric characters. It's a surprisingly good film..." (David Flint, *The Dark Side*, Issue 48, August 1995)

"...this is the finest bluegrass musical/gore movie ever filmed." (*Fangoria's Best and Bloodiest Horror Video*, 1988).

"This immediate follow-up to *Blood Feast* features the usual Herschell Gordon Lewis high-school acting, mannequin-and-ketchup FX and a bluegrass soundtrack provided by The Pleasant Valley Boys... Hee haw!" (Vid Viscount, *Toxic Horror*, Issue 3, April 1990)

Tim Sullivan and David Friedman on the set of the Two Thousand Maniacs remake.

CHAPTER 5
ECLECTIC GEMS
Weird and Wonderful
A Boy and His Dog

Director: L.Q. Jones
Produced by: L.Q. Jones/Alvy Moore
Written by: L.Q. Jones
Cast: Don Johnson; Susanne Benton; Jason Robards; Tim McIntire; Alvy Moore; Helene Winston; Charles McGraw; Hal Baylor; Ron Feinberg; Michael Rupert; Don Carter; Michael Hershman
Special Effects: Frank Rowe
Year: 1975

Plot Synopsis

A nuclear explosion appears—after which we are informed, "World War 4 lasted 5 days." It is 2024 A.D., and Vic (Johnson) roams the barren deserts of America with his dog Blood (voiced by McIntire), who speaks to him telepathically.

Blood tells his owner that a female lies 25 miles away, but by the time Vic arrives she has been raped and killed by a passing gang. Blood teaches Vic some history as they walk, telling him that World War 3 ended in 1983.

Vic insists that the dog find him women to mate with, but Blood expects food in return. They argue over which should come first. Vic steals some food from a gang of travelers who proceed to shoot at him, but he escapes. Later that night, Vic and Blood watch a movie at a scruffy outdoor theater where black and white porn reels are playing.

The next morning, Blood informs Vic that he senses a lone female living underground. Vic opens a cover to an underground house, and finds a beautiful young woman getting dressed (Benton). He confronts her and tells her to undress. She does not resist and strikes up conversation, which confuses Vic. We find out her name is Quilla June

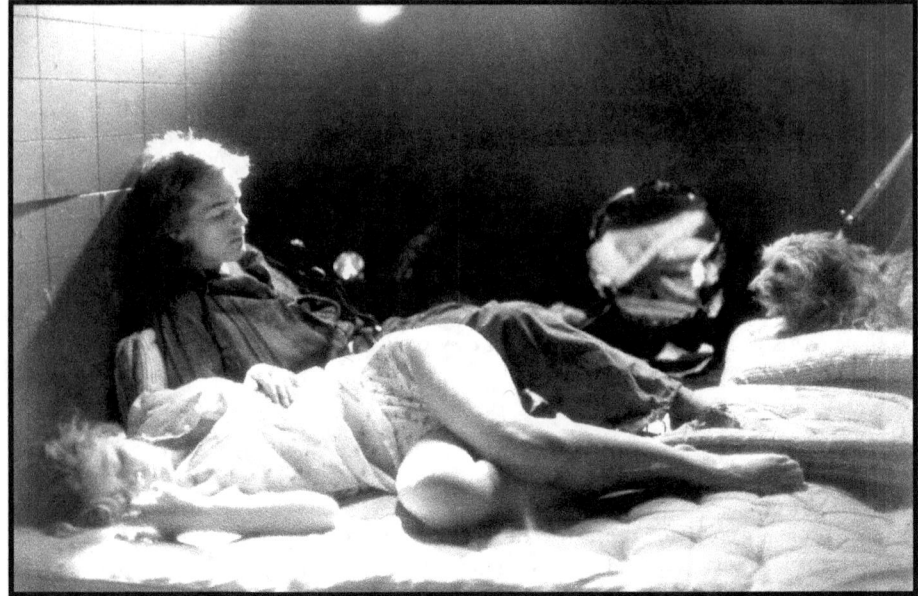

Vic (Don Johnson) and Quilla (Susanne Benton) spend the night together as the annoyed Blood looks on.

Holmes. Blood informs Vic that the hideout is being invaded by another rogue gang, and urges his master to escape. Vic refuses and a gunfight ensues, whereupon he and Quilla June are victorious. Afterward the couple spends all night making love, to the disdain of Blood.

Quilla June informs Vic that she lives "underground" and that he should follow her. Although he refuses, he is smitten enough with her to trace her tracks when she disappears the next morning. Coming to a door in the middle of the desert which will lead him "underground," Vic cautions Blood to stand guard and promises to return.

Vic walks down a dark staircase and lands on some green grass, full of gravestones. A sound system announces, "sound tours into the past." Suddenly he is grabbed from behind and knocked unconscious by a mysterious, heavily built man (Baylor). When Vic awakens he is being washed in a bathtub, while men and women with painted faces look on. A marching band passes by outside. All of the men are dressed in a shirt and dungarees. In what could be a church or a town hall, Lou Craddock (Robards), the "Head of the Committee," lords over events and sentences those who have disobeyed the rules of his society to "the farm" (meaning death).

Quilla June speaks to Craddock and asks if she will be rewarded with a position on the committee for bringing Vic underground. Craddock is largely dismissive of her. Quilla June complains to one of her friends that she is being underappreciated and wants to overturn Craddock.

Vic is led in and told that his job will be to impregnate several young women. However, this is not quite as easy as he thinks; the boy is tied up and has his sperm forcefully sucked out off his body by a machine. Quilla June comes to his rescue and asks him to fight Craddock so that the two can set up a new committee. Vic refuses and a heavily built man, called Michael, strangles some of Quilla June's friends who have assisted in Vic's escape.

Jason Robards as Lou Craddock (far right) is the Head of the Committee who rules the underground society.

Vic shoots at Michael until the bullets finally reveal that he is a robot. "Let's get another Michael out of the warehouse," shouts Craddock casually, as Vic and Quilla June make their escape.

Outside the bunker, Blood is starving and can barely stand. He needs food. Quilla June tells Vic to forget about the dog and to carry on without her. When we fade back into the film, a fire crackles and Blood is on his feet again. "She had particularly good taste," laughs the dog, as he walks into the distance with Vic.

Critique

A nightmare vision of the future, based on a story by Harlan Ellison, *A Boy and His Dog* still retains its ability to unsettle 30 years since its release. The film contains an especially dark and unpleasant ending, whose humorous write-off ("She had particularly good taste," laughs Blood after eating Benton) manages to make the movie's bleak finale all the more hideous. However, the apparent decisiveness with which Johnson has decided to slaughter his female companion manages to fit in well with the overriding tone of *A Boy and His Dog*—where humanity has doomed itself to scavenging for food and sex, and does so without any degree of compassion. It is probably inevitable that the feature's coldness will, even today, isolate some viewers, but there is a grim power to the movie's depiction of a futuristic human race that haunts a war-torn world.[1] This is humanity at its most primal, starting anew, and it is fascinating to watch Johnson and his dog (both dislikable characters from the get-go) treading the desert sands and bickering with one another, sometimes to comical effect, while sniffing out rogue females. Johnson's instinct is to mate, but in this wasteland—where no character ever appears to indicate love—sex is forced and reduced to rape. Thus, when Johnson encounters Benton and she puts up no fight, it makes the boy even angrier and the film's first sign of humanity—in this instance guilt—actually surfaces. It would be nice to say that this

Don Johnson's character fails to win sympathy from the audience—once a misogynist, always a misogynist.

makes Johnson's character more identifiable, or easier to like, but it does not—and his postcoital discussions with Benton are dismissive and isolated. Once a misogynist, always a misogynist, one presumes...

In Robards' underground sanctuary, *A Boy and His Dog* contains at least one extended sequence that represents a nightmare come to life. Awash in bright colors (the all-too-perfect green grass and the dazzling white and blue costumes—both luring the viewer into a false sense of security), this hidden world finally comes to resemble a macabre funhouse, complete with murderous robots and Robards' demented dictator. Initially appearing to us in the form of scenic trees and grassland, which is in stark contrast to the endless desert that we have previously been privy to and appears all the more luxurious and reassuring as a result, the film's underground society might even make George Orwell shudder. Starting from scratch, Robards sentences death upon anyone who fails to comply with his rigid set of rules (which the film never makes entirely clear—all we know is that fucking with this society equals certain doom).

That Robards sends people to their demise in the surroundings of what appears to be a church, while dressed like a pastor, may be making an all-too-illustrative point about the possibilities for abuse in a relationship between religion and state. Certainly in the film's atmosphere of anarchy there appears to be no place for authority outside of this right-wing, reactionary hierarchy, which instills its wisdom through a Biblical-like fear of punishment. There is no denying that Robards is pictured as a brutal and heartless dictator—surrounded by his own riches, while casually passing death sentences upon his luckless subjects—and the message is clear: when rebuilding itself, humanity will commonly look for the easiest option to get itself back on its feet, even if that option means being lorded over by someone of extreme means. Hardly a radical statement, as history teaches us, but nonetheless one that echoes with a harsh, horrible reality.

In a rare turn as a director, Jones—who is most recognizable as a supporting actor in numerous films that include *The Wild Bunch* (1969) and *Casino* (1995)—handles himself well. In a decision that was unusual for a low-budget film back in 1975, he chose to shoot *A Boy and His Dog* in wide-screen, often framing the action in long shots—effectively indicating the stark, vast wasteland that Johnson and his dog walk upon. The end result works well, and although the cinematography is never too flashy, there is a confidence behind the camera that results in some striking moments, as with the aforementioned underground sequence.

Jones also manages to coax a tremendous performance out of Johnson and the rest of his cast. *A Boy and His Dog* remains the best thing that the *Miami Vice* star has ever put his name to, and although he strikes a despicable presence, it is difficult not to feel some pity for the poor chap when, held against his will by Robards, he finds himself tied to a machine that sucks the sperm from his body. Benton, a largely unknown actress, casts an attractive onscreen presence—exuding a false sense of innocence when we first meet her that later evolves into a cast-iron confidence and desire for control. By building up her character's strength as she plans to override the authority of Robards, the film makes it all the more shocking for us to accept her demise—at the hands of her lover, no less. Robards, probably the most famous name in the cast, is in fine form too, although it is difficult not to feel that every human onscreen is being overshadowed by the incredible performance of the movie's dog.[2] At first, the animal's telepathic form of speech seems ridiculous, but the canine is so convincing in every way that it doesn't take long before we are utterly invigorated by the critter's every turn.

Robards is pictured as a brutal and heartless dictator, surrounded by riches while casually passing death sentences upon his luckless subjects.

A Boy and His Dog **plays with the viewer's emotions and teases the audience.**

Playing with the viewer's emotions perfectly, Jones teases us—as *A Boy and His Dog* reaches its nihilistic coda—with the prospect of a happy ending. Of course it is not to be, and the sight of Johnson and his pet dog walking away from a fire that has been used to cook the remains of Benton may have been intended as comical, but ultimately it leaves one feeling rather depressed. Here, the film has gone ahead with its early promise of delivering a bleak, hopeless future—and while, even today, we are used to being reassured with a positive coda, this is not the case with *A Boy and His Dog*. Perhaps this is what is so upsetting about the movie's finale: the director has actually gone ahead with the strength of his convictions and kept the tone of his picture consistent right up until the last second. Jones indicates from the very start of the movie—where we see the utter desperation of mankind in the wake of another World War—that this is one feature that can only end in tears. Kudos to him for making *A Boy and His Dog* one of the oddest, not to mention darkest, futuristic nightmares ever to unfold on the silver screen…and you have to love that theme tune.

Standout Moment
Johnson's awkward, forced romancing of Benton in her underground hideout followed by a night of lovemaking carried out to Blood's sometimes hilarious vocal commentary.

Memories of the Film
"Basically I'm an actor, that is what I do and that is what I enjoy," confirms L.Q. Jones. "When I go into work my job is to please the director. Apart from being an actor, I have a company that makes pictures and when I'm mad enough we go out and make one. I say when I get mad enough—but *A Boy and His Dog* happened because my cin-

While Vic thinks he is manipulating Quilla, it's really the other way around.

ematographer brought in a book and dropped it on my secretary's desk and said, 'L.Q. you want to read this,' and I thought, 'Okay,' and I took it home that night and started reading it about 3:30 in the morning. And I read the first third of it and I stopped and I said, 'What a shame, because this is truly marvelous and I'll get to the end and I'll be disappointed.' Then I'm two-thirds of the way through it and I'm saying exactly the same thing. About 4:30 or 5:00 in the morning and I finish it. I sat there hysterically laughing because of what I'd just read and because the author had pulled it off. So I brought it in the next morning and dropped it on the desk of my producer and said, 'This is what we are going to do next.'"

The ending of *A Boy and His Dog* still holds up as a shocking, but darkly suitable, climax. However, Jones admits that many viewers think Johnson killed Benton in order to eat her—when, in fact, it was to keep his dog alive. "It's really very important to me that people understand that," comments Jones. "I would guess that this is a mistake that 90 percent of people make until they stop and think about it or until I draw it to their attention and it is totally dear to the story. What I was trying to do with that comment, where Vic says he's not hungry, was to emphasize that this has nothing to do with it. The fact is that he *is* hungry, but now you have the real logical part of the story—the world has to keep going, humanity has to move ahead, but he can't commit suicide and let the dog eat him because the dog and Quilla June do not get along. They don't get along at all—she's too conniving and she doesn't give a fig, but the dog does. So if he kills the dog, or lets the dog die, he and Quilla June can't stay alive because they can't compete. So it comes down to the bare necessities—she's the one that's got to go…so that the two of them can keep going. So he does it for the dog and then the dog asks him if he's hungry and he says, 'I don't want any.' Well, he's starving to death, but he damn sure is not going to eat because he loves Quilla June and, other than Blood, it's

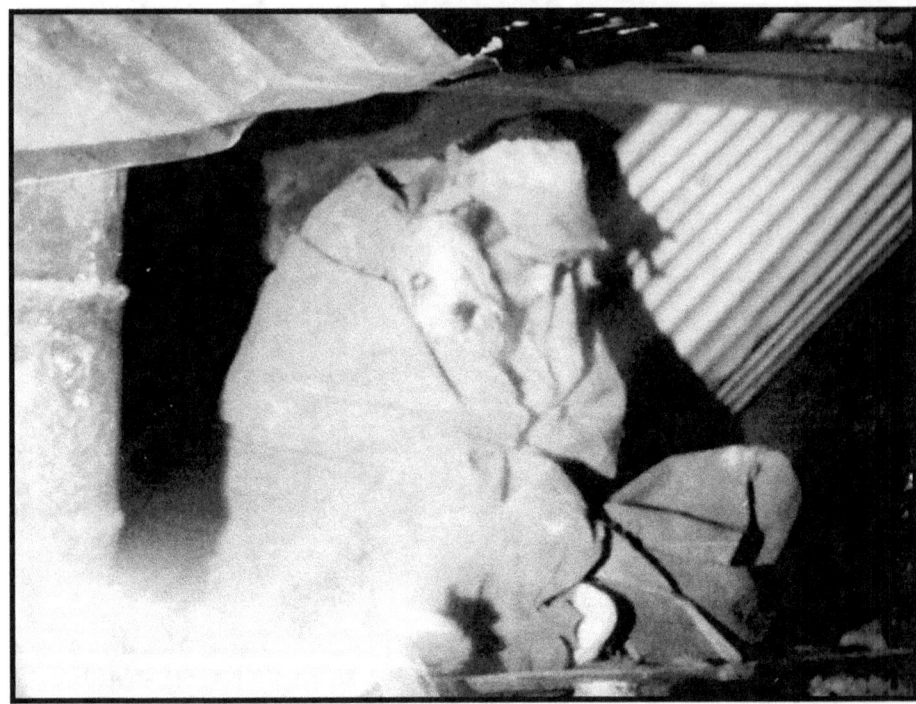

Despite the misleading title, *A Boy and His Dog* is not a movie for children.

the first time he's ever loved anybody. So you can see that it is very dear to me that people understand this."

How was the reaction to this ending back when the film first came out? "Well, I think I can safely say that it is the most unusual ending," laughs the director. "Even by today's standards, we still don't do this. The reaction was this—I've had people throw up, I've had people faint, I've seen people nearly riot. I have been with the picture in groups as small as one and as large as 15,000, so it is awfully hard to know what an audience reaction is going to be. It's one of these pictures where when I say to people, 'I hope you like it,' they think I'm saying it because of the money. But I'm saying it because it is one of these pictures where if you see it and you like it—you'll never forget it, and if you see it and you hate it—you're screwed because you will still never forget it! It's going to be there in your mind and so, when we went out a second time, the people who saw it the first time in the theater brought along parents and brought along children. So DVD will probably bring along a whole bunch of new fans. Back when it came out it was accepted and appreciated the most around colleges. Kids didn't understand what took place, older people were put off by it, and I can't even break it down to that—I'm just saying that in general terms."

Speaking of kids, the title of *A Boy and His Dog* alongside the jovial title music initially indicates, very wrongly, that this is a children's movie. Was Jones every worried that the movie would be interpreted this way and that he might face the wrath of several angry parents as a result? "That was a total concern," he replies. "I actually have a file here of alternate titles for *A Dog and His Dog*. I have maybe a thousand titles lined up here," laughs Jones. "The picture is rated R, we took a chance and included that in

A Boy and His Dog depicts a bleak, hopeless future.

our advertising, which we are not supposed to do. But we wanted people to be aware of the fact that it was an R-rated picture and with a title like *A Boy and his Dog,* this is conjuring up Walt Disney or Huck Finn floating down the Mississippi—and mothers going to pick their children up when it is over—that was a total concern to me.

"I showed my picture to an audience made up of those who were involved in making it. I invited about 30 people to come see the picture. I specifically said that they should not bring children and when I showed up for the screening, lo and behold, there were four children that were between the ages of six and 10. What do I do? I thought the parents should have to explain the thing, so we rattled on with the picture. After the picture had finished I looked up and the children had gone. I thought, 'Uh-oh,' and two days later I called the parents of the children. I was told that 'They loved it—absolutely loved it and they now have a new game in the neighborhood called Blood Says.' So they saw the things they wanted to see and they saw nothing else—Blood was great fun because he was a dog and the fact that he could communicate was super for them. From that point we still put it out R-rated, but anybody could come in and I don't believe many pictures have come out a second time and been that successful, and it might even come out a third time—we're planning that now. *A Boy and His Dog* did far better the second time than it did the first."

Don Johnson is excellent in *A Boy and His Dog*—and even his detractors will likely have to admit that this cult classic sees the actor in fine form. "We went along fine for a good three days and I'd heard he could be hard to work with," mentions Jones. "Well, Don decided that he should be calling the shots. And I said, 'That is a great idea! As soon as you put the money in, then you can do that, now if we have any more of this horseshit you're going to be on the bus and I'll do the part.' Well, that was the end of

L. Q. Jones

that and then we got along great. He did a marvelous job and I can't imagine anyone doing a better job than Don did. I think it was the best thing he ever did or ever will do. Don had already done a couple of fair-sized pictures. But look at the picture and learn from it, because you should never work with animals. They say, 'Never work with animals or children because they'll eat you alive.' Well, how would you like to work with an animal that can talk?"

Did Jones ever feel tempted to have the dog speak onscreen—rather than telepathically? Not an easy thing to pull off in a pre-CGI world, but surely it crossed the director's mind? "You're walking on very thin ice," states Jones. "We're talking about communicating, we're not talking about a dog speaking, so it has to be ESP. So that's the way we wanted to do it from the beginning, and there was never going to be any other way. The dog is the star of the piece—no mistake about that. If you take the star out of your picture then you got nothing left, and we realized that going in, and it's tough to pull off. Besides being tough—when did you ever see the dog looking at his trainer in *A Boy and His Dog*? Never? Well, isn't that amazing? No matter where it is, if you look closely, that's the way he's been trained to work. They do it by hand signal—'Sit up, roll over and blah blah blah.' Our dog never looked at, or for, his trainer—the first time ever in the history of our business that we ever did, and I'm not sure if you'll ever see it again."

How did Jones find the right animal for the part? "Our dog had been in pictures here for a long time," he says. "I'd started looking at dogs, and I thought we'd never find the dog to do the part. I had even outfitted myself in wardrobe so that if we never got the dog we'd do it with a human being and we'd carry on. It would have been a shambles. When we auditioned him, we did that scene in the theater where Blood sits next to the guy, and he did it perfectly. That's when I realized that I got Blood."

Surprisingly, Jones admits that despite several offers he has never opted to do a sequel to *A Boy and His Dog*, despite an idea for it. "I would like to start partially where I left off," he maintains. "Harlan and I came up with a character called Spike, who also happens to be female, and Spike also happens to be 10 times tougher than Vic. Remember at the tail end of the picture? That's where we would start—and right at the tail end of it you'd hear a rifle, and she's been following him for a long time and she wants Blood. This is her way of getting him. Three times every year someone comes in and says, 'We want to do the sequel to *A Boy and His Dog*.' I never see eyeball-to-eyeball with them so it never happens, and so far Harlan has never come up with the story. When it

The finale of *A Boy and His Dog* even today will still shocks audiences.

came out, one critic called me 'an American Fellini.' I could give you a bullshit answer as to why I have not directed many pictures (Jones' other feature is 1964's *The Devil's Bedroom*), but when it comes right down to it I always compare things to *A Boy and His Dog*. My high point came early. *A Boy and His Dog* was brilliant for its day and brilliant for today—so don't screw it up by doing something normal! Why didn't I direct more pictures? I just never found one that was worthwhile."

One director that was clearly inspired by the film was George Miller, whose *Mad Max* trilogy owes a lot to the film. Is Jones aware of this? "I understand that—from people who have talked with Miller—he took *A Boy and His Dog* and went commercial. That's what he did! He was much smarter than I was. I took it and went the other way with it. Does that make me real smart? Probably not. Did it make me real wealthy? I can guarantee you not. But I got to do what I wanted to do. I wish I had the talent that the picture shows! Our picture made the most out of the wide-screen, if you recall the way it is shot we use extreme lefts and extreme rights of the screen. And we do many sequences about half a mile away from the camera. I'm still very proud of *A Boy and His Dog*."

Alternate Critiques

"...overrated...a real shambles...it's a violent, vulgar black comedy." (Allan Bryce, *The Dark Side*, Issue 39, April/May 1994)

"A comic science-fiction nightmare....Distinguished by writer/director L.Q. Jones' offbeat approach and Blood's wonderfully sardonic dialogue." (Michael Gingold, *Fangoria*, Issue 153, June 1996)

"Unpleasant and badly made film....For some fans, a cult film." (*Hoffman's Guide to SF, Horror and Fantasy*, 1991, Corgi)

Cronos

Director: Guillermo Del Toro
Produced by: Bertha Navarro, Arthur H. Gobson
Written by: Guillermo Del Toro
Cast: Federico Luppi; Ron Perlman; Claudio Brook; Margarita Isabel; Tamara Shanath; Daniel Giméz Cacho; Mario Iván Martínez; Juan Carlos Colombo; Farnesio de Bernal; Javier Álvarez; Gerardo Moscoso; Eugenio Lobo
Special Effects: Laurencio Cordero
Year: 1993

Plot Synopsis

In 1536 an alchemist—fleeing the Inquisition—invented a key, known as the Cronos device, that would allow him to gain eternal life. In 1937, the building where the alchemist had been living collapsed and killed him. We see the nude body of a dead man, hung upside down and bloodstained, in the alchemist's apartment—but the ancient man's secret has gone with him to his grave.

In the present day, an old man—Jesús Gris (Luppi), who runs an antique shop—comes across the egg-shaped Cronos device hidden in the base of a statue. Standing by his side as he examines this new antique is his young granddaughter Aurora (Shanath).

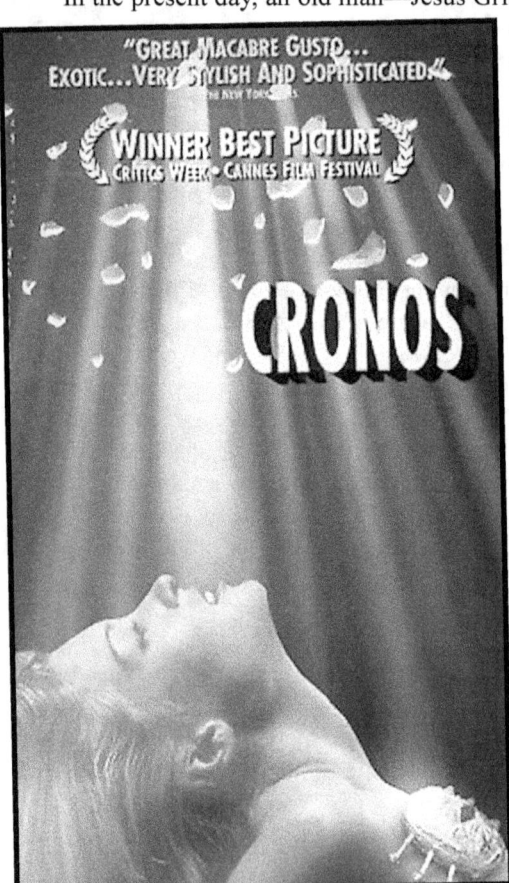

An old dying tycoon, Dieter de la Guardia (Brook), traces the Cronos device to the antique shop, and sends his well-built nephew, Angel de la Guardia (Perlman), to retrieve it for him. However, upon arriving at the shop and buying the statue that once housed the ancient contraption, the old man is upset to find that it is missing. While playing with the Cronos device, Gris is pierced by metal claws, which suddenly sprout from the object. He subsequently finds himself with an insatiable lust for human blood.

Gris approaches Dieter de la Guardia to find out what the device is. He is told that 40 years ago an Alchemist's manuscript was found, "written backwards in Latin," which explained that an insect is captured within the contraption and—in exchange for fresh blood—the creature gives eternal life to the object's keeper. Much to the tycoon's dismay, Gris will not reveal where the contraption is kept.

To the confusion of his granddaughter and wife (Isabel), Gris goes missing at a New Year's Eve ball when he leaves them to go the bathroom. In the bathroom, Gris notices that someone has suffered a slight cut. When the toilet is deserted, he licks the blood from the floor. Suddenly, Angel de la Guardia enters the bathroom and knocks Gris unconscious. The man takes Gris outside and beats him with the intention of finding out where the Cronos device is. After delivering a succession of blows, Angel de la Guardia throws Gris off the edge of a cliff.

The old man's body is found and taken to a funeral parlor where he is presumed dead—but the now-immortal Gris escapes from his coffin and returns to his house. His granddaughter reunites him with the Cronos device and Gris goes on to confront Dieter de la Guardia for information about what is wrong with him.

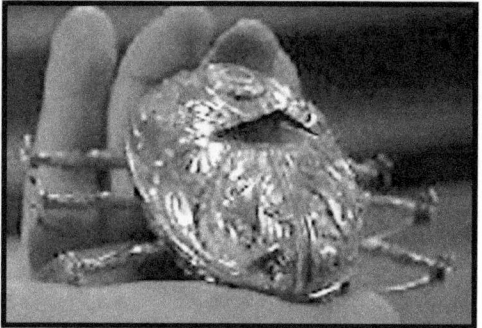

Jesús Gris (Federico Luppi) and Aurora (Tamara Shanath) examine the Cronos device.

Dieter de la Guardia informs Gris that he will live forever as long as he keeps allowing the Cronos to feed from him. The man then stabs Gris and attempts to steal the device for himself, but Aurora comes to her grandfather's rescue and kills the tycoon.

Angel de la Guardia fights Gris on the top of his uncle's residence, in front of a bright neon sign. Finally, the thug falls to his death and Gris survives. Seeing his granddaughter bleeding, Gris almost cannot hold himself back from attacking the little girl, and the result is that he destroys the contraption and ends his days dying in bed—surrounded only by his wife and Aurora.

Critique

An engaging film with beautiful visuals and a morbid feel, though not without some degree of dark humor, *Cronos* is the debut masterpiece from Guillermo Del Toro who would, understandably, find Hollywood knocking at his door following this movie. Despite bigger budgets and studio backing for projects such as *Mimic* (1997) and *Blade 2* (2002), Del Toro has never crafted anything quite as wondrous as *Cronos* while working in North America. Ironically, it was only when he returned to his native Mexico to make 2001's acclaimed *The Devil's Backbone* that the filmmaker equaled the achievement of his first movie. A director with a gift for expressing himself through the most captivating of images, at his best Del Toro is perhaps most reminiscent of Italy's Dario Argento and Mario Bava.

Colors play an effective part in the landscape of *Cronos*. For instance, the lair of Brook's character, Dieter de la Guardia, has a very cold and faded appearance—whereas the antique shop owned by Luppi is bright and colorful. As Luppi becomes more ill, however, his character's surroundings become darker and more sinister—reflective of early German Expressionism—and this is echoed in the old man's clothing as well. Perhaps, therefore, it is inevitable that when the man is lying in his deathbed at the film's finale, Del Toro should choose to light the scene with a redemptive, bright hue. Despite the gorgeous, symbolic color schemes and sets evident throughout *Cronos*, the most dazzling scenes in the film are those that are shot from within the title device. Such an audacious example of pure style brings to mind the sort of ambitious, albeit effectively needless, camera trickery that Argento would attempt while still in the prime of his career. The shot of a bullet traveling through the barrel of a gun in Argento's rarely seen *Opera* (1988), for instance, might be a comparable example.

Cronos has remarkable visuals.

    Cronos is a film noteworthy for more than its visuals, of course. Applause needs to be given to Del Toro's performers, with the lead role of Gris perfectly captured by Luppi and excellent support given by familiar character performer Claudio Brook. Furthermore, the young Margartia Isabel, who never utters a word, gives fantastic screen time for an unknown child actress (*Cronos* was her first film role), perfectly portraying her character's confusion and sympathy for her grandfather. The moment where she is finally persuaded into giving Luppi the Cronos device, which she has taken to hide, is poignant and truly disturbing. During this sequence, the little girl seems reflective of a young child handing her alcoholic relative a bottle of booze. She is at once obedient to her grandfather's demands and yet fully aware of the damage that the mysterious contraption is doing to him. Perlman, an actor who would also go on to bigger things with prominent roles in Hollywood blockbusters such as 1997's *Alien Resurrection* and Del Toro's own *Hellboy*, is similarly wonderful as the bullish Angel de la Guardia, a foul-mouthed buffoon who allows *Cronos* most of its comic relief. An underrated actor of physical comedy, Perlman is both moronic and threatening in his role.

    Although Del Toro's visual connection to Argento and Bava has been touched upon, the director surely owes some of the more disgusting moments in *Cronos* to the "body horror" genre that is typified by Canada's David Cronenberg. Thus, the scene where Luppi reaches into his stomach and pulls away layers of dead flesh reminds one of a similar moment in Cronenberg's *Videodrome* (1982), where James Woods reaches deep within a vagina-shaped puncture that has appeared on his belly and, after rummaging around, inexplicably locates a gun. Such bizarre imagery, written down on paper, does not have quite the same effect as when shown on the screen and, as such, this near-poetic moment—whereupon Gris begins to comprehend the seriousness of his transformation—leaves the viewer both shocked and saddened.

This is because, unlike with most vampire films, Luppi's is a tragic character and we actually care for him. It is not only with revulsion that we watch the scene where the sil-

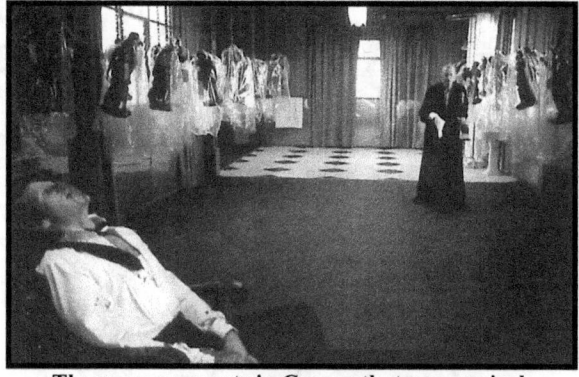
There are moments in Cronos that are magical.

ver-haired character slowly licks blood from the floor of a public toilet, but with concern because he might be caught. Del Toro stages this particular moment with maximum suspense, as we squirm at the thought of the old man being seen by anyone while carrying out this truly disgusting, and degrading, act. The director has stated, in the past, that Luppi's resurrection from the dead is intended to present him as "a Christ figure."[3] If this was indeed the intention, then it seems bizarre that the old man is never seen as a saint, following his return from the dead. Instead, he continues to struggle with his addiction to the Cronos device, before finally finding his own path to redemption.

There are moments in *Cronos* that are magical and, in turn, there are many sequences that are both horrific and tragic. As a debut, the film is wondrous—and while some may feel that Del Toro's substance might be a little overbearing, take solace in the fact that *Cronos* was clearly an attempt by a director to show the world what he was capable of. Young filmmakers take heed—if you only have one chance to let the world know about your talent, make sure to pull out all the stops. Del Toro did and the result is one of the finest tales of terror to come out of the nineties. The film is, without doubt, one of the 10 best genre releases of its decade, and it dragged the vampire film into the 21st century.

Standout Moment

Gris enters the toilets and finds that a man has cut himself. As the wounded chap exits, the old vampire scoops up some of the blood from around the sink, only to be interrupted by another member of the public, who sees the spilt crimson and washes the mess away. With only a little left on the floor of the washroom, Gris slowly, carefully bends down onto all fours and begins to lick up the gore—unaware that Perlman is indeed watching him...

Memories of the Film

"*Cronos* was my first movie," remembers Guillermo Del Toro. "The idea was to do a different take on the vampire genre that was set within the Mexican way of life. So I decided to do this vampire film that was set indoors—a drama about this guy who dies and comes back. In *Cronos* we have this character that is so pathetic and so dysfunctional that he has to drink blood from the floor of a toilet! That was the idea—to make something alternative to the Hollywood vampire productions of the time such as

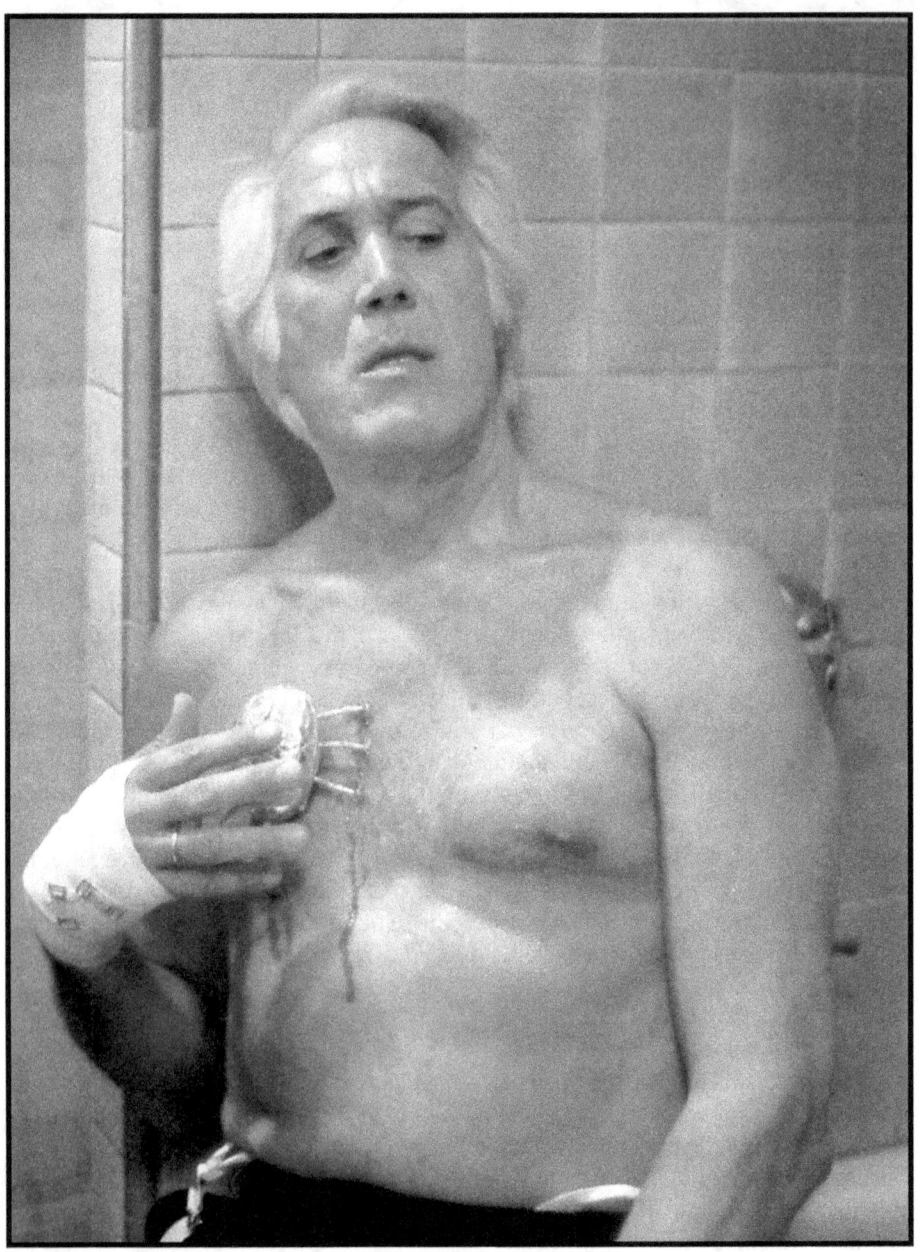
Dieter de la Guardia (Claudio Brook) risks everything for eternal life.

Interview With A Vampire, which has these gorgeous, superb production values. The Francis Ford Coppola *Dracula* as well, which I loved—it is very sumptuous—but it is very easy to drink blood from the neck of Winona Ryder! It is rather more difficult to lick blood from the floor of a toilet."

The director laughs when asked if he made *Cronos* in the hope of kicking off a career as a genre director. "I thought that I was ending it," asserts Del Toro. "The movie that we made was going completely against the grain of what was expected from a Mexican film. So the support for it when it came out was a surprise. I ruined myself economically making *Cronos*...we did not know that anything would come of it—and when it did well, it was very moving for me." With *Cronos,* Del Toro made a genre movie that appeared to have little influence from Hollywood. Indeed, stylistically the film looks to be

Director Del Toro on the set with Perlman and Tamara Shanath.

far more indebted to European horror movies. "For the most part, yes," syas the director. "There are many European horror directors I love—Pupi Avati, Mario Bava, Lucio Fulci—and lately the great horror movies that have come from Korea and Japan. In the 1970s there was this huge resurgence of Euro horror with films like *Daughters of Darkness* and all the Jess Franco stuff. And the guy who did these French movies with vampires...Jean Rollin. So Europe is incredibly interesting in its take on the genre—I also love *Eyes Without a Face* and (René Clair's) *Beauty and the Beast*."

Surprisingly, Del Toro mentions that there was no outlet for horror fans in his native Mexico, at the time of making *Cronos*. "No, there was no scene at all unfortunately," he reveals. "From the very moment I wanted to do fantasy or horror movies I never thought that I would get to do one. These films were nonexistent in Mexico except for a couple of Z-grade, direct-to-video movies that were made for something like two dollars, and here I was wanting to make *Cronos,* which was to be the most expensive Mexican film ever made. Not just that, but it was to be a horror movie! Everyone was against me, because they didn't want me to make this huge error and lose a lot of money..." 2002 saw Del Toro return to vampires with the big-budget *Blade 2*. Does this reveal an interest in the immortal bloodsuckers from the director? "I think vampires are an interesting mythology," maintains the director. "You can put social, sexual, political or religious themes into the story of a vampire. Look at George Romero's film *Martin*, essentially it is a film about a kid who does not fit into society. With *Blade 2* we just wanted to make a great action/adventure film. You see, you can do different interpretations..."

Throughout his career, one thing has been very evident with Del Toro—the director always works from his own script—presumably a personal decision? "Oh, 100 percent," answers Del Toro. "I think that if you don't direct your own script, you are likely to have your script altered by other writers. Things can get muddled when you work from someone else's script." After the "studio interference" that went into his 1997 American movie *Mimic,* Del Toro was happy to return to his more humble routes with *The Devil's Backbone*—an independent movie that stayed true to the artful, renegade spirit of *Cronos*. "When I was offered *Blade 2,* it was before I made *The Devil's Backbone*, but I told the studio that they must let me make *The Devil's Backbone* first. I needed the freedom to do that film," states Del Toro. "I wanted to do *The Devil's Backbone*, quote—unquote, 'for myself,' and then I was willing to do a studio movie. The main

(Left) RON PEARLMAN plays a wealthy executive attempting to find the fountain of youth from an elderly antique dealer (right, played by FREDERICO LUPPI) in Vidmark's CRONOS.

pleasure of making *Blade 2* came from putting all these great monsters onscreen and I think we had a creative bad guy. Yes, ultimately I think we had a really interesting bad guy. I was prepared to do a movie that was going to be different from *The Devil's Backbone*."

Now at the top of Hollywood following such hits as *Blade 2* and 2004's *Hellboy*, Del Toro nonetheless remembers one independent genre classic that affected him and remains a personal favorite. "I became a vegetarian for four years after I saw *The Texas Chain Saw Massacre*, and then I went back to being a carnivore," laughs the director. "After seeing the movie, everyone came out and went for dinner and they were eating meat. I couldn't stand the sight of meat after seeing that film. It just made me want to puke (*laughs*). So, yes, it made an impression on me."

Alternate Critiques

"*Cronos* alternates between the ominous and the outlandish (sometimes blending the two); an out-of-steam anticlimax puts only a slight dent in my admiration for the film and its quirky and stylish qualities. *Cronos* is worth an hour and a half of any horror fan's time." (Dr. Cyclops, *Fangoria*, Issue 141, April 1994)

"Deft, imaginative, original and gruesome variation on the vampire myth, stylishly directed and conjuring an atmosphere of genuine terror." (*Halliwell's Film and Video Guide*)

"...if you prefer a little more thought and heart to your vampires rather than the endless round of neck-biting, then *Cronos* is definitely for you." (Ian Miller, *Shivers*, Issue 14, January 1995)

Dead and Buried

Director: Gary Sherman
Produced by: Ronald Shusett
Written by: Dan O'Bannon/Robert Shusett
Cast: James Farentino; Melody Anderson; Jack Albertson; Dennis Redfield; Nancy Locke; Lisa Blount; Robert Englund; Bill Quinn; Michael Currie; Christopher Allport; Joseph G. Medalis; Macon McCalman
Special Effects: Stan Winston
Year: 1981

Plot Synopsis

George (Allport), a photographer, shoots some pictures on a beach. He finds himself distracted by a beautiful blonde (Blount). The girl asks if he would like to take some pictures of her. He agrees, and she removes her top. "I'm going to put this in *Playboy*," the excited photographer exclaims.

Suddenly George is attacked by a mob. They tie him to a post and soak him in gasoline, finally setting him alight as they photograph his agony. "Welcome to Potter's Bluff," pronounces one of the locals.

Following this grisly opening, we meet Sheriff Gillis (Farentino) and Dobbs (Albertson), a local coroner. They both check out the photographer's overturned car, which houses the man's charred body. To the Sheriff's surprise, the man lets out a scream and is still alive, despite his burned appearance.

The next morning at a cafeteria, the waitress (Linda Turley) who serves a group of men coffee is the same woman who set George on fire. The Sheriff suspects nothing. Harry (Englund) teases him by saying, "If you can't solve a traffic accident, what are you going to do if a murder takes place?" A drunken man (Ed Bakey) walks across a pier only to be slashed with meat hooks by the locals of Potter's Bluff. Once again, the dying man is photographed.

At the mortuary, the Sheriff grills Dobbs about the burned man. He tells Dobbs that he thinks the man in the accident may have been burned before

Sheriff Dan Gillis (James Farentino) finds the peace of his town shattered by a series of grisly murders.

he was put in the car. The Sheriff is suddenly alerted to the dead body of the old drunk.

The Sheriff finds out what hotel the burned photographer was staying in. He speaks to the hotel owner (McCalman) about the man—trying to place his identity. The hotel owner tells the Sheriff that his wife had actually come by to visit the photographer. Back home, the Sheriff's wife Janet (Anderson) admits a passing acquaintance with the man, and says that she visited him to buy some photographic equipment for the school at which she works. Later, the Sheriff asks the school principal (Robert Boler) if he knows about this, but the man states that he does not.

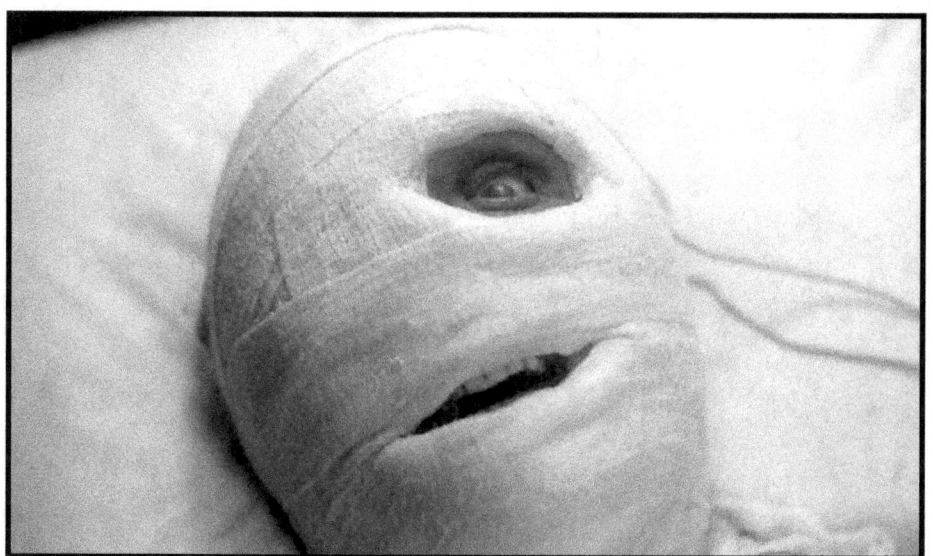

Innocent photographer George (Christopher Allport) is attacked and burned by the local townspeople.

At the hospital, the Sheriff asks to speak to the burned man, but his request is not granted. The blonde lady from the beginning of the film dresses in a nurse's outfit and sneaks into the ward that holds the photographer. When she finds him, the man is bandaged up except for one exposed eyeball. She plunges a hypodermic needle into his pupil and kills him.

A grave is built for the photographer. Dobbs castigates the Sheriff for not finding out more about the man's identity. Back home, the Sheriff cannot bring himself to confront his wife about why she lied to him about buying photographic equipment.

A young couple and their son arrive in Potter's Bluff. They stop to ask directions at the cafeteria and are greeted by the locals, including the photographer, who shows no evidence of being burned alive. After leaving a local restaurant, the family is chased into a remote house and stalked, but they manage to escape.

The Sheriff accidentally runs someone over on the same night, but when he leaves his vehicle to investigate, he finds a still-moving arm clinging to the car's radiator grille. He chases the man that he runs over, but eventually loses sight of him. Back home, the Sheriff once again approaches his wife to see if she knows anything about the strange events and murders, but she denies any knowledge. In her cupboard he finds a book on alchemy and witchcraft, alongside a dagger.

Janet gives her husband a roll of film to be developed. Harry calls the Sheriff to tell him that he has found a deserted car on the beach. The car belonged to the family that appeared to have escaped. Ben, the hotel owner, tells the Sheriff that he just saw the dead photographer walking around. The Sheriff does not believe him.

Meanwhile a female hitchhiker (Lisa Marie) is picked up and killed by the locals—including the drunken man who had been slaughtered earlier in the film. After this murder, the girl is brought back to life at the local mortuary by Dobbs. A scientist (Medalis) who is helping the Sheriff with the case has acid fed into his nose. In gruesome detail, his flesh melts from his skull.

The Sheriff digs up the grave of George to prove he's really dead—but the body is gone, only the heart remains.

The Sheriff digs up the grave of the photographer, following Ben's story. Inside the coffin he finds only a human heart. The Sheriff puts out an arrest warrant for Dobbs and goes into town to pick up the film that he handed in to be developed.

When played, the film shows the Sheriff's wife murdering someone that she is in bed with. The perplexed Sheriff goes straight to the mortuary and finds out that Dobbs has been bringing the dead back to life as murderous zombies. Angered, he shoots Dobbs on the spot. The Sheriff also finds out that his wife is one of the walking dead. After shooting her, he takes her to the cemetery and buries her.

Back at the morgue, however, the Sheriff is in for a nasty surprise when he finds out that the man his wife killed in the film footage was himself. Dobbs tells the Sheriff of his final, vicious secret. He too is one of the man's reanimations.

Critique

If the above plot description sounds like the sort of film you can barely picture existing, then take heed—*Dead and Buried* plays out every bit as madcap as this synopsis indicates...and it is none the worse for it. The feature is a very unnerving experience, with a considerable amount of plot twists and very little adherence to logic, as well as some fantastic special effects courtesy of future Oscar winner Stan Winston. Winston demonstrates his early talents through a number of memorable set pieces, including the now-infamous needle-through-the-eyeball gag and a charred skeleton that suddenly springs back to life. However, the movie's splatter highlight is when Albertson's crazy coroner regenerates the facial features of a murdered female hitchhiker. Reminding us of a time when stop-motion effects were still used (instead of CGI), this is a morbid but fascinating spectacle and holds up rather well. Likewise, although not overly gruesome,[4] *Dead and Buried* does contain a number of jolting murder sequences, each one especially well telegraphed.

Sherman's movie pulls the viewer into a world where, similar to many Italian horror classics (see Argento's *Inferno* or Fulci's *The Beyond*), bizarre things happen without any proper explanation.[5] For instance, the entire point of Albertson bringing the dead back to life to commit murders is never explained—unless we accept the fact that the old man is simply insane. Indeed, there appears to be no other rational explanation for the reanimated homicidal maniacs that live in

Another innocent victim is netted for the crazed Dobbs.

Potter's Bluff (or why the Sheriff and his wife do not hold any murderous desires themselves), other than that more dead bodies provide the town coroner with fresh material to reanimate. Furthermore, despite the initial impression that the residents of Potter's Bluff only slaughter outsiders, this soon comes to be proven otherwise—for instance, a local man is killed walking along the pier, and the scientist helping the Sheriff with his investigation is also annihilated. Considering these instances, it makes no sense that any "real" human beings would still be living in the town, but there are a number of (seemingly) normal residents of Potter's Bluff, each one interacting with the living dead. In defense of these narrative shortcomings, the director does note that the finished product was the subject of haphazard post-production edits (see "Memories of the Film") which, one presumes, may have made *Dead and Buried* a more logical movie.

Yet if this all sounds like someone complaining about the film, it is not. After all, no one ever said horror movies ever had to make sense[6]—and as a scary, surreal viewing experience *Dead and Buried* is one of the best, fully warranting its appearance in this book. This was Sherman's first horror effort since his superior *Death Line* (see Chapter 1), and the wait was well worth it—with some perfectly realized moments of suspense. Coupled with its haunting twist ending, the movie plays out as an extremely stylish variation on the EC Comics of old. The Gothic appearance of Potter's Bluff, for example—which is always enshrouded in mist—is nothing less than gorgeous, and the movie is certainly well made and atmospheric. The film's delicious payoff, whereupon Albertson informs Farentino, "Oh, by the way...one more thing you should know..." also brings to mind the later revelation of 1999's horror blockbuster *The Sixth Sense*. While *Dead and Buried* is nowhere near as sophisticated or tightly plotted as M. Night

Dobbs (Jack Albertson) has a grim secret he's hiding from the Sheriff.

Shyamalan's instant classic, it does happen to feature a similar surprise at the end, revealing to us that the lead character has been dead all along. Played more for the surprise revelation of a *Twilight Zone* episode, writers Dan O'Bannon (also responsible for penning *Alien*) and Ronald Shusett provide the perfect finale for a story that is full of quirky, innovative touches—and it also makes *Dead and Buried* a nearly impossible film to categorize. At once a zombie movie, a mad scientist picture and even a slasher flick, Sherman seems intent on making his movie a true "eclectic gem."

Dead and Buried's best scare sequence is when a family passes through Potter's Bluff and ends up being chased by the locals. This lengthy set piece perfectly captures the sense of claustrophobia and desperation that should accompany any good horror movie, especially when the murderers corner the victims inside a dilapidated old hotel and begin to break through the windows. However, perhaps the most admirable thing about the film is its "take no prisoners" prologue, where Christopher Allport's luck takes a sudden downturn and the inhabitants of Potter's Bluff group together to burn him alive. One of the most unexpectedly vicious, if not explicitly gory, openings to any horror film, Sherman pulls no punches—and it is easy to imagine at least a few horrified audience members demanding their money back after witnessing only the first five minutes. Consequently, one wonders if *Dead and Buried* landed on the U.K.'s "video nasty" list primarily because of this brutal prologue—without doubt the most violent sequence in the entire film. Coupled with a dash of gratuitous nudity, this initial scene leads one to believe that he is watching just another slice of exploitation sleaze—although nothing could be further from the truth, as the remainder of the movie showcases. However, by starting the film with such a brutal set piece, Sherman keeps the viewer off guard for the remainder of his feature—after all, how is he ever going to top such nastiness? Of course, the director does not choose to—but the feeling that the movie just might have worse things in store for us should keep most viewers on the edge of their seat (one might argue that director Dario Argento used a similar trick with his masterpiece *Sus-*

piria—furthering the idea that *Dead and Buried* is inspired by Italian horror flicks).

The most iconic image from *Dead and Buried* remains *An Officer and A Gentleman* starlet Lisa Blount dressed as a nurse, with a needle in her hand, about to plunge the contraption into the exposed eye of a bandaged Allport. Oddly enough, the same year's *Strange Behavior* (see later in this chapter) would also feature a death via needle-in-the-eyeball. Fans are advised to keep an eye out for a young Robert Englund—although his screen time is minimal. Sadly, *Dead and Buried* was Albertson's last role.

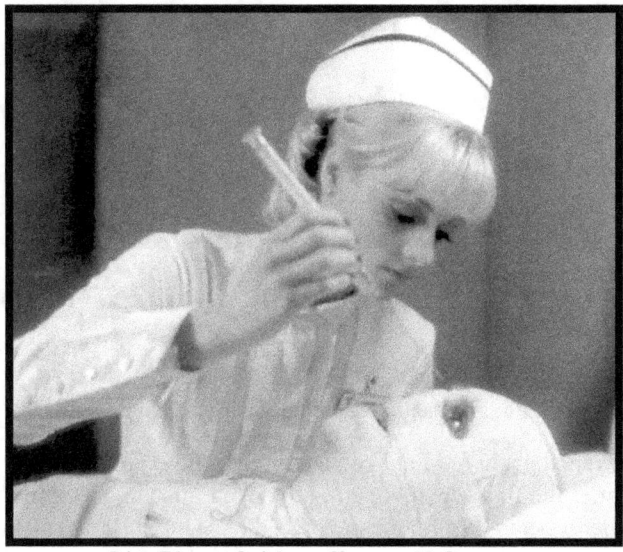

Lisa Blount finishes off poor old George.

Standout Moment

Lisa Blount is deceptively seductive, and decidedly cute, in a nurse's outfit…until she plunges a needle through your eyeball! *Dead and Buried*'s most famous scene is also its most effective.

Memories of the Film

"That's what you've got to do. It was meant to be shocking and it blew a lot of people away," maintains director Gary Sherman when questioned about the horrifically effective opening to *Dead and Buried*. Sherman is equally nonplussed about another horror sequence in the movie—the notorious needle in the eyeball scene. "No, it doesn't make me squirm because I shot it and I was there when Stan Winston devised the effect. Sam was just brilliant. You know I have had the pleasure of working with the greatest special effects people—Rick Baker, Stan and the godfather of them all, Dick Smith, who is a genius. I worked with Dick on *Poltergeist 3*. It was pretty incredible how we did that eyeball effect in *Dead and Buried*. It was not actually Christopher Allport in that scene, it was a dummy under the bandages, which was operated like a puppet. The needle in the eye we shot backwards with Lisa Blount...yeah, we shot her hand in close-up and the little wiggle she did when the needle was put into the eye and then we pulled upward and filmed her taking the needle out. A lot of people would run out of the cinema at that scene. The needle in the eye really tested how squeamish people were.

"One of the reasons I decided to do *Dead and Buried* was that it was originally a black comedy," continues Sherman. "Richard St. Johns at Four Star developed the film and approved the final script. He was the original producer and then Aspen bought the studio that the movie was going to be filmed under—which was Guinness, they had just decided to get into movies back then, but they wanted out of the business pretty

Lisa Blount leads photographer George to his doom.

quickly. Aspen was then under a guy called John Hyde and he had a slightly different idea about the movie. The pre-production took place under Richard and then Hyde...and then there was another new owner, called Mark Damon. The original cut of *Dead and Buried* I truly loved."

Will viewers ever be able to see this 'original cut'? "No, and I'll tell you why," answers Sherman. "Everyone was so excited about my final cut, everyone was so proud. Then Mark Damon took me aside after the first screening and he looked me straight in the eyes and said, 'If I wanted Bergman to do a horror movie, I'd have hired Bergman, now let's cut the bullshit and go and make a proper horror picture.' They then had the big band music that was on the soundtrack remixed and I had to add some scenes with more gore, change some scenes and if I didn't do it then they just would have hired a new director to do it. When they finally showed the film again, after the changes, Robert Raimi at Avco—who was ready to distribute it—asked me, 'What happened to it? I'm now stuck with a movie I don't even want to release.' Then they threatened to sue Avco if they didn't release it, and I was told to just walk away from it...they actually destroyed the original cutting print of *Dead and Buried*. The original version doesn't even exist anymore. I was pretty distraught. I just focused on making *Vice Squad*, my next movie, which turned out to be a huge hit, but I was upset with that as well. In the same way that people didn't seem to get *Death Line*, people didn't seem to get *Vice Squad*. *Vice Squad* was an anti-violence movie, it was saying 'violence against women is an ugly thing folks, a really ugly thing.' Instead critics saw the violence and just choose to say—'This director must really hate women,' which is ridiculous. I love women, that's probably why I've been married so many times," laughs the director.

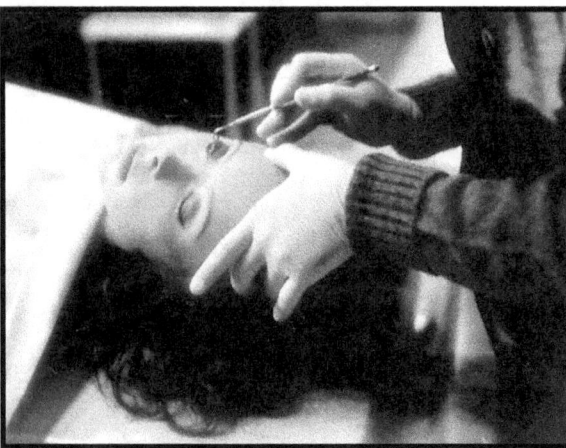

Dead and Buried was banned in Britain.

"The whole thing in *Dead and Buried* was a play being put on by Dobbs for James Farentino's character. The big surprise was that the sheriff was dead all along," remembers Sherman. When asked if he is willing to take some credit for pre-dating the similar twist to *The Sixth Sense*, the director objects. "No, I think

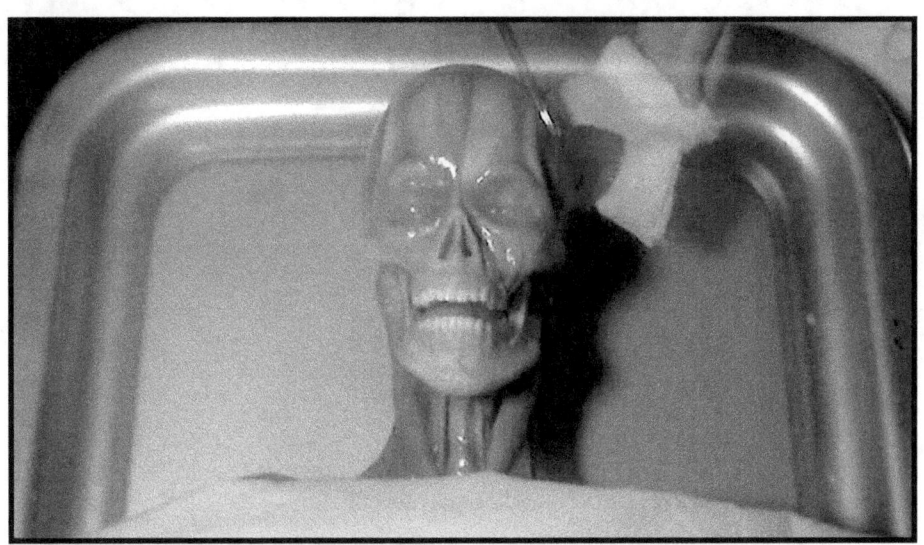
Dead and Buried was meant to be shocking, and it was.

that ending has happened before anyway. I loved *The Sixth Sense*, I thought it was the best horror film made in years, although I've been disappointed by that director's films since. I've seen *The Sixth Sense* six or seven times now, although I must admit I knew what the ending was going to be pretty early on. On the scene when Bruce Willis started following the kid home in the same suit he had been shot in, I thought that something wasn't right. No trained psychiatrist would have done that, and then he sat in the kid's living room and didn't look at the mother and the kid sees dead people...and then I knew he was a ghost. It didn't spoil the film for me though, if anything it enhanced my enjoyment of the movie...."

Sherman is also remarkably upbeat about the "video nasty" that initially greeted his film in the U.K. "Yes I knew about that, and I'm proud of it," laughs the director. "To make a film offensive enough to be banned...that's great! A lot of my friends and family still live in England and I knew what was going on with the horror videos. We had problems with the British censors on *Death Line*, they were offended but they couldn't find anything to cut out."

Alternate Critiques

"Great *Twilight Zone* type of horror movie building to a nifty revelation in the last few seconds..." (Chas Balun, *The Connoisseur's Guide to the Contemporary Horror Film,* Fantaco, 1992)

"...a clever zombie film, albeit one that resembles *The Stepford Wives* more than *Night of the Living Dead*....Most of the film's special effects were created by Stan Winston and have generally stood the test of time." (Stephen Foster, *Shivers*, Issue 107, September 2003)

"The twist ending is a cracker and though there is a fair amount of gore on display, the film is not swamped with it. In fact it mainly relies on good performances and direction to give it its chilling impact." (Allan Bryce, *The Video Nasties*, Stray Cat Press, 1998)

Evilspeak

Director: Eric Weston
Produced by: Gerald Hopman, Sylvio Tabet, Eric Weston
Written by: Joseph Garofalo, Eric Weston
Cast: Clint Howard; R.G. Armstrong; Joseph Cortese; Claude Earl Jones; Haywood Nelson; Don Stark; Charles Tyner; Hamilton Camp; Louie Gravance; Jim Greenleaf; Lynn Hancock; Loren Lester
Special Effects: Harry Woolman
Year: 1981

Plot Synopsis

In the 16th century, Father Lorenzo Esteban (Richard Moll), a Satanist leader, and his followers are told by a church priest to leave their native Spain. Esteban spits in the priest's face, and later carries out the ritual decapitation of a topless woman on the shore of a beach.

Cut to the present day and a military school that is largely attended by the rich children of prestigious figures. A soccer game takes place where Coopersmith (Howard) loses control of the ball, leading to the rival team scoring a goal. A pack of bullies, led by Bubba (Stark), pushes Coopersmith around in the shower room, but the boy is saved by his friend Kowalski (Nelson), a black teenager who seems to be similarly isolated in the school.

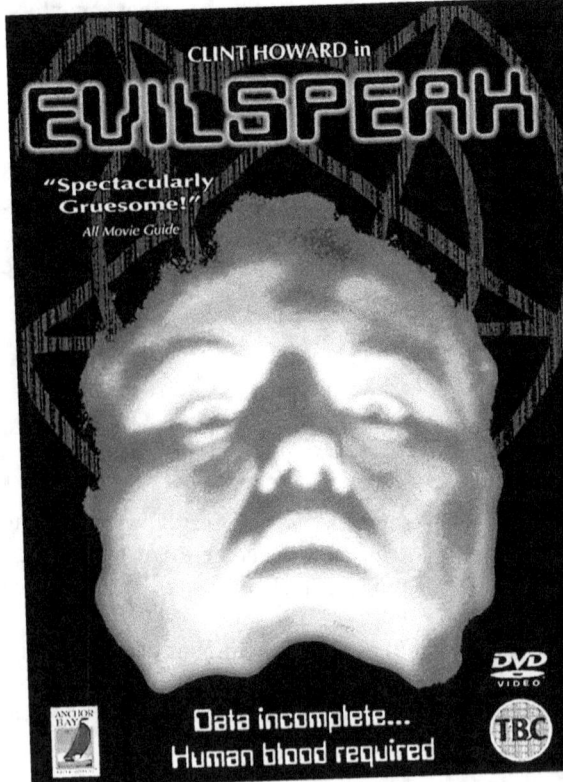

The coach (Earl Jones) informs Bubba that he should try to see to it that Coopersmith cannot play the next game. Colonel Kincaid (Tyner) shows Bubba's mother (Sue Casey)—the wife of a senator—around the college campus. He informs her that the school also takes in "welfare cases," such as Coopersmith—who was left as an orphan when his parents died.

Coopersmith is sent to clean up the basement as punishment (presumably for losing the soccer game). The school's alcoholic sergeant (Armstrong) castigates him for being in the cellar, but Coopersmith explains to him that he has a task to complete. The boy snoops around and discovers a room hidden behind a brick wall. Kincaid

Clint Howard as Stanley Coopersmith, a meek student at an upscale military academy.

wraps up his tour of the campus with Bubba's mother by telling her that the military academy was built as a place of exile for Esteban, prior to his execution. Esteban swore that he would one day return to avenge his death.

In the secret room, Coopersmith hears a voice and finds some ancient artifacts from the time of Father Esteban—including a dusty black book with a pentangle on the front. The boy takes the book and, later that night, he has a nightmare about the Satanist leader. He awakens the next morning to find he has slept in—his alarm clock stolen by the bullies—and his clothes are tied together. Making it into the last few minutes of Latin class, his teacher (Camp) gives him a dressing down. Coopersmith swears to make it up to him with his class project—the replication, in model form, of an ancient catapult as used in old battles.

At computer lessons, Coopersmith translates some of Esteban's book from Latin to English. After class Bubba and his friends push him around again. The school's Reverend (Cortese) passes by and the fight stops. The Reverend exhibits disdain for Coopersmith and he is later taken to Kincaid's office. On the way in he leaves his books on Kincaid's secretary's (Hancock) desk—but Esteban's book slips into the dustbin. In Kincaid's office, Coopersmith is whipped with a cane for not getting along with the other boys. He is sent to help the academy's farmer clean out his pigpens.

Kincaid's secretary finds Esteban's book and tries to pick the pentangle from off the front of it. In doing so, she somehow sends the farmer's livestock into a violent frenzy and the pigs try to attack Coopersmith while he is clearing out their pen.

Back in his dorm, Coopersmith finds his Latin project in tatters, broken by Bubba and his gang, and his book missing. Not realizing that he has left it with Kincaid's secretary, he blames Bubba—but the boy denies ever having seen it. Later at the dinner hall, a friendly cook fries Coopersmith a steak and offers him a puppy as a present. The delighted boy takes it.

Bubba (Don Stark) and his gang scare Coopersmith into organizing a black mass.

Bubba and his gang dress up in animal masks and black robes. They scare Coopersmith—causing him to run into a wall and fall unconscious. When he wakes up, Coopersmith believes he has awoken spirits and becomes even more dedicated to organizing a black mass, for which he needs the "blood of a consecrated host." The drunken Sarge discovers Coopersmith's dog and threatens to rape the boy; however, a strange force breaks the man's neck. The word "Esteban" appears on Coopersmith's computer screen.

Kincaid's secretary comes home with her stolen book and goes for a shower. The farmer's pigs break out from their pen and invade her home—eating her alive while she is still nude. The book vanishes from her mantel.

At the Miss Heavy Artillery Contest, a group of *Playboy*-type models parade in skimpy bikinis for the pleasure of the students and staff. Coopersmith wants a pretty blonde called Kelly Gallagher (Kathy McCullen) to win, but she does not. Afterwards he approaches Kelly to tell her that he was cheering for her. She finds his awkwardness amusing enough to offer him a draw on a joint. Bubba and his friends see what is happening and strip Coopersmith of his trousers. Kincaid arrives and informs Coopersmith that he has been thrown off the soccer team.

Bubba, Kelly and the rest of the gang find Coopersmith's secret room—as well as his pet puppy. Noticing the computer screen asking for blood, Bubba stabs the dog to death. The computer then states that "human blood" is needed.

The next morning, Coopersmith returns to his room. Finding the dog killed, he snaps. He takes holy water from the chapel to help with his black mass. The Latin teacher follows him and, in an extraordinary bout of strength, the boy impales him and drinks his blood. Esteban appears on Coopersmith's face, as he swears to follow Satan.

Coopersmith's possession leads to gory killings as he takes revenge on his tormentors.

The soccer team is at the chapel with the school's Reverend. A nail from the wrist of a statue of Christ comes undone and imbeds itself in the Reverend's head. Coopersmith arrives, carrying a large sword, and unleashes an army of hungry pigs. Everyone in the chapel is either decapitated or digested. Bubba has his heart pulled out by the sergeant, who is resurrected.

A final coda tells us that the chapel burned down, and Coopersmith was considered the only survivor of a freak accident. He is now in an asylum—but his computer screen promises that he will return.

Critique

Originally banned in Great Britain as a "video nasty" in the mid-1980s, *Evilspeak* is in a similar vein to Brian De Palma's classic *Carrie*, with its story of an abused, unattractive teenager who takes revenge upon a number of abusive classmates. As with Sissy Spacek's excellent portrayal of Carrie White, Clint Howard cuts a sympathetic figure as the abused Coopersmith, who is dubbed "Coopershit" by his tormentors, and the actor has rarely been better cast. His unassuming, kindly demeanor makes his torment all the more effective and it is easy to be on Howard's side when he begins tampering with black magic—usually the sort of taboo that indicates a villainous character. Also like *Carrie*, *Evilspeak* presents Christianity in a negative, if not entirely critical, light. For instance, the school's chaplain is a despicable character who encourages the abuse of Howard's character and is even seen to enjoy the parading of scantily clad young females in a bikini contest (puzzlingly, the rest of the school's hierarchy never questions this). The chaplain's demise, at the end of a flying nail that rushes from the hand of a statue of Christ, is also—no doubt—influenced by the grisly end that meets Piper Lau-

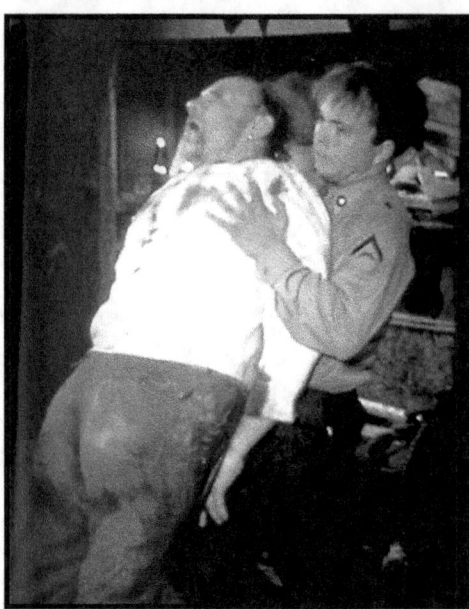

Evilspeak's villains are a repugnant bunch of thugs.

rie in De Palma's film. Rather dubiously, however, it is not through the salvation of the Bible that Howard is "redeemed" but rather through Satanism—which allows him to construct a bloody revenge and, judging from the end scroll, get away with it all. In this sense it is surprising, "video nasty" controversy aside, that *Evilspeak* did not meet with any trouble in its native North America—especially considering the sort of hostility that greeted the U.S. release of Kevin Smith's abysmal *Dogma* in 1999.

Evoking a believable performance from someone who is consistently terrorized (and make no mistake about it, *Evilspeak*'s villains are a repugnant bunch of thugs with no redeeming features), one really wants to see Howard get his retaliation. As other critics have mentioned[7]—after the thugs sacrifice Howard's pet dog, there is little chance of any audience member being able to resist cheering on the final scenes of carnage. Seeing Howard weep while cradling the body of his murdered puppy dog does make for an especially somber moment—even if it is an admittedly cynical attempt to steer our sympathies toward the poor fellow and applaud his upcoming retaliation.

That we are reminded of Howard's background in the movie (he's a "welfare case" and an orphan) and with his peasantry in complete contrast to his wealthy colleagues, his brutal revenge appears all the more fitting. Certainly, it is possible to see *Evilspeak* as being just as much a story of class war as it is about a bullied kid getting his comeuppance. For instance, the only "nice" characters in *Evilspeak*, aside from Howard, are his black friend (who also appears to be alienated, perhaps because of his race) and a working-class cook—whose lack of resources stop him from keeping his litter of dogs. Everyone else is either an upper-class thug, one of whom is even the son of a senator, or a well-maintained teacher at the school.

Howard's social standing is a common point of conjecture in the movie (such as when the head teacher expects the boy to show appreciation for being taken in by the prestigious academy, despite his lowly background) and it is, therefore, difficult not to appreciate his vengeance as a form of class rebellion. Although this does not add any extra depth to the film, it does give Howard's character a bit more clarity and helps us to further sympathize with his ordeal, because there is no evidence that "Coopershit" is being attacked for his chunky, nerdy appearance. In fact, one of the foremost thugs in *Evilspeak* is a gruesome, overweight lad—and his presence in the movie may be in order to alert us to the actualities behind Howard's alienation. As opposed to his lack of physical attractiveness, it seems that the boy is refused a place in the academy's hierarchy solely because he is not "one of them"—he is a refugee and an orphan, not a privileged rich kid.

Despite its low budget, *Evilspeak* is a competently directed horror film with impressive special effects

Despite its low budget, *Evilspeak* is a competently directed horror film with impressive special effects and the shocks are nicely telegraphed. Every sequence of horror ends in a gory payoff for the viewer—such as when the school's deceased caretaker (Cortese), whom Howard kills earlier in the film, comes back to life without any suitable explanation in order to tear out one young thug's heart. It makes little sense, but in the madcap atmosphere that prevails over *Evilspeak*'s especially riotous finale, which sees Howard styling a haircut from hell—quite literally in this case—levitating and doling out his own brand of retribution, it fits in just fine. As hungry pigs flood the Academy's chapel, characters end up beheaded or eaten and it is difficult not to be grabbed by the whole insane spectacle.

Considering the horrible situations that poor Howard encounters during the film (just when things look like they cannot get any worse, the institution's caretaker threatens to rape him—"Now I'm going to show you how I make a little boy into a little girl," he threatens) his ultimate revenge is a bit of a given. Although predictable, however, director Weston wisely throws in a few unexpected moments of lunacy—including the movie's sexy secretary being consumed by rabid pigs. As any Dario Argento fan will attest, horror films do not necessarily need to make any logical sense as long as they present a believable and nightmarish atmosphere, something that *Evilspeak*, in its own B-movie way, manages. The result is an always amusing, and fast-paced, demonic shocker that should find a place in any horror fan's heart. Certainly, as far as eclectic and offbeat genre cinema goes, *Evilspeak* is a wonderful slice of insanity—just leave your brain at the door.

Standout Moment

The school's attractive, but bitchy, secretary takes her final shower when a group of flesh-eating hogs barge through her front door and chow down on her nude body. It makes no sense at all, of course, but that's *Evilspeak* for you...

Evilspeak was also banned in the U.K.

Memories of the Film

"Well yeah, I've been to London—I've never really had my finger on the pulse of what the cinema is like over there. I didn't realize they had restrictions, I thought it was about as wide open as America..." states Clint Howard when he learns that *Evilspeak* was once banned outright in the U.K. "A video nasty! I was in a video nasty—that's a good one," he laughs, punching the air in victory. "But I don't quite understand with *Evilspeak*," the actor continues, "I mean it had demonic overtones but it was only a movie...I wonder if they actually saw it."

Indeed, people who pass comment on *Evilspeak* without having first seen it, is something of a thorn in the side for the film's star. "Yeah, that's a bone I have to pick," maintains the actor. "I met a famous television reviewer of movies. They gave it 'dog of the week' when it came out. At the time they were doing this cute little thing, where they had this little Chihuahua dog that jumped up on the couch, and they announced 'dog of the week.' Now granted, *Evilspeak* is not *One Flew Over the Cuckoo's Nest*, it's not *A Beautiful Mind*, it's not *Chinatown*—it's a horror movie, and I thought it was a pretty good little horror movie. It had its flaws, but I felt like it had a message and it was interesting and it moved along for the people that like horror movies—and I'm proud of *Evilspeak* and I really have a lot of great memories of working on it. But anyway they announced it 'dog of the week' and they had their little bit of fun at our expense. It hurt, I was in my early 20s and it was like, 'Oh shit,' because we knew they were going to review it on the program.

"I talked to this guy later on, this was years later, and I said, 'Hey you guys named a movie I did a long time ago 'dog of the week'—why'd you do that?' And he hadn't even seen it—his staff had seen it, and so it was just an easy one to make 'dog of the week.' Now, the fellow—and I believed him when he said this—he said, 'I can't see all the movies, we have staff that see them.' I mean it didn't stalk me for life or anything because we got some good reviews and it made a little money. *Evilspeak* fell into a difficult situation because it was released by a company that went out of business soon after, so ownership of the movie and the rights to it all became a little muddled. Warner Bros. owned the video distribution rights for a while, and I understand the studios—if they start to sell 'X' amount of copies of a video title they start to owe back (the main crew) in payments. And with Warner Bros., if they know a movie is getting close to reaching that threshold, they will just pull it. They don't want to pay—because they know they're not going to make as much as they're going to have to pay out to the writers and the director....As a piece of business, the people that owned the company didn't make any money from *Evilspeak*...but it's cool to have your movie stamped a video nasty!"

Actress Lynn Hancock undresses in *Evilspeak*.

Despite having gone on to work on many of his brother's (Ron Howard) mainstream films, including a pivotal role in 1995's Oscar-winning *Apollo 13*, the actor admits to having gratitude toward the many low-budget horror films that he has appeared in. "I appreciate this little underground film world," insists Howard. "I know the director of *Evilspeak*—Eric Weston—he's getting old, he's not feeble or anything, but he's an old guy, he's around town, I run into him every once in a while....That was one of the first films I did as an adult—I mean there was *Rock 'n' Roll High School*, but we shot *Rock 'n' Roll High School* in Los Angeles...we shot it in a really horrible neighborhood in East Los Angeles. You know, all these young white guys were driving down to the hood and making a movie! Nobody got hurt or anything but they had to have armed guards on the set of *Rock 'n' Roll High School*! Well, when we shot *Evilspeak*—and I have great stories about *Evilspeak*—we had to have shotgun-carrying security personnel here in Los Angeles, because we shot for like six weeks up in Santa Barbara."

The actor is not kidding when he boasts about having "great stories" about shooting *Evilspeak*—as the following tale indicates. "We came back here and shot at a warehouse/soundstage out in Chatsworth and then they shot it in a bad part of Los Angeles. They shot in an old church. They realized the church was going to get torn down, you know the location manager knew this old church had been condemned. They got permission

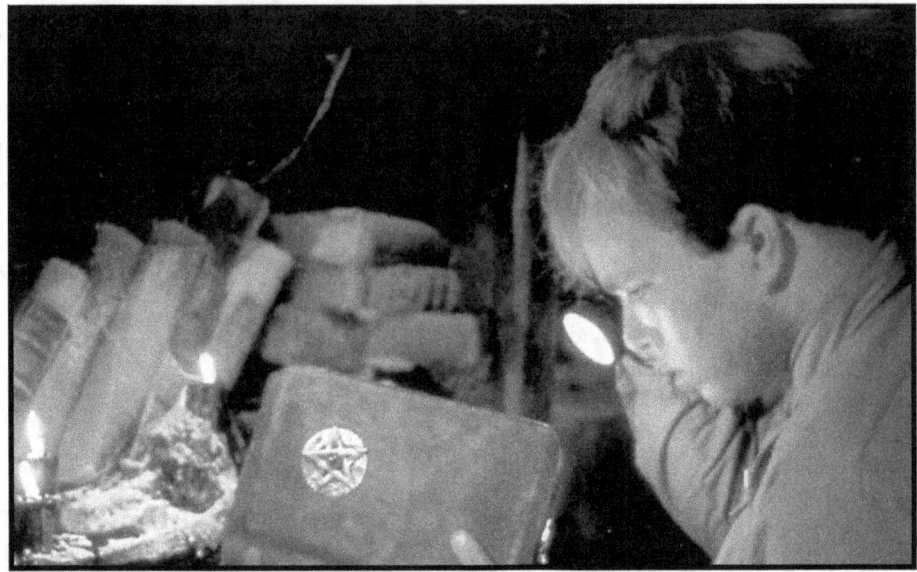

Coopersmith is so abused it is easy to root for him as he demolishes the school and the bullies.

to go in there and refurbish it a little bit in the showbiz way, a little paint, we fixed it up a little bit and then we went and shot in there and then at the end we burned it down. Burning it down was hard though. We were there the second night and this old 80-year-old black minister of the church came back and saw the inside of the church and fell to his knees! He said, 'Praise the Lord, my church has been saved, you've done such a wonderful job, it's like the glory days!' Everybody felt really bad because we were going to torch it three days later.

"Another funny thing—we shot at a monastery, up at Santa Barbara. For Eric to get permission to use this monastery he, in one night, completely changed the script and handed someone at the monastery a script that wasn't called *Evilspeak*. It didn't have anything to do with, you know, flesh-munching pigs and shit. So anyway—I was out on my own…it was a great experience as a young adult actor. Eric Weston and the cinematographer, Irv Goodnoff, and I kind of became collaborators. They knew I had a lot of experience, even for a 21- or 22-year-old kid. I mean, I had been around the business a long time and everyone, and Eric was in his 30s or whatever, really worked together to make that movie. It was a great experience. Such a great part! If I had it to do over again, I'd do things a little different but a lot of that movie works just fine. And Eric did a great job shooting it—it does not look like a little low-budget horror movie…"

Playing such a sympathetic character did call for Howard to practice some method acting. *"You know—I kind of kept to myself,"* reveals the actor. "Don Stark, a character actor who I see at auditions from time to time, he played the head bully. And Don—very early on, like the first or second day—he came up to me said, 'Listen, if you don't mind, I'm going to keep my distance…you're not supposed to be my friend.' And there was a contentious relationship between us. We didn't have a lot of scenes together—they were off doing their thing…I had so much to do in that movie myself. It was a nice chemistry, I don't mean nice as in friendly, I mean nice because the (bullies) palled around together—and I liked the guys, it wasn't as if we were real to the bone mortal enemies or anything…I worked a lot longer hours than they did. I remember up in Santa Barbara I was working all day, and I was drinking at the time—I'd get, like, a pint of Scotch after work and just shoot that pint of Scotch down. I don't drink anymore—I've been sober for a while—but I thought it was a great experience…"

Howard is also candid when reliving his experience of *Evilspeak*'s most powerful scene—where he cradles his murdered puppy dog. "Listen, that was a real easy emotional moment to play. I love animals, I had a great cat pass away and I have an old cat living in my house right now that I've had (for a long time) and I'll cry when he dies. And that moment where I'm holding the dog and rocking back and forth—you always try as an actor…you always try and find a way to draw real emotion—and that was easy. And I happened to actually be around the set that day and…I mean they didn't kill the dog—of course they didn't kill the dog—but Eric the director and Loren Lester, this other actor, and Jim Greenleaf—they were all 'How do we do this?' and Don was very careful about the dog because it was a little puppy.

"They actually had a little puppy and like what happens on a lot of movie sets, and what happens in life, they started with a litter of puppies and then one of them died and one of them ran off or something, and disappeared! Finally they ended up kind of down to the last…they didn't have a lot of extra puppies (*laughs*). So they did the scene with the dog and of course the dog grew. I mean it wasn't a big-budget movie—they only had one set of puppies. That movie probably took about six weeks to film—a dog grows quite a bit in six weeks—and by the end it's like, 'This dog doesn't match anymore.' You know…it's not going to have some sort of revelatory mark on show business or something—but it's a good little film that I'd like people to be able to rent or buy or steal…"

Out of all his films, Howard even goes so far to rate *Evilspeak* as his fondest acting job. "Well…it was probably my favorite experience. I was coming of age—I was out on my own for the first time. Listen, I've had a lot of wonderful experiences, I've worked on movies that have been better than *Evilspeak* and I have fun about 99 percent of the time that I work. I had a wonderful experience working on *Apollo 13*…working on *The Missing*—it was a very hard day, I was actually in Santa Fe for a week but the actual filming was one long day, a very gratifying day of work. But for overall experience, working on *Evilspeak* didn't change my life or anything but it was one of those periods in my life…it was cool."

Alternate Critiques

"An extremely imaginative and energetic outing, the film's highlights include the scenes in which the pigs invade a luxurious bathroom and devour its occupants and, later, run riot in a blazing chapel." (*The Aurum Film Encyclopedia: Horror*, Aurum Press, 1993)

"Some flashy direction…and a campy cast…make this nice, sick fun." (James O'Neill, *Terror on Tape*, Billboard Books, 1994)

"The final 10 minutes are so blood-drenched you'll probably find yourself rewatching just to make sure you've properly consumed every magnificent latex moment." (Rob Freese, *Videoscope*, Issue 52, Fall 2004)

Strange Behavior

Director: Michael Laughlin
Produced by: John Barnett/Antony I. Ginnane
Written by: Bill Condon/Michael Laughlin
Cast: Michael Murphy; Louise Fletcher; Dan Shor; Fiona Lewis; Arthur Dignam; Dey Young; Marc McClure; Scott Brady; Charles Lane; Elizabeth Cheshire; Beryl Te Wiata; Jim Boelsen
Special Effects: Craig Reardon
Year: 1981

Plot Synopsis

A teenager sits reading in his room when the electricity suddenly goes out. Lighting a candle and exploring the house, he is suddenly stabbed to death by a shadowy figure.

Following this incident, we are introduced to Pete Brady (Shor) and his alcoholic father John (Murphy), who is the chief of police in Gaylesberg—a typical American middle-class suburb. The Bradys also employ a housekeeper called Miss Haskell (Wiata), who complains about the mess of the surroundings. Pete drives to school, and John leaves for work, where he learns that the mayor's son is missing.

After school, Pete is told by his best friend Oliver (McClure) about a way to make some fast money. Oliver is currently acting as a guinea pig for the local university's medical department. Intrigued, Pete accompanies Oliver to the research laboratory, where they sit in on a class about behavior and watch an old video lecture from the late Dr. Le Sange (Digman), who was once a leading voice on this topic.

Afterwards, Pete is introduced to Dr. Parkinson (Lewis), who makes an appointment for him the next day. She asks the boy whether or not he is related to John Brady. When Pete admits that he is, Parkinson advises him to keep quiet about coming to the laboratory.

Back home, John Brady is drunk, but his girlfriend Barbara (Fletcher) is there to look after him. She receives a warm greeting from Pete, who asks: "When are you two going to get married?" He then leaves to join a Halloween party.

At the party, Pete and his friends dance to loud music. Outside, Waldo (Boelsen) and Lucy (Cheshire)—a young couple—kiss in a parked car. A stranger wearing a black cape and a Tor Johnson mask watches them.

A Halloween party is the scene of murder and mayhem in *Strange Behavior*.

The mysterious assailant approaches the car and stabs Waldo to death. He then chases Lucy back to the house where the party is being held. Lucy trips and falls into a pool, enabling the stranger to corner her but, alerted by the girl's screams, some partygoers come to her rescue. The murderer runs and, later removing his mask, reveals himself to be Oliver.

The next day, John questions Oliver about the previous night—with Pete present. Oliver remembers nothing, stating that he thinks he drank too much and slept through the events.

Back at the research laboratory, a pretty receptionist called Caroline (Young) talks to an overweight girl named Paula (B. Courtenay Leigh). Paula explains that, after undergoing Parkinson's experiments, she no longer has a desire to eat junk food. Pete arrives for his appointment with the doctor. Meanwhile, the town's forces find the dead body of the mayor's son in a farmyard, dressed up as a scarecrow.

After agreeing to take a new pill given to him by Dr. Parkinson, Pete asks Caroline out. She agrees and Pete takes her to lunch. Caroline tells Pete about some of the horrific animal experiments that have been taking place in the laboratory. Later, Pete stays the night at Caroline's dormitory.

Miss Haskell arrives at another house for work. She calls out for a boy—Timothy—that she is to look after. Having not obtained a reply, the housekeeper searches the residence. She opens the door of the upstairs bathroom to find Timothy (Neil McLachlan) being cut up by Paula, the overweight girl from the clinic. Hurrying downstairs to phone the police, the housekeeper ends up being stabbed and having her throat cut.

The next morning, John believes that the murders might be linked to the laboratory and chooses to investigate. Pete turns up for a morning experiment at the University research facility, but this one involves him being tied up and restrained by Parkinson, which sends the boy into a panic. Before she can begin her experiment, John Brady comes to investigate the murders—which he believes could be linked to the laboratory—but he finds nothing. Once the police leave the faculty, Parkinson plunges a needle deep into his left eye of Pete, injecting him with a mysterious substance.

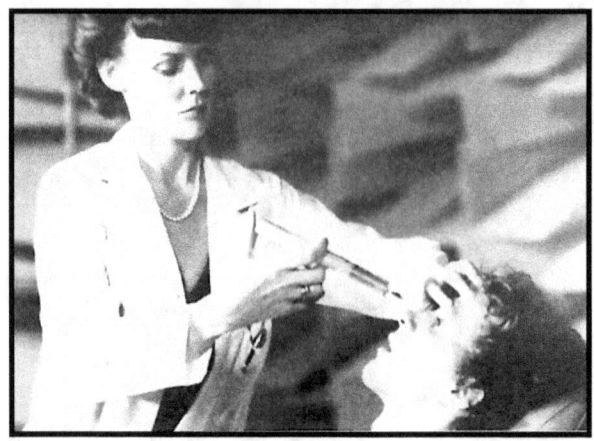

Dr. Parkinson (Fiona Lewis) plunges a needle deep into the eye of Pete Brady (Dan Shor).

Waking up with no recollection of being injected, Pete takes Caroline out for a meal, but before they can order he runs to the bathroom and urinates blood. He decides to return home with Caroline.

John explains to Barbara that he expects Dr. Le Sange had something to do with the death of his late wife, who he explains died many years ago in mysterious circumstances. On a whim, John goes to the cemetery where he digs up his wife's grave—the coffin is empty except for two leg bones. Barbara explains to Pete that his mother was rumored to have had an affair with Dr. Le Sange, who John believes killed his wife.

Later that night, John takes a gun and breaks into the research lab, with Pete and Caroline tracking him in a car. Pete suddenly takes a turn for the worse, knocks out his girlfriend and enters the lab where Parkinson instructs him to tie up his father. The thought-to-be-dead Dr. Le Sange appears and tells Pete to cut his wrists. Pete obliges, and following this the doctor asks him to murder his father. Pete responds by killing Le Sange. John's suspicions now confirmed, and Parkinson arrested, the police chief finally marries Barbara.

Critique

Strange Behavior marked the writing debut of Bill Condon, who is now an established director in his own right, having made 1995's average, but stylish, sequel *Candyman 2: Farewell to the Flesh* and 1999's impressive *Gods and Monsters*. For the latter work, Condon won an Oscar for his screenplay, and he found himself nominated for a second time in 2003 for adapting the successful stage musical *Chicago* to the big screen. Despite his current mainstream status, however, the writer/director remains proud of his more humble beginnings in low-budget genre work (see "Memories of the Film"). Both Condon and director Laughlin would work together again on 1983's science fiction movie *Strange Invaders*, which also featured Louise Fletcher and Dey Young in the cast. *Strange Behavior* is the superior film, however, and you have to love any movie that features a psychopath wearing a Tor Johnson mask!

A cross between a mad scientist film and a more traditional 1980s slasher picture (there is even an homage to the opening tracking sequence from *Halloween*), *Strange Behavior* also throws in an effective subplot about Murphy's dead wife and the sort of accomplished acting and characterization that is usually not seen in a teen horror film. Perhaps indicating Condon's professed love of musicals, something that would most obviously surface in *Chicago*, *Strange Behavior* also features one of the genre's most inappropriate moments, when the young characters bond together for a choreographed dance scene in the middle of their Halloween party. Completely out of sync with the rest of the film (following this musical number, the only one in the film, a violent murder

An Off-kilter atmosphere permeates the movie from beginning to end.

sequence begins), Laughlin's decision to include this sequence certainly shows some bravery. Acting like an interlude from the proper action, this moment adds to the off-kilter atmosphere that permeates the movie from beginning to end. From the almost impossibly quaint and clean suburb (*Strange Behavior* was shot in New Zealand, despite its American setting), to the many irrational moments of horror, the film carries a freaky feeling to it, right from its first moment of teenager death. The final "twist" is also nicely set up and delivered with enough gusto for it to carry a decent sting in its tail—even making one forget that the actual purpose behind Lewis' violent experiments has not really been made clear.

What also makes *Strange Behavior* a memorable cult oddity is its classy direction. With surprisingly lavish use of wide-screen photography (following *Halloween,* a handful of B-horror movies capitalized on the use of Scope, but few really made use of the form—*Strange Behavior* is a welcome exception), the film looks and feels professional. The scenes of terror are also nicely staged, and sometimes prolonged, adding to the audience's unease. Without doubt, it is Shor receiving a needle through his eyeball that stays in the memory longest—not only because of the obvious nastiness of the action, but due also to the time that passes before the act is completed. For instance, as Lewis prepares Shor for his jab, she is interrupted by the police and must attend to their questions. All the while, Shor sits restrained in a chair screaming for help. As would typically happen in a horror narrative, the hero would be rescued, but not so with *Strange Behavior*. Instead, having sent the police on their way, Lewis goes back to work and casually places the needle deep into Shor's eyeball. With no cutaway, the sequence is likely to cause at least a few audience members to turn and face the wall. Poor Shor also gets to suffer further when he is shown urinating blood—an obvious depiction of body horror but one that, nevertheless, carries the ability to make the viewer cringe.

Featuring such vile human experiments taking place with the backdrop of a vivisection laboratory (Young comments on the nasty reality of animal experimentation more than once), *Strange Behavior* was released at just the right time. 1981 revealed the horrors of animal experimentation through the now notorious Silver Spring Monkey

Dr. Le Sangel (Arthur Dignam) is using teenagers as guinea pigs.

Barbara Moorehead (Louise Fletcher) and John Brady (Michael Murphy) have a tenuous relationship.

case (which is largely said to have been the reason behind the rise of PETA[8]). Understandably appalled by the horrific conditions and the abuse of caged primates, the everyday public was suddenly given visual evidence of the horrors of vivisection. Although the theme is not as blatant as in something such as Wells' timeless novel *The Island of Doctor Moreau* it is, nonetheless, extremely evident in *Strange Behavior* and works effectively to create a sense of scientific irresponsibility that is vital to the plot. Furthermore, it is admittedly amusing to see Young talk to Shor, in vivid detail, about the animal abuse in the laboratory just before ordering liver from a restaurant menu.

The cast of *Strange Behavior* also adds to the film's considerable appeal. Oscar winner Louise Fletcher, puzzlingly, chose to follow up her star-making role in *One Flew Over the Cuckoo's Nest* with appearances in a variety of B fantasy and horror movies, making her perhaps the female equivalent of Rod Steiger. Regardless of how bad some of these films are (and *The Exorcist 2* is very bad indeed), Fletcher usually adds a convincing performance to the proceedings. Playing against type as the likeable girlfriend of the police chief in *Strange Behavior*, Fletcher at least temporarily sheds the super-bitch role, which would accompany her into films that include *Invaders from Mars* (1986) and *Flowers in the Attic* (1987) following her Oscar win as Nurse Ratched. As well as familiar character actor Michael Murphy and a seductively deadly turn from Fiona Lewis, *Strange Behavior* gives a rare leading role to the lovely Dey Young (the mother of *Cabin Fever* starlet Jordan Ladd), even if we never get to hear her scream or engage in any nooky.

Standout Moment

Shor takes what can only be described as an extremely unpleasant toilet break—urinating blood. It looks painful and, as a result, it is hardly surprising that this scene is hard to forget.

Oliver (Marc McClure) unknowingly commits murder during the Halloween party.

Memories of the Film

"I always loved horror movies, and at this time I had just started writing scripts for Mike Laughlin," states cowriter Bill Condon. "Also, I had failed to get a few movies off the ground—this was back in my early 20s, when I was getting my first taste of the studio system, and loving horror films and Hitchcock I found that these were relatively easy movies to get made. Also, the indie scene was booming again following *Halloween*'s success, and after being delayed on other projects I gave it a shot..."

Asked if he is still satisfied by the scenes of horror in *Strange Behavior*, Condon feels that time takes away some of the effect. "You know, horror films age and I'm not so sure these scenes would be quite so gruesome today," he begins. "I find something visceral to be exciting and it's great to be in the theater when you get that big jump from an audience. There are different ways to do that—I think the scariest moment in *Strange Behavior* is when the girl played by Elizabeth Cheshire is running away from the character of Mark and he stabs her in the back of her calf. Something about that scene is just so exposed, and I still really react to it...but then maybe you have to be a bit of a sadist to work with these sort of images anyway."

Then there is the nice sense of absurdity—with the killer donning a Tor Johnson mask at one point. Was this the writer's idea? "Yes, definitely. All that stuff was mine," recalls Condon. "I supervised the party sequence where all the kids are dressed as movie characters, the film was intended as a real look back at a certain type of low-budget, mad scientist horror film..." There is also the underlying theme of vivisection—was this intentional? "I guess so...it was certainly built into that whole idea. I've actually just been

Actor Michael Murphy on the set.

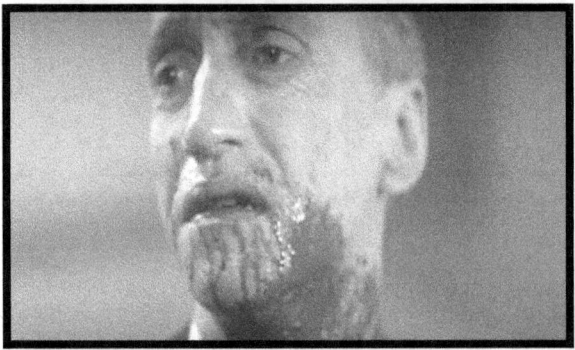

Strange Behavior is a cross between a mad scientist movie and a slasher film.

to the Kinsey Institute" (note: Condon's next film is about the famous doctor) "where I've been watching hours of footage of animals fucking (*laughs*) and the experience reminded me a bit of Dr. Nagel's lab in *Strange Behavior*. I find the idea of the abuse of science really fascinating, so there might be some deeper intent, but the film certainly makes fun of science..."

Why was *Strange Behavior* shot in New Zealand but set in America? "Money! We only had $1 million dollars and there was this tax scheme in New Zealand, paid by the government at the time, which made filming there much easier. We were shooting in this sleepy, small town in Auckland in January and trying to make it resemble this small American town, but watching the movie you still get the feeling that something is just not quite right. That something is slightly 'off'—and that excited me—it felt really eerie." Looking back at these early films, which include Condon's directorial debut *Sister, Sister* in 1987, Condon is forthcoming about his influences.

"Lots of different movies (influenced me), obviously having done *Gods and Monsters* there's a huge influence from James Whale. *The Old Dark House*—we copied a scene from that in *Strange Behavior* when the first victim is killed. The humor and horror that Whale combined in his films is a huge influence, that great eccentricity. In *Sister, Sister* we had the Jewish lady in New Jersey who owed a lot to the maid in *Bride of Frankenstein*, and the set on *Sister, Sister* was straight out of *Old Dark House*—the rainy night, the spooky old house, no way out for those that enter. When I was starting to write the script I was thinking, "Louisiana, swamp and murders," and then Joel Cohen was working on it as well, and eventually it was a more basic *Friday the 13th* slaughter movie. It had some good ideas

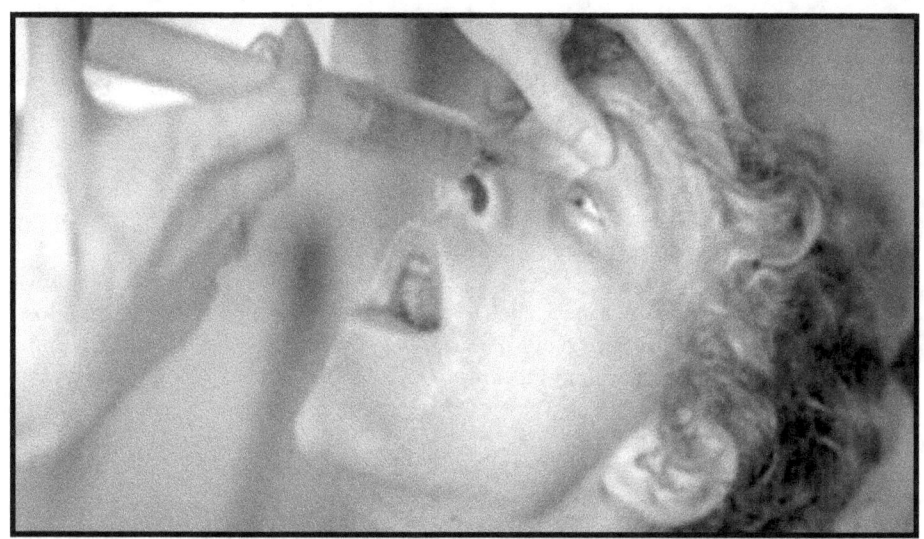

Actor Shor receives this book's second needle in the eye!

though, themes of Catholic repression and the Southern Gothic and the alligator farm that the brother and the sister owned...*Sister, Sister* never got many good reviews but I remember one positive review it got—maybe the only one it received—and it was in *The L.A. Weekly*. The reviewer said that it was 'a *Twilight Zone* episode written by Tennessee Williams,' which I liked."

Alternate Critiques

"An odd, amusing little film... slickly produced, well-acted and tightly scripted—a knowledgeable, sly homage to '50s genre films without the smirking." (Chas Balun, *The Connoisseur's Guide to the Contemporary Horror Film,* Fantaco, 1992)

"An odd title...Lots of interesting little touches (like the killer wearing a Tor Johnson mask), but the final product doesn't add up to much." (Allan Bryce, *The Dark Side*, Issue 45, April/May 1995)

"The pace and the narrative structures seem all wrong: things that should be suspenseful are merely tedious, and the big revelations are only surprising because the script has never prepared us for them." (L.A. Morse, *Video Trash and Treasures*, HarperCollins, 1989)

CHAPTER 6:
FUTURE CLASSICS
Recent Cult Horror Films That We Might Just Be Discussing for Years to Come
Ginger Snaps

Director: John Fawcett
Produced by: Steve Hoban, Karen Lee Hall
Written by: Karen Walton
Cast: Emily Perkins; Katharine Isabelle; Kris Lemche; Mimi Rogers; Jesse Moss; Danielle Hampton; John Bourgeois; Peter Keleghan; Christopher Redman; Jimmy MacInnis; Lindsay Leese; Wendii Fulford
Special Effects: Paul Jones
Year: 2000

Plot Synopsis

Bailey Downs looks just like any other upper-middle-class suburb…until a child finds a human hand in his garden sand pit and a young mother discovers the dead body of her pet dog—its carcass cut in half.

The Fitzgerald sisters—Ginger (Isabelle) and Brigitte (Perkins), are two teenaged Goths who live in Bailey Downs. They photograph each other in various different death scenes for a class project. The next day at school, the girls' teacher, Mr. Wayne (Keleghan), states that he is "sickened" and asks to see the sisters after class.

At hockey practice, a boy named Jason (Moss) tells his friends that he has a thing for Ginger, the prettier of the two sisters. The captain of the hockey team is a cheerleader type named Trina (Hampton). She knocks Brigitte down and the girl rolls into the remains of another dead dog—this one lying on the hockey field. After school, Trina scores some dope from the local drug dealer, Sam (Lemche). Jason asks Ginger out on a date, but she refuses him.

Back home, the Fitzgerald sisters sit with their liberal-minded mother (Rogers) and their perpetually silent father (Bourgeois). Ginger complains

Sisters Brigitte (Katharine Isabelle) and Ginger (Emily Perkins) are held after school because of their sick death photographs.

of stomach pains and her mother talks about menstruation. Embarrassed, the two girls leave the table. That evening the girls leave the house while their parents are out getting counseling. They wander to a nearby park, where they find the body of another half-consumed dog.

Ginger is suddenly pounced upon by a mysterious, four-legged creature and dragged into some woodland. Brigitte runs after her sister and the wolf charges from the woods onto the road, whereby it is run over by Sam.

Brigitte helps Ginger back home, but the girl refuses medical help. In fact, Ginger's wounds are starting to heal. To make matters worse, Ginger has begun her first period. The girls begin to grow apart and the next day at school, Ginger accepts Jason's offer to smoke some pot with him.

Sam approaches Brigitte, believing that she was the one attacked in the woods, and says that he thinks he hit a lycanthrope in his car. Trina passes Sam's van with her dog and her pet goes wild when it sees Ginger. Later, Ginger finds hair growing out of her wounds.

Ginger's mother discovers some bloody underwear while doing her washing. Once again she chooses to raise the subject of menstruation at the dinner table, much to Brigitte and Ginger's chagrin.

The next day at school, Ginger dresses sexily. During the night, Brigitte looks over Ginger's body while she is asleep and discovers that she is growing a tail. The following day, Brigitte asks Sam for help. Sure that he killed the werewolf with his car, he urges her to "throw out the Hollywood rules." Meanwhile Ginger makes out with Jason in his car. She dominates him and finally bites him.

The local dog population doesn't fare very well in *Ginger Snaps*.

Returning home, Ginger vomits blood in the bathroom. She tells Brigitte that she has killed the neighbor's dog. Brigitte gives her a silver belly-button ring in the hope of stopping the transformation. She also tapes Ginger's tail to her thigh so that no one at school will notice it.

Jason tells his friends that Ginger "rocked" his world, but he has blood on his crotch. He later urinates blood.

During a school hockey game, Trina attacks Brigitte again, but this time Ginger intervenes, knocking Trina to the ground and beating her fiercely. Brigitte tells Ginger that she must have infected Jason, because she had unprotected sex with him.

Having looked into folklore, Sam tells Brigitte that there is a common plant, a relation to wolfbane, that grows in spring that might work to offset the transformation. As it is still winter, however, there is no way to obtain it.

Trina arrives at the Fitzgerald house to confront Brigitte and Ginger. Against Brigitte's protests, Ginger violently drags the girl inside the family house. Trina shuffles loose and grabs a knife from the kitchen cabinet, spilling a pint of milk in the process. Trina slips on the spilt milk and splits her head on the kitchen cabinet. She dies instantly. The girls take her body and put it in the basement freezer. Later they bury it in a shallow grave in their shed, but two of Trina's fingers fall off due to the deep freeze.

At school the next day, Jason confronts Brigitte to ask what has happened to him. Since sleeping with Brigitte, he has developed a strange facial disease and he has also eaten his dog. Some hope comes when the Fitzgeralds' mother brings home some of the plant that Brigitte and Sam need. "I picked it up at the craft shop," she explains.

The next morning, Brigitte locks Ginger in the bathroom and takes the plant to Sam's greenhouse. Sam mixes up a potion, but tells Brigitte to test it on someone else first. She does so—injecting Jason, who returns to normal. Safe in the knowledge that the potion works, Brigitte returns to inject Ginger—but her sister has escaped.

A fantastical fright flick with a powerful human center, *Ginger Snaps* was perhaps the first instant-classic horror movie of the new millennium.

At school there is a search for information regarding the disappearance of Trina. Mr. Wayne asks to see Ginger. She kills him in his office. Mrs. Fitzgerald finds the two fingers of Trina in the garden and digs up the shallow grave in the shed to discover the girl's body.

Brigitte locates Ginger and tries to convince her sister to come back home with her. Ginger instead attacks and kills a janitor and asks Brigitte to join her. Ginger is transforming into a werewolf slowly but surely. When Brigitte refuses, Ginger takes off and heads to the school Halloween party.

Mrs. Fitzgerald pulls over to pick up Brigitte and explains that she has found Trina's body. She suggests blowing up the house to cover the evidence, killing her husband in the process, and taking off to "start anew." Wanting none of this, Brigitte instead attends the Halloween party where she finds her sister trying to seduce Sam. Brigitte infects herself with Ginger's blood and takes her sister outside, convincing her to come back home. Sam knocks Ginger out with a spade when he sees this—but Brigitte explains that the cure works, and the two take Ginger's unconscious body back home.

By the time Sam pulls up at the Fitzgerald household, Ginger has transformed. She bursts out of the van. Ginger and Sam hurry to mix up some of their potion. Sam tries to inject Ginger with it, but he is attacked and killed. Now a fully changed werewolf, Ginger chases her sister with the intent to kill.

After a lengthy chase around the house, Brigitte finally kills her sister by stabbing her through the chest with a carving knife. As the wolf dies, Brigitte lies next to what used to be her best friend and sister.

Critique

What is there not to love about *Ginger Snaps*? It brought the werewolf genre back into vogue (two similar-themed films, *Dog Soldiers* and Wes Craven's *Cursed,* swiftly

One of the photos staged by the sisters for their school project

followed[1]) and equated poor Katharine Isabelle's transformation from female to lycanthrope with all the growing pains of puberty. Just as the troubled Goth teenager begins menstruating, she is attacked by a werewolf and subsequently begins to grow hair where it is less than welcome. She also takes on unpredictable mood swings, much to the chagrin of her less-attractive sister, Brigitte (brilliantly performed by Perkins, whose short locks are disguised by a wig). A fantastical fright flick with a powerful human center, *Ginger Snaps* was perhaps the first instant-classic horror movie of the new millennium. Even after subsequent viewings, the film's jet-black humor, tremendous low-budget special effects and solemn, even underplayed ending never lose their appeal.

Written by a woman, *Ginger Snaps* also confronts male viewers with some blatantly honest feminine images that they may not like to see—from the blood-stained underwear to Isabelle's feeling ill for "female" reasons ("The words 'just' and 'cramps' do not go together," she deadpans). Even the onslaught of Isabelle's hair growth, a sure sign of puberty, is dealt with in humorous terms as—finding that she is sprouting locks of fur from above her breasts—the teenager hilariously maintains "I can't have a hairy chest...that's fucked."

Furthermore, when Isabelle worries about what her schoolmates might think of her after she sleeps with Moss, her naïve sister advises her to just pass the onus back onto her male counterpart. "It doesn't work like that," sighs Isabelle, with a hint of truth that successfully highlights the inequality between male and female promiscuity. In a genre that is predominantly associated, rightly or wrongly, with an overwhelming male following, it is refreshing to see a movie that tries to cut through such a stereotype and present an almost all-girl horror movie. Certainly the male presence in *Ginger Snaps* (predominantly highlighted by Lemche's drug dealer and Moss' libido-driven Jock) is minimal, and the central focus of the film is undeniably Isabelle and Perkins—their love and devotion for each other helping to steer a wonderfully conceived narrative.

Ginger Snaps **equates Ginger's transformation from female to lycanthrope with all the growing pains of puberty.**

Ginger Snaps also has its tongue firmly placed in its cheek, although the many laughs and quotable lines never get in the way of the scares or the gore—making the feature a worthy successor to its obvious inspiration, *An American Werewolf in London*. Like the John Landis classic, *Ginger Snaps* is also forthright about its mythology—"Let's forget the Hollywood rules," quips Lemche early on, after Perkins suggests that they might need a silver bullet. This is a movie where the monster can just as easily die from a car accident or a knife wound as from any of the old hokey cinematic devices. What this, arguably, succeeds in doing is adding further humanity to its onscreen creature. Isabelle's ordeal is handled with such care and sensitivity that even when she finally completes her mutation (into a refreshingly non-CGI wolf-woman), the viewer is still well aware of the human being that lurks underneath the fur and claws. That this otherwise ferocious beast can be executed in the most simple of methods makes the mythology of *Ginger Snaps* far more contemporary and easy to accept. Unlike even the Landis film, there is no full moon to usher forward the final transformation. Instead, Isabelle's progression into a werewolf is treated as inevitable—a slow-moving infection, which has a finality about it that is virtually unstoppable. The film also highlights that this "infection" could be viewed as a metaphor for sexually transmitted diseases—especially after Isabelle transfers her condition to her lover.

However, *Ginger Snaps* is as much a movie about teen rebellion as it is about period pains and devoured victims. The film's two sisters, reclusive and alienated at their high school and in their home life, find their confidence and voice through the film's ordeal. Ginger especially discovers her sexuality virtually overnight—and the werewolf curse initially seems to be a positive thing. Whereas the teenager is initially unable to talk to boys (her reaction to being asked out is to stare at the ground and mutter a quick, embarrassed rejection), following her run-in with a lycanthrope she is suddenly

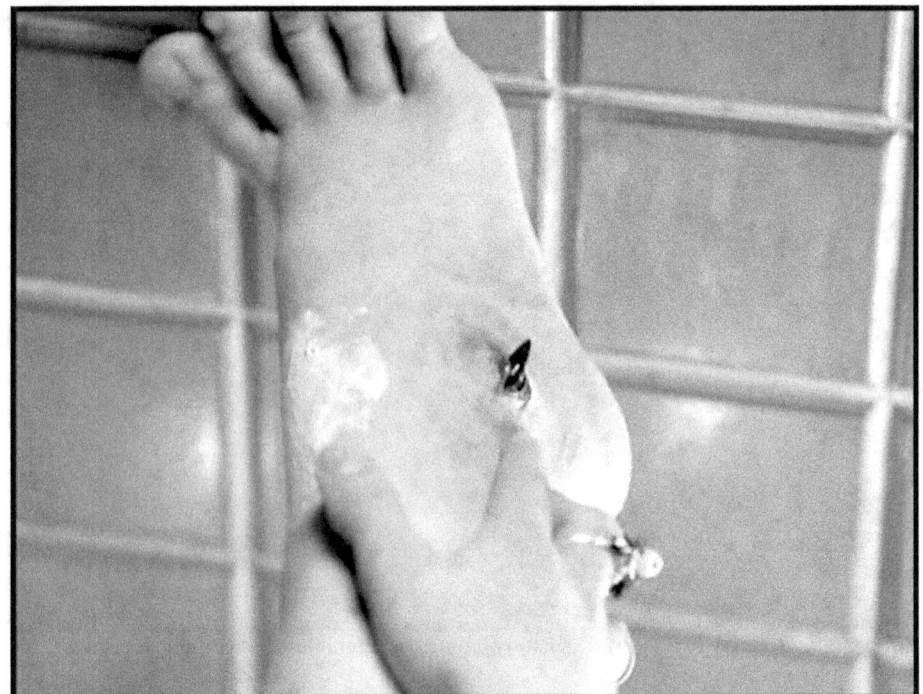

"I think there is an aspect in the transformation from child to adult that is similar to transformation from a moral human with conscience into an immoral creature capable of terrible things."

the aggressor. Her woman-on-top, teeth-bared foreplay with Moss is priceless. The poor boy doesn't know whether to thank his good luck or to be scared out of his wits. Credit also has to extend to Mimi Rogers, whose "liberal parenting" provides the film with a lot of laughs. A New Age, open-minded parent, she is also horribly off-target in discussing matters of a personal nature. Declaring, proudly, at the dinner table that her daughter got her period is extremely funny, but one really does feel sorry for her poor offspring who, understandably, react with firm embarrassment. Although *Ginger Snaps* was not a huge hit in the United States (and the subsequent U.S. DVD release was also lackluster—try to track down the Canadian or U.K. release), and unfairly dumped to video, it is such an endearing movie that one cannot help but feel its following will only continue to grow.

Standout Moment

Isabelle mounts Moss in an all-too-rarely-seen moment of a horror movie female dominating a sexual situation. With *force*...

Memories of the Film

"I had produced a short film in 1992 called *Half Nelson* that John Fawcett directed," states producer Steve Hoban. "I then produced another short in 1996 called *Elevated* that was written by Karen Walton. So when John and Karen decided to team up on a teen-girl werewolf movie, they figured, based on their past experiences working with me plus the fact that I had previously produced a very low-budget kind of horror feature called *Blood & Donuts*, that I would be a good match to help them develop and eventually produce the film. In fact, shortly after the shooting of *Half Nelson,* John says he pitched the idea for *Ginger Snaps* to me and, supposedly, I didn't think it was a very good idea. I have no recollection of this and think John really just made it up.

"But I really liked the idea of a movie that dealt with the difficulties of growing up but [was] told using the metaphor of a bloody werewolf yarn. I also felt that John, Karen and I were all at about the same places in our careers and made a strong team for independent financiers to rally behind. *Ginger Snaps* really did update both the wolfman and the werewolf film. It presents teenaged characters, specifically teenaged girls, in a stylized but emotionally honest way that tied in frighteningly well with our gritty human-transforming-into-monster story. I think there is an aspect in the transformation from child to adult that is similar to transformation from a moral human with conscience into an immoral creature capable of terrible things. Part of maturing is learning to control unsocial behavior. Brigitte learns this but Ginger, of course, does not. I think this kind of story using werewolves had never been done before."

The cast of *Ginger Snaps* is excellent and the two young leads—Isabelle and Perkins—are especially outstanding. Was it difficult to find the right players for the film? "Casting was very difficult," answers Hoban. "From the outset we decided it was crucial to have actors who either were teenagers, or would be completely believable as teenagers. We felt much of the strength of the movie depended upon our teenaged girls and the other kids feeling like teenagers. If they had been actors in their 20s pretending to be teenagers, then I think the whole movie would have felt less honest. A 28-year-old Ginger would have killed our audience's suspension of disbelief more than our five-foot, two-inch ex-jockey in the rubber werewolf suit," laughs the producer. "But, yes, casting for the girls was particularly difficult. We had casting calls in Toronto, Montreal, New York, Los Angeles and Vancouver. Toronto casting provided a unique problem since we had just been very publicly vilified, in the print media, on the radio and on television for supposedly using Canadian taxpayer money to make a slasher movie about teenagers murdering each other. The story started with a couple of Toronto casting directors who obviously can't read very well, and to whom we had sent the script. As a result, a lot of agents would not support their clients reading for the roles. It was remarkable how unprofes-

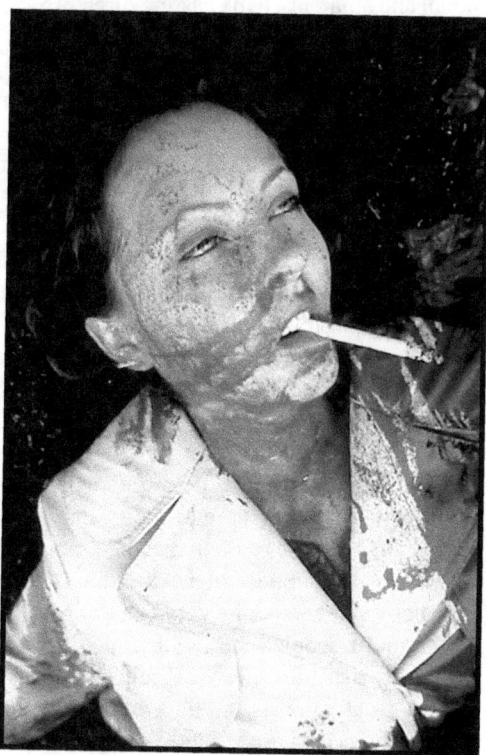

Ginger Snaps **isn't shy about the gore.**

Sadly, *Ginger Snaps* never received much respect in the U.S.

sional and amateurish the casting directors and many Toronto agents were. Fortunately, we did find very good candidates for the girls in New York and Vancouver and ended up getting both Emily Perkins and Katy Isabelle from Vancouver."

Although *Ginger Snaps* has its tongue firmly in cheek for a lot of its running time, it also contains a number of gory moments. Was anything cut from the film? "We did cut some scenes out of the film, but none of it was the gore," recalls Hoban. "We like gore! One scene we did cut was a fun moment in which 'Mom,' played by Mimi Rogers, shows up at the party at the end of act two looking for her daughters. She has some crazy idea that she is somehow responsible for what they are going through and now she is going to rescue them. However, this subplot never really resolved anything and as good as Mimi was, every moment she was on the screen at that point in the movie was going to distract from the evolving relationship between Ginger and Brigitte."

Sadly, despite wide theatrical success in Canada and Europe, *Ginger Snaps* never received the same respect in the States. "The film was always intended to be a genre film that veered into art-house territory, which often means being less commercial," admits the producer. "So we had no problems drifting away from straight-ahead commercial considerations. In the case of the ending to *Ginger Snaps*, we debated on many ways to finish it, but none of them had the dramatic power and honesty of what is in the film. Yes, it was a disappointment (that the film never went theatrical in North America). Especially since we came very close to getting a studio release on 2,000 screens. There were a lot of people who thought the film was good enough and appealing enough to justify the risk of a theatrical release. Unfortunately, not enough of the right people wanted to take the risk in the end, so it went straight-to-video, where it was a hit. I think it could have done well theatrically in the U.S., but who knows. In Canada the film is already being referred to as a bit of a classic, and there haven't been a lot of good

Katharine Isabelle as Ginger

Canadian horror movies in a long time. But unless director John Fawcett or one of our great cast members becomes really big, I suspect it will remain one of those well-made, somewhat influential films that almost made it..."

Through playing the more introverted of the two sisters in the *Ginger Snaps* series, actress Emily Perkins has made an immediate impression on horror movie fans as the hunchbacked, Goth teenager Brigitte, and the young actress admits to relishing her role in these movies. "It was always pretty easy to empathize with Brigitte," exclaims Perkins. "When I was younger, that was the side of me that I kept hidden, I was more of a people pleaser, so there was a cathartic element to playing her, it was really fun." How did this young Canadian become involved in a series of werewolf movies? "Well...I actually just auditioned," admits Perkins. "It was interesting because Katharine Isabelle and I had the same agent, so we auditioned together." With both characters cast, Perkins then had the challenge of acting under a long, shaggy black wig in *Ginger Snaps*—a far cry from her natural short hair. "Yes, I wore a wig," laughs the actress. "It was a bit strange at first, but it became easier as I got more into the character.

"It's totally different acting in the movie and then seeing it later in the cinema," continues the actress, commenting on being center stage in a gory horror flick. "There's so many people around when you're working on a film—you even get a choice of the flavor of blood you want to swallow. I would be asked, 'Would you like the orange or the licorice blood?' (*Laughs*). Same when you have to vomit blood, you get the choice of the chicken or the vegetarian option. I always think that if Julia Roberts was to act in one of these films, she'd get the choice of the asparagus or the lobster—don't you think?"

According to the director, casting for the film was difficult.

Ginger Snaps has made Perkins a recognizable face in the horror genre—so is the actress a fan of this type of movie? "Yes, I like horror films," she replies. "They don't engage me on an emotional, gut level but I think they are interesting to analyze. The monster usually represents marginal characters in society, lesbians or whatever else threatens patriarchy (*laughs*). As a feminist I tend to view horror films through a feminist lens, and I find it hard to get scared. I also like fun, campy horror movies." Does the actress have any favorites? "I don't know off-hand," maintains Perkins. "I thought *The Others* was very good. I don't see too many horror movies just now because I have two kids, so it's usually *Finding Nemo* and family films that I watch." What about *Dog Soldiers*—the other werewolf hit that was released on the back of *Ginger Snaps*? "Sure, I enjoyed *Dog Soldiers*," says the actress. But more or less than *Ginger Snaps*? "I can't comment on that, of course," she laughs, adding, "I'm biased." Like *Dog Soldiers*, *Ginger Snaps* was a hit internationally, but did not fare so well in America. Does Perkins have any insight into why this might have been? "Yes, *Ginger Snaps* did have more success abroad than in the U.S.—it was a Canadian indie movie and not ashamed of that, there were a lot of recognizable Canadian elements in the film," states Perkins. "These Canadian elements weren't covered up and perhaps this is why it wasn't as big in the U.S.—but I like to think that international audiences are a bit more open to films from other countries."

"I hope that doing the *Ginger Snaps* movies will lead to more auditions," continues the actress. "I only had five over the last year. A lot of the productions in Vancouver are American television shows and I'm a little different, I don't really fit the mold for them. I'm not a 'babe' (*laughs*). But I'm hoping to get more opportunities on the back of the *Ginger Snaps* sequels, and to make more original projects."

Alternate Critiques

"A regulation monster of the kind seen in too many *Howling* sequels makes an appearance in the finale, but director John Fawcett works hard to produce a truly emotional climax." (Kim Newman, *Empire*, Issue 145, July 2001)

"...the kids *will* love it...as long as they think *An American Werewolf in Paris* is better than *An American Werewolf in London*." (Alex Godfrey, *Hotdog*, Issue 13, July 2001)

"John Fawcett's hormonally charged *Ginger Snaps* updates *I Was A Teenage Werewolf* with a fun, female twist." (Paul Corupe, *Rue Morgue*, Issue 41, Sept/Oct 2004)

Jeepers Creepers

Director: Victor Salva
Produced by: Barry Opper, Tom Luse
Written by: Victor Salva
Cast: Gina Philips; Justin Long; Jonathan Breck; Patricia Belcher; Eileen Brennan; Brandon Smith; Peggy Sheffield; Jeffrey William Evans; Patrick Cherry; Jon Beshara; Avis-Marie Barnes; Steve Raulerson
Special Effects: Brian Penikas (creature & makeup effects supervisor)
Year: 2001

Plot Synopsis

Darius Jenner (Long) and his sister Trish (Philips) drive home from college. Trish has just split up with her boyfriend and, as such, has chosen to share a car with her brother. They take a back road home, and the road is deserted. Suddenly a banged-up truck speeds up behind them, trying to shove them from the road. The two youngsters manage to maneuver themselves so that the truck passes them by. The truck's license plate reads "Beating U."

Later, Darius and Trish pass by an old church. They notice the "Beating U" truck pulled up outside, and see a mysterious figure (Breck) wearing a cowboy hat and off-loading what looks to be a dead body down a large hole in the ground. Darius attempts to use his cell phone to call for the police, but he cannot obtain reception. The figure (identified in the credits as "The Creeper") gets in his truck and once again endeavors to drive Darius and his sister from the road; this time he succeeds and the youngsters swerve into a field.

As the truck disappears into the distance, Darius decides—against his sister's wishes—to go back to the church and see if it really was a human body being dumped in the ground. If so, he reasons, they have a duty to see if the person might still be alive.

At the church, Darius crawls down a large waste pipe—which

Trish (Gina Philips) and her brother Darius (Justin Long) receive a strange warning, but are unable to make the police believe their story.

is where the "body" was thrown down—with a flashlight. However, he ends up falling down the pipe and landing in a vast underground pit. He discovers the wrapped-up body of a teenaged boy, barely still alive, and with his stomach stitched up. The boy dies in front of Darius. Using his flashlight to look for a way out, Darius sees dead bodies everywhere—cemented into the walls and covering the ceiling.

Trish waits for her brother to return to the car. When he does, he is dirty and unable to speak. He tells her that they have to find the police. They stop at a roadside diner and ask for help. The diner's phone rings and Darius picks it up. The voice of a black woman is on the other end. "Have you seen the cats yet?" she asks. "I saw you with lots of cats." She explains that she sees Darius and Trish and tells the boy to run whenever he hears a song with the lyrics "Jeepers Creepers, where'd you get those peepers?"

The police arrive and find it hard to believe Darius' story. Outside, Darius finds his car has been raided and his laundry has been spilled across the ground. Darius and Trish drive to the police station with two officers (Beshara and Barnes) following them. The officers find out that the church, which Darius reported finding the bodies in, has been set on fire. On the radio in his car Darius hears the "Jeepers Creepers" song.

The Creeper appears on top of the police car and kills the two officers. One of the victims' heads is thrown over the dashboard of Darius' vehicle. Darius and Trish draw to a stop. They see The Creeper pick up the head and bite the tongue out. Trish and Darius drive away and pull over at a lone farmhouse to see if they can use the phone.

An old lady answers the door (Brennan)—and Darius notices that she has lots of pet cats. Remembering what the voice on the phone said to him about seeing "lots of cats," Darius urges Trish to get back in the car and keep driving. Suddenly, The Creeper appears in the garden. The old lady gets a shotgun and fires at it, but the creature leaps up and flies into her house. Trish and Darius escape back into their car. The Creeper kills the old lady when she goes back into her house to battle it with her gun.

Trish and Darius meet an old woman (Eileen Brennan) with a house full of cats, just as they were warned over the phone.

Back in the car, Trish runs their mysterious stalker over, again and again. They drive away, but we see the flattened Creeper sprout wings out of its back and return to normal.

Darius and Trish arrive at the police station. They phone home to explain what has happened. An elderly black woman (Belcher) enters the station and explains that she was the voice on the phone back in the diner. She introduces herself as a psychic, although the police sergeant (Smith) indicates that she is mad. "Every 23rd spring, for 23 days, he gets to eat," she explains to Darius and Trish. She sings the "Jeepers Creepers" song and states that "I hear it playing while one of you is screaming." She then explains that either Trish or Darius has something that The Creeper needs. Down in the prison cells, The Creeper feeds on one of the convicts. When this is discovered, the police officers all group together to kill the mysterious creature—but their firepower fails to take it down.

The psychic tries to help Trish and Darius escape from the station. The Creeper catches the psychic but, after smelling her, it lets her go unscathed. In a deserted room in the station, Trish and Darius hide—but The Creeper locates them and takes Darius in his arms. The police arrive, but The Creeper dives out the window, with Darius, and flies away.

The next morning, Trish asks the psychic what she really saw in her visions. She replies by stating that she is just a crazy old lady.

We arrive in the basement of a deserted factory building where we hear the screams of Darius. We enter into a small room where The Creeper whistles and stitches up some flesh. The dead body of Darius hangs there. His eyes have been removed.

The distinctive Long was a regular on the television series *Ed*.

Critique

Jeepers Creepers introduced horror fans to what was, arguably, the first great movie monster of the millennium. Not since Freddy Krueger, or possibly Pinhead from the *Hellraiser* series, had there been a horror film villain that was popular enough to capture the imagination through a captivating backstory and an effective design. The Creeper, played by Jonathan Breck, has both—and his appearance is nothing less than fascinating, to the point that Breck owns the screen whenever his green-skinned anti-hero appears. Perhaps inspired by the iconic half-man, half-beast creation of *The Creature from the Black Lagoon* (which is one of director Salva's favorite films), The Creeper is surprisingly man-like when we first glimpse him, through the eyes of the film's actor Justin Long, and this allows Salva to surprise us even further when—bit by bit—he unravels the character as being truly "not of this world."

Sure, something is not quite right about the sight of Breck, balanced on top of a speeding police car, attacking two police officers—but this is a horror movie and if Jason and Michael Myers can rise from the grave over and over again, why should this surprise us? It is not until we see Breck actually fly, and sprout his wings, that we really begin to comprehend that this is not just some run-of-the-mill screen slasher. Salva wisely saves his biggest surprise for last when The Creeper lets out a scream and his entire face begins to hideously mutate—his mouth revealing a set of animalistic fangs. After a decade of nondescript cinematic creatures (one would surely have to search hard to think of a memorable monster from the nineties), *Jeepers Creepers* proved to be a breath of fresh air, and it was not much of a surprise when the feature spawned a legacy of its own with 2003's similarly excellent sequel.

Some viewers were, perhaps understandably, disappointed by the movie's split personality (something Salva himself touches upon in "Memories of the Film"). Beginning as a dark, psychological chiller, complete with a coven of dead bodies—one of modern horror's most ghoulish sights—*Jeepers Creepers* spins into something completely different about halfway through its running time. Turning into a more straightforward B movie, with additional scenes of gross comedy, the skin-crawling fear that the film has initially mustered up vanishes until a sudden, but nonetheless shocking, climax. Salva handles this transformation as best he can, proving himself to be an expert filmmaker in the process, and although the movie's tone is certainly not consistent, its characterization, direction and visuals are.

Philips is an appealing and strong heroine.

Certainly, once the terror begins, the film's teen leads act in a sensible manner—from Long attempting to use his cell phone to Philips finding the time to call home once she is in the (relative) safety of a police station.

Even when the narrative insists that the two must go back and explore The Creeper's lair, after they see him throw a dead body into the ground, Salva makes sure that this decision is not taken lightly. Subsequently, Long's argument with his sister ("What if it was one of us down there?") places the viewer in an awkward situation. Fully aware that we are watching a horror film, the viewer's foremost reaction is to urge Long and Philips to drive away; however, Salva cleverly plays upon our own conscience with this sequence and, ultimately, we are made to feel the same guilt that Philips ends up experiencing. Indeed—what if it happened to be us down there? Or what if we could be the one to save somebody's life? While in many genre films characters that return to the scene of a crime are usually hard to sympathize with (especially when they meet their inevitable end), through paying attention to his script and the words of his characters, Salva never fails to make the actions of his leading actors anything less than believable.

Of course, there is still the question of Salva's use of gross humor—which sits alongside the onscreen scares and violence. Considering the lambasting that some genre critics gave Wes Craven's tremendous *Scream* for daring to weave in a few

Jeepers Creepers contains a number of good scares.

laughs with its terror,[2] *Jeepers Creepers* is even less likely to find favor with those who dislike this practice. While these complaints appear futile, especially considering the unintentional comedy value inherent in many "classics" of the genre, it is worth noting that the stylish look of *Jeepers Creepers* at least means that the comedy remains distinctively bleak. Therefore, while we might titter at the sight of The Creeper French-kissing a decapitated head and pulling out its tongue with his teeth, the sequence is shot in such a dark, ominous manner that the viewer's feeling of threat never quite disappears.

This is also true when The Creeper is revealed to us as a scaly, winged carnivore—it takes away a lot of the anonymity of the character but also allows for a fantastical, supernatural element to surge into the narrative that is hard not to be captivated by. Furthermore, one thing that *Jeepers Creepers* is not is predictable. In fact, for a movie that has obvious leanings toward the teen horror genre, its ending is a complete surprise—far nastier than anyone would have the right to expect. Following this unsavory climax, the film's end credits appear decidedly intrusive (as Salva himself explains, *Jeepers Creepers 2* is effectively the second half of the first film's original script rather than an actual sequel).

Far from presenting just another dumb teen horror movie, Salva gives us identifiable characters in *Jeepers Creepers* and his picture holds up well over subsequent viewings. Never too gruesome, but certainly containing a number of good jumps and macabre images, the film begins with just enough mystery to provoke interest and will likely remain an enjoyable thrill ride for future generations of genre viewers. Kudos to Salva as well for creating a female character that has much more to do than run away and scream—Philips, instead, makes for a courageous and worthy heroine. Don't be shocked if this is one monster franchise that spins more installments.

Standout Moment

The Creeper's underground lair—a gruesome but nonetheless spectacular sight that lingers in the mind long after it has disappeared from the screen.

Memories of the Film

"The first film was actually badly compromised, and with the sequel we were given twice the money and twice the time, which allowed me to make the sequel more like how I wanted to make the first movie," states Victor Salva, reflecting on the cult hit that made him a genre name. "I mean, I love all my films," continues the director. "A filmmaker is like a proud father, so saying I'm not happy with it would not be completely accurate. The time and budget restraints meant that I had to make some very big cuts in the script. The first half of the film is actually very accurate to what I wanted, but the third act of *Jeepers Creepers* is not what I had planned, the film ends very suddenly and that's because I couldn't shoot my original third act. I'm very grateful that people love the first film, and a lot of people resent that the movie turns out to be something totally different from what they expect. Halfway through they don't exactly know what all this is, and I've been told it loses its strength, mystery and appeal when The Creeper turns out to be some kind of monster. I have got some disappointment with it, but I still think it's well made and really good. But, yeah, I had other plans for the original film."

Some might agree with Salva's criticism of the original movie—at the time of *Jeepers Creepers'* release, some critics expressed disappointment that the feature's initial suspense and mystery gave way to a loud and violent creature feature. "I really stay away from reviewers," asserts Salva. "I haven't read any of the reviews for the second film, but I know that the critics over here in America haven't been very kind.[3] It's a very strange world, you make a film with this single vision and yet you have the studio wanting to reshape things and then when the movie is finally finished, it's at the feet of the reviewers. Woody Allen said something very true—he said, 'Never let the voices of others into your head.' I used to read reviews, but I started asking, 'Who am I making my film for? For this critic because he said I did this and that wrong?' I'm so glad that *Jeepers Creepers* and *Powder* have resonated with audiences. It's not a good idea to try and make a film that will appeal to the widest denominator, that's how so many bad films end up coming out of the studio process. A friend of mine, for some reason, keeps me informed of the reviews, which I'm not sure is such a friendly thing to do," laughs the director.

It has been said many times that the big studios are almost ashamed to make horror movies. Having made his two *Jeepers Creepers* films for MGM, would Salva agree with this? "Yes, I think that comment is true for a couple of reasons," states the filmmaker. "Horror is not seen as a prestigious genre, and the horror audience is commercially narrow, whereas the audience for a romantic comedy is much wider. However, horror films

Movie vet Eileen Brennan is a welcome addition to any cast.

The Creeper (Jonathan Breck) has plans for the doomed Darius.

are considered inexpensive to make and a way of making cash. The genre is usually the star—you don't need a star to make a good horror picture. I guess the exception might be something like the Dreamworks version of *The Ring*—which cost 40 or 50 million dollars to make, but I think the studios generally see the appeal of big-budget horror as limited. I made *Jeepers Creepers* for the teenaged boy in me who still loves a good horror movie and loves even more a good creature movie—in other words, I am a fan too. And as selfish or self-centered as it may sound, I really don't make my movies for anyone but the person inside me. That is really the only person I know well enough that I feel capable of fashioning stories for.

"Do I hope others will see my story the way I do and enjoy it? Of course! My wish and the wish of every filmmaker is that their story is well received across the globe! But when all the layers of commerce and artifice are peeled away, it is still just a movie for me. Produced for the public. And this is where art and commerce collide and it is usually a very bloody battle, because down deep every studio executive knows that the filmmaker makes films for himself, with the studio hoping that they can skew the director's take on the story toward as much mass appeal as possible.

"Many a great movie has been dismantled and destroyed in the name of box office, as we well know. I have gone on a little too long about this partially because some of the criticism that I have read about *Jeepers Creepers 2* is that it wasn't enough like the first film. So I want to say that, while I enjoyed the tone, the brother and sister and how they reacted to all dark scariness and the slow reveal and evolution of what turns out to be The Creeper in *Jeepers Creepers*—I knew that if I did in fact go down this very long road of making a sequel to my story, that I would not be interested in making another movie of similar tone and similar beats. My biggest incentive to do the sequel was that it was a way to try and do the bigger beats of the original film that were taken away from me, when poor planning and budgeting had a disastrous crush on the making of the original."

Coming after his 1999 drama *Rites of Passage*, *Jeepers Creepers* was quite a transition for Salva. Does the director see himself returning to helming more alterna-

" I made *Jeepers Creepers* for the teenaged boy in me who still loves a good horror movie."

tive, serious films? "Well, I have tried to," replies Salva. "I love film—this is really the truth. Horror is just one of the things I like to do. I'd love to emulate Francis or Alan Parker—they have gone to each genre and done something in each of them. I don't want to be thought of as 'Victor Salva the horror guy.' Even after two monster movies in a row, I have other projects I want to get done. I have a sci-fi picture I want to do, it's not a futuristic sci-fi film, it's more dramatic, and I've written dramas and several thrillers. I don't want to end up being pigeonholed. I mean, I know a lot of horror filmmakers personally, and it's great company to be in…"

When Salva was writing the first *Jeepers Creepers,* did he expect to introduce a new screen villain to sit alongside the likes of Freddy and Jason? "I don't know how to treat that," responds the director. "It's maybe wishful thinking because he's the newest monster. Being part of that echelon would be truly wonderful, but it's not for me to decide if he belongs there." Like Freddy Krueger, The Creeper has moments of comic relief. "Yes, we wanted The Creeper to wink at the cast, tear a tongue out of a severed head…we let The Creeper be a little de-monstrous in his wickedness," laughs Salva. "As long as it was true to itself and not lampooning, we went with it. Probably the best example is The Creeper sniffing the kids, and how he gestures at them. We were a little afraid that he would become this wisecracking Freddy Krueger type. Were we going too far? Was it becoming too cute instead of too creepy? But at the first preview all these touches went down very well, so we kept them in."

What attracted Francis Ford Coppola to produce the *Jeepers Creepers* films? "Well, he produced my first feature, I don't know if you'd call it a horror movie—maybe more of a thriller, a film called *Clownhouse*," states Salva. "I think Francis saw *Jeepers* as a commercial film, as something that could make money and lead to investment in

The Creeper is stalking the guy not the girl in *Jeepers Creepers*.

other kinds of movies." As with many great horror films, *Jeepers Creepers* benefits from having a fantastic scream queen in actress Gina Phillips—although Salva admits that he did not try to discover the next Jamie Lee Curtis. "I didn't cast with an eye on discovering a new scream queen," he admits. "Although since you mention her, I have loved Jamie Lee Curtis since I first laid eyes on her in *Halloween*, and she has become such a wonderful actress and, I sense, a very wonderful person.

"I wanted an actress who could be real enough to pull us into and ground us in the world of *Jeepers Creepers*, and both of these kids have the very tough job of convincing the audience scene by scene that this is really happening and as I do in every film, I just went with the very best actor I could find for the part. Gina's chemistry with Justin was equally important, and the two related to each other like a brother and sister almost instantly, but the truth is that Gina Philips is a terrific actress who understood the part of Trish incredibly well. I know she prepared for the part with an intense focus on detail, and I think it was finally her authenticity that got her the part. She was just a very fine actress doing a very fine job in the role of Trisha Jenner."

Philips also serves as something of a distraction in the plot. Contrary to genre stereotypes, The Creeper is interested in stalking and killing her brother and not her. "Yeah, that's right," states the director. "I got very tired of seeing women slaughtered and raped in all these genre pictures. I have a very hard time with the violence in my films. That may sound absurd because so many violent things happen in Victor Salva movies, but I really couldn't get behind the idea of perpetuating the very tired and damaging misogynistic bullshit that populates so many horror pictures. Being a gay man, I didn't have or harbor any feelings about the girls who rejected me in high school, so maybe I don't feel like I have to take it out on every good-looking girl who wanders into Poho County in any of my films. I enjoy letting them kick ass, be smart and have a point of view.

"However, the dilemma of who gets it—because in horror films someone has to get it—falls to the guys. I enjoy presenting a creature in the way of The Creeper who essentially has to feed off males—because his body, which he is trying to regenerate every 23 years, is a male body and while there are a few parts that could be interchangeable between males and females, The Creeper's very selective feeding gives me a great excuse to let the girls off the hook for once and let the guys be the object of desire for a while. It fits my sensibilities better and presents a very refreshing—and hopefully surprising—beat at the end of *Jeepers Creepers*. Best of both worlds."

Jeepers Creepers **made a cult star of Jonathan Breck.**

Just as *Jeepers Creepers* made Victor Salva famous in the horror world, so too did it make a cult figure out of its star—Jonathan Breck, who plays the film's monstrous stalker. "You know, I've gotten into the genre, more since I became an actor, because that's kind of where my career has gone to," reflects Breck. "As a kid I wasn't a big fan of horror because I was the scaredy cat, I was the kid that the guys picked on—the guy they loved to scare. My dad's favorite prank, when I was growing up, was to go outside in the middle of the night, go around the house and scratch on the screen outside my bedroom window, which would absolutely terrify me.

"So maybe that's why I got into horror, because I had some issues to work out—but I enjoy it now and I'm a fan. I think it's kind of interesting that before I got the *Jeepers* job, I hadn't really done a lot of horror and I didn't know a lot about the genre. And my first thought was, 'Wow, this is so weird,' but I think it kind of served me well, as I didn't go into the role with subconsciously, or consciously, any idea of any horror icon before me. I didn't have any thoughts of, 'Oh I'm going to do this here,' or 'I'm going to do that there.' I think that helped me, as we were able to bring a character to life that was fresh and had a new dimension, and I'm not sure we would have been able to do that if I was an aficionado of the genre."

So how did Breck react to being chosen for the role? "Well, it was one of these weird roles where they sent me a paragraph description of the character and that was back when I went and auditioned for the first movie," he mentions. "It was a big audition…and apparently they'd been looking for this character for months and they were down to the wire, they needed somebody right away. So all they did was fax me the paragraph of what the character description was and I had about a week to work it out—they just wanted me to come in the room and show them what I thought the character was about. And for whatever reason I just started playing around and I had a very strong feeling about the way he would move, the way he would sit, how he would stalk his victims and how he would attack.

"So I went in the room and had these very strong opinions about what I thought the character was and fortunately they responded to it. Also—I shaved my head, which

The makeup for The Creeper took three hours to apply and two to remove.

helped a lot with the intensity of him, because Victor wasn't sure—on the first movie—how much prosthetics were going to be involved. Matter of fact, when they made the deal and the role was offered to me, Victor said to me, 'I really love your look, so minimal prosthetics on you where I can.' Then of course we know what happened, and when I got to the set it went much further…there's nothing left of me but my eyes and even with that I wore contacts for the first one. So why choose me? I guess I just had an innate understanding of who the character was and how to play him, and I've always been an actor that likes to pay a lot of attention to detail."

Did acting under a huge amount of makeup prove to be tough for Breck? "The makeup would take three hours on a good day and seven on a bad one—and then we'd work for a full day and it took two hours to get out of it, so it makes for a long day," he laughs. "It's uncomfortable to be covered in that stuff…but actually while they mold all that stuff to me, it becomes almost like a second skin, so after a while you get kind of used to it. But the hot days are hard because there's no relief. I can't get out it and each lunch or anything like that, and you know there's really no relaxing. I mean, you've probably heard before that moviemaking is 90 percent sitting around and 10 percent work. Well, while with other actors, with that 90 percent of the time they can go in their trailer and read a book, watch a film or whatever, but I'm just sitting there. So this role becomes a process of stamina to maintain your energy and be ready for those 30 minutes, or hour or two, where you really have to be on. The rest of the time it's about manipulating your energy and keeping your spirits up."

There was some criticism about how *Jeepers Creepers* began as this really tense little horror film, and then spiraled into being a crazy monster movie—how would Breck address this criticism? "Well, I think you described it well," replies the actor. "It's almost like two different movies. The first part of the movie is very moody and creepy and settles in on you—it's uncomfortable, and the second half is a much more in-your-face monster movie. And I think that any time a movie tries to straddle genres, they have a hard time succeeding, because people go in expecting one thing and they're halfway through the movie and it turns into something else. You know, I was in the movie a lot more, but then as we got closer to making the movie I got cut out more and more…because they ran out of money.

"But in the original script I was in the first 10 minutes and then as we lost more and more money, I got cut out more. So I know, and this isn't an excuse, that a lot of the reason the movie turned out the way it did was down to budgetary reasons. We had

The underground lair of the monster is a moody set design.

another 20 pages in the script, and when I arrived in Florida where we shot the first film and they had a new script for me...they said, 'You better look at this one,' and when I did, the last 20 pages had been cut. They decided the last 20 pages were too expensive, it was going to involve a lot of digital effects, and there was an extensive chase scene. There was to be a magnificent chase scene in *Jeepers,* one where I'm on top of the van and the kids are driving and I'm fighting with them...so you get a lot of that with the bus in *Jeepers Creepers 2.* A lot of the action that we weren't able to put into part one, Victor put into the sequel. He effectively called the second one his 'little action picture.'"

Recently we're seen *Alien Vs. Predator* and *Freddy Vs. Jason*—if The Creeper could fight any movie monster, who would it be? "I actually get asked that question a lot," replies Breck—"over who's going to win between Freddy and Jason. I mean, this is moviemaking and I've learned never to second-guess them. You don't know what they're gonna come up with. Who would I like to fight? I think I'd like to go after Godzilla or something like that."

Alternate Critiques

"Victor Salva's solidly creepy, '70s-style horror film has decent characterizations and a gloomy atmosphere that cuts deeper than most teens-in-terror flicks." (Kim Newman, *Empire*, Issue 149, November 2001)

"Writer/director Victor Salva has got some moves, but it's not genuinely scary or genuinely funny. So what's the point?" (Peter Bradshaw, *The Guardian*, 10/19/01)

"...writer-director Victor Salva's *Jeepers Creepers* is an enjoyable horror flick... Salva brings a reasonable imagination to play on a powerful memory." (Philip French, *The Observer*, 10/21/01)

King of the Ants

Director: Stuart Gordon
Produced by: David Michael Latt/Duffy Hecht
Written by: Charles Higson
Cast: Chris McKenna; Kari Wuhrer; Daniel Baldwin; George Wendt; Timm Sharp; Ron Livingston; Vernon Wells; Lionel Mark Smith; Carlie Westerman; Steve Heller
Year: 2003

Plot Synopsis

A young house painter named Sean (McKenna) meets an obese, friendly manual laborer while decorating a house. The laborer introduces himself as Duke (Wendt). "Is this all you want to do?" asks Duke. He promises to call Sean if he can find him further work.

Duke phones Sean to tell him that he is to meet Ray (Baldwin), the owner of a building company who might have some employment for him. The three men have a short conversation in which Ray asks Sean to follow around an accountant at city hall called Eric (Livingston). Sean does so, taking pictures of Eric as he goes about his day-to-day work. Sean also develops an attraction to Eric's beautiful wife Susan (Wuhrer), who works at a local mission for the homeless.

One evening, a drunken Ray picks Sean up in his car. He offers Sean a cash reward if he can kill Eric for him. They agree on $13,000. The next day, Sean enters Eric's house and bludgeons the man to death.

When Sean returns home, he vomits. He then tries to get in touch with Ray and Duke, but to no avail. Finally Duke agrees to meet Sean at the local zoo. Once there, Sean is throttled by Duke and told to leave town. Duke explains that they wanted Eric to be "shook up," but not dead. They never expected Sean would be able to kill him.

Scared, Sean takes some files to his friend George (Sharp), who works at a dog shelter. Sean is later picked up and forced into a van by Duke

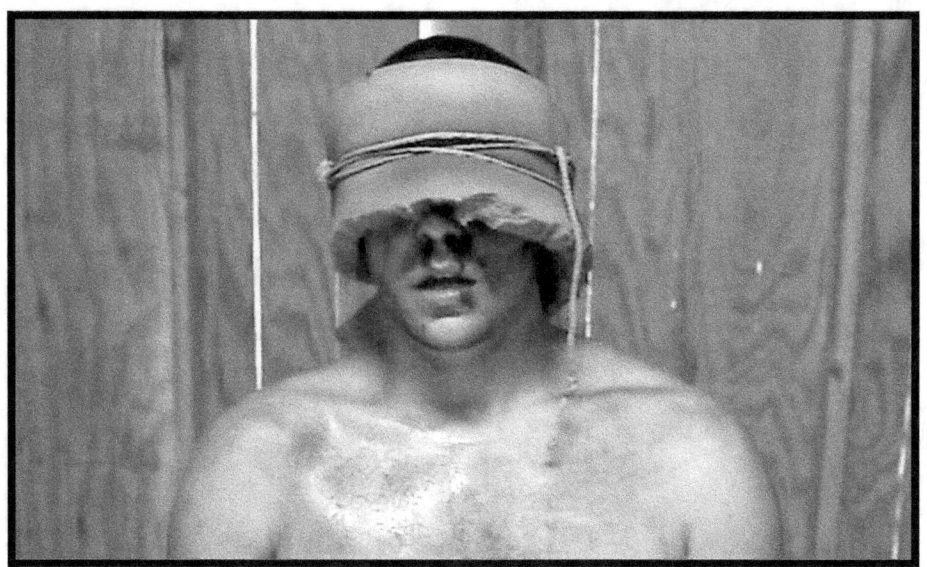

Sean (Chris McKenna) is beaten by the thugs who hired him to kill a man.

and two more of Ray's henchmen—Carl (Smith) and Beckett (Wells). In the van, Sean explains that if anything happens to him the truth will come out. As a result, the men drive Sean to Ray's house—located in the middle of the desert. They lock Sean in a wooden hut. Left alone, Sean masturbates and imagines making love to Eric's wife, Susan.

When Ray arrives, the men force Sean onto a chair and pour alcohol down his throat. Ray explains that he is not going to kill Sean, but rather he is going to turn him into a vegetable. The men wrap a foam blindfold around Sean's head and eyes and wallop him once with a golf club to the cranium.

Sean awakens with a pounding headache. He begins to hallucinate about Susan. The next morning, the men return to once again use the golf club on Sean's head. More hallucinations follow—this time Sean imagines Susan as a hermaphrodite. Beckett takes pity on Sean and allows him to leave the shed for a brief walk.

After another thump with the golf club, Sean imagines Susan as a grotesque monster, eating her own shit. The next day, Sean ties the foam blindfold around his head and sits in the chair. The men are shocked.

Beckett again allows Sean to leave the hut. He offers him a glass bottle of beer. Sean breaks the bottle in half and tries to slit his own throat. The men decide that they cannot leave their prisoner alone anymore.

Duke stays with Sean in the hut. Sean dives at him, knocks him over and bites the man's throat out. Duke dies. Sean beats Carl with a hosepipe as he tries to escape. Suddenly George arrives and urges Sean to get into his van. George has read the files that Sean left with him.

George tells Sean, whose face is a bruised and distorted mess, that he has to turn himself in for Eric's murder. Sean refuses, and George tells him to leave the van. Sean walks to the mission where Susan works. Taking pity on him, Susan spends the next few weeks nursing him back to health. When Sean is recovered, Susan takes him into her house. Sean still carries his files, sealed away in an envelope.

Sean is attracted to Susan (Kari Wuhrer) but the relationship will spell her doom.

Susan's young daughter Catlin takes to Sean and he settles into the household well. One weekend, Susan sends Catlin away with her relatives so that she and Sean can be together. They make love. The next morning, Sean leaves Susan's house to meet up with George. However, in a fleeting moment, Susan recognizes him as the man who once sat outside her home.

Suspicious, Susan opens up Sean's secret envelope. She finds the pictures that he took of her and Eric, and also his notes on the killing. When Sean returns, Susan confronts him and begins to beat him. Sean tries to resist retaliating, but he finally throws Susan against a wall. She hits her head and dies instantly.

Sean leaves the house and returns to Ray's pad in the desert. He calls Ray and asks him to come to the desert. Sean finds Duke's body stored in a refrigerator. Sean decapitates Duke and burns the head. Ray arrives with Beckett and Carl. They find Duke's mutilated body.

Sean wounds Beckett and Carl with an axe. They lie dying inside the house. Sean throws gasoline into Ray's eyes. Ray pulls out a gun, but he cannot see to shoot. Sean sets him on fire, and sets the house alight with Beckett and Carl still inside.

Critique

A blistering, brutal film—*King of the Ants* remains criminally underseen, although it is undoubtedly the finest film that Stuart Gordon has lent his talents to since 1985's startling debut *Re-Animator*. Since then, Gordon has taken on a whole host of projects but none of them have ever allowed him to cross over to the mainstream in the way that, for instance, John Carpenter or Wes Craven have. This may be because Gordon tackles films that—even for the scope that the genre affords to fantastical plots—contain elements that are far too bizarre and incomprehensible for many viewers to get their heads around. This, coupled with his focus on especially bloody set pieces, has resulted in such interesting items as *From Beyond* (1986) and *Dolls* (1987) being viewed as little more than subversive cult curios.

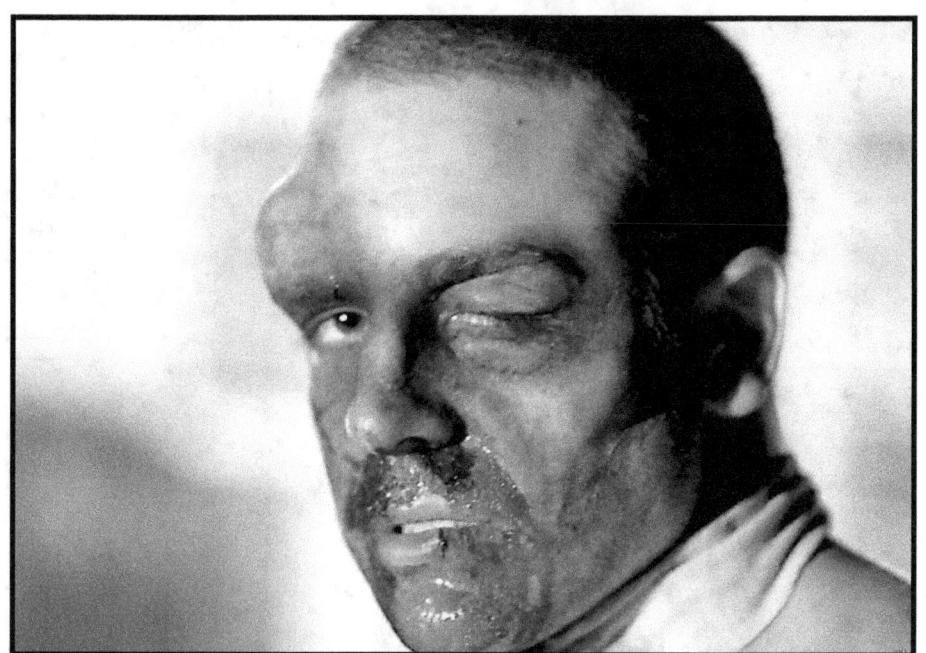

***King of the Ants* has that definite Stuart Gordon look.**

As a result, Gordon remains a distinct cult personality, albeit one with a notable individualism which is perhaps most evident in his 2001 film *Dagon*—a weirdly intriguing mess that few directors would even dare to attempt. 2003's *King of the Ants* showcases a more serious, studied side of Gordon—although the filmmaker's love of outlandish, violent material is in evidence throughout. This factor alone might be enough to alienate a wider audience, which is something of a shame considering that *King of the Ants* also contains a radical and purposely muddled view of "right" and "wrong" that all but banishes "good" and "bad" characters and instead lets in a flourish of gray. In our post-September 11th world, where cinema in general appears to be so much more interested in giving us straightforward plots of good vs. evil, *King of the Ants* is a study of humanity's potential for barbarity—in the face of deprivation—that delivers its message with an almighty wallop to the head. And in the case of Chris McKenna's character, you can read that last line literally…

King of the Ants is a low-budget feature that benefits not only from Gordon's seasoned expertise in the director's chair, but also from a first-rate cast. McKenna, an unknown actor, takes on the lead role with confidence and admirable gusto—his transformation from hard-up, good-guy drifter to murderous thug is brilliantly calculated. His awkward killing of Livingston is hard to endure (there is no fast kill, but rather a slow and methodical death)—made all the worse by the actor's apparent tenderness toward his victim just before he finishes him off. Considering that this is McKenna's first lead role, his emotive, and shockingly frank, performance is very impressive. Female costar and B-movie maiden Wuhrer is a remarkably beautiful onscreen presence, and her natural, dark good looks are slightly reminiscent of Ashley Judd. Perhaps more familiar from such recent schlock as *Anaconda* (1997) and *Eight Legged Freaks* (2002), the actress certainly proves her worth as a more serious performer in *King of the Ants*.

Sean's hallucinations picture Susan as a hideous monster.

From her appearance as a shit-eating monster, to the sight of her harassing McKenna with a power drill during one of the actor's many hallucinations, and finally shedding her clothes for some copious nude scenes, Wuhrer is in top form throughout. Her violent confrontation with McKenna, whereupon she realizes that her new lover is also her husband's murderer, is nothing less than believable and her character's genuine grief makes for what is probably the only humanity in the entire picture.

As McKenna's tormentors, Baldwin and Wendt, in particular, carry a vile presence, and their torture of the young actor is extremely difficult to watch. It also helps to put the viewer in a distinctly awkward situation. Having witnessed McKenna brutalize and kill an innocent man (Livingston), we are suddenly placed in the position of watching him being horrifically beaten. Gordon wisely spends enough time with McKenna's character, prior to his slaughter of Livingston, for us to grasp his innocence and his financial desperation. Although McKenna's murder of an innocent man is a ghastly, revolting sight, it is difficult not to change one's emotions from disgust to pity, as McKenna is captured and tortured by a bunch of repugnant hoodlums. Interestingly, *King of the Ants* then turns this sympathy on its head and the movie's horrifying finale reminds us of what we really should have known all along: McKenna is a sadistic, desperately violent man.

Admirably, Gordon's camera takes a distant stance from the action—never judging the characters and never directing the audience's emotions. *King of the Ants* is a movie that asks viewers to watch the unfolding horrors and make their own minds up as to how they feel when the end credits roll. Nothing is solved in the film—four violent men die and one violent man lives—and the true tragedy involves the death of Wuhrer and her husband, a young, loving couple. There is no feel-good ending and any emotional investment that we may have had in McKenna—following his beatings—evaporates after his involvement with Wuhrer surfaces. "These days and times, you gotta do exactly what you can to survive," states Baldwin when he first meets McKenna. This is probably the underlying theme of *King of the Ants*—greed keeps the Western world moving along, regardless of the victims in its wake. If we are to take anything away from Gordon's modern masterpiece, then it is surely that—in a culture where humanity is taught to look out for themselves first and others later—morality can only shatter. And for the relevance of the title, you'll just have to see the movie for yourself.

Standout Moment

McKenna's brutal revenge. Distant, harrowing and quite thoroughly disturbing.

Memories of the Film

"A friend of mine told me to read the script," comments star Chris McKenna, when asked how he was cast as the lead in *King of the Ants*. "I read it and I loved it. In fact, I read it over and over again. That's the God's honest truth. It's not something I would normally do, but I really loved the script that much and I was convinced immediately that I was the only person who could play this role the right way. I just had to convince Stuart Gordon of that and all the other producers. So, I went into the audition with that intention and I guess it worked. Stuart said he'd love to work with me and I said I'd love to work with him. About 36 hours before the start of the shoot, I found out that I was finally cast. Everyone else was cast but me. I walked into the room where the whole cast was sitting and they were there waiting expectantly for their lead. I was terrified but exhilarated."

What were the challenges, for the actor, of portraying a character that's tortured and driven to madness? "I had to do some soul-searching, I suppose," reflects McKenna. "I

George Wendt is Duke, who drags Sean into this world of violence.

stayed alone. I had my girlfriend move out for the month so I could spend more time by myself to find in me the darkness that (my character) Sean had to have. Sean was a loner so I figured I would emulate that lifestyle. There were also physical challenges, of course. I was bruised and beaten up by the end of the film something awful, as were George, Vernon, Lonnie and Kari. We all took a beating physically.

"Mentally, I had some difficulty with nightmares. It was certainly all worth it and I think it all helped. I would do it all again, that's for sure, and Stuart's a wonderful man and a great director—he's like Santa Claus. Everyone says that about him and it's true. He never stops smiling no matter what's going on and no matter how horrible the problems are on the set. He's always happy, he's always 'up,' he's always optimistic and he always makes it work. Stuart was wonderful. He knew when everything was going well and he wouldn't touch anything. If any of us had a problem, he knew just what to say. It's that kind of know-how and savvy that makes him a great director and a great guy.

"I mean, I was absolutely terrified that I was the only one on the call sheet that I had never heard of. But from the very start, George walked up to Stuart right after our read-through and said, 'This kid's gonna be good.' Stuart told me that story just because I'm sure he knew that I was nervous. People were nothing but supportive to me. I heard nothing but positive things after every scene that I did. No matter how nervous I was, everyone was there right behind me. Everyone believed in me, and as a result, I believed in myself. It was very intimidating, yet it was certainly a blessing because they knew how to make it work. They're all great actors who make it really easy to turn in a good performance when you have such a great cast around you. I got along with everybody, and everybody seemed to be very happy with the results of the film."

Despite the brutality and nihilism of the completed film, the actor does admit that the shoot also provided some fun times. "There were plenty of light moments on the set," laughs McKenna. "Stuart is a funny guy, George is hysterical, Vernon, Lonnie,

Daniel and Kari—we all had a great time on the set. It's probably hard to tell by watching the film, but there were jokes left and right. During our rehearsal of the love scene, Kari would be saying, 'Will you pay more attention to my breasts?' Then when Vernon and I were wrestling and calling each other names we would say to each other, 'Are you whipped?' or 'You hit like a girl!' We were joking and having a good time. We had to. We spent so much time together under such grueling conditions that the only way to get through it was to laugh. So we had a great time. During one of the masturbation scenes in the shed, I got ahold of Kari's prosthetic penis from one of the earlier scenes. During the filming of it the last day, David Latt, the producer, put me up to it and I pulled my hand out from under the sheet holding up this prosthetic penis and screaming in terror (*laughs*) which got a big laugh from everybody! I think we have it on film somewhere. They're keeping it hostage."

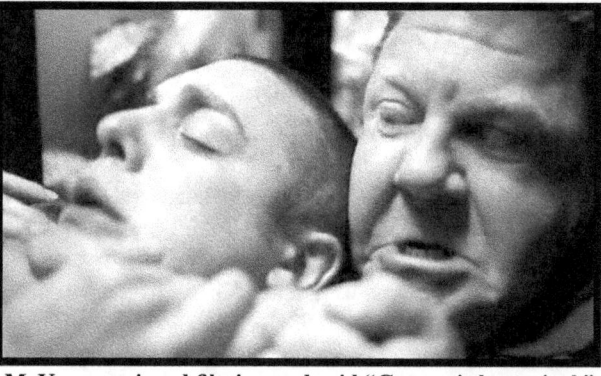

McKenna enjoyed filming and said "George is hysterical."

McKenna's reaction to the finished film was overwhelmingly positive. "I watched it with Stuart Gordon and we had a great time," says the young performer. "I was so nervous how it was turning out, but I had a big smile on my face for an hour and a half as the movie played out. I couldn't believe how it had all worked and that my performance, as far as I could tell, was working the way I wanted it to, and the film was working the way I wanted it to, and the way I imagined it would. I couldn't have been happier. At the Seattle Film Festival, I walked out of the theater halfway through and stood to the side so I could watch everyone's faces instead of the film. I watched people with their mouths open, people covering their eyes, people cheering, people laughing, people clapping. I had never seen anything like that before where my performance or something I was involved in, [got] that big of a reaction out of the crowd. People were actually getting emotionally involved in the movie and characters. That was very special to me. I'll never forget that first time I saw it with an audience."

Alternate Critiques

"Newcomer Chris McKenna is excellent as a young manual laborer....The reason this film is so effective is it's brilliantly written and brilliantly acted, and shows once again what a fine and versatile filmmaker Stuart Gordon is." (Allan Bryce, *The Dark Side*, Issue 109, June/July 2004)

"Stuart Gordon exploded into the horror film world with his unforgettable *Re-Animator*....His latest, *King of the Ants*, may be his best film since his auspicious debut." (Ross Williams, *Film Threat* [online])

"...an absorbing portrait of a rising serial killer filled with deft twists and turns." (Alan Jones, *Shivers*, Issue 110, February 2004)

R.S.V.P.

Director: Mark Anthony Galluzzo
Produced by: Mark Anthony Galluzzo
Written by: Mark Anthony Galluzzo
Cast: Glenn Quinn; Jason Mewes; Majandra Delfino; Daniel Joseph; Grace Zabriskie; Jonathan Banks; Rick Otto; Lucas Babin; Brandi Andres; Nora Zehetner; Jeanne Chinn; Reno Wilson
Special Effects: David J. Barker/Kirby Brothers
Year: 2002

Plot Synopsis

A man climbs through an apartment window and murders a young, sleeping couple. The police arrive on the scene to find the words, "Why did the quick brown fox jump over the lazy dog?" sketched in blood on the wall. This is actually a visual document of the topic being discussed in a criminal psychology lecture by Professor Hal Evans (Quinn). The "brown fox" was the moniker of a famous mass murderer who went uncaught for three years.

Following the class, Quinn discusses serial murder with one of his pupils—Nick (Otto). "To do this you have to have a plan," muses Nick to his friend Jimmy (Babin). Jimmy is distracted by the appearance of his girlfriend Jordan (Andres), who happens to be Nick's ex-girlfriend. Nick explains to another of his friends, Garrett (Wilson), that there are no hard feelings between the two.

Jimmy has invited his classmates to Las Vegas for an end-of-semester party. In a roadside bar Jimmy, Nick and Evans discuss serial murder further. Nick acknowledges the classic Alfred Hitchcock film *Rope* in which two students of criminal psychology kill one of their classmates in an almost-perfect murder.

Nick paces around his large suite in Las Vegas alone. He appears restless. Terry (Mewes), a fast-talking, long-haired stoner, arrives with

John (Daniel Joseph) clutches his bong at an end-of-semester party.

some dope to smoke. Soon other guests begin to arrive, including Garrett and his girlfriend Cricket (Chinn), John (Joseph) and Jordan. Nick seems increasingly nervous, especially around Jordan, who wants to know why her boyfriend is not at his own party. Nevertheless, the booze and drugs continue to flow.

Jimmy's patriotic uncle (Banks) and aunt (Zabriskie) arrive with their attractive daughter Leigh (Zehetner). Nick instantly begins chatting up Leigh. Jimmy's aunt is a card reader and she agrees to read Nick's future. She slaps down the "death" card, but also says that she sees "fame" in his future.

When Jordan thinks that she hears a thumping noise, Nick turns up his stereo as loud as possible. The noise is soon forgotten about. The party's final guest, Evans, turns up. Jimmy's aunt and uncle decide to leave. In the corridor, Nick bludgeons them both to death and carries their bodies away.

In the suite, Evans speaks about his admiration of bullfighting. He gets into a fight with John, who believes that he is disturbed. Evans ends up on the receiving end of a beating before the two are separated.

Nick invites Leigh into the bathroom, where they begin to make out. Admiring his reflection in the bathroom mirror, Nick suddenly breaks the girl's neck and dumps her body in the bathtub. When Cricket and Garrett and leave the party, Nick runs out into the corridor and nail guns them both.

Nick's neighbor, Callie (Delfino) surprises him by gate-crashing the party. He takes her inside and introduces her to the other guests. Jordan insists that Nick call Jimmy. He seems to do so, having a conversation with him on the phone, but when Jordan tries to take over the call the line is dead.

Callie takes out a Twister board and the drunken guests start to play. Nick puts some poison in Terry's wine. He then climbs up to the hotel balcony and strangles John. Back in the suite Terry begins to cough and passes out from the poison in his drink. No

R.S.V.P. tagline: Nicky's having a party...and everyone's dying to be there.

one has a phone to call the emergency services. Nick takes Callie into the kitchen and drowns her in a pot of boiling water.

Jordan tries to leave the suite, but Nick stops her. Evans catches on as to what his serial murder-obsessed student is doing. He is trying to carry out the perfect murder spree. We learn that Nick killed Jimmy earlier, by suffocation, and his dead body now resides inside a cabinet which dinner has been served on—just as in *Rope*. Nick intends to frame Evans for the killings—after murdering him in "self-defense."

Nick pulls out a handgun. Evans is killed but Jordan escapes onto the roof of the hotel where Terry, previously assumed to be dead by Nick, comes to her rescue and slices his adversary's legs with a knife. Nick topples to his doom and Terry lies upon the balcony of the hotel, joking with Jordan that he's going to have to find some new friends.

Critique

Having previously made the excellent, but underrated, independent drama *Trash* (which featured future stars Jeremy Sisto and Jamie Pressly in lead roles—possibly launching their careers), director Galluzzo makes an impressive genre debut with *R.S.V.P.* and stakes his claim as a true *auteur*. Writing, directing and producing the movie, as well as lending his talents to the film's slick cinematography and even the stunts, Galluzzo crafts a wickedly dark movie that has its roots in Hitchcock's classic *Rope*—to the point of referencing the film's plot in a *Scream*-style moment of postmodernism. While this sort of self-parody is tricky to realize in a "straight" horror feature, *R.S.V.P.* does it well by never overdoing such winks to the audience and instead treating its scenes of mayhem with deft seriousness while still playing on the viewer's knowledge of the Hitchcock release.

Thus, while James Stewart's professor brought his murderous students into line during the finale of *Rope*, Galluzzo has his psychotic killer (brilliantly essayed by the relatively unknown Otto) actually slay his superior (*Angel* star Quinn) in an unexpected twist. It is very much a rerun of the classic *Frankenstein* story—Quinn, possibly every bit as unlikable as his lunatic counterpart, has created a monster out of his student and must face the result. The professor is utterly obsessed with blood sport and serial murder but without even a hint of condescension for such acts—and so when he ultimately meets his end, there is a genuine feeling of just desserts, especially when the viewer has had to suffer through his pretentious and obnoxious defense of bullfighting. Quinn—in what would sadly be his final movie role—is excellent throughout, genuinely reflecting the possibility of a future leading man that would, of course, be squashed only shortly after *R.S.V.P.* wrapped up.

Of course, Quinn and Otto are not the only scumbags in Galluzzo's movie. Indeed, as with *Rope*, *R.S.V.P.* does not have one likeable character in the entire cast and even after the murder spree has finished, and Otto is dead, the movie's two survivors show no noticeable remorse—sitting atop their lavish Las Vegas hotel and joking about the situation. It is likely that Galluzzo's cynical approach is not for everyone, but his dislike of "yuppie" culture and the media's treatment of serial murderers as celebrities is evident throughout the feature—and it is refreshing to see the genre being used to, literally, slaughter some of society's less appealing characters. In a hugely entertaining sequence, Galluzzo has Otto, Quinn and Babin discuss some people that deserve to meet their end. Among those listed (which the audience may find slightly cathartic) are cigarette manufacturers, traffic cops, politicians, tax men and meter maids and, strangely enough, Americans themselves. The suggestion being that the country needs to start over. However, in light of Otto's thirst for fame and recognition (perhaps a comment on the *Big Brother* reality TV-show generation) it is difficult to believe that such desperation is relative only to the States—especially considering the international appeal that "reality" television has gained. In saying this, *R.S.V.P.* is, without doubt, every bit an American story—from the mannerisms of the characters to the setting of Las Vegas, which could not be any more perfect for the movie's events. Long seen as the city of wealth, consumerism and, of course, sin, Galluzzo's Las Vegas houses a group of obnoxious youngsters who dress well, look good and yet appear remarkably dull and bereft of personality. If ever an onscreen cast cried out to be destroyed, then this is it.

The deaths in *R.S.V.P.* take place largely offscreen, but in true slasher film style a plethora of weapons are used in the slaughter. Galluzzo wears his love of the genre on his sleeve, and well-versed fans will likely recognize a violent nail gunning (shades of *The Toolbox Murders*) and a nasty face roasting (*Deep Red*, *My Bloody Valentine*) as being among the nods to previous movies. The murders are all impressively staged—very theatrical and even operatic (Galluzzo's use of music on the soundtrack complements *R.S.V.P.*

Kevin Smith's favorite actor, Jason Mewes, is the star of *R.S.V.P.*

the onscreen action well)—and Otto wears a violent streak a mile wide that always indicates to the audience that no one is safe for long while he is around. Although much of the film is played for laughs, there are some nice jumps in here, and a growing sense of unease throughout.

Certainly, *R.S.V.P.* is infinitely better-acted, directed and shot than most of its peers, and Galluzzo is clearly a talent to watch. The cinematography in the film, which looks as if it was executed on a budget far larger than the film had (apparently less than $1.5 million), is outstanding, and the there are some razor-sharp lines. Jason Mewes is also in fine form in the sort of role he has become famous for playing—that of a stoner with little motivation in life outside of girls and parties. Filmed while Mewes was still recovering from a devastating heroin addiction, it's surprising how sharp his performance is, and a testament to Galluzzo as a director. Although the rest of the cast is less known, Andres casts a strong presence as Jordan. Not your typical slasher film "final girl" (that would surely require a lot more screaming), she is extremely attractive and carries her part with confidence. Although *R.S.V.P.* went largely underseen, even despite being selected for Sundance, the movie showcases a slew of youthful talent, both in front of and behind the camera, that commands our attention.

Standout Moment
The gorgeous Nora Zehetner thinks she's about to get it on with Otto when he suddenly, and without warning, snaps her neck. It's the film's first truly shocking scene of violence—and the beginning of the end for most of the cast...

Memories of the Film
"I wanted to see if I could do the film with a visual style that wouldn't get stale," reveals director Galluzzo. "My biggest objection to most one-set books or plays, that are turned into movies, is that they still keep the three-wall structure. It's very flat—and it gets boring. So I specifically designed the set to provide maximum visual options by incorporating numerous planes of actions, octagonal shapes, obstructions such as pillars, chandeliers, bulky furniture, multiple levels. You name it, we added it! We also put a roof on the set and proceeded to shoot it like an actual location. This made the lighting appear more natural, and for the most part viewers assume that the set is a real penthouse.

"I was a horror junkie as a kid...*Night of the Living Dead, Friday the 13th, A Nightmare on Elm Street*—these are my favorites, but you got to take the *Scream* series into account as well. If for nothing more than how they showed the audience exactly how the genre works," states the director when quizzed about his love of horror films. "I'd say Frank Capra's *Arsenic and Old Lace* ended up a big influence on the final presentation—in fact, we deliberately attempted to add its zany, frantic energy to the *Rope* plot of a hidden murder victim and party scenario. Finally we tossed in some of Agatha Christie's *Ten Little Indians* to raise the stakes...or maybe I should say the body count. But I thought we were actually pretty restrained in regards to graphic bloodshed and sort of went with an old-school style of the lead-up and strike without lingering on the damage. However, I've had quite a few people tell me how gory my film is, so I must be getting jaded out here in Hollywood.

"It really just started out as an exploration of modern culture and the concept of fame vs. infamy and the way that the media hypes both equally," explains the direc-

Things get hot for one of the unsuspecting party guests.

tor—speaking about the motivation behind *R.S.V.P.* "If you look at the U.S. today, the youth are gagging for fame. *American Idol, Survivor, Project Green Light*...we've sort of created a fame lottery. Of course with *R.S.V.P* we took it down a very macabre path and used a psychopath who is killing people to be recognized as being the best at something." Gullazzo then proceeds to talk about the psychology that drives the murderous lead character played by Rick Otto. "He is trying to impress, and even one up, his college professor, who has filled his head with all these breathy tales of serial killers. In truth, Otto's character doesn't even care if he is caught and has to go to trial, since he would relish the spotlight and the chance to go toe to toe with the F.B.I.

"The lead characters played by Glenn Quinn and Rick Otto dominate the film and by nature they are not the kind you'd like to have over to meet mother. I suppose, in the end, we really wanted to touch on Social Darwinism, Nietzsche, and the fame vs. infamy debate." Is *R.S.V.P.* the first horror film to actually quote from Nietzsche? "As far as I know we probably are," laughs Galluzzo. "We intended to have a whole Nietzsche subplot, but had to cut it for time. Though I can assure you I'm not the first to pilfer Friedrich—in fact, *Conan the Barbarian*, of all films, opens with a quote from him. Then again, that's what you get when Oliver Stone helps write your action script!" So what about the other, less than likeable, characters in the movie? "As for the other characters in *R.S.V.P.*—I don't know if I would class them as being unlikable...but this might be down to my continued exposure to a certain city on the west coast of America," laughs the director—referring to Los Angeles.

The director also explains his motivation behind the film's various murders. "I sort of tried to find a means of death that matched the character's personality or occupation. Thus, the rock 'n' roll guy gets strangled by his own guitar string, we poisoned

The egotistical Nick (Rick Otto) plans on committing the perfect serial murders.

the stoner, and the construction worker gets the nail gun to the forehead." The film's biggest name star is "Jay and Silent Bob" icon Jason Mewes, and *R.S.V.P.* gives the actor another very similar role to play. Was there ever any worry about typecasting? "Not really," confirms Galluzzo. "I actually wrote the role for someone else as it so happens, which might surprise some viewers. Also, the role that Jason plays is supposed to be the one guy who is invited to every party in town because he brings the weed—he knows everyone and everyone knows him. Finally, there was the character point that he has taken so many drugs that you can't poison him! He's like Keith Richards, I guess—he'd snort anthrax if he could get his hands on it."

Alternate Critiques

"Galluzzo's one-liners aren't great, but the movie is a cut above garbage like *Soul Survivors*. Oddly, this film has gone straight to DVD when lesser productions have nabbed theatricals. It's well worth taking a look at." (Richard Marshall, *DVD World*, Issue 11, April 2004)

"Diabolically clever…a matter of increasing suspense!" (Kevin Thomas, *The L.A. Times*, 2003)

"An experiment in unpleasantness! The most despicable cast of characters to descend on Las Vegas since Peter Berg's *Very Bad Things*!" (Scott Foundas, *Variety*, 2003)

Wrong Turn

Director: Rob Schmidt
Produced by: Brian J. Gilbert, Robert Kulzer, Stan Winston
Written by: Alan McElroy
Cast: Desmond Harrington; Eliza Dushku; Emmanuelle Chrigui; Jeremy Sisto; Kevin Zegers; Lindy Booth; Julian Richings; Garry Robbins; Ted Clark; Yvonne Gaudry; Joel Harris; David Huband; Wayne Robson; James Downing
Special Effects: Stan Winston Studio
Year: 2003

Plot Synopsis

A young couple (Gaudry and Huband) climb a mountain in the vast woodland of West Virginia. The man makes it to the top first, leaving his girlfriend stuck halfway down. She struggles and asks for help. A noise is heard and her boyfriend's dead body appears at the top of the mountain. The girl cuts herself free and drops to the ground. She tries to run but trips over a line of barbed wire and is pulled offscreen.

Chris (Harrington) is a doctor on his way to a conference. Stuck in a traffic jam, he decides to take a back road through the West Virginia woods after locating a map at a run-down gas station. He crashes into a camper van that has pulled over due to a line of barbed wire planted in the road. Five young people have been planning to take a vacation in the outdoors. Chris meets Carly (Chrigui) and Scott (Sisto), who are just recently engaged, and a pretty brunette called Jessie (Dushku). The four decide to go and look for help, leaving behind Evan (Zegers) and Francine (Booth), who smoke dope and make out.

Chris notices a campfire in the woods as the four continue their walk. They finally reach a dead end and decide to take another route.

Back at the site of the crash, Evan hears a noise in the woods and goes to investigate. When his girlfriend does not hear

Jessie (Eliza Dushku), Chris (Desmond Harrington), Carly (Emmanuelle Chriqui) and Scott (Jeremy Sisto) take a deadly *Wrong Turn*.

from him again, she follows suit—discovering her boyfriend's shoe and his ear on the ground. From behind, she is hooked in the mouth with a shaft of barbed wire by a mysterious stalker.

Chris and his three companions arrive outside an old shack. Desperate to use a telephone, they walk into the abandoned house, which is unkempt and horribly dirty. Carly goes to find a toilet. Chris discovers body parts in the fridge, and Carly finds a dead body in a bathtub. As the four decide to leave, a van pulls up outside and they are forced to hide. Chris and Jessie hide under a bed, while Scott and Carly take refuge in a cupboard. They watch two huge, deformed mountain men (Clark and Robbins) and their skinny, monstrous brother (Richings) enter with the dead body of Francine. The men cut her up on a table and fall asleep, after which the four youngsters escape from the house but awake the men in the process. The three villains jump in their van and give chase.

The youngsters arrive in a scrap yard full of cars and tents, presumably taken from previous victims. The mountain men leave their van and fire at Chris, shooting him in the leg. Scott diverts the mountain men by running into the deep woods, allowing Chris and the two girls to steal the van. The three pull the van up when they see Scott emerge from the woods, but he is shot by an arrow and killed. A roadblock soon stops the van from going much further.

The three leave and take shelter in a huge watchtower, where they find lights and a radio. As nightfall approaches, the passing mountain men hear the noise of the radio and burn the tower. Chris convinces the girls that they can stay alive by jumping from the tower into the trees. They do so, but are then tracked by the skinniest of the mountain men, who follows them from tree to tree—firing arrows. He finally catches

The stranded travelers will find no help in this filthy shack.

up with Carly and beheads her. Chris and Jessie manage to push him from atop a tree, and eventually lose the men—taking shelter in a cave for the remainder of the night. Jessie tells Chris that she split up with her boyfriend and her friends took her out on this trip into the wilderness.

Jessie has a dream that the men kill her. When she awakes, she and Chris leave the cave and continue their hike to safety. The three men surprise them and Jessie is taken captive.

Chris sees a police car and runs for help, but the officer (Harris) is shot in the face with an arrow and dies. One of the mountain men takes the vehicle, with Chris gripping on underneath the car. The police car pulls up at the men's shack, where Jessie is tied up.

Chris appears from under the car and lights fire to the hut. He then drives the vehicle into the house and fights the three mountain men. Jessie gets free and helps him, shooting one of the maniacs with an arrow and slashing another with a machete. As the two leave the house, Chris shoots the police car and blows up the house. He and Jessie drive away to safety in the mountain men's van.

However, later that night a state trooper—investigating the site of the damage—is attacked by the skinniest of the three mountain men, who is still not dead.

Critique

Although *Wrong Turn* demonstrates an obvious fondness for such 1970s horror classics as *The Texas Chain Saw Massacre* and *The Hills Have Eyes,* it actually plays out as an unacknowledged remake of Jeff Lieberman's 1980 film *Just Before Dawn.* Although not as famous as the Craven or Hooper movies, *Just Before Dawn* also took the *Deliverance*-inspired premise of pitting unprepared city dwellers against backwoods

Chris convinces the girls that they can stay alive by jumping from the tower into the trees.

residents who don't take too kindly to trespassers. The end result features the "townies" resorting to varying degrees of viciousness in order to stay alive (in Lieberman's movie, one would-be victim kills her antagonist by forcing her entire arm down his throat). *Just Before Dawn* also features two monstrous, inbred brothers (unlike *Wrong Turn*, however, they are masked—this being the period of *Halloween* after all), and the movie is a tightly directed, genuinely chilling fable that has, somehow, escaped a release during the DVD boom.

In saying this, *Wrong Turn* betters *Just Before Dawn* by featuring superior performances from its young cast, creepier villains, an increased number of gruesome set pieces, and excellent special effects from Stan Winston. Even so, considering that 2003's excellent remake of *The Texas Chain Saw Massacre* opted to retain the same title as Tobe Hooper's original hit despite having very little in common with its forefather, it does seem puzzling that *Wrong Turn* did not choose to be more forthright with its most obvious inspiration and find a way to use the *Just Before Dawn* moniker. Indeed, despite replacing *Just Before Dawn*'s mountain setting of Oregon with West Virginia, and adding an extra killer to the mix, *Wrong Turn* is pretty much the same film only with all the benefits that CGI and better production values bring to the admittedly scant storyline.

Whatever the case may be, there is no denying that *Wrong Turn* is perhaps best placed within the recent outbreak of genre remakes such as *Chain Saw*, *Dawn of the Dead* and Tobe Hooper's *Toolbox Murders* (both 2004) and the forthcoming *2001 Maniacs*. With the feel of 1970s horror permeating the movie, *Wrong Turn* is inevitably predictable (count down the deaths of the supporting characters until the leads triumph over their adversaries) but—much like its inspirations and its aforementioned contem-

Wrong Turn **has a sharp, visceral brutality that carries a considerable punch.**

poraries—the movie has a sharp, visceral brutality that carries a considerable punch. The end result makes for one of the most gruesome mainstream genre releases in recent memory and there is no denying that Schmidt, and screenwriter McElroy, have put a lot of thought into how to splatter their characters. Even for the most jaded viewer, there are some wicked little surprises on offer here. Moreover, the feature moves along at one hell of a pace and Schmidt's flair for creeping up on the viewer and shouting "boo!" is extremely well done.

Make no mistake: for all its debt to past classics, *Wrong Turn* features a number of gut-wrenching moments that are entirely its own. Top of the list has to be the wonderfully staged sequence where Schmidt has his four young leads trapped in the rundown old shack of his repugnant cannibalistic villains. With two characters hiding in a cupboard (in a magnificent moment of computer-enhanced camera trickery, we get to zoom through a hole in the hiding place and straight into Chrigui's pupil as she watches the terror unfold) and another two located under a bed, *Wrong Turn* really jacks up the suspense. It is hard not empathize with the foursome as they watch the dead body of their friend (Booth) thrown on top of a table and subsequently dismembered by the grunting thugs who have killed her. Even if the hapless onlookers close their eyes, Schmidt makes it very clear to us that there is no escaping the ghastly sound effects and, in doing so, he puts some of the more squeamish audience members in a similar predicament to his actors.

It is a moment of perfectly realized horror—and *Wrong Turn* succeeds admirably in following this up with further intense scenes such as Jeremy Sisto's untimely demise and the excellent, drawn-out escape through the tree tops, whereby Chrigui is eventually killed. Although there have been some (perfectly valid) complaints about the use of

CGI in the genre, *Wrong Turn* creates some of its backdrops and effects digitally and the result is seamless. Similarly, the beheading of Chrigui, followed by her body dropping to the ground and a shot of her diluting pupil, is a digitally produced moment of mayhem that stands up with some of the best demises in slasher movie history.

As with such contemporaries as the *Texas Chain Saw* and *Toolbox Murders* remakes, *Wrong Turn* wisely casts its movie with Hollywood up-and-comers who can actually act. This is not a film that has young actors merely substituting for a pound or two of meat, ripe to be hacked up by some passing maniac—but rather a movie that opts for fleshed out, believable characters. Although Harrington's transformation from stern-faced businessman to Indiana Jones-type hero is slightly difficult to buy into, his female counterpart, played by Dushku, casts an alluring presence as the movie's heroine and her eventual descent into brutality is nicely realized.

Dushku explains, in one pivotal moment, how she personally feels responsible for her friends' deaths (she had broken

Wrong Turn has believable, fleshed out characters.

up with her boyfriend and pushed for a backwoods trip with them to forget about it). As a result, her final retribution toward the mountain men carries a cathartic air to it, and although the actress does not quite manage to portray her climactic self-defense with the flavor of dementia that one might expect from a young girl who has seen her friends slaughtered, she nevertheless does a good job of trying. Unlike Rob Zombie's 2003 release *House of 1000 Corpses*—which also attempted to recapture the tone, and brutality, of 1970s exploitation horror but ended up being merely unlikable—*Wrong Turn* gives the viewers characters to remain focused on and to really pull for. This

The girls are chased by Three Finger (Julian Richings), the skinniest of the mountain men.

vital ingredient, overlooked in Zombie's movie as well as in the recent *Cabin Fever*, is what really makes for a great horror film. Fully understanding this, Schmidt crafts an edge-of-the-seat classic in *Wrong Turn* that sets the bar for any future filmmakers who might think of treading into the woods for another *Deliverance*-meets-*Texas Chain Saw* take-off. Only the ill-advised credits sequence that creates a set-up for a sequel leaves a bitter taste in the mouth.

Standout Moment

The entire sequence in the cannibal's mountain hideout...Don't. Make. A. Sound.

Memories of the Film

"I made short films, first on video and then on 8mm and 16mm film. Then I entered film festivals, went to film school, watched a lot of movies, often two a day..." states director Rob Schmidt, reflecting upon what got him started as a film director. "I got involved with *Wrong Turn* because I had wanted to do a horror film for a long time," he continues. "In my first reading I thought it was a very simple, tight horror film. The idea was to make a straight ahead, 1970s-style horror movie. It is made to scare you and in my experience, adding gags damages a film's ability to scare. *Wrong Turn* isn't original—it introduced people and killed them off in horrible ways, but it was scary. I could do without the sequel-establishing ending, but I love the rest of the movie..."

If Schmidt was unhappy with the ending, does this indicate he did not receive final cut on the film? "Well, you know, in the U.S. you don't usually get final cut," he answers. "I believe that in Europe some sort of legal thing protects your final cut, but

Urban meets redneck in *Wrong Turn*, and it's not a good thing.

in the U.S. it is not set up that way. You have some consultation on it, I mean—I love that film and I am very, very happy with it. We had lots of discussion about the ending, and I always wanted it to end with Eliza and—driving away, but the producers wanted something that would lead into making another movie. I liked the idea of the two lead characters, having gone through this adventure together, driving away in their vehicle and if I got everything I wanted in life I'd be very happy. I love horror films and I had wanted to make one since I was a kid. They're one of the coolest type of movies to make, because you get real visceral reactions from the audience when they're working. One of the great pleasures of my career to date was seeing *Wrong Turn* with our first test audience. But I'm comfortable with the ending we have, and yesterday I was called about doing the sequel; the sales of the DVD has had something to do with it..."

How did the Oscar-winning special effects guru Stan Winston get involved with *Wrong Turn*? "You know, Stan found *Wrong Turn*," states Schmidt. "Brian Gilbert, who is the president of Stan's company, funded it. Stan Winston wanted to produce a series of creature-based horror films and he was combing for scripts, and that's how *Wrong Turn* got discovered. Working with Stan is like working with a brilliant, charming uncle that has your back. He has a terrific sense of humor and he brings a really great vibe to the work."

Was it a disappointment for the director that the film did not have the theatrical success that contemporaries such as *I Know What You Did Last Summer* and *Scream* had? "Well, you know, I don't have experience of marketing movies," answers Schmidt. "I would have liked there to be a bigger campaign for *Wrong Turn*, it was very conservative—a theatrical run of 1,600 theaters, when other horror films might get a release on 2,800 to 8,000 theaters. But that was the business strategy and the studio figured that it would make most of its money on home video, so they just put it out on a limited number of screens. I'm not a business or marketing person, but it worked out well enough for them to want to do a sequel. Why it didn't do better business than *Scream*—well, *Scream* was the sort of movie you'd go and watch as part of a gang of friends. When you go and see it you're seeing stars—beautiful people up on the screen, and that is all part of the appeal. As for *I Know What You Did Last Summer*—I don't know why we weren't as big a success. I spoke with one of the producers of that movie, and he is a smart guy. I don't understand why the film was such a success. Honestly, I have come this far with little knowledge of the marketing side. For the most part, the people who run companies know what they have to do to keep their company profitable. They usually know what people want to see. I don't know the economics involved with *Wrong Turn* or *I Know What You Did Last Summer*."

Was there any intentional comment from the director on the more liberal side of America, represented by the youngsters in *Wrong Turn*, meeting the regressive, Southern area of the country? "I should tell you that originally with *Wrong Turn* we wrote the lead part for a black man," answers Schmidt. "I would have loved to make that movie, it would have contrasted things even more starkly, the urban meeting the rural. The film is certainly based upon the premise of this entire fear, the fear of people who live out in the middle of nowhere and who might hate you—or eat you! Certainly this is a big part of how horror movies function. When we held screenings of *Wrong Turn* at malls, I really liked it when kids come out mimicking (the killer) Three Fingers' laugh. I can imagine them going camping and doing that laugh—it's something primal, just this basic fear of otherness.

"But something I've discovered since I began making movies for a living is how hard it is to find a star that equated with being financially reliable with one sort of movie—horror, comedy or action or whatever. In that age group of 20 to 25, there are not many black

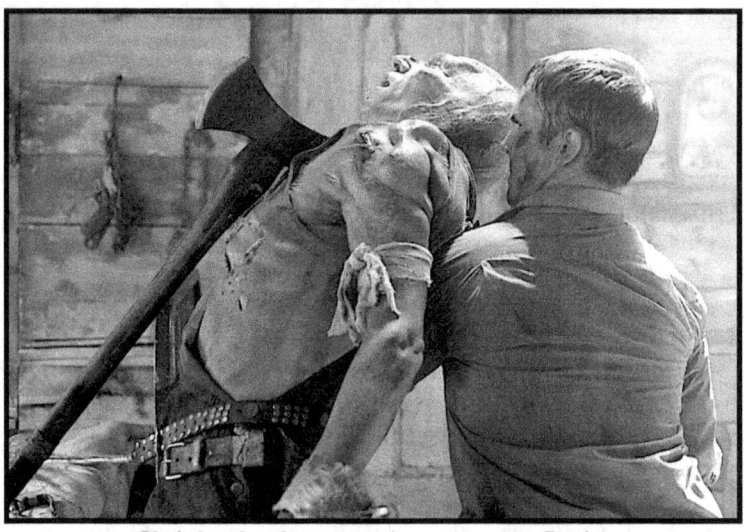

Chris battles the mountain men to save Jessie.

actors who people will agree to cast in a lead role of a film. It all comes down to finance and it sucks. I'll give you an example—people would tell me that in Japan they won't go and see a film with a black guy as the lead, and I told them I thought *Night of the Living Dead* was a huge hit in Japan. I tell you something else, in the original script, with the cabin sequence—you know, when they are all sneaking out of the cabin. Well, in the original sequence, Lindy Booth is put on the table and the mountain men fuck her dead body, with Desmond and Eliza still hiding underneath the table. It was an amazing moment in the script, you feel really alone, it doesn't get anymore nightmarish than this. We couldn't put it in the movie, though, because if we shot that scene we would have been the first studio movie with necrophilia, which for me as a filmmaker was 'right on' (*laughs*). I thought I would be making some screen history. But very few people would want that sort of film as part of their history, and that shows how challenging the casting process is."

Was there ever any discussion about *Wrong Turn* stealing some of the thunder from *The Texas Chainsaw Massacre* remake? "You know, we had some very direct discussions about how *Wrong Turn* would fare if it came out after *The Texas Chainsaw Massacre*," admits the director. "The two companies discussed the release date of *The Texas Chainsaw Massacre*, and we put our release date earlier than it should have been. But that's business..."

Alternate Critiques

"Overall, *Wrong Turn* isn't a revolution in horror, but it's definitely worth checking out. Just don't book a camping holiday after seeing it." (*Movie Insider*, Issue 6, 2004)

"Some of the deaths are impressively brutal...But at 84 minutes, there's little time to get bored, even if you've seen this all before." (Mark Kermode, *The Observer*, 06/03)

"There's very little in *Wrong Turn* that wasn't done first in *Deliverance*, *The Texas Chain Saw Massacre* or *The Hills Have Eyes*, but Schmidt manages to keep the atmosphere creepy." (Steven Foster, *Shivers*, Issue 111, March 2004)

Footnotes

Chapter 1
1. Oddly enough Rick Baker himself remains not so impressed with the final result. "David Naughton's hands are inside this rubber hand and we had this ribcage on him and this kind of ruff of hair, because the wolf had this big mane and this pretty human face and you're standing there trying to eat some fish and chips. Well, I'm looking at him and I'm going, 'This is the stupidest-looking thing.' It reminded me of one of those goon things in Popeye—and I still think it's stupid looking." (As told to the author of this book, *Shivers*, Issue 113, June 2004)
2. "...the transformation scenes...suffer from a lack of urgency and drama that so effectively showcased the transformation scene in *The Howling*," comments critic Chas Balun. (*The Connoisseur's Guide to the Contemporary Horror Film,* Fantaco, 1992)
3. "Warner Bros. had the U.S. rights and they decided that *Black Christmas* was a bad title, that people would think it was a blaxploitation movie about Santa Claus. So they changed the title to *Stranger in the House* and altered the ad campaign. And it laid an egg. Bob had to go down there and make an appeal to them before they would change it and release it properly, and sure enough, it did very well." John Saxon explains the reasons behind the delay of the film in the U.S. to Keith Bearden. (*Fangoria*, Issue 159, January 1997)
4. "I think I can say that you don't need to go back with that sort of thing after having done it twice...I'm really not sure I could still make that kind of film." Wes Craven speaks to the author of this book in *Shivers* (Issue 108, October 2003)
5. The full quote from King reads, "...if you have seen one film by Wes Craven, for instance, it is safe enough, I think, to skip the others. The genre labors under enough critical disapproval and outright dislike; one need not make a bad situation worse by underwriting films of porno-violence..." (*Danse Macabre*, 1981, Warner Books)
6. "*The Hills Have Eyes* also deals in a series of cosmic images of ritualized violence. The film is full of elemental imagery, particularly of blood, and shadows across fire," states Mikita Brottman—somewhat bafflingly. (*Meat Is Murder*, Headpress, 1997)
7. As told to the author. (*Firelight Shocks*, Issue 2, 2000)
8. As author Darryl Jones aptly pinpoints, "Standard in Cronenberg's work is an anti-corporatism, a recurring interest in the ways in which the products of science are manipulated and perverted by corporate interests..." (*Horror: A Thematic History in Fiction and Film*, Oxford University Press, 2002)
9. "...a man whose eyes have never left (the future)." (Chas Balun, *The Connoisseur's Guide to the Contemporary Horror Film,* Fantaco, 1992)

Chapter 2
1. The budget for *Alligator* was $1 million. (Keith Bearden, *Fangoria*, Issue 142, May 1994)
2. "And as the relationships between East and West went into deeper cold storage and the possibility of yet another war did not seem *so* impossible, so we could align our fear at the prospect with the idea of invasion from outer space by monstrous entities." (Richard Davies, *The Encyclopedia of Horror*, Hamlyn, 1981)
3. "I was drinking a case of 16-ounce tallboys a night, and there's one novel, *Cujo*, that I barely remember writing at all," states King. (*About Writing*, 2000, Hodder and Staughton)
4. "Tobe had walked off and the producers came up to me and said, 'You're going to have to direct the ending!'" states Burns. (Stefan Jaworzyn, *The Texas Chain Saw Massacre Companion*, Titan, 2003). However, according to Robert Englund, "The editor and Carolyn Jones (finished it)...they kind of monkeyed with it, so it's really not all Tobe's." (Doug Brod, *Bloody Best of Fangoria*, Vol.7)

5. Indeed, when the writer of this book was helping to organize Hooper's presence at San Francisco's annual Fearless Tales Genre Festival, the directed requested that *Eaten Alive* be shown as part of a night honoring his work. Sadly this was easier said than done, and in the end *The Texas Chainsaw Massacre 2* was brought in as a late replacement.

6. "Commentators have noted that *Death Trap* bears a resemblance to some comic stories published by EC in the 1950s, such as 'Horror We? How's Bayou?' and in particular 'Country Clubbing.'" (Kerekes and Slater, *See No Evil*, Headpress, 2000)

7. Unless one wants to read the movie, as critic Carol J. Clover does, as being along the line of some kind of feminist tract. "Possession via oral penetration...bodies penetrated, invaded, and colonized—bodies convulsed by some alien force....And insofar as that story turns on bodily orifices, holes—natural passages to an inner body—it would appear to be a story built around the female body." (*Men Women and Chainsaws*, BFI, 1992)

Chapter 3

1. In *Friday the 13th Part 3*

2. "In *Alone in the Dark*, writer-director Sholder suggests that asylum may be the outside world," states critic John McCarty (*Movie Psychos and Madmen*, Citadel, 1993)

3. This character trait would also be used in 2001's *Valentine*, including as part of the movie's final "twist."

4. When Paramount released the movie in the U.S., it was cut by three minutes, perhaps resulting in many viewers wondering what the fuss was all about. Suitably, uncut foreign cassettes have been the only way that Americans have been able to see the uncut version of *Intruder* for some time. (Source: Tim Lucas, *Gorezone*, Issue 11, January 1990)

5. For an alternate opinion, critic Stephen Thrower—the editor of the excellent but now-defunct *Eyeball* magazine—has argued in favor of most of these movies. He defends *The New York Ripper* (a film where a naked woman has her breasts slashed with a razor blade in firm close-up) against accusations of misogyny, at length, in *Beyond Terror: The Films of Lucio Fulci* (FAB Press, 1999). Of *Don't Go in the House* he writes that the film "is, like *Maniac*, seemingly disinterested in making its nastiness into *Halloween*-ish fun...I like that in a movie." (*Eyeball*, Issue No. 5, Spring 1998)

6. As told to Christopher Koetting, Issue 147, October 1995

7. The others were *Bloody Moon* (1980), *The Boogeyman* (1980) and its sequel *Revenge of the Boogeyman* (1982), *The Burning* (1980), *Don't Go in the House* (1979), *Don't Go in the Woods* (1980), *The Driller Killer* (1979), *The Funhouse* (1981), *Madhouse* (1981), *Mardi Gras Massacre* (1981), *Nightmare Maker* (1981), *Nightmares in a Damaged Brain* (1981), *Pranks* (1981), *Terror Eyes* (1980), *The Toolbox Murders* (1978), *Unhinged* (1982) and *Visiting Hours* (1981). Mario Bava's seminal 1972 picture *Blood Bath* (a.k.a. *Bay of Blood/Twitch of the Death Nerve*) was an early slasher prototype that also made the "video nasties" list.

8. Critic and television personality Jonathan Ross perhaps sums up the appearance of *Night of the Demon*'s monster the best, describing the film as "atmospheric and successfully spooky right up until the very end, when a big, clumsy, dumb-looking monster appeared and spoiled it all." *(The Incredibly Strange Film Book*, Simon & Schuster, 1991)

Chapter 4

1. At the time of this book's writing, Henenlotter has been busy trying to raise funds for his first directorial project since 1992's sequel *Basket Case 3: The Progeny*. The title of Henenlotter's new script is *Sick in the Head*. The director also commented upon the reason behind the space between films back in late 1995: "It's hard for me to get other projects that *aren't* horror-related," (emphasis theirs) he told Curt McAllister in *Alternative Cinema* (Issue 4, Winter 1995).

2. "I don't see *Brain Damage* relating to any real-life drug issues in that way because it is not a pro-drug film and it's not an anti-drug film. It's a monster movie....At one point in the writing

of the script I became aware of how druggy the story was getting....I tried to write around it, to avoid having Elmer inject Brian with drugs and so on. I tried several ways around it, and it just wouldn't work." (Robert Martin, *Fangoria*, Issue 71, February 1988)

3. "At times it gets a little heavy-handed with the (hopefully) unintentional anti-drug allegory," states Steven Puchalski. (*Slimetime*, Headpress, 1996).

4. This is a point also picked up on by Carol J. Clover (*Men Women and Chainsaws*, BFI, 1992)

5. "Hooper had originally been considered to direct *Motel Hell* for Universal, but Universal thought it was too extreme." (Stefan Jaworzyn, *The Texas Chain Saw Massacre Companion*, Titan, 2003)

6. The late James Ferman, the Secretary of the Board, and the person responsible for withholding U.K. cinema and video releases to the first three *Chainsaw* films, was responsible for this quote. (Tom Dewe Matthews, *Censored*, Chatto, 1994)

7. For instance, in speaking about the slasher movie *Slumber Party Massacre* (1982), in which the murderer uses a power drill to kill his female victims, critic John McCarty writes: "It doesn't take much interpretation to view the maniac's drill as a surrogate penis—especially since his female victims are often framed between his towering spread legs, cringing in fear, and he is often seen fondling the drill in a suggestive manner." (*Movie Psychos and Madmen*, Citadel, 1993)

8. Hooper has also stated that the final cut was taken from his hands. "My cut ran to just over two hours....Cannon has no interest in mood or atmosphere, they just want the basics. Strangely they cut some very expensive effects sequences out," explained the director to Philip Nutman in 1987. (*Bloody Best of Fangoria*, Vol.7) For some of the sequel's deleted scenes, check out Elite Entertainment's original laserdisc release of the film.

9. Laurence Boyce, *Hotdog*, Issue 39, 2003.

10. According to Troma's official press release for the film.

11. Kaufman is especially outspoken about what he perceives as a bias in the American ratings board that acts to keep the smaller studio down. He has spoken, in the past, of "a very convenient double standard that seems to protect those Clint Eastwood movies that show people getting shot in the forehead, but in *Troma's War*, we couldn't do that....So, it's a very tough thing for independents and as a result, you can see many independents have gone out of business. To some extent, I'm sure this has contributed to it." (David Henry Jacobs, *Toxic*, Issue 2, February 1990)

12. Not as strange as it sounds, considering Kaufman's owns views toward the modern climate of aggressive business practice. "In the old days, there were lots of little [movie] theater companies; now, all of them have merged and merged and merged, so you only have maybe two or three chains in each area. And those giant chains are not interested in dealing with an offbeat, unrated movie." (David Henry Jacobs, *Toxic*, Issue 2, February 1990)

Chapter 5

1. Certainly, such Cold War-era horror pictures as *The Day the Earth Stood Still* (1951), *Invasion of the Body Snatchers* (1956) and *The Man From Planet X* (1951) can be seen to be "best understood as a group, reflective of the concerns of the society and the times which produced them." (Darryl Jones, *Horror: A Thematic History in Fiction and Film*, Oxford University Press, 2002). Likewise, *A Boy and His Dog*'s story of a run-down, post-war world and an authoritative government comes at a time when America had been engaged in the Vietnam War. The film joins other movies of the period such as *Deathdream* (1972) and the vicious *Last House on the Left* (1972) in depicting young characters that have become numb to death and violence.

2. "The same dog was used in *The Brady Bunch*." (Allan Bryce, *The Dark Side*, Issue 39, April/May 1994).

3. As told to Caroline Vie (*Fangoria*, Issue 132, May 1994)

4. Indeed, even Leslie Halliwell, not by any account a fan of the modern day "splatter" movie, saw fit to credit *Dead and Buried* as being "comparatively discreet." (*The Dead That Walk*, Grafton, 1986)

5. The critic Kim Newman has also noted that *Dead and Buried* feels "like a Fulci movie." (*Screen Violence*, Bloomsbury, 1996)
6. Johnathan Lake Crane goes so far as to say, "Fans like killers who star in movies that do not make conventional sense." (*Terror and Everyday Life*, Sage, 1994)
7. "After Howard's tormentors," comments critic Phil Hardy "have stabbed his puppy, one really *wants* to see them get their porcine comeuppance" (emphasis his). (*The Aurum Film Encyclopedia: Horror*, Aurum Press, 1993)
8. For more information, see Deborah Blum's *The Monkey Wars* (Oxford University Press, 1996).

Chapter 6

1. *Ginger Snaps* was also the first successful Canadian horror film in some time. A welcome return from the country that gave us *Black Christmas*, *The Changeling*, David Cronenberg, *Deranged*, *Happy Birthday to Me*, *My Bloody Valentine* et al.
2. Stephen Thrower, for example, rants against postmodern horror in his lengthy opening essay in *The Flesh and Blood Compendium* (FAB Press, 2003).
3. The reviews for the sequel in the U.K. were decidedly mixed, with some altogether scathing. *Empire* magazine was especially catty, stating, "There's a real possibility that you'll wet your pants watching this, but it sure as hell won't be the result of being terrified." (Scott Russon, Issue 171, September 2003)

If you enjoyed this book
write for a free catalog
or visit our website at
www.midmar.com

Midnight Marquee Press, Inc.
9721 Britinay Lane
Baltimore, MD 21234

410-665-1198

www.ingramcontent.com/pod-product-compliance
Lightning Source LLC
LaVergne TN
LVHW021654060526
838200LV00050B/2350